They Gathered at the River

They Gathered at the River

River THE STORY OF THE GREAT REVIVALISTS AND THEIR IMPACT UPON RELIGION IN AMERICA

by

BERNARD A. WEISBERGER

With Illustrations

OCTAGON BOOKS

A DIVISION OF FARRAR, STRAUS AND GIROUX

New York   1979

Copyright © 1958, By Bernard A. Weisberger

Reprinted 1979
by special arrangement with Little, Brown & Company

OCTAGON BOOKS
A DIVISION OF FARRAR, STRAUS & GIROUX, INC.
19 Union Square West
New York, N.Y. 10003

Library of Congress Cataloging in Publication Data

Weisberger, Bernard A   1922-
    They gathered at the river.

    Reprint of the ed. published by Little, Brown, Boston.
    Bibliography: p.
    Includes index.
    1. Revivals—United States. 2. Evangelists.   I. Title.
BV3773.W4   1979   269'.2'0922   78-27278
ISBN 0-374-98338-0

Manufactured by Braun-Brumfield, Inc.
Ann Arbor, Michigan
Printed in the United States of America

To
Avery O. Craven

Now when they heard this, they were pricked in their heart, and said unto Peter and to the rest of the apostles, Men and brethren, what shall we do?

Then Peter said unto them, Repent, and be baptized every one of you in the name of Jesus Christ for the remission of sins, and ye shall receive the gift of the Holy Ghost.

For the promise is unto you, and to your children, and to all that are afar off, even as many as the Lord our God shall call.

And with many other words did he testify and exhort, saying, Save yourselves from this untoward generation.

Then they that gladly received his word were baptized: and the same day there were added unto them about three thousand souls.

THE ACTS 2:37-41

Shall we gather at the river
Where bright angel feet have trod;
With its crystal tide forever
Flowing by the throne of God?

Chorus

Yes, we'll gather at the river,
The beautiful, the beautiful river;
Gather with the saints at the river,
That flows by the throne of God.

Ere we reach the shining river
Lay we every burden down;
Grace our spirits will deliver,
And provide a robe and crown.

(*Chorus*)

Soon we'll reach the silver river,
Soon our pilgrimage will cease,
Soon our happy hearts will quiver
With the melody of peace.

(*Chorus*)

ROBERT LOWRY

Preface

A BOOK ought to make its way into the world unencumbered by the parental fussings and apologies of its author. On the other hand, it deserves a fair start, without the handicap of extravagant claims made for it. This book touches on sensitive areas, and therefore certain disavowals are necessary, so that it may at least draw fire on the basis of what it *is*, rather than what it is *not*.

First of all, it is not a general account of religious enthusiasm or of evangelism in America. It is a history of revivals and revivalists, and both words have a very specific meaning in United States church history, which I hope will be clear before my story has gone very far. That meaning was not served very well by the word *revival* itself, which came into use around 1800. Ministers chose it deliberately to scold a naughty world by the suggestion that it was necessary to "revive" the piety of an earlier day, when Americans supposedly had more respect for God and His anointed. Rebuke was built into the term. To confuse matters further, the preachers who specialized in the conduct of revivals later began to call themselves evangelists, a word which has the general import, merely, of one who brings a gospel. There are innumerable "evangelists" and many kinds of "revival," but this book is about traveling preachers who made a specialty, and finally a profession, out of the management of a particular institution — *the* revival — in certain American Protestant denominations.

Hence, I have not considered merely popular preachers, even when they were effective in winning church members, if they did not make revivals their whole duty. I have left out the missionaries to the heathen both at home and abroad. I have also omitted the enthusiasts who strayed from the fold and founded their own churches. I have thus overlooked a good number of saints and charlatans, who deserve books to themselves, but are only indirectly a part of the revival tale.

Secondly, I want to emphasize that this is a book about religion, and not a religious book. In the past, most histories of revivalism looked no further for explanation than the sovereign pleasure of God. As a historian, I have tried to interpret revivals in purely secular terms. In this I claim some warrant from the later revivalists themselves, who insisted that God worked through means in the natural world and through agencies in the world of man. History may properly concern itself with the development of those means and agencies, and no more. It is up to others to look for deeper causes, and nothing that I say is intended to forestall such a search.

Similarly, I have consciously avoided a discussion of the psychological phenomenon of "conversion" — another word with a special meaning in this chronicle — or of the moral effect of revivals on groups and individuals. Neither of these subjects can really be evaluated under the conditions set by historical discipline, and those conditions are my chosen limits.

I have had to treat theological doctrines very briefly, and inevitably have done them some violence in the process. It is, after all, impossible to explain Arminianism and Calvinism, for example, in one paragraph without appearing to reduce the differences between them to quibbling matters. I offer my apologies to serious students of theology, but I can claim some support from the revivalists once again. They made a consistent practice of reducing doctrines to their barest essentials.

There are, however, purely historical problems that I have not touched. I have tried to explain the events I describe in terms of nineteenth-century America, but I know that revivals have occurred in other countries and other periods, and my notions are by no means intended for universal application. I should like to see those other stories told. Other matters of considerable moment have been neglected, too, such as the place of popular preaching and folk hymns in the development of American culture, or the whole impact of evangelical religion on our social, intellectual and economic life. Many a good book is waiting to be written about the part which the old-time faith played in our national shaping, and the time may be at hand for their appearance.

We are only beginning to take a good, retrospective look at our background of orthodoxy. Until the beginning of the twentieth century it was treated, if at all, with too much reverence. Then came thirty or forty years of revolt in America against Victorian propriety and everything connected with it. Perhaps we are now at the age of maturity, when we can look at our forefathers neither in awe nor in anger, as children do, but with understanding and forgiveness. In the words of a popular revival hymn:

> Fields are white, and harvests waiting.
> Who will bear the sheaves away?

B.A.W.

Novi, Michigan

Acknowledgments

AS USUAL, it is impossible to make individual acknowledgment to friends and colleagues whose ideas have been consciously or unconsciously borrowed. I do, however, want to express my collective thanks to those who have talked about the subject matter of this book with me since I began to write it.

I am very grateful to the Social Science Research Council for a grant which allowed me to spend one uninterrupted summer of work, part of it at the Library of Congress. I also wish to thank Wayne State University for providing funds for three trips to research libraries and for making possible the typing of the manuscript.

I am glad to express my appreciation to the librarians at the Garrett Biblical Institute, the University of Michigan, the Library of Congress, Oberlin College, and Wayne State University. I particularly want to thank Miss Nondis Meyer, in charge of interlibrary loans at Wayne State, who worked especially hard to procure materials, and Miss Mary Venn, of the Oberlin College library, for extra effort and kindness. I also want to say a special word of appreciation for Mr. Bernard DeRemer, archivist of the Moody Bible Institute, who took considerable trouble to help me during research there, and to thank the institute for permission to use Moody's letters.

Thanks are also due to the trustees of Oberlin College for permission to use the photograph of Charles G. Finney which appears in the book and to Mrs. Edwin Fishel for timely help with the picture of a camp meeting.

It is too bad that acknowledgments to wives have become something of a convention, thus robbing the words of their meaning. I wish I could invent a special vocabulary of love and thanks for June Weisberger. She read every chapter carefully, intelligently and critically, and also located and secured the illustrations. In addition, she relieved me of innumerable responsibilities in the home, and she bore with affectionate patience all the many demands of a writing husband.

A last, heartfelt and cheerfully made acknowledgment is contained in the dedication.

Contents

(Illustrations appear between pages 114-115)

They Gathered at the River

CHAPTER I

Woe unto Thee, Chorazin

IN 1798, a solemn group of Presbyterian ministers met in assembly to consider a dreadful fact. Their fellow citizens of the new American republic were falling away from the orthodox habits of their forefathers. The infant country had beaten the British, but seemed to be no match for Satan. The dreadful fact had to be faced and put on record. Ominously, the assembly's report concluded "that the eternal God has a controversy with this nation." [1]

It was a bitter consideration to clergymen worn old in years of authority. To a youthful generation of preachers just out of school, however, the situation was a challenge. They were ready and willing to take God's part in the controversy. By the time they, in turn, became gray-haired old men, baptizing their third generation of parishioners, they could look back on their work with satisfaction. In 1838, only forty years later, the United States was satisfactorily reconciled to God. Few public policies were launched except in His name, and few politicians were willing to risk the united condemnation of His spokesmen, the ministers. Church membership had grown steadily. Religious newspapers were not only bought, but read. Almost every college and private school in the country was operated, from boards of trustees down to senior tutors, by ministers and devout laymen. National societies had been formed to print Bibles, establish Sunday schools, send missions to the heathen, and guide lawmakers in the paths of righteousness. Few villages were without local chapters of these organizations, so that a great network of Christian enterprises was one of the things holding American society together.

Most of this was the work of one generation. And most of

these enterprises — colleges, newspapers and benevolent societies — had come about as the fruit of what were called "revivals of religion." It was an impressive testimony to what the term meant. Yet it was work undertaken entirely in the spirit of counterattack, and with the awful urgency of the defensive. At the beginning of national life, American Christianity's first order of business was to take up a quarrel with the temporal world. From the start, the revival was no passively received blessing. It was a weapon aimed at sin, and it was meant to be used and to hit hard.

There was plenty of sin to worry about in the seventeen-nineties. Looking about them, orthodox believers saw a "melancholy and truly alarming situation." [2] From New England parsonages, the world appeared far backslidden. There were towns in Connecticut where the local congregation could claim only four or five new members a year.[3] People died or went West at a faster rate than they joined the church of God. What could be expected from "the rising generation," in that case, except indifference to holy things? [4] A cold mist smudged the religious horizon in the land of Puritan and Pilgrim. In more than one village, the "house of God was much forsaken on the sabbath, especially if the weather was unpleasant." [5] Was it possible that "the Sabbath would be lost, and every appearance of religion vanish, yea that our Zion must die, without an helper, and that infidels would laugh at her dying groans"? [6]

Danger also threatened elsewhere than in the outposts of Zion manned by Yankees. The colonial South had been the particular fortress of the American adherents of the Church of England. When the Revolution cut the umbilicus, they organized themselves as the Protestant Episcopal Church in the United States, adopting a charter at a convention in 1789 attended by two bishops, twenty clergy and sixteen laymen. Yet twenty-two years later, another national convocation could show an increase of only five clergy and four laymen.[7] In that same year of 1811, moreover, William Meade, later a bishop of Virginia, presented himself for ordination at Williamsburg. Meade had just been graduated from William and Mary, founded in 1693 so that the

Church of England might rear up her colonial sons to be "piously educated."[8] Now, Meade's planter friends wondered why "a gentleman, college-bred," should apply to become a parson. At the ordination service his relatives — seventeen of them — made up the whole congregation. Still, Meade should not have been surprised. The college students, who knew more of horseflesh and wine than theology, had only recently held a debate on "whether Christianity had been injurious or beneficial to mankind."[9]

The colleges, in fact, were a trial to godly minds. At Princeton, a great nursery of Presbyterian ministers, there were in 1782 only two professing Christians among the students.[10] Three years later, a nineteen-year-old New Haven youth, entering Yale, discovered to his horror that the scholars were gambling, tippling and likely doing worse things still. The fashionable Yale men of that year read French skeptics and deists over their pints of flip and gaily nicknamed themselves "Rousseau" and "d'Alembert."[11] To young Lyman Beecher this was a shock that he distinctly recalled when he was past eighty, and it gave him warrant for a later apprehension that the schools were raising up "a brood of infidels, heretics and profligates — a generation prepared . . . to assail . . . our most sacred institutions."[12] College was a trial to the piety of young men cut out for preachers.

Foreign visitors of an evangelical turn gazed sadly at decayed church buildings in Virginia. Sunday in the Carolinas was a day of "riot and drunkenness." The backwoods thronged with "unbaptized infidels."[13] Religious exertions seemed unquestionably in demand. Otherwise it would be more tolerable for Tyre and Sidon at the day of judgment than for the cities of America.

There were three particulars to the indictment brought against America by its clerical leaders. The first charge was intellectual: the nation had succumbed to Beelzebub in adopting newfangled and "infidel" doctrines. The second was social and political: it had thrust the church out of its rightful place at the head of society. The third was harder to characterize, but exclusively American. Those who had gone West were abandoning old churches and showing no enthusiasm for building new ones. The frontier was destitute of religion.

There was some backbone in all these charges. Deism *had* enjoyed a popularity in respectable society that racked orthodox Christians with the pangs of martyrdom. This "religion of reason" took a benevolent view of the Lord as a wise and sympathetic Creator who had laid out the universe according to a sagacious blueprint and then given man, through reason, the ability to understand the plan and conform to it. It was a tidy, eighteenth-century notion, and entirely at war with the Puritan belief that man was a fallen creature, utterly unable to escape damnation except through the sovereign grace of God, which no human goodness could command or buy.

Yet under one name or another, deism's man-centered and rationalistic outlook was supported by distinguished laymen. Not many of the fathers of the Revolution espoused it as openly as, say, Benjamin Franklin, but not many of them were noted for outspoken Christian pietism, either. In 1784 Ethan Allen, the Revolutionary hero who had allegedly captured Ticonderoga "in the name of God and the Continental Congress," relegated God to second place. He issued a book, *Reason the Only Oracle of Man*, a long attack on revealed religion. In 1794 Tom Paine, still remembered as the champion pamphleteer of American independence, printed *The Age of Reason*, a vigorous (and vigorously damned) work of deistic tendencies. In 1802 Elihu Palmer, a recreant New England Baptist minister, published still a third popular volume in the library of "infidelism," his *Principles of Nature*.[14] The ideas of Paine, Allen and Palmer were widely discussed and adopted with special warmth by American sympathizers with the French Revolution. Almost all these sympathizers were gathered into the Democratic-Republican party being formed under the leadership of Thomas Jefferson. Feelings about the "religion of reason," then, became entangled with sympathy for democracy and with local party ends, and the entire issue was superheated by the injection into it of all the name-calling, shouting, exaggerating steam of party politics.

So when Joseph Priestley, an English Unitarian whose views

were said to hew close to the deist line, was treated to a round of
Democratic-Republican banquets on a visit here in 1794, scandalized churchmen cried out that the United States was poisoned
by the existence of an anticlerical party.[15] When a French Ori-
entalist, Constantin Volney, issued a work entitled *Ruins: or a
Survey of the Revolution of Empires*, which defied Biblical history by tracing the common roots of Christianity and other Eastern religions, the orthodox were horrified by the rumor that one
of its translators into English was Thomas Jefferson.[16] Jefferson
vied with Paine for the role of best-hated man among conservative Christians. His library and his cosmopolitan dinner table
were both wide-open to radical viewpoints. A Virginia senator
once complained that in Jefferson's home he found himself defending "the character of Jesus," and could get no support from
any of the company except the first cashier of the Bank of the
United States, David Franks, a Jew.[17]

The deists were even strong enough to organize societies in
New York and Philadelphia, and to launch newspapers, the
Temple of Reason and the *Theophilanthropist*, that is, "lover of
God and Man." [18] The latter publication pledged itself, in 1810,
to spread the beliefs that God's "mysteries are the means most
conducive to human happiness," and his ceremonials "acts of charity, benevolence, generosity, and public spirit." These ideas
were natural to the human mind, said the editor, and from them
"nothing but the most villainous imposture could have deluded
it." [19]

To a believer in supernatural Christianity in 1810 this was not
only fatuous, but subversive, and for years orthodox writers
could shudder retrospectively over those clouded days when infidelity "showed herself in the workshop, the counting room,
and the parlor, in colleges . . . in halls of legislation, and . . .
the press." [20] Rational religion was marked as one of the first targets of revival effort.

Meantime, clergymen were suffering other trials as irksome as
"reason's" attack on their beliefs. Their social standing was slipping. In Puritan New England for a century and a half the ministers had kept order in an unruly schoolroom of a world. They

had chosen the legislators and prayed over them; they had sent the armies of Gideon against the red-skinned Canaanites; they had whipped the Quakers, hung the witches, made sure the foundations of the school system, and trained up their own successors at Harvard and Yale. In smaller towns the minister was shut close in his study for ten and twelve hours a day, wrestling with the mysteries of eternity. When he appeared in company in a "full-bottomed, powdered wig, full, flowing coat, with ample cuffs, [and] silver knee- and shoe-buckles," he was a majestic sight.[21] He not only served his congregation; he ruled it. When he climbed into the pulpit on Sunday in his long black gown and white neckbands, he looked every inch God's lieutenant. There was no quarter either for Satan or for the congregation. It was supposedly considered a privilege, after two hours of sermon, to watch the hoarse and perspiring divine turn over the sandglass to begin one more.[22] In nine of the thirteen colonies at the Revolution's beginning there was an established, tax-supported church, so that the sovereignty of the law backed up the already overpowering respect for the cloth.[23]

But the postwar generation was more disposed to sit in the seat of the scornful. The leaders of the fight for liberty were laymen, for the most part. And while in New England the preachers did more than their bit for independence, the Anglican churchmen, strong in the other colonies, were a long time in getting over the handicap of their official connection with the English Government.[24]

The rise of anticlericalism in the Jeffersonian ranks, too, was not only an intellectual setback, but a political disaster in the making. An irresistible move towards disestablishment gathered momentum. By the end of the war, the Anglican Church, with the sanctions of patriotism against it, was deprived of state support in those colonies which had maintained it. The Congregationalists hung on as the tax-supported church in New Hampshire until 1817, in Connecticut until 1818, and until 1833 in Massachusetts.[25]

This was not entirely the work of Antichrist. The unestablished, or "dissenting," denominations were understandably interested in putting an end to public support for rival faiths. The Jeffersonian ranks were filled with frontiersmen, many of them good Baptists, Methodists and Presbyterians. Besides, most of the planters who supported the Democratic-Republicans were at least nominal Episcopalians. Nevertheless, the fight for separation crumbled the clergy's immunity to public criticism. The glory of the Lord still shone round about ministers, but not so strongly that they could not be attacked and beaten at the polls. The more perceptive of them knew that their exalted position could never be the same. The "onset" against the establishment, Lyman Beecher wrote from Connecticut, was "systematic, keen, and persevering"; its object, "to scatter and destroy us." [26]

Disestablishment was a symptom, too, not a cause — an omen of increasing self-confidence among the laity, hearkening to the pipes of democracy. It might substitute a mere "vast community of small change" for "an ancient treasure of precious vessels," but that was the way the electorate wanted it, and as the base of suffrage widened, the electorate began to write the rules. A social revolution could not be checked by a few thunderbolts from Sinai.

Worse than direct attack, which could be resisted with dignity, was ridicule. The secular press, in 1800, could print jokes which vainly invoked the awful name of Jehovah — like the epitaph for a man with a large mouth, which concluded: "Reader tread lightly on this sod/For if he gapes, you're gone, by G——!" [27] In Pennsylvania, a frontier lawyer, judge and politician, Hugh Henry Brackenridge, was composing installments of the first American novel, a rambling romance entitled *Modern Chivalry*. Its hero was a Captain Farrago, who traveled about with an earthy and illiterate Irish servant, Teague O'Regan. In one chapter, Teague thought of passing himself off for a minister, whereupon his master lectured him on that high calling.

> Teague, said he, do you know what you are about? . . . Are you apprised of the difficulty of this work? The first thing you will have to do, is to take a text; and when that is done, you

will have to split it into parts. There are what are called heads; and these you must divide into firstlys, and secondlys, and thirdlys, and fourthlys and so on, till you come to twentiethlys, perhaps. Are you furnished with a concordance? or do you know what a concordance is? Can you find a text to suit your purpose when you want it? Can you explain the scriptures; the meaning of Daniel's ram and the he-goat, or the seven trumpets in the Revelations? You are mistaken if you think your Irish will pass for Hebrew.[28]

Those were hard words for pious men to digest in a land which Puritan saints had cut out of the wilderness. They were even harder coming from a press whose first printed work, in the English colonies of North America, had been a psalmbook. A revival of religion would have to restore, among other things, the public dignity of those whose calling was to serve God.

As for the early effects of the westward movement on American Christianity, they were simple and terrible. Like the magnetic mountain in the legend, which jerked the nails out of passing ships and so destroyed them, the frontier sucked congregations out of settled tabernacles. Westward the unpromising raw materials of empire took their way — farmers, speculators, miners, hunters, printers, lawyers, "merchants, millers, blacksmiths, artisans, rogues and saints — all rubbing elbows on the trails that led to the mecca beyond the mountains." [29] By the mid-point of the nineteenth century, the five states of the old Northwest Territory *alone* — Ohio, Indiana, Illinois, Michigan and Wisconsin — contained four and one half million souls, more than the entire population of the country in 1789.[30]

Taken collectively, the American church was no broadbacked hippopotamus, but even so it was not nimble enough to keep up with a migration as swift-footed as this. In a few cases the pioneers left in groups, complete with ministers and apostolic blessings, to win the wilderness for God. Most settlers, however, sniffed cheap land in the breeze, and set out by single families for the frontier, where they were soon, in Henry Adams's phrase, "cutting into the forests with the energy of so many beavers, and with no more express moral purpose than the beavers they drove away." [31] Building temples to God and rearing courts of law played second fiddle to more expedient considerations.

Eastern churchmen, therefore, were faced with a frightening prospect. Hundreds of thousands of humans lived in the new settlements without the ministrations of organized religion, hair-hung and breeze-shaken over the vault of hell. More than future life was at stake. The church was a guardian of public morality and good order, a great pier on which stable society rested. But frontiersmen, gambling daily with death, and often energizing themselves with jolts of raw liquor to overcome the malarial squalor of log-cabin life, tended to outrun both written and eternal law. Violence and new settlement were perpetual yokefellows.

To religious-minded visitors, as a result, every frontier community was a Sodom unredeemed. The Reverend Timothy Dwight, president of Yale, described the Maine frontier in 1797 as the haunt of "vicious men" who had fled society to give more liberal rein to their "idle and licentious dispositions." [32] This view might be written off to the account of educated Calvinistic stiffness. But Lorenzo Dow, a lowly born Connecticut Methodist, insisted in the same year that the people of western New York were "the offscouring of the earth." [33] Even Peter Cartwright, an Illinois Methodist preacher who was born, raised and remained contented in the West all his days, said that the Kentucky of his boyhood, in the seventeen-nineties, was the abode of "murderers, horse thieves, highway robbers, and counterfeiters." [34]

Nor was the unregenerate frontier a mere passing trial. The rush to new lands was a steady thing, never letting up, and the worst of it was that as the West grew in power, its redemption became even more urgent, for the stakes were higher. An agent of a national missionary society wrote in 1830:

> Look at . . . the "valley of the Mississippi." In twenty years if it should continue to increase as it has done . . . it will con-

tain a majority of the people of the United States . . . The destinies of the Union will be in their hands. If that portion of the country be not brought under the influence of religion *now*, it cannot, to human view, be done at all. . . . *Now or never is* the watchword . . . in reference to that region.[35]

If the future character of the nation depended upon saving the West for God, a further conclusion was inevitable for the ardent patriots of that era. As a Princeton theology professor pointed out, the American national character was of "unutterable importance to the world." Therefore, those who walked not in the way of the ungodly might well ask themselves "whether a generation ever lived on whose fidelity so much depended." [36] The salvation of the whole earth might depend on bringing the pioneers into the fold.

"Infidelity," disestablishment and migration were therefore three prongs of the Devil's pitchfork, prodding the evangelical clergy to action. Because they numbered among them men of zeal and toughness, there was to be action in good and sufficient measure. Revivals would furnish some of the most dramatic high lights of that action.

Yet the revival was not the recourse of *all* American Christians. It belonged pre-eminently to one group — vastly numerous, but clearly definable, with a local habitation and a name. This was the rural and small-town middle class. This group above all demanded a new vitality in religion, to match its own. Yet it was this group to which none of the available solutions of the churches' problems appealed, except the renewal of a real or imaginary "old-time" faith. In fact, it was this segment of society which felt a religious crisis when others were disposed to be at ease in Zion.

In reality, the picture was not uniformly black. If the jaws of hell were yawning for America in 1790, it was strange that only forty years later Alexis de Tocqueville could find "no country in the whole world in which the Christian religion retains a greater influence over the souls of men than in America." [37]

Could an evil tree bring forth good fruit? It could, because the roots were really sound.

The religious "decline" of the waning eighteenth century was testified to mostly by men who later became profoundly zestful clergymen. To them every unconverted soul, every peg of spirits beyond moderation, every Sabbath giggle or "God-damn" were fearful reminders of the destruction promised at the last trump. The old Puritan idea that Satan was still going up and down in the earth and walking to and fro in it died hard. The witness of desolation in the colleges, for example, was borne mostly by grown men, remembering the impressions of late adolescence; and what was more natural than for piously reared boys to see, in sophomore high jinks, the lecherous cavortings of the damned? [38]

Visible signs of grace were ignored. The churches were meeting many of their challenges very well, all in all. Despite the fact that most of them had roots in the Old World — the Presbyterians in Scotland, the Methodists and Episcopalians in the Church of England, and other communions in Rome, in Holland and in Germany — they had organized nationally with surprisingly little tumult. The Methodists and Anglicans had, without schisms, cut the ties with England by 1789. Even the few American Catholics had, by that year, their own prefect apostolic, appointed by Rome to take over from the vicar apostolic in London. The Dutch Reformed Church in America was a going concern in 1794, and various Lutheran bodies had by then set up independent synods.[39]

Nor were the churches, taken all together, losing their flocks. Those which were willing to make room for common folk had no lack of applicants. Methodism in America, for example, had only begun in the seventeen-sixties, with the first New York worshipers holding services in a rigging loft. Yet by 1818 Methodists claimed close to a quarter of a million souls in the United States.[40] Most of these were recruited on the frontier, where Methodist evangelists were tireless, but the Methodists had even invaded New England under the noses of the lordly Congregationalists and Presbyterians. The trouble was that the descendants of the Puritan churches did not consider this a gain for religion. Almost every Presbyterian and Congregational minister ordained in the country between 1758 and 1789 had some college training, but the Methodist ministry was then largely self-educated.[41] The Methodists were considered an ill-born and ranting sect, somewhat akin to the "holiness" churches and Jehovah's Witnesses of the present. Their worshipers sang, shouted and clapped in meetings, and no Calvinistic minister of the omnipotent Jehovah could clasp to his bosom a fellow cleric who was believed to use such expressions as: "Let us rush upon the thick bosses of God, determined that we will have mercy."[42] Hence when Jesse Lee finally organized a New England Methodist "conference," with 481 members in 1792, the New England clergy did not exactly see the light dawning amid the darkness of religious decline.[43] To other eyes, however, Methodist success was a proof that religion and equalitarian democracy might be able to get along together after all.

The same conclusion might be drawn from the rise of the Baptists, whose churches were in fine health. During the period beginning in 1784 and ending in 1812 they grew from 8 churches to 239 in New York State alone; from 266 churches to 430 in New England; from 169 to 897 in Virginia, Georgia, Kentucky and Tennessee.[44] But the Baptists, too, drew heavily on the unschooled for shepherds and flock both, and in the old Puritan commonwealths they had a hereditary taint of heresy. Men were undoubtedly still alive in 1800 whose grandfathers had seen the door of a Baptist meetinghouse nailed shut in Boston in 1678.[45]

In time the Baptists and Methodists would gain in respectability — like democracy itself — and would be joined in the revival movement with the churches which had been the parade marshals of colonial society. But this was not true for the first quarter of the nineteenth century, and so Baptist and Methodist growth was not regarded as a cheering sign that the church was sound at the core. And in a day of bitter religious controversy, leaders of the most successful Protestant churches took no pleasure in the prosperity of smaller denominations, and were positively alarmed by growth among Catholics.

That was one ray of hope ignored. There were others. Some Christians, at least, were doing their best to bring their beliefs into line with the humanitarian and rationalistic attitude which had exploded in the American and French revolutions. The rise of Unitarianism in the United States was an honest attempt to make the lion of God's ineffably mighty power lie down with the lamb of His affection for the creatures made in His own image. The argument over the Trinity was secondary. The implicit Unitarian insistence on God's respect for human intellect and character in the universe was something of a compromise between revealed Christianity and the despised "religion of reason." [46] By the side of the Unitarians rose the Universalists, holding that in the final judgment *all* mankind was to be saved from damnation. Strict Calvinists of that day believed at the very least that these positions limited God's majesty and tended to make him a respecter of persons.

The Unitarians made inroads at Harvard and in Boston, and could claim in 1812 that "most . . . Boston clergy and respectable laymen" belonged in their fold.[47] A religion which dug itself in among the best minds of the intellectual capital of the United States was not to be measured by mere numbers. This was especially true when the controversies it raised up in the parish broke apart eighty-one Congregational churches in New England by 1820.[48] From an impartial point of view, the rise of Unitarianism was a success story in which Christianity kept its hold on a portion of the educated upper classes in Federalist New England. Those who bewailed the "skepticism" of the age, however, were inclined to overlook it.

The frontier was not entirely lost to religion, either. Many of the lamentations over its fallen state came from fund-raising missionary agencies and therefore, as a matter of tradition and need, were bordered in black. Actually, the congregations of the East were quick to recognize the needs of "thousands and millions of our guilty race . . . on the frontiers" and to "put forth every exertion for the spread of that precious Gospel, which is the grand charter of our eternal inheritance." [49] As early as 1788, Congregational associations in Connecticut were sending traveling ministers to the wilds of New York and Vermont. By 1798 a statewide missionary society had been formed. Every ordained clergyman who braved the rigors of a preaching tour in western New York and New England got four and one half dollars a week from the treasury. An equal amount went to his congregation to hire a replacement so that they might not thirst for the word of God in the minister's absence.[50]

Thereafter, lawyers could hardly draw charters of incorporation fast enough. Massachusetts Baptists organized a home missionary society in 1802; Connecticut Episcopalians in 1808. The Congregationalists of the Bay State forged a missionary group in 1799; those of New Hampshire in 1801; and those of Vermont in 1807. That was fast work, since Vermont itself was still mostly a frontier. But nothing stood still where the westward movement was concerned; by 1816 Connecticut churches were worrying about how to get missionaries to places *inside* the state which were too poor to support a minister because most of the congregation had cut out for the new lands.[51] There were county and city societies, too, and something new — women's organizations. In 1800 the Boston Female Society for Missionary Purposes was born, and in 1804 New Hampshire brought forth the Female Cent Institute — a band of ladies who volunteered to contribute one penny per week to bring light to the darkness of Maine, Vermont and points west.[52]

Thus the heathen of Western America were kept in touch with the charter of their inheritance. It took organization, money and sweat. Even in a so-called "decline of the churches," religious Americans were able plentifully to supply all three.

The warnings of doom, clearly, were coming from classes not fundamentally affected by the hopeful movements of missionary work and liberal religion.

The home missionary crusade was all very well, but it did nothing in particular for the very people who sponsored it. It suited the frontier at its crudest, but once a region had passed beyond wearing buckskins and using whiskey for currency, its own settlers felt themselves to be a cut above the semisavages further out towards the edge of civilization. In towns which had gotten past log cabins to frame houses, and gardens, and painted chapels, and marked streets — and, of course, in the two-century-old towns of the East — congregations opened their pocketbooks for the relief of the destitute on the frontier, without thinking of immediate religious benefits to themselves. It was a goodly work to send Bibles and preachers to Western men and women still smelling faintly of gun grease and past sins, but it was an effort directed outwards — aimed by those who were stable, orderly, propertied, socialized — towards those still on the make, still in peril of soul. Eastern parishioners were not likely to see a religious blessing for themselves in the home missionary's works.

The marriage of human reason and divine guidance was something for the urban few. The country gentlemen of the old landholding upper classes remained Episcopalian, largely by habit. A few social leaders of the rising cities were willing to compromise on Unitarianism, yet even this was true only in Boston to any large extent. But a religion hugged close by patrician Boston was not an answer to the needs of the New England countryside. Lyman Beecher, when he was a Presbyterian minister in the "hub of the universe," never missed a chance to point out that the Unitarians were aristocrats who ground the faces of the poor. He said that their control of Harvard was "silently putting sentinels in all the churches, legislators in the hall and judges on the bench, and scattering everywhere physicians, lawyers and merchants." [53] Hard-working farmers and self-taught small-town leaders were apt to share Beecher's resentment over the fact that in the contest for church members, "Unitarianism . . . had a better chance, on the score of *talents, learning, wealth* and popular favor," than the faithful.[54] In the villages it was easy to wax indignant over the opposition to revivals, as Beecher described it in the flinty prose which made it a delight to read his version of church history.

The *upper class* put mouth to ear, and hand to pocket, and said *St-boy!* There was an intense, malignant enragement for a

time. Showers of lies were rained about us every day. . . .
Wives and daughters were forbidden to attend our meetings;
and the whole weight of *political, literary* and *social* influence
was turned against us, and the lash of ridicule laid on without
stint.[55]

This note was to be sounded again and again — this insistence
on separation from the fallen "lower classes," on the one hand,
and the deluded but fashionable sinners of liberal "high society," on the other. One has to subtract, then, from the "dark"
religious picture, the frontiersmen with their coonskin democracy, their Baptist and Methodist meetings, and their missionary
preachers. One must subtract the arrived urbanites, embracing
liberalism, and also the smaller pietistic sects, and the churches,
such as the Dutch Reformed and Lutheran, which rested most
heavily on non-English-speaking groups. And the gentlemen
treading the Episcopalian road to heaven must be subtracted,
too, from the estimate of church decadence.

What is left is a rural class halfway between rawness and cos-
mopolitanism. The America ready to be revived was an America
of one- and two-church towns — of meetinghouses and county-
courthouse lawyers; doctors in buggies who took their fees,
often enough, in eggs and firewood; parlor prayer meetings;
genealogy treasured up by widows and spinsters over the teacups; and general stores where men gathered to curse the city
bankers. This America was the home of the evangelical religion
which felt threatened by the world, yet superior to it.

It was here, where the greatest part of the population lived
until the twentieth century, that native American Protestantism
would develop its culture and values. It had to do without state
support most of the time, and without the props of tradition
so important in the Old World. Its strength was in the "self-
conscious . . . middle class . . . self-reliant, activist, practical
and prosperous." [56] It had to develop "the Christian system in
its practical and moral aspects rather than in its theoretical and
theological." [57]

That would not always be easy. Democracy gave the American church its strength, but it set a number of snares for its

feet. Ministers were important, but laymen called the tunes. Self-appointed prophets carried away whole congregations with them on newly discovered pathways to salvation. Politics had its own gospel, always challenging the evangelical message for attention. Religion in the New Jerusalem would have to develop a gospel equally intense and magnetic.

The nineteenth-century revival was, of all answers to these problems, the most exciting and the most arguable and the most lasting in its effects. "I was baptized into the revival spirit," wrote Lyman Beecher, who turned twenty-one in 1796.[58] But that spirit would be a flexible thing, able to change with the times. Beecher's generation wanted to employ the revival to make the world over in the image of Scripture. But first they would have to make something usable of the revival itself. And though they did not know it, in so doing they would borrow freely from both the liberal Christians and the frontiersmen they looked down upon from the height of the sure word of God.

For among the props on which revivalism rested, two were fundamental. One was the importance of emotion in religion. The other was the significance of the individual. It was his salvation that would always be the first and foremost goal.

In 1800 two of these props were being hewed out of native timber. A wild, free, singing flavor was introducing itself into religion on the frontier, flinging the gates of redemption brazenly and invitingly ajar. In the flickering light of Kentucky campfires, amid hallelujahs and handclaps, the Great Revival of 1800 was beginning to make a tradition.

CHAPTER II

Walking and Leaping and Praising God

IF SATAN kept close track of human affairs in 1797, he might have taken a warning from the experience of a certain Kentucky hunter who one day trapped a bear at the foot of a tree and swung at him with an ax. The bear knocked the ax away and sank his teeth into the hunter's left arm. Promptly the Kentuckian plunged *his* teeth into the bear's nose and his free thumb into the animal's eye socket. At that point, friends came up and dispatched the beast. Later, the hunter was asked if bears gave him much trouble generally. His answer was no. "They can't stand Kentucky play," he said. "Biting and gouging are too much for them." [1]

The portent would have been plain for Satan. When he met with Americans on the frontier, there was going to be gouging and biting. From 1798 to about 1810, certain communities of the half-tamed forest met the enemy in Christian battle, in what was sometimes called the Western or Kentucky or Great Revival. This revival was not the first on the American continent. A so-called "Great Awakening" had lit fires of religious zeal along the seaboard in the seventeen-forties. But holy enthusiasm among the squirrel hunters of Kentucky, western Virginia, the Carolinas and Tennessee was something special. They had concepts of pious experience that went with braining bears and battling Indians. Theology was presented to them by men whose faith was strong, but who "murdered the king's English almost every lick." [2] They received it with tears and shouts and such wild dances as David performed before the ark of the Lord. For a few passionate years, something amounting to godly hysteria crackled and smoked in the backwoods settlements. But this was only the flash of initial combustion. Within a decade the Western revival was institutionalized, more or less, in the camp meeting, which abounded in demonstrative energy, certainly, but kept within control. Its enthusiasm was carried through the clearings in the saddlebags of a traveling, evangelistic ministry, mostly of the then "lower-class" Methodist Church. These men were native timber, with the bark on. They were undistinguishable in dress, manner or rhetoric from the rest of the pioneers, except that they brought to the job of converting sinners the same quick-triggered zest which their neighbors directed against the British, or land speculators, or excise men. Yet they, too, for all their individuality, preached mostly within the bounds of rule and discipline.

Therefore, by 1830 the *genuinely* frenzied and spontaneous frontier revival was largely a memory. It survived where settlement was brand new, and in islands of population, mostly Southern, where frontier attitudes somehow never quite changed — in the remoter mountain counties, and among certain Negroes.[3] What remained was still lusty, but somewhat more ritualized and predictable. Yet the early binge of unharnessed emotionalism left its mark on parts of American Protestantism. It bequeathed a tradition of unpolished preaching by plain men, lay exhorters in all but name. It left another pattern, of mass participation in special meetings gotten up exclusively to save souls. It shaped a kind of religious thinking that was intensely individual, making the apex of Christian experience for each separate man and woman a *personal* change of heart which came about suddenly and publicly and under excruciating emotional pressure.

These things were part of the frontier revival, and when the settled churches embraced a brand of revivalism, they became part of the nation's religious life. The churches of the older regions did not plan it that way. They did their best to domesticate and polish whatever it was that they took from the wilderness, but afterwards they were never quite the same. However indirectly they borrowed from the camp meeting, they were touched with the frontier spirit. In every public exercise carried on in that spirit there was just a suspicion of the circus. The camp meeting, though it might be frontier religion's "harvest time," flourished along with the "militia muster, the cabin-raising, and the political barbecue." [4] The whole history of American revivals would lightly or heavily underscore that fact.

In 1798 the Presbyterian Church's general assembly asked that a day be set aside for fasting, humiliation and prayer to redeem the religious life of the West from Egyptian darkness.[5] At that very time, however, renewals of pious enthusiasm were already breaking up the soil for the planting of churches in western Kentucky. The most pungent of these were the joint work of the Lord and a tall, angular Presbyterian preacher with keen black eyes and a "bold and uncompromising manner," the Reverend James McGready.[6]

McGready was born in Pennsylvania, of Scotch-Irish stock. These Ulster Scots had come to the American colonies in vast numbers during the eighteenth century. Mostly poor in the things of this world, they had settled along the frontier, where land was cheap, and where they worked, fought, and prayed heartily. It was said of them that, like their Presbyterian Scottish ancestors, when the crops failed, they could live on the shorter catechism. McGready's family took him, as a child, to Guilford County, in western North Carolina.

Under a childhood diet of hard work and doctrine, McGready soon showed signs of sanctification. From his seventh year he never omitted his prayers, and as an adolescent he was preserved from swearing, intoxication and Sabbath-breaking. A visiting uncle, struck by these evidences, persuaded the family to commit him to the study of the gospel. The boy was sent to the home of the Reverend John McMillan, in Pennsylvania. McMillan, a Princeton graduate, tutored young men in theology for part of the day, and they worked out their board and tuition on his farm in their free time — a rough, but satisfactory, form of frontier scholarship aid. Soon, a bout with smallpox brought McGready face to face with the question of whether or not he was prepared for eternity. He wrestled with it, and on the first Sunday after his recovery, was "converted." [7]

In 1788 McGready was licensed, when "about 30 years of age," to preach in the presbytery of Redstone, in western Pennsylvania. Some time thereafter he moved back to his home territory of North Carolina, preaching in Guilford and Orange counties. It presently became evident that he was going to allow no concessions of any kind to the prince of darkness, even if it meant a fight with a deluded congregation. The custom then prevailed of abating the gloom of a funeral with a few servings of liquor. McGready denounced it and refused to officiate at any burial where drinks were available. Some of the laity to whom this was a relatively innocuous social custom were unpleasantly impressed.

Next, McGready began to preach against the "formality and deadness" of the churches in his part of the country. He soon had some communicants convinced of their sinfulness and need of divine aid. Apparently, not everyone was affected in the same way. Some church members were not docile under scoldings from the pulpit, for frontier congregations were not overawed by the cloth. Their ministers wore buckskin breeches and were demonstrably human. McGready abruptly moved to Kentucky in 1798,[8] and a legend circulated that he had been requested to do so in an anonymous letter written in blood.[9] It was a vigorous beginning for a ministry, but even more exciting things were in store.

In Kentucky, McGready had the management of three small congregations at Red River, Gasper River and Muddy River. They were all in Logan County, in the southwestern corner of the state, described by one frontier parson as a "Rogues' Harbor," abounding in desperadoes and unregenerate doings.[10] The new minister soon displayed vigorous abilities in exhortation. He would "so describe Heaven" that the ague-ridden and calloused congregation would "almost see its glories and long to be there." Significantly, he would also "so array hell and its horrors before the wicked, that they would tremble and quake, imagining a lake of fire and brimstone yawning to overwhelm them, and the wrath of God thrusting them down the horrible abyss." [11] And McGready concentrated these eloquent sermons on a particular question: "Is religion a sensible thing? If I were converted, would I feel it and know it?" Under the goading of this question, with the lake of fire and brimstone smoking in the background, a "very general awakening" took place. By the summer of 1798, many were "struck with an awful sense of their lost estate."

In July of 1799, McGready's power over audiences began to be witnessed visibly. During a service prior to the Lord's Supper at the Red River church, some of the "boldest, most daring sinners in the county covered their faces and wept bitterly." Next month, when the same sacrament was administered at Gasper River, "many fell to the ground, and lay powerless, groaning, praying and crying for mercy." A woman screamed to Mc-Gready, "I have no religion; I am going to hell." A gray-haired old man, with his wife and children, sobbed, "We are all going to hell together . . . we will all be damned." [12]

In a little while, winter froze the trails and suspended religious meetings, but in the lonely cabins, through the long nights, the anxieties of the past summer had time to work. In June of 1800, at Red River, McGready had his Pentecost.

The occasion was another sacramental service, at which new members were admitted. McGready was not alone at this one. William Hodges and John Rankin, Presbyterian preachers, were assisting at the service, and in addition two brothers, both ministers, were present. They were John and William McGee. William was a Presbyterian, John a Methodist. Their presence was not unusual. Frontier preachers were scarce enough to know each other, and a religious service was also a social occasion and therefore a treat for the settlers, so that several ministers were often invited to share in the affair and lengthen it.

McGready, Hodges and Rankin spoke; possibly one or both of the McGees did so as well. What they said is not recorded, but a solemnity settled over the house, during which the preachers, with the exception of the two brothers, stepped outside to rest. William McGee, powerfully wrought upon, walked up to the pulpit, "scarce knowing what he did," and slumped to a sitting position beside it. John was wrestling with himself. As a Methodist, he thought the time ripe for a strong emotional appeal, but it was assumed that Presbyterian meetings were supposed to be conducted quietly and with order. Finally, however, his zeal overwhelmed him. He rose and with a trembling voice urged the congregation to submit to "the Lord Omnipotent." As he warmed up, he began to twist his way between the log benches, "shouting and exhorting with all possible energy and ecstacy [*sic*]."

Whereupon the dam broke for the repressed and terrified sinners of Red River. In a moment, the floor was "covered with the slain; their screams for mercy pierced the heavens." Soon, according to McGready, one could see "profane swearers, and Sabbath-breakers pricked to the heart and crying out 'what shall we do to be saved?' " as well as the more interesting sight of "little children of ten, eleven and twelve years of age, praying, and crying for redemption, in the blood of Jesus, in agonies of distress." [13]

Despite this widespread tumult, only ten people were "savingly brought home to Christ," but McGready, unlike some later revivalists, was interested in intensity of experience rather than statistical victories. He was evidently satisfied when he moved on to Muddy River for a meeting there and similar scenes took place.

> The nights were truly awful; the camp-ground was well illuminated, the people were differently exercised all over the ground — some exhorting, some shouting, some praying, and some crying for mercy, while others lay as dead on the ground. Some of the spiritually wounded fled to the woods, and their groans could be heard all through the surrounding groves, as the groans of dying men.[14]

Next month, events of greater significance took place. Flushed with success, McGready had advance notice given of the next sacramental service at the Gasper River church. When word of this spread through the settlements, a number of pioneers headed, in wagons, in the saddle, and on moccasined feet, for Gasper River, to be baptized in the Spirit. McGready said they came from as far as one hundred miles away — a trip of over a week in some cases. The Lord's work was spreading phenomenally. Here was no single flock, but an entire territory catching fire. The multitude of visitors was too large to be put up by the brethren of Gasper River, so many came with tents and provisions — cold pork, slabs of corn bread, roasted fowls, and perhaps whiskey, too, to stay out the three-day meeting. Later it was claimed that this was the first camp meeting — that is, the first religious service of several days' length, held outdoors, for a group that was obliged to take shelter on the spot because of the distance from home.[15]

A mixture of motives brought the Kentuckians from far and near to the log church at Gasper River. They were looking for a rare chance to hobnob with neighbors unseen for a year at a stretch. They hoped for entertainment in the form of rousing sermons, and a chance to let out feelings which were cramped up by a hog and hominy existence. But it is important to remember that fundamentally they were expecting to be converted by divine influence. Put simply, they came expecting a miracle.

"Except a man be born again, he cannot see the kingdom of God," Jesus told Nicodemus, the Pharisee who came to him by night.[16] To certain Protestant believers in America in 1800, this "new birth" was the central point in religious life. It outweighed good works and dogmas and sacraments, and the true church was built around it. Church bodies of this persuasion somewhat loosely carried the name "evangelical," and the major evangelical denominations in the United States were the Congregational, Presbyterian, Methodist and Baptist churches and their various offshoots.

All these churches agreed that man, sinful by nature since Adam's fall, deserved damnation eternally. They agreed, too, that the death of Christ made atonement for the sins of men and opened the prospect of heaven to the human race — not as a matter of justice, but as a free act of God's sovereign grace. From that point onward, they were often poles apart on questions of belief. How large a part of the human race would be saved? Could a sinner help in the work of grace by good deeds? What were the duties and perils of those who were saved from damnation? What was the place of a church in this scheme of affairs? Over these and hundreds of associated problems theologians fought long and often bitterly.

Yet, in 1800, these evangelical communions did share one other vastly important expectation. They believed that those destined for eternal life went through a definite, palpable religious experience. First a man (or woman) felt a gnawing sense of guilt and wickedness, and then a frightening awareness that hell was an entirely just punishment for such a wretch as he. Thus, "broken down before the Lord," the sinner, stripped of pride and self-esteem, was ready to throw himself on God's mercy. Now, if God had chosen him for salvation, he might read the promises in the Bible and feel that they applied to him. He could pass from being "convicted" of sin and "anxious" for his soul, to a state described as "hopeful." Lastly, he might have a climactic emotional experience, some special "baptism of the Spirit," some inward, unmistakable sign that pardon was extended and a crown of glory laid up for him in heaven. This was regeneration. Without it all men and women, no matter how shining their virtues or pious their deeds, were sinners. But the sinner who had this experience was "saved," or "converted," or "born again," or "made a Christian," the exact term differing with the time and place.[17]

The Puritan fathers of New England insisted that only those who were saved could be church members in the most complete sense. In order to be fully received into their Presbyterian and Congregational congregations, newcomers had to "make confession of their faith and declare what work of grace the Lord had wrought in them." [18] It was assumed that the work was a lengthy one, proceeding by degrees from preparation "through calling, faith, justification, adoption, sanctification." [19] Some men and women attended services faithfully for years before they could testify to experiencing salvation. Assurance was a slow-ripening fruit.

Yet it did not have to be. God could, if he chose, convert one sinner in a flash — as He had done with Saul of Tarsus — or three thousand, as he had done on the day of Pentecost. Sometimes, instead of causing the seed of rebirth to mature gradually, sinner by sinner, He might shower His grace simultaneously on whole congregations of lost souls. Overnight, church membership could make a dramatic upward surge. Testimonies of conversion would pour thick and fast into the delighted ears of ministers, hastening to welcome crowds of new sheep into the fold. When such things happened, churchmen knew that they were experiencing a "revival of religion."

A revival was a joyful thing. It was also an extraordinary thing — a miracle within a miracle. For conversion itself was a supernatural affair. The Holy Spirit purged away the corruptions of a soul and changed it from black to white. It was clearly a work of God outside the sequence of natural events, even when it took years. When the work of grace occurred in a flash, it was even more visibly a divine intervention. A true believer, watching such a conversion, trembled at the nearness of God.

This was the miracle which the roughly dressed men and women converging on Gasper River were expecting. They wanted to witness and share in a mighty baptism of the Holy Ghost. When they received it, they would show it in ways considerably stronger than trembling. For a sudden conversion was a tidal wave of feeling. When the traditionally slow cycle of guilt, despair, hope and assurance was compressed into a few days or hours, its emotional states were agonizingly intensified. The terrors of hell and the joys of eternal bliss took on cutting edges which knifed deep into self-control. At the very least, tears might be expected when the sinner was "first . . . nailed on the cross of natural despair and agony, and then in the twinkling of an eye . . . miraculously released." [20] In the settled towns of the East, however, where conventions of propriety had hard-

ened, tears were about the most that could be anticipated in the
way of demonstration.

The frontiersman was different. He lived, worked and died
hard. It was natural that he should convert hard; that he should
cry aloud in wrestling with his guilt; and that he should leap
and twist and shout in rejoicing over his forgiveness. The revival was something of a blessing to the settlers for this reason.
They lived always in the shadow of the terror by night, the
arrow by noonday, and the pestilence that walked in darkness.
Yet a rigorous code prevented them from expressing self-pity,
or fear, or the need of each other, or wonder at their own sur-
vival. They needed iron in their souls to stay alive, and the iron
did not let them unbend. But in religious life, they were willing
to suspend the rules. Then starved feelings feasted to the full
on terror and glory, in public, and without shame. On the frontier, Puritan theology lost some of its New England formality
and stood revealed for the heart-shaking thing it was.[21]

At Gasper River, that revelation was not long in coming. The
settlement was soon crowded with lean and travel-worn worshipers. When it was clear that the meetinghouse would not
hold the crowd, the men got to work with their axes and built
themselves split-log benches, resting on sticks, and outdoor
preaching stands. Services were removed to God's first temples.[22]

On Saturday, under the preaching of McGready, William
McGee and others, the fountains of the great deep were broken
up. Presently, everywhere there were "sinners lying powerless
praying and crying for mercy." In the special vocabulary of
revivalism, however, children were "sinners," too, if they had
not undergone the saving crisis. Nobody thought it strange,
therefore, for a little girl, who had been crouching with her
head in her mother's lap, to start up and shout:

> "O he is willing, he is willing — he is come, he is come — O,
> what a sweet Christ he is — O, what a precious Christ he is —
> O, what a fullness I see in him — O, what a beauty I see in him
> — O, why was it that I never could believe! that I never could
> come to Christ before, when Christ was so willing to save
> me?" [23]

Amid such outbursts, the work went on, with the groans of the "awakened" ringing through the meetinghouse and grove. When the preachers were exhausted, the insatiable worshipers gathered in knots to pray together and, if lucky, "to tell the sweet wonders which they saw in Christ." The night hours crept on into the morning, and this alone was enough to make the event memorable in the minds of people who had to rise with the roosters every day of their lives. Sleepless and light-headed, the "mourners" — that is, the unconverted — endured fresh showers of brimstone and gracious promises in alterna-tion all through Sunday and Sunday night. On Monday, a "vast concourse of people" were there, grown men and women, children, graybeards and Negroes, too, still throbbing with fatigue, fear and exhilaration. On Tuesday morning, after four days and nights, the meeting broke up. Satan had been well bitten and gouged. Forty-five had professed salvation, a number small in itself, but to preachers in the sparsely peopled back-woods as numerous as the sands of the sea.[24]

By the end of 1800, much of southwestern Kentucky and part of Tennessee had caught the revival fire, and now it spread northward. One of McGready's converts in his North Carolina days had been Barton Warren Stone, a Marylander by birth who had come to Carolina in the foot-loose way of the pioneer, studied at a frontier academy, and been saved by the Guilford County revivalist. He had gone into the Presbyterian ministry then, and eventually had taken charge of two congregations at Concord and Cane Ridge, in Bourbon County, Kentucky, near the present city of Lexington.[25]

Stone came down to Logan County to see what was going on, and went back to use the techniques of the master in his own spiritual fief. He was soon joined by others, most notably Richard McNemar. McNemar, two years the senior of Stone, was a Pennsylvanian. He, too, was a Western Presbyterian pas-tor, raised to revere the eternal God and to farm. He had held a pulpit in Cane Ridge before Stone got there, and also served at Turtle Creek, Ohio, and Cabin Creek, Kentucky.[26]

Soon Stone, McNemar and kindred spirits had the settlements

which clung to the creeks and rivers resounding to the cries of the distressed at camp meetings. Within a year after the Logan County revival of 1800, the monster meeting of the region's history took place at Cane Ridge. It was another sacramental service, to culminate in the administration of the Lord's Supper, and was announced for August 6, 1801. Somehow, a current of excitement ran from cabin to cabin, and when the appointed day came, an unbelievable crowd was gathered to be washed of its sins.

The preachers congregated at Cane Ridge had never seen anything like it. Some of them guessed that 20,000 people were on hand. One put it as high as 25,000, a fantastic total in view of the fact that in 1800 there were not more than a quarter of a million people in Kentucky, so scattered that Lexington, the state's largest city, had only 1795 residents.[27] But all the figures were somewhat imprecise. One man counted 147 wagons on the ground Saturday morning, and even allowing for horseback riders and those on foot, that would have meant a much smaller meeting.[28]

Whatever the numbers, there was abundant confusion. Technically, the meeting was Presbyterian, but Baptist and Methodist preachers had come to join in, and there was room for them. Even a Boanerges, a "son of thunder," could not reach a mob of such dimensions alone, so several preaching stands were set up. At eleven on Saturday morning two Presbyterian ministers were holding forth in the meetinghouse. One hundred and fifty yards away, another Presbyterian brought the good news of salvation to a crowd around his feet. Off in another direction a Methodist had an audience pressing close to him. Nearby was a knot of Negroes, one of them loudly exhorting the others. Besides the preachers, some of the worshipers, undistracted by the competition, were telling private gatherings of *their* experiences. One account said there were as many as 300 of these laymen "testifying." The ministers were handing out lead tokens to admit people to the communion, with no questions asked about denomination, and on Saturday morning alone 750 were distributed.[29]

The crowds were without form and void. They collected,

listened, shouted "Amen!" and "Hallelujah!" and then broke up and drifted away to find friends, or refreshment, or more preaching.[30] The din must have been enormous; the "stricken" were groaning, the preachers shouted, crowds of the unredeemed contributed a number of hecklers, children unquestionably cried, and horses stamped their hoofs and whinnied. There was a sound like the "roar of Niagara." At night, when campfires threw grotesque shadows of trees across the scene, the whole crowd seemed "agitated as if by a storm." [31] It rained and thundered, to make things more spectacularly impressive. Those without tents got drenched, but the work went on.[32]

It was a time to improvise. Exhorters who could not find a preaching stand climbed onto stumps or wagons. The Reverend William Burke, a Methodist, could find no regular spot unoccupied on Sunday morning, but he discovered a fallen tree on which he could stand fifteen feet above the ground. A brother Methodist tied an umbrella to a pole and held it over his head while he spoke. In moments, Burke claimed, ten thousand people were massed before him.[33]

Even if there had been only these things — the shouts, the wagons, the murmurous, plastic crowds, surging in the half darkness under the rain-beaten branches, Cane Ridge would have burned itself for life into the memories of men who were there. But stranger things were said to have happened; the power of the Lord was shown as it was when cloven tongues of fire sat upon the apostles and amid a rushing, mighty wind they spoke to an untoward generation of Parthians, Medes and Elamites, each in his own tongue. For at Cane Ridge, many men testified to the physical power of the Holy Spirit's baptism, which unstrung the knees and melted, with fervent heat, the hearts of the worshipers.

The Methodist preacher William Burke, speaking from beneath his umbrella, said that under the word of God, hundreds fell prostrate on the ground before him, and lay in agonies of distress, with a sinner occasionally jumping to his feet to give vent to "shouts of triumph." [34] These were probably believers. But scoffers, too, were affected. One man, a "blasphemer," sat mounted on a horse, smiling at these unbridled religious passions, when he suddenly reeled and fell from his saddle, where he lay unconscious for thirty hours. When awakened, he could not account for anything that had occurred during his trance.[35] Little children, too, were brought visibly into the kingdom of God, like the seven-year-old girl, sitting on her father's shoulder, who exhorted the crowd for a time and then slumped with weariness. "Poor thing, she had better be put down," a bystander said. The child roused herself and said, "Don't call me poor, for Christ is my brother, God my father, and I have a kingdom to inherit, therefore don't call me poor, for I am rich in the blood of the Lamb." [36]

Some of these stories were tricks of memory, probably, played on men who had been giddy with piety. But strange things were unquestionably happening. James B. Finley was a witness who learned at firsthand of the tremendous, churning emotional pressures of the great meeting. Finley became a Methodist minister later in life, but in 1801 he was an unlikely candidate for godly exercises. Although his father was a Presbyterian minister, the young Finley liked to whirligig at a dance, and he could hold his own in a bare-knuckle fight and take his dram of raw spirits — all these being mortal sins to frontier churchmen. He had been twenty in 1800, bred up for a doctor by his father, but seduced from his Latin, Greek and mathematics by a passionate love of hunting in the wilderness, then alive with game. Now he was living in a bark-covered cabin in southwestern Ohio, on a tract which he had grubbed clear with his ax and planted in Indian corn. Except for a slight advantage in education, he was a typical young man of the frontier.

He went to Cane Ridge out of curiosity, determined that this wild-eyed religion should not move him. His father was a Princeton graduate, and he himself had book learning and a stout constitution — enough, surely, to allow him to resist any mere "nervous excitability." Yet as he watched the meeting he suddenly became aware that his heart was thundering. His knees became jellylike, and, sitting down on a log, he looked on wide-eyed as five hundred people collapsed with "shrieks and shouts that rent the very heavens" under the spell of an exhorter. Finley scrambled to his feet and rushed back into the woods, with a feeling of suffocation. He found a log hut where liquors were kept, and at this "tavern" he had a nerve-stiffening shot of brandy. So fortified, he went back to the meeting and wandered from crowd to crowd, but it seemed that his mind insisted on raking up every sin he had ever committed, until he felt that he would die if he did not get relief. After a night spent sleeping in a haystack with his guilt for company, he started back home, and burst into an irrational fit of crying on the way. The next day at evening he crept into the woods to pray, but when his knees touched the ground, he gave a shout and fell prostrate. Neighbors found him and put him to bed. When he awoke, he had a sudden feeling of release, and he went on home, uncontrollably laughing, weeping and shouting most of the way.[37] That was how the Kentucky revival worked on one man who was neither a mystic nor a zealot.

Under such compulsions, the neuromuscular system suddenly chose to render its own testimony. At Cane Ridge and elsewhere in the frontier world, during these years, men and women were suddenly swept up in various "exercises" which reflected, to the backwoods mind, especially bountiful gifts of the Holy Spirit.

There was, for one thing, catalepsy, as in the case of Rachel Martin. She was a Kentucky girl who was smitten with a sense of her lost estate and lay for nine days, neither moving, nor uttering speech, nor taking food, until she obtained blessed assurance.[38]

Then, most spectacularly, there were the "jerks," a spasmodic twitching of the entire body of the transported penitent. Richard McNemar said that the victim bounced about like a ball, or hopped from place to place with head, limbs and trunk shaking "as if they must . . . fly asunder." Sometimes the movement would be so quick that the kerchiefs on women's heads would be snapped off.[39] Peter Cartwright, an Illinois Methodist parson, said that even the hairpins flew out, but Cartwright was not above the frontier trick of embroidering a story.[40] James Finley saw another form of the jerks in 1804, in Tennessee. The penitents bent backward and forward rapidly, their heads nearly touching the ground at the end of each stroke.[41] Lorenzo Dow, a wandering apostle who had spells and saw visions, claimed to have seen the "exercise" in Tennessee in that same year. At one meeting ground there was a thoughtful touch. Saplings had been cut and peeled, making short posts in the ground to which the afflicted could cling to steady themselves between spasms. The earth around them was kicked up and scuffed like the ground under the feet of a horse stamping off flies. The faces of the victims, Dow said, bore a "heavenly smile" during the fit.[42] Jacob Young, another traveling Methodist, said that ladies pouring tea were sometimes taken with the jerks at home and involuntarily flung their cups upward to break against the ceiling.[43]

There were other evidences of strange fire, too — the "laughing exercise," when uncontrollable guffaws exploded in the congregation, although "the manner was devout even when the laugh was boisterous"; the "singing exercise," in which the worshiper chanted melodiously, to the captivation of those nearby, and in which the sound issued entirely from the breast, and not the nose or throat; and the "barking exercise," when the smitten gathered on their knees at the foot of a tree, barking and snapping in order to "tree the Devil."[44]

Many stories of unusual transports of holy joy and anguish were undoubtedly stretched. Some came from supporters of the revivals, accepting all that they heard in the firm belief that "with God nothing shall be impossible." Others were planted by opponents, who were trying to underscore the element of caricature in the meetings. But there was good evidence that the spirit often overcame the believers in one way or another. The Reverend Archibald Alexander, in a dignified Connecticut church publication, said that "falling down" created a problem at first during the Cane Ridge affair, but later on grew so familiar that it disturbed nobody.[45] A Kentucky gentleman wrote to his brother in Virginia that he had seen a meeting where hundreds lay prostrate on the ground, and no mere uneducated riffraff or hysterical children, either, but "the learned pastor, the steady patriot, and the obedient son . . . the honorable matron and the virtuous maiden crying, Jesus, thou son of the most high God, have mercy on us." [46]

Claims were made that not all of the ecstasy was spiritual. A conservative Presbyterian minister noted rancorously in his diary of Cane Ridge, "Becca Bell — who often fell, is now big with child to a wicked trifling school master of the name of Brown. . . . Raglin's daughter seems careless. . . . Kitty Cummings got careless. . . . Polly Moffitt was with child to Petty and died miserably in child bed." [47] Finley, too, remembered later that men "furious with the effects of the maddening bowl" would outrage all decency by their conduct.[48] There was plenty of the where-withal to fill the bowl, too. Some men brought their own supplies, and some of "Satan's emissaries," with a shrewd sense of business, set up barrels as close as they could get to the meeting and went into business.[49] There were enemies of the camp meetings who were quick to sneer that "more souls were begot than saved" as the intoxication of the gatherings whirled away restraint after restraint.

There was, however, no way to prove that the emotional exhilaration of camp-meeting religion was the undoing of frontier virgins. The crowds were composed both of worshipers and of numbers of families who came merely to enjoy the show. When several hundred lonely men and women were brought together for three or four days in an informal outdoor setting, nature took its course among the awakened and the unredeemed alike. As time went on, the meetings were organized and policed, so that temptations were reduced and suspicious characters discouraged away. Once the novelty wore off, the gatherings were dominated beyond challenge by the God-fearing.

It was just as difficult to support the claim that the revival alone elevated the frontier's moral tone. The sins which McGready, Stone, McNemar and the others scourged were mostly personal and sumptuary — gambling, drinking, horse racing, cockfighting, swearing and dueling. As churches grew in number, the practice of these arts declined. But as churches multiplied, so did schoolhouses, courts of law, newspapers and other tranquilizing agencies. All played a part in sanding the ragged edges off the backwoods character.

With or without dancing, laughing, singing, rolling, barking and jerking, revivalism rolled over Kentucky, Tennessee and southern Ohio between 1800 and 1804, and thence spread elsewhere. At Waxhaws, in South Carolina, in 1801, there was a monster meeting with three thousand souls and twenty ministers looking up to the Southern skies for grace. A description of it carried the unlikely news that "illiterate negroes" and children from five to eight years old were moved to speak "of their views of the mediatorial glories of Christ; his fullness and sufficiency to save to the uttermost . . . the holiness of God, and the purity of the divine law."[50] Someone evidently was a better minister than he was a reporter of frontier dialect.

In the congregations of the Reverend Elisha Macurdy and the Reverend Thomas Marquis, in western Pennsylvania, the spirit of God moved over the face of the deep at sacramental services. Some fell to the ground, overborne by "the distressing anguish of a wounded spirit." Meetings crept on into the small hours of the morning. Candles were lit, and in the smoky cabin, with the shadows dancing grotesquely, and the atmosphere favorable to conjurations and visions, "many cried out." Soon, in one Pennsylvania revival after another, Satan was handled as roughly as the collectors of the Federal whiskey tax had been seven years before. In North Carolina, McGready's old pasture, the exhortation of a convert to "stand still and see the salvation of God" brought sobs, groans and cries from the packed house. Throughout the South, ministers who had been at revivals in Kentucky and Tennessee visited meetinghouses and bore the sacred flame to Georgia and Virginia.[51]

So the great revival rolled its turbulent way across the frontier world, a crude triangle of rugged territory and hard-working people, its base running from western New England to Georgia, its apex thrust deep into the valley of the Ohio and its tributaries.

The revival should have brought unanimous rejoicing in the religious world. The "unchurched" Western territory, the cause of so much despair and so many missionary societies, now seemed to be ablaze with piety. Thousands were listening eagerly to the gospel and crowding to enroll themselves among the saved. It was easy to thank the Lord enthusiastically for such undeserved, but welcome, mercies.

Yet from the very start there was another side to revivalism. It brought important innovations with it — fiery preaching, and meetings that lasted for whole days and nights together, and tumultuous emotional outbursts by the congregation. These could be dangerous. The revival was a medicine for ailing frontier denominations, starved for support. Yet like most frontier remedies, it was "heroic." It could kill as well as cure, and at the very least it was liable to rack the patient with spasms, purges and sweats. In a church, these symptoms took the form of schisms. They were not long in showing up after the Kentucky revival. By 1809, the Presbyterian Church in the West had split asunder, not once, but twice.

The Presbyterians were vulnerable, because there were, at this time, two Presbyterian worlds. The Presbyterianism of New England and the mid-Atlantic states was the child of seventeenth-century Puritanism. It was intellectually majestic, training its ministers, mainly at Princeton and Yale, to deliver sermons heavily weighted with learning in ancient and modern tongues. Its congregations were drawn from the successful classes of the countryside and supporting towns.

But as one moved southward and westward, one found Presbyterian flocks gathered mostly from the Scotch-Irish who were taming the frontier. Their pastors were educated usually at backwoods "log colleges." The learning of these men was far from contemptible, but their congregations were less contented with the dry bones of theology, hungrier to be stirred up in their worship. These differences were a mirror of a gap dividing two Americas — a settled and orderly one, facing the Atlantic, and another across the Appalachians which was crude, restless and more than a little violent. The two were constantly blending and acting upon each other.

The revival, however, was a wedge driven sharply between the two Presbyterian universes. Suddenly, contrasts between them stood out in unmistakable relief. There was, for one thing, the matter of homiletic technique — the question of how to preach.

The established method in the East was to choose a text, deduce a doctrine from it, and lead the doctrine through an hour or two of "application," honeycombed with theological pits and snares. But the revivalists believed that the word of God should be "quick and powerful" — in Saint Paul's language, "sharper than any two edged-sword, piercing even to the dividing asunder of the soul and the spirit, and of the joints and marrow." [52] To camp-meeting apostles, an "intellectual" sermon left "the heart without interest and the conscience without alarm." [53]

And that was the battle — between preaching aimed at the head and at the "joints and marrow." The revivalist thought that his whole duty was to convulse the conscience. He sharpened the message of man's guilt to a point, by repetition, and drove it into the sinner's heart. The prophets of the Kentucky awakening believed in "experimental" religion. Today, the word would be "experiential" or "experienced," but the point was that the sinner had to *feel* in his very bones the smoldering of guilt, abasement, hope and assurance.

Conservative Presbyterians did not see it that way. "I would not give this old handkerchief for all the experimental religion in the world," one of them said.[54] Others distrusted the acrobatics of the jerks. Satan, too, could make men and women dance a frenzied jig. There were ministers who were wary of "protracted meetings, night meetings . . . weeping in the pulpit . . . singing hymns, all noise — shouting, groaning, or crying out for mercy." Some of them, trained in medicine, outraged revivalists by treating fallen "mourners" like victims of a fit, instead of rejoicing over the imminent conversion.[55] It rankled a preacher like Stone or McGready, after he had exhorted a man halfway to salvation, to see someone else hold a bottle of camphor under his nose and open one of his veins. Between the believers in "experimental religion" and their conservative brethren a gap began to widen.

The breach gaped even more when the two groups read the Westminster Confession, which governed the Presbyterian Church. At that time, the confession held closely to the Calvinistic doctrine of election, which stated that God had chosen only a small part of mankind to be saved and had determined beforehand

who these "saints" would be. Those elected were "predestined"
— certain to go to heaven. All others were just as certainly
doomed. Nothing — no effort of will or agony of repentance —
could change the awful decree.

A belief like that was a millstone around a revivalist's neck.
To be aroused, sinners in his audience simply *had* to feel that
there was more hope for them than predestination allowed, *some*
reasonable chance that salvation was available. Bit by bit, revival-
minded Presbyterians drifted from the "pessimism" of ultra-
orthodoxy. Frontiersmen, who often took land without asking
and lifted their caps to nobody, were apt to lose interest altogether in a heaven whose gates were barred to all except a small
aristocracy of "saints." By 1803, Stone and McNemar were concerned lest the narrow view of election should be "the means of
strengthening sinners in their unbelief." [56] Eventually, they
feared, even preachers might stop worrying about that tiny and
unknowable chance of conversion, and take their comfort in the
empty outward observances of religion. And that would be an
end of the evangelical spirit.

From here it was an easy step to the devaluation of a learned
ministry. Better a humble, but converted, pastor than one who
was brilliant but not saved. What was the point, anyway, of
scholarly sermons to explain the ways of righteousness? A converted heart did what was right instinctively, by reflex. After all,
the apostles had known less of the law than the scribes and
Pharisees.

The seeds of separation were planted, then. A new group was
emerging in the West. They had come to believe that a guilty
sinner might well roar, faint, leap and twitch, as he struggled
toward the light. They also believed that election might be more
freely accessible than the confession allowed — that the kingdom
of heaven was really democratic, as frontiersmen had a right to
expect.

It was not long before the harvest of controversy was gathered
in. The Presbyterian Church operated under a federal organization, so that its internal conflicts had a tendency to show up
along geographical lines. Congregations were grouped together

under presbyteries, which were governing bodies composed of laymen and ministers. The presbyteries were linked in regional associations, with ruling boards known as synods. Periodically, the synods met in a general assembly of the entire church.[57] In 1801, the Kentucky Synod set up a new presbytery in southwestern Kentucky, where McGready's fires were burning. This Cumberland Presbytery promptly used its authority to ordain a number of new preachers who were something unusual in Presbyterian ministerial circles. They had no seminary training and were established men, with farms and families, who had taught themselves to "exhort." They were all ardent revivalists. Conservatives in the synod branded them as "illiterate," and began a long, bitter battle to dissolve the new presbytery. Finally, in 1809 the general assembly, which was the Presbyterian Congress and Supreme Court, agreed to doom the new body. Thereupon, the Cumberland men seceded and organized separately as the Cumberland Presbyterian Church. It remained a separate church until 1906.[58]

Meanwhile, the Kentucky Synod turned its attention to the north, and began to prepare charges of heresy against Stone, McNemar and three other revivalists. The "heretics" did not wait for trial. They withdrew and organized an independent Springfield Presbytery. Popularly named "New Lights," they soon controlled more than fifteen congregations. By 1804, however, the New Lights were moving too fast even for nominal Presbyterianism. They dissolved their organization and proclaimed a new church, carrying the simple name of "Christian." Its only creed was to be the Bible. Congregations would choose their own ministers and support them by voluntary offerings. Those ministers were to be selected only on the basis of their "soundness in the faith, acquaintance with experimental religion, gravity and aptness to teach," and their sermons were to avoid "philosophy, vain deceit," and "traditions of men."[59] In short, they were to be a band of revivalistic brothers.

Even then, some of the New Lights could find no resting place for the soles of their feet. In 1805, McNemar and some of his associates went over to the Shakers, a small sect whose members lived in little communistic commonwealths, where they practiced celibacy and worshipped the Lord with vigorous bodily exercises which gave them their name.[60] Stone, meanwhile, remained in the Christian Church, which was fortified by union with certain dissenting Methodists and Baptists.[61] In time, he became interested in the teachings of the Campbellites, or Disciples of Christ, another small, Bible-centered body founded in the West. In 1832 he led some of his fellow Christians over to a union with the followers of Thomas and Alexander Campbell, and became, at last, a patriarch among the Disciples.[62]

McGready himself was not a seceder. In 1809 he came before the Transylvania Presbytery to make "due submission to the discipline of our church in every point of view." [63] Thus, the John the Baptist of the Western awakening made amends for driving Presbyterians into the arms of Cumberlanders, Christians, Shakers and Disciples. He was a hard man to comprehend, but there was one illuminating story about him. In 1806 he was once discovered dead drunk. Sadly, he made his explanation. After a long, hard trip, he had been offered a sweetened drink, which he took gratefully and copiously, unaware that it was strongly spiked. He was, of course, bitterly sorry.[64] Perhaps revivalism had come to him in just the same way!

At any rate, by 1809 the fight was in the open and the problem was clear, if not easy. Revivalism was a blessing in the number and vigor of its converts. Yet its ecstasies and its short-circuiting of doctrine could lead whole congregations into the quicksands of heresy. Was there some way to save the energy of revivalism and yet purge away its grossness and discipline its results? Conservative evangelical ministers throughout the country would long grapple with this question.

In the interim of hesitation the revival would not cool down. An agency was busily at work institutionalizing it and spreading it over the entire West — an agency so perfectly fitted to that job that it might have been designed for the purpose. Its name was the Methodist Episcopal Church.

Presbyterianism had trouble containing the passions of the revival. Methodism was made for it. Methodist theology was more hospitable to its central ideas. The social classes from whom early Methodism recruited were less rattled by its turbulence. The Methodist plan of organization was ideally suited for making the church a transmission belt of religious values in the West.

The strict Calvinism of the Presbyterian and Congregational churches in that day was a tightly closed system. The elect were foreordained from eternity. The unregenerate could not change their fate. Even their attempts to repent were not signs of holiness, but arose out of mere selfish fear. On the other hand, the elect could not resist salvation, and once touched with grace, they could not backslide. In ministerial shorthand, "predestination, unconditional election, irresistability, and perseverance" were formidable walls, sheltering the small community of "saints." [65]

The Methodists, in clear contrast, believed in a modified kind of Arminianism, a doctrine taking its name from Jacobus Arminius, a seventeenth-century Dutch theologian. In their view, God would save "those whom He foresaw would persevere to the end," and damn "those who should continue in their unbelief." So election and reprobation were, in a measure, *conditional*, dependent partly on the behavior of the sinner. In addition, the death of Christ made atonement for the whole human race, but only those who believed in Him could enjoy its benefits. Redeeming grace could "be resisted and rendered ineffectual by perverse *will* of the impenitent sinner," and, once regenerated, even saints might relapse and "die in their sins." [66]

Thus fortified with "conditional election" and "free will," the Methodists had a head start in adopting the revival tradition. Salvation was *potentially* available to all. The sincere penitent might expect that the help of the Holy Spirit would not be denied to him. The miscreant who grew old in his sins might be passing up a genuine chance at heaven, not merely a speculative and unlikely one. On this basis it made sense to exhort the crowd to repent, to believe, to wriggle free of the suction of hell.

Besides this, a doctrine which allowed an individual some say in his (or her) eternal destiny harmonized better with democratic theory, and Methodism was thus several steps ahead in the race for converts in the new and professedly equalitarian America. As it happened, Methodists worked mostly among the pushing lower classes neglected by the successful colonial churches. They were a new church in 1800, only thirty-five years old in America, in need of converts, and quite willing to "make Methodists of the raw materials which the frontier presented." [67]

Nor did Methodists fear "enthusiasts." They were fighting in England and America against what they considered heartless and cold formality, and they recruited among the lowly, where the belief in supernatural doings reigned, uncorrupted by the educated rationalism of the Enlightenment. A pioneer American Methodist like Richard Whatcoat found nothing strange in the experience of one "Nancy Jeferis," whom he visited in Virginia in 1789. She had "Lost her Speech four days & Nights But God was with her She saw a Glorious place and heared heavenly Music; and also Heard the Screeks & Crys of Damned Souls." [68] The same night that Whatcoat visited Nancy, he went to the prayer meeting where "one woman Brok oute in prayer with all her Might in Dutch." Next month, when Bishop Asbury — Francis Asbury, patron saint of American Methodism — preached a discourse in "Accamack Courthouse," the Lord's power "Came Down upon the people so that Maney began to praise the Lord Call upon his Name and Exhort the people &c." [69] All of this was acceptable, if not normal Methodist procedure.

Hence the Methodist reputation, at the time, for noise and excitement. At Cane Ridge, one Presbyterian minister wrote of the people falling down around him, and reported unhappily that this *"was a new thing among Presbyterians,"* not among Methodists.[70] For the entire first half of the nineteenth century, millions of Americans shared the belief of an Arkansas Presbyterian who wrote in 1846 that the piety of Methodist parsons was "very low, except when the fit is on them."[71] Nevertheless, bodily vigor in religion coincided nicely with the emotional demands of the wilderness, and precisely because early Methodists did not turn their backs on groans and jerks, they could slay their thousands while the other denominations counted their hundreds.

But the Methodists had something more than democracy and enthusiasm on their side. Western Baptists, too, were down-to-earth in their membership, to name only one example. The Methodists had an extra advantage in a unique scheme of organization both flexible and autocratic. They had few seminaries and widely scattered flocks, so they recruited untrained preachers and kept them on the move. Individual Methodist congregations, called "classes," were linked into "circuits," which embraced a number of classes close enough together to be reached by a man on horseback in a circular tour of two or three months. Circuits were gathered into "districts," and districts into regional "conferences," which were represented in a general conference of the entire church every four years.

The wheel horse of the system was the traveling minister, or circuit rider. A class member with some speaking talent could be licensed as an "exhorter," to try his abilities on friends and neighbors. He could then advance to become a circuit rider. Eventually, he might rise to be a district superintendent, or "presiding elder." At the general conferences, the presiding elders elected bishops from among themselves from time to time, though not many — only twelve in the first fifty years of the church in America.[72]

The circuit riders were a superbly mobile force, ready to go anywhere, at any time, where sinners were in need of the saving word. No settlement was too rundown or too remote for them. They roughed it along the trails in snow and rain, taking their chances on bears, wolves, cutthroats and Indians. They put up where they could find local hospitality, which usually meant corn bread and pork and a spot for sleeping on the dirt floor by the fire. They spent a good part of their lives hungry, wet, cold, verminous and saddlesore, and if they did not die young of consumption, they could expect an old age of rheumatism and dyspepsia. But they went almost literally everywhere. A disgruntled Kentucky Presbyterian once was "ambitious to find a family whose cabin had not been entered by a Methodist preacher. In several days I travelled from settlement to settlement . . . but into every hovel I entered I learned that the Methodist missionary had been there before me." [73] A folk saying was even more succinct. When blizzards howled or cloudbursts pelted down, people said that "nobody was out but crows and Methodist preachers."

Yet the "Methodist preachers" were part of a well-disciplined force. The circuit riders were chosen by the presiding elders, and new presiding elders were made by the bishops. Approval came from the top down. Besides this, elders continually visited their subordinate circuits, and bishops wore themselves into exhaustion by constant rounds of inspection covering whole conferences. The traveling was miserable, and the pay, for a long time, sixty-four dollars a year. The reward, however, was not only a harvest of souls for the Lord, but a solid church. Circuit riders could not strike off into schismatic paths, carrying faithful congregations after them. Bishops and elders were always appearing to test classes for doctrinal soundness. In addition, the circuit riders themselves were shifted to a new circuit every year or two by the inflexible command of the *Discipline*, the Methodist rulebook. So in spite of the fact that frontier Methodist ministers were completely on their own for months at a time, the church had a remarkable unity. Until the trouble over slavery broke it apart in 1844, it suffered only two extremely minor secessions, both of them over questions of organization.[74]

The American Wesleyans, therefore, had nothing to fear from the heat and fury of the revival. It worked on their side, as the sinners of the clearings, roused from their indifference, were collected wholesale into Methodist classes by the tireless circuit riders. The Methodists had grown from 15,000 souls in 1785 to 850,000 by 1840, in good part because of their identification with the revivalist viewpoint.[75] The contribution was not all one-sided, however. From bishops to exhorters, the Methodists, in turn, were wide-ranging salesmen of the revival point of view, and they froze into revivalism itself a number of practices which lingered long after the last circuit rider had hung up his saddle-bags. Things that were novelties in 1800 came to be at home in American religious life when the evangelists of circuit, district and conference were through with them.[76]

For one thing, they brought the supernatural world close. It was easy for them, countrymen as they were. Frontier boys grew up believing that Satan was as real as General Washington, and hell as palpable as Pittsburgh. Dreams had meaning, and the activities of beasts were oracles to the knowing. Birth, love and death were assisted or held back by incantations.[77] When a boy raised in this way became a preacher, it was not hard to reconcile his folk inheritance and his Christianity.

So Lorenzo Dow could be a seer and a traveling Methodist prophet at the same time. The Methodists did not allow him formally to be one of them, because he would not stay put on circuits. But he sturdily insisted that "God did own the Methodists," and with or without a license from any conference, he assisted at their camp meetings all over the country.[78] Lorenzo, who called himself an "eccentric Cosmopolite," had a vivid dream life. He spoke with the prophet Nathan at the age of twelve, and at thirteen was taken to heaven in a whirlwind, where he saw God, Jesus and the angel Gabriel.[79] God even told him in advance that the British would burn Washington in the War of 1812.[80] Divine wrath was ready to punish Lorenzo's enemies, too. Soon after a group of rowdies broke up one of Dow's meetings in Virginia, the ringleader had his nose bitten off in a fight, and another member of the gang broke his neck in a fall from a horse — clearly, "chastisement from the Lord." [81]

Dow was unbalanced, but the circuit rider Peter Cartwright was a shrewd and practical backwoodsman, with no nonsense about him. Yet Cartwright was converted when a voice from heaven said, "Peter, look at me." [82] James Finley, after his conversion, took to a circuit rider's life when he opened the Bible at random and found a passage in Deuteronomy: "Thy shoes shall be as iron and brass," an assurance from above that he was qualified.[83] Jacob Young, another itinerant, doubted the genuineness of his own conversion, until, one night, "the Savior appeared with the book of life in his hand" and showed Young his name properly inscribed there.[84]

Years later, revivalists would talk easily of Jesus, leaning over the battlements of heaven to see how individual sinners reacted to sermons. Or they would dramatize conversations between the

Devil and backsliders, or dying children and choirs of angels. When they did so, they were awakening old ghosts. Long after popular education had limited the role of superstition, they played on half-conscious memories of a time when circuit riders taught that God and His hosts were very near.

Another thing the mounted Methodist clergymen did to perfection was to raise the emotional content of preaching to excruciating levels. For them, the "new birth" had pangs which cut to the bone, and they meant for their listeners to share the intensity. Finley, when the Spirit finally found him, long after Cane Ridge, shivered alone in a hollow log, weeping and reading the Bible for days at a stretch.[85] Cartwright was struck down by a flash of divine light all around him.[86] Young was unconscious for a few hours when first smitten with conviction, and fainted again when he was at last "translated from the power of darkness into the kingdom of God's dear Son." [87] Men who "got religion" in such ways thought that preaching was a failure if it did not induce an identical saving agony in their listeners. Worship without excitement — without tears of glory and shouts of penitence — was "*a sham.*" A service lacking in thunder and lightning might just as well be carried on by machines.[88] Feeling this way, the Cartwrights and Finleys and hundreds of their fellows carried the throat-tightening, pulse-fluttering stimulation of frontier religion to every lonely cabin in the West. They spread the spirit of the Kentucky awakenings across an entire section of the country. In time to come, the revival as a kind of theatrical excitement in religious dress would rest on foundations which they helped to set in place.

Above all, the Methodist itinerants liked plain talk. Their sermons were short and pungent, aimed at holding crowds which were quick to show scorn or boredom. Proudly, the circuit riders boasted that they read nothing but the Bible, the hymnbook and the *Discipline*. By the eighteen-fifties, when Methodist colleges were raising a new generation of ministers, an aging Finley complained that the "multiplication of books" would result in "diverting the mind from the Bible." [89] Cartwright detested educated young ministers; they reminded him of "a gosling that had got the straddles by wading in the dew." [90] Mostly these were patriarchal grumblings, not the guns of a formal revolt against "intellect." Yet somehow, there was a breach that these men sensed and believed in — the breach between an "evangelistic" ministry and an "educated" ministry. In all the history of revivalism, it would never be closed.

Of course, the plain-spoken Methodists could be ridiculed by secular writers, and they were. Johnson Hooper, a Southern humorist of the eighteen-forties, caricatured the struggles of a preacher with a reluctant convert at an Alabama camp meeting:

> Then he tried to argy wi' me — but bless the Lord! — he couldn't do that nother! Ha! Lord! I tuk him fust in the Old Testament — bless the Lord! — and I argyed him all thro' Kings — then I throwed him into Proverbs — and from that, here we had it up and down, kleer down to the New Testament, and then I begun to see it work him! Then we got into Matthy, and from Matthy right straight along to Acts; and *thar* I throwed him! . . . Yes L-o-r-d! and h-e-r-e he is! [91]

Hooper had his central character, a picaresque rascal named Simon Suggs, pretend to be converted, take up a collection to spread the good word in his own town, and decamp with the money. That was a staple of frontier humor. Mark Twain lifted it bodily into *Huckleberry Finn* when he had the King work the same game on a camp meeting in Pokeville.[92] But the Methodist itinerants had the last laugh. Their preaching might be foolishness to some, but their audiences suffered them gladly, and the church in the West was built in considerable measure on their work. Thanks to them, it was in good part a revivalistic church.

The legacies of the circuit riders endured long after the spread of settlement and education made their calling obsolete. They had spread the potent, pervasive, democratic and irresistible Arminian theology up and down the West, and it was to be the hallmark of revival preaching ever after. Because their lack of education made them laymen in all but name, they had proved by their work that laymen could be the backbone of evangelism, and the revivalists who came after them were for the most part innocent of formal theological training, though they might acquire degrees of divinity in the course of their labors.

They created an atmosphere of intensity and zeal which lingered after them, and they gave respectability, of a sort, to plain, ungrammatical and almost chatty talk about eternal concerns. They turned Jesus, the hosts of heaven and the powers of hell into villains and heroes as recognizable as Indians and claim-jumpers. The revival of the nineteenth century finally came to be a series of mass meetings addressed in plain language with emotional zest by a man untutored in technical divinity. Such meetings first took place on the frontier under the revivalistic Presbyterians; such meetings were riveted into American experience by the traveling Methodists.

Yet before the rough and shaggy frontier camp meeting could become part of a national tradition, it had to be refined, combed and groomed for marriage to the respectable religiosity of already established regions. Revivalism did not come to the cities hot, smoking and direct from the Kentucky campfires. It underwent a period of probation and polishing. Even as the victory shouts were rising from Red River and Cane Ridge, another kind of revival — fundamentally similar, but adapted to vastly different local conditions — was taking place in the Presbyterian and Congregationalist church houses of New England and New York. The Atlantic phase of the Great Revival of 1800 was enlisting its champions. They were better bred and cultivated than the Western messengers whom God was sending before His face. But they were equally full of holy concern.

CHAPTER III

And Some, Pastors and Teachers

ONE November day in 1792, a twenty-two-year-old youth named Edward Griffin took his youngest sister to a prayer meeting in their home town of East Haddam, Connecticut. He was glad of the chance to do so. A serious-minded boy, two years out of Yale, he had abruptly given up plans for law in favor of the ministry, and was "reading" theology at New Haven when, during a visit home, he became aware of the fact that he was the only "professor of religion" in a family of ten. This was an especially "trying" fact for a fledgling shepherd of God to digest, and Griffin had been brooding about it for a while when his sister gratifyingly agreed to visit the prayer meeting in his company.

There, he had a victory in store for him. As they left, the girl burst into tears and said, "The singing of those christians [*sic*] convinces me that they have something which I want." Griffin hurried her home and then went to call together his family and that of his uncle, who lived in the neighborhood. While his sister "lay weeping in anguish of spirit," he delivered an impromptu sermon, urging them all to submit to the Lord. Under the circumstances, he was quite effective. He converted his sister, his mother, a sister-in-law and a few other kinsmen. And that, he later wrote, "was the beginning of American revivals so far as they fell under my personal observation." [1]

Griffin's "personal observation" was limited. American revivals had begun well before his efforts. But there was something significant in his hearthside appeal for converts. It showed the threads of a new pattern emerging in the Northeast. In the next few years, while frontier preachers like McGready were leading their deerskin-clad hundreds to the throne of grace, redemption of the fallen on a grand scale was also taking place in New England, New York, New Jersey and Pennsylvania. Yet there was a difference in the Lord's doings east and west of the Alleghenies, which was reflected in miniature in Griffin's first victory as a soul saver.

Griffin was a college-trained man. His education did not include fist fighting and beaver trapping, which was often enough the case with Western evangelists. His hand held a Bible easily. It had never been shaped around a gunstock or a skinning knife. His first missionary effort did not take place in a cabin lit by pine knots, but in the oppressively proper parlor of a small-town Connecticut dwelling. And this meant something. As he knew it, revivalism had a flavor of home about it, of something close-knit and watchful for indecorum. To be converted in Kentucky was likely enough an exercise of the body; in Connecticut it was an exercise mostly of the mind.

Many minds were deeply affected when revivals began to warm the religious atmosphere of New England towns, flowing together into a discernible tide by 1800. Churchmen called them "an uninterrupted series of . . . celestial visitations." [2] But in secular terms, they were palpable reactions to the need to match religion with social change in New England. Spreading over the first quarter of the nineteenth century, they spelled out the effort of a whole generation of rural Christians to fuse together an inherited faith and a new set of values which were democratic, practical and optimistic.

The fusion could be made, but not without unforeseen results. To allow for the practice of revivalism, Calvinist theology had to undergo considerable modification. It had to leave more room for human hope and reason. It had to pose a universe still governed by a sovereign Jehovah, but not in a completely arbitrary fashion — rather, through moral principle, to which men might (with His help) conform. Such new views, however, laid upon the shoulders of the pious a duty to *act*, as well as believe. So revivalism spilled over into social and community activities. Saint Paul and John Calvin were levied upon to underwrite or refashion the ethics of nineteenth-century American society. And this in turn added new responsibilities to the high calling of the pastors. Ministers who would take the lead in promoting revivals and moral reformation had to spend an inordinate amount of time sitting in meetings and walking to and fro among the congregations. They became men on the move, and such men do not long remain what they were in a tradition-bound society. So all in all, New England revivalism helped to fit out American Christianity with a set of working clothes. It was not the opium, but the adrenaline, of the people.

When Edward Griffin put the beginning of American revivalism in 1792, he was actually more than fifty years out of date. When "respectable" Eastern ministers spoke with scorn of the "extravagances" of Methodist or frontier worship, they did so with painful, self-conscious memories. For the eastern seaboard had felt the power of a tremendous revival in the seventeen-forties, known as the Great Awakening. An awakening it certainly was, but it had also been a religious explosion. Griffin's generation, looking backward, found it both fascinating and frightening.

Well into the eighteenth century, the Congregational and Presbyterian churches of New England continued to assume that the only "true" church members were the elect of God, who had experienced conversion. Yet there were problems in operating a church on earth when only God knew who the real members were. Not everyone could boldly and positively testify that his conversion was genuine. As the zeal of the first founders cooled, fewer men and women were found to bear public witness that they had "experienced religion." In order to keep membership from shrinking drastically, many churches had to settle for the Half-Way Covenant of 1662. By its terms the "unawakened" could enjoy a kind of partial membership, baptizing their children and joining in congregational activities, but not taking full communion. This was enough church affiliation for most political and social purposes, so that gradually the "saved" sank to a tiny minority. Orthodox writers grieved over mere formalism and worldliness in the churches, and wondered if New England had not "in great measure forgot the errand of our Fathers." [3]

But in 1734, a corner of the Yankee world suddenly experienced a vast change. In the little Massachusetts town of Northampton, the Reverend Jonathan Edwards had spiritual charge of two hundred families, suffering an "extraordinary dulness in religion." There was little self-examination and, on the other hand, a good deal of "licentiousness . . . night walking, and frequenting the tavern, and lewd practices." In December, 1734, however, "the Spirit of God began extraordinarily to set in." A "great and earnest concern about the great things of . . . the eternal world" swept the town. Soon, the only preoccupation of the townspeople was "to get the kingdom of heaven, and every one appeared pressing into it." At communion services, converted sinners began to appear — one hundred before one sacrament, sixty at another, and so on until the number of communicants (as opposed to mere halfway members) was six hundred and twenty, "almost all our adult persons."[4]

Edwards called this a "surprising work of God," and properly said little about the effect of his own sermons and influence. Yet the work at Northampton was only part of a renaissance of piety stirring churches throughout the colonies. In 1720, Theodore J. Frelinghuysen, a minister of the Dutch Reformed Church in New Jersey, had stirred the feelings of his solid Raritan valley farmer parishioners with a series of "impassioned" appeals and enjoyed a great "ingathering of new members." Next, the fire spread to the Scotch-Irish Presbyterians of the middle colonies. In a little school derisively dubbed a "Log College" by more bookish clergymen, a Pennsylvania preacher named William Tennent was turning out a number of ministers of "flaming evangelical zeal." Whatever their scholarly failings, his alumni soon had revivals flourishing, particularly in New Jersey. After a time, Log College men dominated a newly created New Brunswick Presbytery. Soon there was an argument with conservatives over the question of "educated" versus "converted" ministers, and there was an exact preview of what happened, nearly seventy years later, to the Cumberland Presbytery. The New Brunswick Presbytery was expelled from the parent body, and the whole Presbyterian Church was divided into "New Side" men, favoring the revival system, and their "Old Side" opponents.

Undiscouraged by opposition, the New Side forces organized a separate New York Synod and sent missionaries into the Southern colonies. The tang of Log College preaching was brought into an atmosphere chilled by Anglican formality. Under the special leadership of the Reverend Samuel Davies, revivalistic Presbyterian congregations took root in Virginia. In Virginia and the Carolinas both, the Baptists commenced to flourish noisily under an "uneducated" and often part-time frontier ministry. The Methodists, a step behind, were to come along on the eve of the Revolution and profit by the rebellion against the "establishment." [5] The groundwork of the movement everywhere was laid by social change. The state-supported churches in the colonies were tightly controlled by the upper-class descendants of the first-comers. In the course of a century they had taken over the best lands, the richest trades, and the front pews in the houses of worship. Recently arrived Scotch-Irish, German and other immigrants were resentful. When they flocked to revival meetings, they were, in part, registering a protest against the idea that salvation, too, was a monopoly of the colonial aristocrats.

In 1739, the whole awakening received a gigantic stimulus with the arrival in Delaware of George Whitefield, mass evangelism's true father. Whitefield, a close friend of the Wesleys, founders of Methodism, had packed churches in England with warmly emotional appeals for conversion. Now he brought his powerful voice and magnetic style to the colonies, and preached his way through Georgia, the Carolinas, Virginia, Maryland, Pennsylvania and New York. In Philadelphia he spoke outdoors, and even the worldly-wise Benjamin Franklin was impressed, especially when the audience "admir'd and respected him, not withstanding his . . . assuring them they were naturally *half beasts and half devils.*" It was a surprise to the deistic Franklin to walk through the streets of his city and hear psalms ringing out from house after house. He understood it better, however, when he himself later fell victim to the power of the preacher, not in the matter of religion, but of money. Whitefield was raising funds for an orphanage in Georgia, on a plan which Poor Richard disapproved. Yet after listening to Whitefield's talk, Franklin emptied his pockets into the collection dish.

The shrewd philosopher noted some of the sources of the evangelist's power. Whitefield's voice could reach thirty thousand people. (Franklin tested it himself by standing half a mile away, where he could still make out the words, and then computing the number of listeners who could stand elbow to elbow in a circle with a half-mile radius.) The Whitefield technique of alternately scolding and cajoling kept the audience constantly involved in his talk. And, because he traveled, Whitefield reaped the advantages of novelty and constant practice. He could repeat the same sermon in different places, until "every accent, every emphasis, every modulation of voice, was so perfectly well turn'd . . . that, without being interested in the subject, one could not help being pleas'd with the discourse; a pleasure of much the same kind with that receiv'd from an excellent piece of musick." [6] For two hundred years, successful evangelists would follow the same pattern.

It remained for Whitefield, in 1740, to cross-pollinate the New England revival begun by Edwards with that of the Middle colonies. A number of Boston ministers invited him to their town, and again a precedent was set unknowingly, for every outstandingly successful revivalist of later years would eventually find his way to the largest cities. Whitefield spoke in Boston itself, and at Harvard, and finally went to Northampton to deliver four talks to Edwards's congregation.[7] Then he journeyed on through the towns of Connecticut, where the crowds came in from the surrounding farms so thickly that it was "like a steady stream of horses and their riders scarcely a horse more than his length behind another all of a lather," all to see a man who "looked as if he was Cloathed with authority from ye great god." Men were ready for a preacher who gave "churchgoing America its first taste of the theatre under the flag of salvation."[8]

Whitefield left New England after a month, and the revival blazed behind him. Soon Boston played host to Gilbert Tennent, the son of the Log College's founder, and sinners were reminded of the "awful danger" of their going to hell, and the "amazing miseries of that place of torment." Visitors "in deep concern about their souls" began thronging to ministers' doors. Special weekday evening lectures in the churches drew capacity audiences, and private prayer groups multiplied in the city, so that preachers were constantly busy trying to visit them all.⁹ Meanwhile, Edwards and other ministers began to visit neighboring towns to deliver "revival sermons." When Edwards spoke at Enfield, Connecticut, about "Sinners in the Hands of an Angry God," he was merciless. He described God holding men over the flames in the way that one held a loathsome spider over a candle. He speculated on how it would feel to have the searing agony of a burn drawn out through eternity. He told listeners that the ground beneath their feet was a rotten flooring over a blazing pit, ready to give way in seconds. It was strong medicine for men and women to whom those flames were unmistakably real. Sobs and gasps rose to such a crescendo that Edwards sometimes had to pause in his delivery, his voice drowned out.¹⁰ The sermon was almost his undoing. Later generations of Americans almost forgot that he was a keen psychologist, a brilliant philosopher and the third president of Princeton. They remembered him, inaccurately, only as one more dramatic preacher of hell and damnation.

By 1741, all the elements of the revival were in play — the visitors in the pulpits, the threats of hell-fire, the traveling spellbinders, the prayer meetings and special gatherings, the rush of members — and also the controversies and secessions. One final hallmark was not yet visible, however. There was no hysteria. That came, too, and when it did, it carried a shock that jarred the revival party in New England to its foundations. Suddenly the awakening turned riotous, not in the backwoods, but in conservative Connecticut, and under the leadership of a stanch descendant of the Puritans.

The Reverend James Davenport, of Southold, Long Island, was clearly cut out for respectable caution in all walks of life. He came from the family of John Davenport, who had founded New Haven in 1638, and he was a graduate of Yale. When George

Whitefield came on the scene, however, Davenport was so impressed that he determined to become an evangelist himself. He made a spectacular beginning. He gathered his own congregation together and talked to them for nearly "twenty-four hours without interruption." He spoke easily of his "converts," as if he had God's certain knowledge of who would be saved.[11] Then he swung out on a tour of Connecticut towns, inviting himself into the churches of brother ministers and leading their charges in strange ways. Davenport gave "unrestrained liberty," one of those Connecticut pastors recalled, "*to noise and outcry*." Those who groaned and quaked at one moment and shouted with joy in the next were "instantly proclaimed *converts*" and others were invited to follow them. Davenport was also a great "favorer of *visions, trances, imaginations and powerful impressions*." Sixty years before Cane Ridge, Connecticut towns knew the lurid convulsions of unrestrained religious enthusiasm.

That was not all. Davenport urged his converts to "exhort *publicly*," and when ordained preachers objected, he began to drop unflattering references to "*letter learned rabbies* [sic], *scribes and Pharisees, and unconverted ministers*." This was explosive. The ministry, venerated if not always followed, was the bedrock of New England society. Moreover, the Congregational Church was the official church of Connecticut, and therefore a political institution, not to be undermined without risk. Yet Davenport pressed on and began to examine ministers on their own spiritual state. Those who submitted were likely to be labeled "unconverted," and those who refused were likewise in danger of Davenport's calling them "Christless." Since the zealous apostle was enormously popular, a minister who stood out against him ran a sizable risk to his own reputation.[12] Many of them could only stand by helplessly as the meetings grew wilder; women fainted, men shouted, and children sat frozen and wide-eyed at the excitement. In a climactic gathering in New London, Davenport had his followers hurl their fine clothes and idolatrous personal ornaments, together with certain "unscriptural" books, into bonfires.[13]

That broke the back of Davenport's movement. A Yankee Savonarola was altogether too much. The New England churches recoiled. In May, 1743, the annual convention of Massachusetts Congregational ministers issued a "Testimony" condemning a long list of revivalistic practices which led to "disorderly tumults and indecent behavior." [14] Condemnatory books and pamphlets sprang from the presses. The weightiest action came from the Connecticut colonial legislature, which passed acts that cut off the salary of any "established" minister who entered another's parish without express invitation. Preachers who were guilty of the same offense, but not on the public payroll, would be fined. Whole congregations which were guilty of dissenting from the official creed of Connecticut Congregationalism, the Saybrook Platform of 1708, could also lose their tax support. [15]

The revolt then flickered out. Davenport himself retreated and ended the war on the unconverted. A few Connecticut congregations set up on their own as "separates," and some went over to the Baptists. But in spite of another "Testimony" from over one hundred ministers in four colonies, praising the "late happy Revival," [16] the "extraordinary season" was over. Meantime, the revival ran out of energy elsewhere. Throughout the colonies, the agitation of special "awakenings" died down. Whitefield, on later visits, was met with far less tumult. Jonathan Edwards himself turned to work on the intricate and forbidding volumes of theology which would make him famous. For years his followers and their opponents kept the presses busy with controversy — New Lights, Old Lights, New Divinity, Old Divinity, Edwardeans, neo-Edwardeans and other persuasions raining learned pamphlets upon each other. [17] But the war was confined to paper, and eventually, in 1758, even Old Side and New Side Presbyterians reunited.

That was the Great Awakening, as it lingered in the consciousness of the clergymen of the seventeen-nineties. Beset as they were by alleged "infidelity" and apathy, it had vast attractions. It had aroused the churches to brisk activity in the world; dozens

of missionary, benevolent and educational enterprises had sprung
into life under religious guidance. (Rutgers, Dartmouth, Princeton and Brown were only the most famous of many schools which
could trace their founding impulse to the awakening.) [18] The
increase in church membership was even more impressive. From
1740 to 1742, between 25,000 and 50,000 members were added
to the New England churches alone. Between 1740 and 1760, 150
new Congregational bodies were formed, to say nothing of the
steadily proliferating Baptists.[19] Most of these members, too, were
"regenerate" and therefore supposedly active and conscientious
Christians in every sense. It was entirely natural, on the eve of
the nineteenth century, to think that a resurgence of revivals was
the very thing needed to restore the kingdom of God in America.

Yet there was that disturbing obverse side of the revival. The
Great Awakening had, after all, split the Presbyterian Church. It
had threatened a split in the Dutch Reformed Church. It had
sown the seeds of discord among New England Congregationalists, set laymen on high, and made ministers the targets of public
abuse. It had weakened the steady habits and good order which
made religion a social cement. Accepted, the revival was dangerously inflammatory. Resisted, it could split believers into warring
armies. There was something fundamentally dangerous about
this movement, something that made for upheaval, uprooting good
and bad alike.

So the men of Edward Griffin's day pondered their duties.
In the end, the threat of a weakened church tipped the balance,
and they chose to adopt revivals. They could not, of course, create revivals. From first to last, those were manifestations of the
divine will. Yet feeble men could pray, and wait hopefully for the
rain of grace. Therefore, church literature began to urge that
Christians assemble and entreat God for new signs of His favor.
Along with petitions to the Lord went a great deal of human
effort, for however much they denied the effectiveness of man's
work, ministers of the new America were incapable of prayer
without lively action to implement it. Among the ordained of
God, as elsewhere in the United States of 1800, passive waiting
was an impossibility.

By and by, the showers of mercy began to come. It was possible to keep a weather chart of them, because in 1800 men were learning that a movement publicized is a movement strengthened. In that year, a number of "Reverend Messieurs" launched a magazine, to be published at Hartford, which would present, among other things, "narratives of revivals of religion in particular places." [20] Dozens of Connecticut pastors pushed aside unfinished essays on regeneration and natural ability and wrote to the editors concerning "displays of sovereign grace" among their charges. So the fifteen volumes of the *Connecticut Evangelical Magazine* became a running history of revivalism in that state at the turn of the nineteenth century.

The letters clearly showed two things. First of all, the ministers were keeping the revivals firmly in their own hands and using only the "ordinary" means of grace — extra lectures delivered by themselves, prayer meetings and visits to the homes of the faithful. Secondly, a mighty effort was being made to preserve the doctrinal purity of Calvinism. Conversions were made solely at God's pleasure, for the benefit of a completely undeserving set of sinners. Moreover, there was always something speculative hanging over them. In short, there was a determined effort to avoid the burned fingers of the seventeen-forties, as well as the irrepressible yeastiness of the Western revivals, tidings of which were beginning to make their way back eastward.

Thus the Reverend "Mr. Backus" of Somers, Connecticut, wrote that in 1797 and 1798 his church had gained fifty-two members, "most of whom *professed* to have experienced a saving change." The awakening was "not . . . attended with outcry or noise." The new saints had been led to glory first by a "full discovery of their moral pollution," and even now "none manifested high confidence of their conversion." [21] Davenport's error of hastily proclaiming "*converts*" was not to be repeated.

Similar restraint marked other reports. A minister of Bristol allowed himself the statement, in 1799, that some of his flock had "received comfort." In Torrington, a pastor gladly reported that it had "pleased the great Head of the Church . . . to show forth his presence," but the result was only that a goodly number had obtained "hope of their reconciliation" — above all, there was no "wild enthusiasm or disorder." [22] At Windsor, the Reverend William F. Miller instituted weekly prayer meetings in February of 1799, and started to deliver three or four sermons a week in addition to one on the Sabbath. The result was an addition of fifty-four members in a year. Miller was quick to point out that the divine law, which had once seemed harsh to the newly born Christians, was now delighted in as "holy, just and good." [23] The Reverend Elijah Lyman, of Brookfield, took pains to record of a group of new converts that "the doctrine of election, in particular, which some could not endure but with abhorrence, and which they were wont to esteem very discouraging to sinners, now became their only encouragement . . . and was sweeter to them than honey and the honey combs." [24] Edward Griffin, now a full-fledged minister, "enjoyed" a revival and also said that those under conviction "were now wrapt up in admiration of the laws and absolute government of God, which had before been the object of so much cavil and disgust." [25] All these reservations had some very specific grounds. The Methodists of New England were gaining headway with their Arminian notion that God might save all who believed in Him; the Unitarians were giving utterance to their deistic notion that man was not innately a depraved creature. The orthodox churches needed revivals to stem the tide, but the revivals had to stay within the fence of approved doctrine.

By 1800, these small, but cheering, episodes were numerous. Had they remained localized in this way, they might have presently died out, looking for all the world like the sporadic manifestations of God's pleasure which they were supposed to be. But the Lord was also pleased to raise up at this point a number of men who were keenly aware that the church needed a defense in a rapidly changing world, and that religious enthusiasm, controlled and moderated, was essential to the very preservation of religion as they saw it. God's pleasure would have to be solicited a little more ardently, His word explained in terms that made sense to contemporaries, His faithful stimulated to a life of regular activity on His behalf, if infidelity was not to gain the upper hand in the long run. Of this new generation of New England Protestant leaders, four were outstanding, and their careers touched and twined at significant points for them all. They were Timothy Dwight, primarily a college president; Asahel Nettleton, a traveling evangelist; Nathaniel Taylor, a theologian; and Lyman Beecher, a little of everything — mostly dynamite.

In the beginning was Dwight. The grandson of Jonathan Edwards, he was born in Northampton eleven years after that great man had terrified the sinners of Enfield. Graduated from Yale in 1769, Dwight studied for the ministry, served as a chaplain in the Revolution, then returned to a Connecticut pulpit. His energy was enormous. He composed epic poems, dabbled in nature study, and was a tireless outdoor traveler, recording his impressions in voluminous journals. He plunged into the theological and political controversies of the day, and emerged as an unrelenting enemy of Jeffersonian Republicanism, "liberal" religion and infidelity — all three of which were, to him, virtually identical. He called for a return to the deep-bottomed and steady-riding society of the forefathers, unshaken by storms, with the officers secure on the quarter-deck and the crew safely in the forecastle. The church had been the keel of that society and it must be restored to vigor. From his pulpit, denunciations volleyed and thundered around the "infidels" who had "the malice and atheism of the Dragon, the cruelty and rapacity of the Beast . . . the fraud and deceit of the false Prophet." [26] The Republicans were accused of aiming to "change our holy worship into a dance of Jacobin phrenzy," and the result of their teaching would be to see "the Bible cast into a bonfire, the vessels of the sacramental supper borne by an ass in public procession . . . our sons become the disciples of Voltaire . . . our daughters the concubines of the Illuminati." [27] While he had breath, Timothy Dwight did not intend to let this happen.

For Dwight the method of battling the Antichrist was through the awakening of sinners in revivals. This could be accomplished by a liberal use of the means appointed by God — prayer, repentance and scriptural studies. The special awakening might be the

Lord's work, but man was not to sit idly awaiting the blessing. In 1795, Dwight was appointed the president of Yale College. Almost immediately he "launched the batteries of . . . revivalism" against the young men of the school, arguing, persuading, driving, bringing the relentless pressure of his energy and talent to bear on their youthful minds — until he made the college thoroughly evangelical. Yale went through revivals in 1802, 1807, 1812, 1815 and 1820, and even in intermittent periods seemed to fit the description by Benjamin Silliman. "Yale College," he wrote to his mother in 1802, "is a little temple." Since Yale was training much of the intellectual leadership of New England, not to say the country, this was a fact of transcendent importance in American history. Dwight's election to the presidency of Yale was a famous victory for revivalism and all it stood for, if not entirely for the New Divinity followers of Edwards.[28]

It was not long before graduates of the "new" Yale created by Dwight were showing others the way to salvation. One of them became a successful wandering awakener, and thus an heir to Whitefield. It was a dangerous legacy, because after James Davenport the churches were suspicious of popular messiahs who had the power to scatter confusion among the believers if they chose. But there was no need to fear Asahel Nettleton. He was not cut out to be an independent religious firebrand. Welcomed by some as "the greatest benefactor which God has given to this nation," he was basically a retiring person, and what was more, he was "deeply impressed with the importance of a settled ministry" (and with what he had heard concerning the career of Davenport).[29] His work was "uniformly discreet, and such as met the hearty approbation of judicious pastors." [30] Yet, unwittingly, he was to make drastic changes in the role of those very pastors.

Nettleton was born in North Killingworth, Connecticut, in 1783, the oldest son of a farmer in "moderate, but comfortable, circumstances," [31] a typical social background for a clergyman of the day. His family was not "Christian." His parents were church members only under the still-existing Half-Way Covenant. Despite these impious surroundings, Asahel was an impressionable boy. Once, while he was looking at a sunset, the thought that "he and all men must die" came to him and he began to cry. This and other "religious impressions" made him ripe for plucking when the revival of 1800 swept into North Killingworth. For a long period the word *eternity* "sounded louder than any voice" to him. A final conversion struggle was triggered by a spasm of guilt that overcame him after he attended a ball for Thanksgiving, and from it he at last emerged a "professor of religion." [32]

He now decided to be a missionary, crammed in the preparatory studies between chores, and got himself into Yale with the entering class of 1805, in which he claimed to be the only convert — a claim open to considerable doubt. His roommate remembered him as only an average student, a quiet, older boy of the pious type. Boys of that kind are unobtrusively at home in a small, denominational college, and Yale was just such a college in 1805. But in the autumn of 1807, a revival swept the school and Nettleton came into his own as a counselor. He was always free with his time and prepared with appropriate consolation to distraught teen-agers shuddering with the fear of damnation. He had taken the first unsuspecting step towards his vocation.

Then, chance led him further along the road to evangelism. In his junior year at Yale, Nettleton had met Samuel J. Mills, then a student at Williams College. Two years later, Mills, after attending Andover Theological Seminary, had talked the Congregational churches of Massachusetts into forming the American Board of Commissioners for Foreign Missions. Forty thousand dollars was raised, and in 1812 five young Yankee clergymen were ready to carry the gospel to India.[33] Mills had earmarked Nettleton for a pilot missionary group, and now urged him to join. But Nettleton, in the meanwhile, had gone into debt to finish his course at Yale and his studies for ordination. He had to stay and work off these obligations, so he ruefully passed up this chance to go abroad.

Since he hoped to leave soon, however, he did not want to take a settled pulpit. The Connecticut Congregational association, accordingly, sent him out as a missionary to preach in certain hinterland churches "desolated" by the westward movement. So successful was Nettleton as a traveling man that he remained one the rest of his life. Thus, by accident, he became a professional specialist in revivals.

For eight years he jogged from town to town in Connecticut. His revivals were not spectacular. He did not precipitate exciting fights with the ordained ministers. Nor were his sermons particularly pungent. His preaching was "solemn, affectionate, and remarkably plain." [34] It did not attempt to stir the audience; in fact, if the meeting began to show signs of violent feeling, Nettleton was apt to break it up. [35] He had, perhaps, slight awareness of how useful drama could be. In one of his first sermons he rose, looked around the assembly and began:

> "What is that murmur which I hear? — I wish I had a new heart. What shall I do? — They tell me to repent — I can't repent — I wish they would give me some other direction."

In this vein he went on for a time, "personating the awakened sinner." [36] But as a rule his discourses were "highly intellectual." [37] As a rhetorician, Nettleton did not precisely crackle.

> "But what must be the state of every sinner out of Christ? Sinner, in what court will you plead? At the tribunal of justice, or of mercy? It is with the kindest intention that you are now called upon to hear, that the sentence of eternal death is pronounced upon you, and that this sentence is holy, just, and good." [38]

His straightforwardly "doctrinal" preaching made heavy demands on listeners' attention.

> "But future events must become *certain* of existence before their existence can be *certainly known*. Though what is foreknown is equally certain of existence; yet mere knowledge cannot be the ground of this certainty. On the contrary, in the order of nature, absolute certainty is the ground of all knowledge." [39]

Yet he was a success; revivals followed in the towns he visited as surely as the night the day, and he and others delighted to record them in what was then the standard jargon of the evangelical clergy. In one place, "the Spirit of God accompanied his labors, and several interesting cases of hopeful conversion occurred"; in another, "a large number became, hopefully, subjects of renewing grace." In the "waste place" of East Granby, in Bridgewater, where "great stupidity prevailed among the people at large," in Torrington, and in town after town "the . . . fruits were gathered" in the shape of new members after Nettleton's sermons — each one "an arrow from the Almighty's quiver" — had done their work.[40]

Part of the reason lay in Nettleton's own perseverance. He was no pulpit spellbinder, but he was assiduous in "faithful private conversation." He followed aroused sinners to their homes, and put no limit on the amount of time he would spend with each one. His general air of lugubriousness convinced the smitten that he was genuinely concerned over their condition, and this touch of human kindness was apparently a more convincing demonstration of the redeeming power of love than a blood-and-thunder discourse.[41] If other evangelists hit upon the potency of mass appeal, Nettleton's discovery was the efficacy of the personal approach after the meeting. He could be, on paper, a crabbed controversialist, like almost every minister of the day, but he was gentle in his personal contacts.

More than this, the ground was prepared for him. The victories of Nettleton were scored in small towns, where the soil was the foundation of a regular way of life, and where the church and village were the religious and political manifestations of a homogeneous and self-confident society. Although it was on the way to becoming a factory state, Connecticut in 1820 turned out a mere two million dollars' worth of manufactures. Only New Haven, Hartford and Middleton had more than five thousand inhabitants, New Haven numbering just 8327. Immigration was passing the state by.[42] In towns of two and three and four hundred families, intimately linked in thought and feeling, it was necessary only to establish the idea that a revival was in the wind in order for it to sweep from house to house. Nor was the idea a hard one to accept. A revival was exciting, even without the dances and acrobatics of the camp meeting. For ministers and congregations believing in the literal inspiration of the Bible it was a mighty thing to feel that God Himself — God who had routed the Philistines, swept Elijah to heaven in a fiery chariot, or sent the mighty rushing wind to convert three thousand at once — God who weighed the mountains in a balance and meted the heavens with a span — might actually be showing Himself in the familiar world of main street, parsonage, kitchen garden and gristmill. In the world of Derby, South Britain, Danbury, North Lyme, Bolton, Chester and Torrington, the "village street merged imperceptibly with the golden streets of the New Jerusalem." [43] Was it any wonder that an evangelist was accepted as a heaven-sent messenger who lifted the isolated little town out of itself and bathed it for a time in an exciting glow from a light that never was on land or sea?

So Nettleton, in the eight years after his departure from Yale, became the nonpareil revivalist in the small-town world of the Nutmeg State. In the summer of 1819, he broke out into wider spheres. On a visit to Saratoga Springs, for a rest, he fell in with a minister of a nearby town who got him to conduct a meeting or two. There he was noticed by a minister of Schenectady, New York, a Dr. McAuley. McAuley invited Nettleton to his church for a time. Presently, Schenectady was buzzing with talk of the kingdom, and in the area around the city some eight hundred souls were newly born.[44]

Having a foothold in New York, Nettleton improved it for a time and then went to Yale, where the 1820 revival was in progress. In five autumn weeks eighty citizens of New Haven and twenty-five of Yale's sons were brought to "rejoice in hope." The pattern of a Yale revival was exhausting. Students not only went to chapel twice on Sundays, but they had religious meetings on Tuesday and Saturday nights, prayer meeting on Fridays and private conventicles in the dormitories. All this was in addition to normal academic duties, for every missed recitation had to be made up before examinations. It was no wonder that Connecticut was "almost totally an ecclesiastical state" with such a training ground for its leadership.[45] From Yale, Nettleton sallied forth into Massachusetts. Here, too, success followed his efforts.

But now Nettleton reached the end of his career. In the autumn of 1822, a bout of typhus laid him low. He did not recover for two years, and when he did, he was too weak for sustained preaching. In addition, the pattern of revivalism was about to change and leave him excluded. He made occasional trips as far south as Virginia, and went to England in 1831. In 1833 he accepted a chair in a new theological seminary founded at East Windsor, Connecticut, and there in 1844 he died.[46]

With his characteristically retiring air, Nettleton did not seem to be a forceful or significant figure as he wandered from hamlet to hamlet. Yet his continued success in revivals did much to create the professional idea. For if Nettleton brought showers of blessing, there was no reason why he should not make a full-time duty of pleading Zion's cause more widely. It was impossible to follow Nettleton and believe that revivals were purely transient evidences of God's generosity, likely to strike anywhere without warning or preparation. Moreover, it was impossible for a regular, Sunday-in, Sunday-out pastor to match the slight touch of glamour that even the sorrowfully reserved Nettleton, with his old honors thick upon him, brought along when he came into town. Given a Nettleton, the way was open to specialization in arousing the unsaved, and that specialization robbed the settled clergy, for good or for ill, of a vital function. However deferential to the men of God in the towns which he visited, Nettleton was doing his bit to cut down the scope of the regular ministry.

Nettleton's inoffensive manners kept him, more or less, a shadowy figure. But Lyman Beecher blazed like a star in Connecticut's firmament. For a full fifty years as minister, pamphleteer, educator and father, Beecher's one idea in life was "the promotion of revivals of religion . . . as a prominent instrumentality for the conversion of the world, and the speedy introduction of the millennial reign of our Lord Jesus Christ."[47] American spaciousness was never more dazzling. Most mortals would have found the conversion of one congregation a satisfying task, without worrying about the entire world or the millennium. But Beecher, though he claimed to defend a sixteenth-century Calvinist orthodoxy, was all nineteenth century. His life was a mirror of the

easy confidence of the down-to-earth, independent agrarian middle class of the American Republic before the Civil War. He *did*
things. As a religious leader, he never used a doctrine or a "means"
without consciously shaping it towards the advancement of his
kind of church. In his hands, the revival was knowingly used to
goad fellow Americans along the path to glory marked out by
evangelical teachings.

From boyhood he was made for success as his world understood it. He was born in 1775, in Connecticut, to a prosperous
Guilford farmer and blacksmith who could afford a hired man
and had four or five thousand dollars laid up, unthreatened by
moth and rust, before he died. Lyman was a third child and
showed his distinguishing marks early. He was fond of one of
his grandmothers, and said that "as soon as ever I saw her coming, I *clicked it* into the house, crying 'Granny's coming!
Granny's coming!'" [48] All his life, when Beecher was stirred
up about a coming event, good or bad, he would *click it* to find
an audience and shout his news. And he would express himself
in the same vocabulary, bearing about it the tang of homemade
mince pie. His loosely knit, contumacious and probably inaccurate
autobiography stands out as a gem of ministerial writing, because
Beecher was never cursed with the curious conviction of his
Bible-steeped colleagues that a good Christian leader in the nineteenth century needed to talk like a seventeenth-century translation of an ancient Hebrew book.

Lyman's mother (one of David Beecher's five wives) died when
he was a child, and the boy was sent to the farm of his uncle,
Lot Benton, who was a model of a self-sufficient yeoman good
enough to have stepped out of an economic history. Uncle Lot
had forty head of cattle, forty sheep and two horses. He made
and mended his own tools, harness and plow. He raised oats,
corn, grass and flax; his own boys cut his firewood and sheared
his sheep; his womenfolk baked their own bread and spun Lot's
wool and flax into garments. Here was a world that needed almost nothing essential from anywhere else. It was natural for
those who grew up in it to assume that the universe was merely
a larger edition. They neither knew nor needed to know of out-

side ways or values. If God governed the Creation by law, it must be the same law that operated in Connecticut. Life at Uncle Lot's was complete without once breaking the circle of the horizon.

Lyman grew healthy on rye bread, butter, buckwheat cakes, pie, salt pork, corned beef, vegetables and Indian pudding. He hunted, fished and waxed husky. But when he was eighteen, Uncle Lot made him plow a fifteen-acre patch, "steep as the roof of a house," with a clumsy, homemade plow. This kind of outdoor exercise did not appeal to the boy. He took to daydreaming and wandered out of the furrows — always, of course, by accident. Uncle Lot had not heard of psychologically caused errors, but he had not made a prosperous life by dodging realities, either. Lyman was plainly not going to be a farmer. Instead, Lot offered him a chance at college. The first step to success, for the nephew, led away from pasture and barn.[49]

Lyman was sent off to Yale, poorly prepared either for learning or piety. He was "not much of a reader," and his religion was entirely practical. The sermons he heard puzzled him, but once another boy reproached him for playing on Sunday and told him that God would put him in a fire and burn him forever. "That took hold," Beecher said. "I understood what fire was, and what forever was. What emotion I had, thinking, No end! No end! *It has been a sort of mainspring ever since.*"[50]

Yale, in 1793, was not much of a college to open windows wider on the world for Beecher. He remembered that the entire physical-science equipment consisted of a rusty orrery, a four-foot telescope, a decrepit air pump, a prism and an elastic hoop to demonstrate centrifugal force. Other facilities for reading and instruction were not much better. But in 1795 Timothy Dwight appeared, and he was a university in himself. Beecher loved him to distraction. Dwight expanded the horizons of his student body, mostly the gawky sons of country farmers and preachers, even while restoring "orthodoxy" and battling French philosophy. He made them feel that they could, by proper use of the means of grace, act as instruments of God in the mighty struggle to redeem the saved. He awakened them to the austere majesty of the Puritan drama of man's weakness, God's might, and the battle for

souls between good and evil. There was excitement in contempla-
tion of the gulf between man's vileness and God's goodness, and
high challenge in calling upon God's mercy and man's ability in
order to help cross the gulf. When Lyman Beecher was a senile
octogenarian, he still remembered. He was asked what the greatest
of all things was. "It is not theology," said the old man, "it is not
controversy, but it is to save souls," and he lapsed again into the
deep shadow.[51]

By the time of Beecher's graduation, Dwight had convinced
him that he should prepare for the ministry. During a vacation
he had had his first religious "experience." And while putting in
a year of postgraduate study in theology, he was, in accordance
with the accepted Calvinistic canon, appalled by his own "sinful,
stupid heart." [52] Gradually, however, the light came "by degrees."
Beecher could not stay sunk in a "dark, sullen, unfeeling state"
for long. He knew himself well enough. "I was made for action,"
he said. "The Lord drove me, but I was ready." Dwight was
making him ready for a specific destiny, too, as he drove him
through a reading course with three other boys, all of them meeting in the doctor's study weekly to read papers on set topics.
"Dwight was . . . a revival preacher," Beecher noted, "and a
new era of revivals was commencing. There had been a general
suspension of revivals . . . during the Revolution; but a new day
was dawning as I came on the stage, and I was baptized into the
revival spirit." [53]

Fresh from this baptism, he took up his first preaching charge
in the village of East Hampton, Long Island, socially speaking
then a province of Connecticut. He served a Presbyterian congregation for three hundred dollars a year plus his firewood, but
without the extra inducement of his predecessor, a quarter share
in all whales stranded on the beach. Almost at once, he offered
battle. There was an academy in town, and two of the teachers
in it were "skeptical." The new minister went straight to work.
He did not assault the "infidels" directly, but neither did he
waste any time preaching on safe abstractions until he knew the
congregation better. "I always preached right to the conscience.
Every sermon with my eye on the gun to hit somebody. Went

through the doctrines; showed what they didn't mean; what they did; then the argument; knocked away objections, and drove home on the conscience." [54] When he was through, he declared with majestic simplicity, "infidelity was ended." A year after reaching the town as a candidate for the church, and four months after marrying Roxana Foote, he had his first revival. One Sunday before evening meeting he heard that two sons of one of his deacons were "under conviction." He flew to them, and "oh how I preached! I spilled over." In six weeks, eighty were converted (Beecher had no hesitation about using the phrase straightforwardly) and fifty joined the church. He had begun.[55]

For ten years Beecher remained in East Hampton, tormented by the Yankee urge to work. While others built factories, hewed down forests and sent clippers to China, Beecher rescued souls. Yet there was a limit to this activity, and the man grew restless. He fished, he hunted, he cut wood and hiked across the marshes. Once a whale was sighted offshore. He leaped into a boat and joined with joy in a back-breaking ten-mile chase. He liked to scrape a fiddle now and then and play pranks of a startling nature with his growing family — such pranks as swinging his eldest daughter, Catharine, out of the garret window by her hands. His surplus of energy was a permanent problem. Needing money in East Hampton, he tried to teach school, but it was pure agony to sit still while others were reciting or studying. Later in life, when he could not ramble outdoors, he sawed cords of wood for himself and his neighbors. When that gave out, he had a pile of sand dumped in his cellar and shoveled it furiously from one corner to the other. And still he was restless. What he needed was controversy; a bout with God's enemies to put his strength to use. Other ministers spoke of winning victories for Christ; Beecher would say that he wanted to throw the Devil one more time.[56]

At last, in 1806, he got into a fight that reached beyond the town limits of East Hampton. At that year's session of his presbytery, he preached a sermon against dueling. The inspiration was largely political. Less than two years before, Aaron Burr had killed Alexander Hamilton, the peerless champion of the Federalist Party, in a duel in New Jersey. Beecher was already worried over the way in which Jefferson's party was "swelling higher, and beating more and more fiercely on old Federalism," which was the support of the established church in New England. The sermon fairly sizzled. Scouting the concept of a gentleman's "honor," Beecher announced that a man might be "a gambler, a prodigal, a fornicator, an adulterer, a drunkard, a murderer, and not violate the laws of honor." But retribution was in store. God was just. "His sword is impatient of confinement; ten thousand plagues stand ready to execute His wrath; conflagration, tempest, earthquake, war, famine, and pestilence, wait His command only, to cleanse the land from blood." This was the forked-lightning style of the revivalist, for certain. The sermon was reprinted, and with its circulation, Lyman Beecher had accomplished three characteristic objects. He had married eternal and temporal concerns, enlisted God on the side of a secular reform and entered the lists of controversy on the side of political conservatism.[57] He had also made his name known to others.

The next year, at the General Assembly of the Presbyterian Church, he met Edward Griffin, now a pastor in Newark, who had a revival going in which two hundred and fifty had been converted, from nine-year-old children to persons of seventy, including numbers of drunkards, apostates and infidels. Beecher was stirred to action. He went back to revive East Hampton again, and he did not merely pray for a blessing, either.

> I began to predict, and was so earnest and confident that a great work was at hand that some of the good people wondered. They made me think of hens in the night, when you carry a candle into the hen-roost, how they open first one eye and then the other, half asleep. . . . Finally I resolved that I would preach the doctrine of Election. I knew what that doctrine was and what it would do. So I took for my text Eph. 1, 3-6 and went to work. My object was to preach cut and thrust, hip and thigh, and not to ease off. I had been working a good part of a year with my heart burning, and they feeling nothing. Now I took hold without mittens.

Without mittens, he told them that God would "arouse the stupid" and "awaken the secure," that He would "cut off self-righteous hopes . . . harrow up the selfish hearts of sinners" and in good time "confound, humble and convert them." That started the work. Eyes glittered in the church like stars on a winter night, and Beecher fired election into them eight more times. At the end of it, the church had a hundred new members.[58]

One of the sermons in this series, "The Government of God Desirable," was Beecher's justification for his frank efforts to promote revivals. The Almighty, it said, governs the earth "as a part of His moral kingdom." Men were "*still entirely free and accountable for all the deeds done in the body*." Finally, God would "send to hell none who are not opposed to Him, and to holiness, and to heaven." [59] That sounded suspiciously as if Beecher were defending man's freedom of will, and proclaiming that those who were damned were not damned merely by God's arbitrary pleasure — the doctrine of predestination in its naked form — but were damned because, in some avoidable way, they had rejected Him. This sounded almost Methodistic, and Beecher admitted that the sermon had "a run through the Calvinistic world, and also with many who called themselves Arminians." The long-range effect of this kind of thinking was to justify efforts in the here and now to reconcile sinful men to God, through evangelism. The ground was also cleared for greater efforts by the churches in the way of reform. If God governed the universe by a moral system, then good morals were more important than ever in achieving salvation. The Holy Spirit would be helped in the work of redemption if men could behave in a way approved by God even *before* they were regenerated. The Bible showed such a way, with its reduction of God's mandates to specific orders and prohibitions. Later on, Beecher would speak of a reformation of morals as "practical and desirable," and of the Bible as "a code of laws." Slowly, emphasis was shifting from the eternal to the tangible — to realities with which Beecher's countrymen were self-confidently at home: the *government* of God, the *laws* of the Scriptures, a *systematic* moral order. God seemed to work by plan, after all, and His creatures might justifiably do the same to hasten the advent of His salvation.

Beecher's sermons attracted attention, and ultimately the offer of a church in Litchfield, Connecticut. He took it gladly. A larger salary for his growing family was only one of Litchfield's advantages. It was a bigger town; it was distinguished by the presence of the pioneer law school of Judge Tapping Reeve; it was under the shadow of Yale, and better suited in every way for publicizing the views of a verbal preacher. So Beecher went there in 1810, moving along the predestined orbit of success, from rural isolation to population center — Uncle Lot, to East Hampton, to Litchfield.

Revivals came first. Within a short time he was giving his two Sunday sermons, lecturing as many as nine times during the week, and trotting from house to house in the morning to plead with the unconverted. "I never heard the like," exclaimed an enthusiastic parishioner. "He is determined we shall all be converted." [60] From 1812 to 1817, little Charles Beecher could hardly remember a communion time when there were not additions to the church. In 1821, Nettleton was called in to assist at a fresh ingathering. Beecher, contrasting the ways of the slow-moving evangelist with his own, wrote huffily to one of his sons that Nettleton seemed "indisposed to make any more work for himself." Poor Nettleton was yoked with a tiger.

Beecher was impatient because he was now praying for revivals as a matter of desperate political need. Connecticut was in upheaval in the fifteen years of his Litchfield pastorate. [61] Federalism was on the defensive. The dissenting — that is, non-Congregational — churches were making common cause with Republicans. The War of 1812 and then the drain of emigration and finally the coming of factories brought social unrest and economic dislocation. Pressures were building up for an alteration in the old and steady ways of rule by a tripartite alliance of the wealthiest traders, the largest farmers, and the ministers.

Nowhere were they more evident than in the drive to disestablish Congregationalism as the state-supported church in Connecticut. Lyman Beecher was stung into vigorous defensive action. It was not merely a question of tax support. The issue was whether or not orthodoxy could keep its hold on a restless population seduced into worldliness by promises of political power, cheap land, new markets and jobs. Around him, Beecher gathered friends to conduct a pamphlet war on the "toleration" party.[62]

Revivals now were part of a campaign to build up the old faith, and Beecher began to extend their influence by trading pulpits occasionally with neighboring ministers, a new thing for him. Next, he took the lead in prodding the Congregational churches of Connecticut to organize societies — one for the enforcement of temperance in 1812, and another more ambitious one for the Suppression of Vice and the Promotion of Good Morals. These had a purpose. They drew ministers together, and they furnished the occasion for attacks on "Sabbath-breakers, rum-selling, tippling folk, infidels and ruff-scuff generally" — all of whom Beecher was quick to identify with enemies of the establishment and with "democrats." [63]

Beecher lost his fight. Methodists and Baptists waxed numerous. Finally, the upper-class Episcopalians joined with their lowly fellow "dissenters" in the Toleration Party, and in 1818, disestablishment was carried out.[64] Catharine Beecher found her usually bubbling father, the day after the news came, sitting in a kitchen chair with his chin on his chest and his arms hanging down, thinking glumly about "THE CHURCH OF GOD."

And yet, in losing, Beecher and his cause had won. For within a short time — at least according to his recollection in old age — he saw a great light. Reform societies and revivals were an answer in themselves! They could appeal to the public mind as vividly as the allurements of politics. They themselves could be a refuge in times of economic disorder. Beecher, lifelong enemy of democracy, had suddenly discovered the power of public opinion. The quest for security in the breakup of an old society could work *for* the church. The old ministry of the "standing order" was gone, with its gowns and bands, its treatises on theology, its majestic isolation and its certainty of respect for its opinions. But the "new" ministers were not powerless. "*By voluntary efforts, societies, missions and revivals, they exert a deeper influence than ever they could by queues, and shoe-buckles, and cocked hats, and gold-headed canes.*" [65]

Revivals stood out in a new light. They could kindle the flame of enthusiasm in masses of people. That enthusiasm could then be directed into societies for moral improvement. Moral improvement would create a society of better men — men riper for regeneration, if not already regenerated. The hosts of hell would be routed, the community of the righteous would expand, and who could say, then, that the millennium might not be in the offing? From the day of the disestablishment, Beecher said, "I worked as hard as mortal man could, and at the same time preached for revivals with all my might, and with success." [66] At last, in Beecher's mind, there shone the clear image of a most blessed goal, a millennium that he could *work* for!

Yet swinging the siege enginery of democracy — community pressure — into play was not Beecher's job alone. Elsewhere in America other men were hastening along the road to other heavenly cities, organized along unconventional economic or social lines. Indeed, all of America worked hard and expected improvement, followed inevitably by "perfection." Out of this came a curious paradox. Revivalism became part of what one writer has called "freedom's ferment." A movement originally seized on by religious conservatives to resist change fell in step with the cadence of nineteenth-century American progressivism. Each would march a long way in the slightly incongruous company of the other.

Beecher's eye could not see to the furthest end of the road ahead in 1818. With the cocked-hat and gold-headed-cane clergy gone, the theology which supported them would have to disappear as well. Beecher, however, was absorbed in a new fight — this time with Unitarianism, which had steadily gained in influence, particularly among well-off Bostonians. At once he patched up his quarrel with Connecticut dissenters and turned to face the new enemy. "Unitarians will gain the victory if we are left without revivals, but they will perish by the breath of His mouth and the brightness of His coming if revivals prevail," he wrote to a friend.[67]

There was a revealing social motive in the war on the Uni-

.tarians. Beecher had good enough theological reason to fight
them. Their renunciation of the trinitarian concept of God, of
man's innate and incurable sinfulness and of his inescapable predestination to damnation cut the ground from beneath the feet
of both traditional Calvinism *and* revivalism. But another significant strain ran through the attacks on Unitarianism which
Beecher made in sermons, in private correspondence, in pamphlets and in letters to the orthodox paper, the *Christian Spectator.* Unitarians were apt to be better educated. They easily
financed publication of their "floods of heresy." [68] They recruited largely from the professional classes. Their dominance
of Harvard gave them the power to put "sentinels in all the
churches, legislators in the hall and judges on the bench" and to
scatter everywhere "physicians, lawyers and merchants." In all,
their "concentration and moneyed resources" gave them an enormous advantage.[69] Years later, his famous daughter Harriet echoed
what Beecher unquestionably believed at the time:

> All the literary men of Massachusetts were Unitarian. All the
> trustees and professors of Harvard College were Unitarians. All
> the elite of wealth and fashion crowded Unitarian churches.[70]

So Beecher was fighting the battle of rural society — of Uncle
Lot. He had already condemned the "ruff-scuff" of Connecticut
Republicanism and the rum sellers and infidels whom he believed
to be sprung from the "lower classes" of society. Yet when the
enemy turned out to be Unitarianism, entrenched in Boston, he
bitterly complained of it as a phenomenon of the cultivated,
professionally established, and wealthy urbanites. Through all
revivalism to follow his for a century, there would run this formal assault upon the two great classes of unconverted — on the
one side the deluded masses, who must be saved from the rum
seller and the Sunday theater; and on the other, the corrupted
rich with their novel unorthodoxies. And perhaps the intensity
of the "war" — as well as the success of the revival — could be
explained to some degree by the fact that the countryside was
beleaguered by change. Immigration, the industrial revolution and
new forms of transportation all joined to depopulate the country-

side, shake up its social patterns, rob it of leadership and jerk it in and out of booms and depressions beyond its control. The "revival" by its very name harked back to the old order of things, the day of the supremacy of self-sufficient yeomen. It also promised a "new birth" and an eternal assurance and refuge. Either way, it belonged in an age when fundamental questions were painfully forced on mankind by economic growth.

In 1826, Beecher was enabled to carry the campaign to the enemy. By then he was one of the better-known ministers in the country, in both the Congregational and Presbyterian churches, which were closely allied. It was not surprising that the Hanover Street church, in Boston, should make overtures to him. Once again, Beecher pleaded the inadequacy of his salary as an excuse for leaving his old congregation — five more little Beechers had been added to the household, including Harriet and Henry Ward. He needed no urging, however, to take on the Unitarians in their homeland. In March of 1826, the fifty-year-old man, with his second wife and his nine children, came to Boston. After twenty-seven years, he was in the stronghold of the wicked.

He found a demanding situation. The orthodox churches were on the defensive. Many congregations had gone over to Unitarianism. The strictly trinitarian minorities in them insisted on their right to retain the church properties, but the courts took a different view, and many of the faithful had been literally thrown out of the chapels raised by the hands of their Puritan forefathers. Beecher, anxious to hearten the retreating Congregationalists, now learned to refine the revival as armament. He began a series of special "inquiry" meetings and got assistants to cover the entire room, probing the state of each person present. Organization was succeeding one-man effort. When these helpers "brought back reports of awakenings," Beecher hustled to visit the "convicted," whom he "*struck*, just according to character and state." With those who believed already, he would use "plain instruction"; with those who pleaded their own "inability," he "rose into the field of metaphysics." When he met skeptics, he put himself "on the highest key . . . and made them feel that somebody else knew something besides themselves," until they "came, meek as lambs." And some hard cases, he admitted, he "never made out any thing with."

Soon his old Connecticut enemies, the Baptists, joined in. Presently meetings were going on in widely scattered parts of town. Beecher laughed with joy to hear the bells ringing out in the evening. At communion time, there were seventy converts in his church alone. Yet to the end, he was bitter about the Unitarian reaction. He accused them of raining "showers of lies" on him and, what rankled even more, of snubbing him. "It was two years before the leaders of the Unitarians began to change their tactics and treat me gentlemanly," he grumbled in retirement.[71]

As 1827 dawned, Beecher seemed securely established. He had made the revival a superb defensive instrument, he thought, for those evangelical churches which he accepted. Through the reformation societies in which he was taking a hand, he was finding a way to impose the discipline of those churches on countless numbers of Americans whose loyalty was competed for by other kinds of betterment programs. Personally, he had a good pulpit in a great and exciting city, and he was the acknowledged field marshal of New England orthodoxy.

Then, suddenly, a crisis occurred as a new kind of revival came roaring in from western New York, carrying with it some of the spaciousness and barbaric yawp of the old frontier awakenings of 1800.

By 1825, severe problems were arising, because neither Dwight, nor Nettleton, nor Beecher had faced certain implications in revivalism. For one thing, revivals were taking place outside New England and the Congregational-Presbyterian fold there. In fact, they were no longer isolated manifestations. The Great Awakening of 1800 was permanent. In 1818, the editor of a religious paper in Albany brought out a volume listing the awakenings which had occurred in the previous two years. He levied on the letters of forty-seven ministers of different denominations and on the narratives of synods, presbyteries, conventions and associations. What emerged was a record of continuous awakenings in the small villages of the country — page on page of testimony to the work of regeneration in Danville, Marshfield, Canterbury, Unadilla, Romulus, Genoa, Cayuga and a thousand identical towns.[72] The Methodists were continuing to build, and in Massachusetts and Connecticut, and on Long Island, in the very sanctuaries of the churches which once scorned the Wesleyans, camp meetings were held wherein sinners cried for mercy, shouted glory and fell in rigid trances. In the South, revivals of the Methodist and Baptist type went on, unshackled and undecorous as the frontier itself.[73] Moreover, a new corps of revivalists, born when Beecher and Nettleton were at Yale, was preparing to take the field.

The revival in the Eastern United States was no longer the property of a small but devoted band of Dwight's disciples, if indeed it ever had been. Revivalism was developing techniques of its own; a "host of ardent, devoted revival men," raised in the school created by Beechers and Nettletons, had sprung up. The host were becoming "more and more experienced," and as they did so, the original goals of revivalism were in danger of being obscured.[74] What would happen, say, if mass conversion became merely an end in itself? Or if the "means of grace" — prayer meetings and the like — turned out to be carefully tailored so as to produce results? Where, then, was God's unpredictable intervention?

An even more burning question was whether God, as depicted by Calvinist orthodoxy, had survived the revival movement at all. The theological system developed by the followers of Jonathan Edwards in the period of the American Revolution had been explicit on certain points. Man was sinful by nature and incapable of good acts unless God chose to convert him. He could not "will" himself to salvation, for his will was not free, or rather, it was limited. He could independently follow his impulses towards sinfulness; in that sense he was "free" and responsible for his wickedness, and therefore God's damnation of him was just. But on the other hand, he could do nothing about the origin of those impulses. His will in that sense was not his own, and by just so much was God's sovereignty absolute. Thus God's absolute sovereignty and man's responsibility for his sins were neatly welded together. Any attempt by an unconverted heart to lift itself towards grace was a defiance of God's will — a man simply could not *want* to be holy, because the power to originate such a "want" was not his own. So all "exercises" of the unconverted were mere selfishness — inspired by fear or the desire to appear pious. Only the converted could pray with a "right" heart.

It was obvious from the start that this doctrine could not coexist with revivalism. To bring men to prayer meetings, to urge repentance on them, to plunge them into self-examination and religious exercises *before* they were converted would be to encourage them in sin by a strict construction of these "neo-Edwardean" doctrines. Dwight and Beecher solved this simply enough by ignoring doctrines when they had to. If a literal belief in "inability" meant that the sinner could not really pray properly until he knew he was converted, then a literal belief in "inability" would have to give way. Man's utter *dependence* on God to make him fit for holiness would have to be soft-pedaled, and reliance on study, prayer and penitence would have to be stressed.

The theological ins and outs of the controversy were tortuous. However, Beecher had moved in the direction of crystallizing the revivalists' position with the East Hampton sermon in which he had roundly declared that all men were *"entirely free and accountable"* and that God would "send to hell none who are not opposed to Him." In short, while he did not technically depart from a Calvinistic position, Beecher was hinting that even unregenerate men *could* repent, and that they would go to hell, not by God's fiat, but because they thoroughly deserved it, if they did *not* repent.

Beecher was too busy to write these views into doctrinal sermons. His attitude was determined by the goal at which he aimed; he would preach whatever the situation called for. When he got to Boston, he discovered that the people "did not need high-toned Calvinism on the point of dependence" but a "vigorous prescription of free-agency" to fit them to battle the Unitarians, and he gave it to them. He boasted of lifting people out of "the sloughs of high Calvinism." Once he was arguing with Dwight that it was the sinner's duty to repent immediately on realizing his condition. Dwight was not sure that this was entirely possible, but he certainly thought that every means of grace — mostly reading and prayer — ought to be used on the stubborn heart of the would-be convert. Oh, well, Beecher said in effect, you would simply give the sinner "a larger dose of *means*" than of repentance.[75] Lyman Beecher's mind dealt roughly with metaphysical subtleties; he had no time for them when action called.

He got more scholarly backing, however, from the last of Dwight's great trio of pupils, Nathaniel Taylor, Beecher's life-long friend, next to whom he would finally be buried in New Haven. Taylor came to the Center Church in New Haven in 1812, four years after graduating from Yale. In 1822, when Yale established a permanent chair in theology, he was called to occupy it. For many years in his ministerial study he was absorbed in working on a new system of divinity which left man free to repent and virtually promised that he would be saved if he did. At Yale he was able to pass these notions on to a generation of students going out to New England pulpits. Under Taylor's teaching, men were still saved by God, but they were supposed to use their reason to see the justice of His intelligible and regular moral system. What was more, they could improve their lives and the lives of those around them, as both a prelude and a testimony of conversion. Taylor wrote the theoretical justification for Lyman Beecher's scheme of revivals and reform.

But "Taylorism" and "Beecherism" plainly narrowed the difference between Calvinism and Arminianism, and a hard core of strict Calvinists chafed and fretted as they saw the ancient bastions being torn down. The conflict was muted in Connecticut while orthodox forces hung together to fight disestablishment and then Unitarianism. But in 1828, war broke out in earnest with the publication of one of Taylor's sermons, and the upshot was a series of pamphlet battles and the creation, in 1833, of a new and "orthodox" theological school at East Windsor, Connecticut.[76]

So in the end, after all Nettleton's judiciousness, the revival in New England brought schism to the Congregational churches once again. Ultimately, the defenders of strict Calvinism were the losers. As Baptists, Methodists and prorevival Congregationalists and Presbyterians drew closer together, in the conduct of revivals, the old lines blurred, and American Protestantism found itself dividing along new lines — revival-oriented churches and the others. Lyman Beecher, towards the close of his life, found himself the defendant in a heresy trial before a conservative, or antirevival, Presbyterian court.

The seed of disunion was still concealed in the revival. Other difficulties also strewed the way of the church which leaned upon the revival too heavily. The rise of specialists in revivalism, moving from pulpit to pulpit with the powerful forces of anticipation, publicity and novelty working for them, began to break down the grasp of the settled minister on his flock. And the crystallization of the results of a wave of conversions was a time-consuming job. With prayer meetings to attend and missionary, benevolent and reform societies to counsel, ministers were far too busy for the continuous study and writing of Edwardean days. Beecher knew that, when he was old. He remembered Uncle Lot's old Parson Bray, who preached twice on Sundays, went to funerals and gave a quarterly sacramental lecture, and needed to do no more. "Nowadays," reminisced the man who had done so much to bring on the change, "they wear a man out in a few years. They make him a slave, worse than on the plantation. The old way was healthier." [77]

There were still opportunities to be a learned minister, but they depended increasingly on getting a chair at a theological school. With learning retreating to the seminaries, and evangelism falling into the hands of experts, the preachers themselves were pushed towards a more exclusively organizational and social role, broken by the regular Sunday sermon. Their luster was dimmed a little when they sat beside the visiting evangelist, whose rousing appeal was fresh. And laymen could draw up petitions and occupy the chair at meetings just as well, and donate more. Reform societies and revivals might enable "energetic, active, prosperous and practical Christianity" to marry itself to politics and put its stamp and seal on American institutions. But this would be achieved, in part, at the expense of the regular American Protestant ministry. What would its new role be?

All these questions had not yet been faced in 1825. Something was needed to bring them to the surface. But suppose a man turned up who would bring to the pulpit what was essentially a layman's view? Suppose a man appeared who would become the well-dramatized *personal* leader of the revival hosts? Suppose that such a man made logic run second to emotionalism, and brought the lusty breath of the Western revival into the East? Suppose that he spurred his converts into furious activity aimed at remolding certain "sinful" social institutions? Then all the problems would be laid bare. Then the revival would be forced to move closer to its democratic associations and break openly with its past in "high-toned" Calvinism.

That man appeared like a cloud on the horizon in 1826. His name was Charles G. Finney, and he came with a sword in his hand, ready to "slay" his adversaries in the name of Christ. A new phase of American church history was opening.

CHAPTER IV

Out of His Mouth Goeth a Sharp Sword

LIKE most of his kind, Charles Grandison Finney, champion revivalist, was a devout temperance man. He drank unstintingly of one liquor, however — the wine of success. He was a man who "made good" in his chosen work of bringing men to Christ, just as others were climbing the peaks of achievement in trade, journalism or politics. When he came on the revival scene overnight in 1824, it was still dominated in the East by the alumni of Timothy Dwight's Yale, and in the West by the rough-cut spellbinders of the camp meetings. Twenty years later Finney was the best-known "soul winner" north of the Ohio and the Potomac, a public figure and a type, like Horace Greeley or Daniel Webster or John Jacob Astor.

He was wonderfully equipped to be a catalytic agent, bringing together the lay-directed pietistic vigor of the West and the respectable, seminary-bred religious enthusiasm of New England. He was raised on the Yankee frontier of western New York in the first quarter of the nineteenth century, a region geographically and culturally midway between the two. Intellectually he was fit to stand between the plain-spoken prophets of Cumberland Presbyterianism and such graduate theologians as Lyman Beecher and Nathaniel Taylor. He was mostly self-educated in religion, which he largely ignored until his thirtieth year and then clasped possessively. He crammed in enough private study to be ordained by the Presbyterians, but in effect he always remained a layman. Never having sat at the feet of scholars in divinity as a youth, Finney had no hesitation about writing his own doctrinal platform in a bold script.

On the other hand, he was no "common man." Trained as a lawyer, he had a piercingly logical mind and an argumentative knack that brought the worldly dissenter to his knees. He boasted, correctly, that his success was greatest with members of the rising professional and business classes — the lawyers and merchants of the enlightened eighteen-twenties and -thirties, who had gotten enough learning and self-importance to reject a Christianity based on pure authority. He made it as sensible for them as compound interest or writs of jurisdiction.

Yet the frontier strain showed through the acquired learning. Along with the formal creed lingered the countryman's folk religion of spells and superstitions. Finney still believed that God literally smote down unbelievers for their presumption. Satan was still a personal enemy who might try to kill him by overturning a buggy.[1] His sense of proportion was faltering. One moment he would speak of final judgments and salvation, and in the next, fume over something as trivial as a ruffled shirt on a minister of God.[2] He could paint the love of Christ in melting colors, yet he was arrogantly happy to see "sinners" humbled and broken down. Plainly, he enjoyed it when the frock-coated dandy or the well-dressed village belle knelt before him, disheveled and shaken by sobs wrung from hearts which he had filled with terror. As he grew older he mellowed, but a trace of bigotry flavored all his days.

Above all, Finney had the unbelievable energy and concentration of his kind and class in America. Nothing mattered but the saving of a wicked world — not leisure, not friendship, not even the bride of two days whom he left for a six-month preaching tour. And being the sort of blunt, practical and active man whom plain Americans understood, he won them. He did not study the popular mind; he had it. There was nothing sacerdotal or remote about Finney in the pulpit. The man in the front pew recognized another edition of himself up there, speaking a language elevated enough for respect, but plain enough for comprehension. This preacher did not beckon men into a world of mysteries and symbols. One could be a Finney convert and a man of affairs as well; a success in the countinghouse or courtroom.

So Finney traveled upwards, away from his beginnings. He won popularity, first in the farming villages of rural New York, and then in the rising market and manufacturing towns that lined the Erie Canal. He went from there to crowded houses in Philadelphia, Boston and Providence, and at last to a settled pulpit in New York City itself. From there, God called him to become a professor and then president of Oberlin College. More theology crept into his sermons. Personal visits to "break down" sinners were replaced by organized appeals, formal campaigns. His doctrine softened, and he began to argue that sinful man could be "perfectly" holy. To the waning forces of strict Calvinism he became a religious radical. Moreover, men went forth from his lectures to champion a multitude of reforms.

Nevertheless, he was, at his life's end, a man of prominence and position. One could afford a touch of softness when acceptance in society was guaranteed, and nothing in the doctrines of Charles Finney remotely threatened the economic underpinnings of society. Revivalism had popular trappings and equalitarian slogans; it had democratic implications — but like Finney himself, it had a touch of conservatism at the core.

Finney was a Connecticut Yankee, born in 1792 in Litchfield County, across the path of the westward migration of New Englanders towards the more promising lands of the Great Lakes plains. In 1812, of western New York's two hundred thousand souls, two thirds were New England born.[3] Finney's father was tumbled along in the rush. He moved into the wilderness that was Oneida County, taking along a family which included his two-year-old son, Charles Grandison, grandiloquently named for the hero of a moral novel by Samuel Richardson. When the boy was sixteen, they moved to Henderson, on the Lake Ontario shore. In both places churches were scarce. It was for settlements like these that the home missionary societies of Connecticut marshaled their pennies.

Young Charles attended the common schools of the winter season in his childhood, and at the end of his teens was sent back to Warren, his Connecticut birthplace, for the unusual privilege of attending a kind of high school. He met formal religion there, embodied in the Reverend Peter Starr, and was not impressed. Minister Starr delivered sermons in a monotone, punctuated by verses from his heavy pulpit Bible. To mark the places, he put his fingers between the pages, and droned on, liberating his fingers one by one. When he was down to the last finger, the congregation, too, could look forward to being set free shortly.

Charles thought of attending Yale College, but his school "preceptor" told him that he could cover the curriculum by himself in two years. Never lacking in self-confidence, Finney accepted the judgment with alacrity. He taught school in New Jersey for a while, and looked for new horizons. He wanted to set up a private school in the South. On a visit home, however, his worried parents put in a claim on their wandering boy, now twenty-five years old and without prospects. They persuaded him to move to Adams, in Jefferson County, not far from Henderson, and study law with Benjamin Wright. He agreed to this, pushed easily through a reading course, joined the bar and settled down to practice.

Finney had reason to be satisfied with himself. He was a striking six-footer, popular with the young set in town. He played the cello and sang in the church choir. The womenfolk probably regarded him as the village catch. He could look forward to a comfortable life of legal advancement, some land speculation if he chose, or a political career if it suited him. He was a young Augustine in a provincial Carthage — not dissolute, perhaps, but worldly for a provincial.

And then, on the verge of his twenty-ninth birthday, almost overnight, Charles Finney was converted!

Looking back on it as an old man, it suited both his doctrine and his conceit to make it appear a wholly unexpected miracle. It was hardly so. He grew up in a world which might be churchless, but was unswervingly Christian, and in Adams he had been dutifully attending the Presbyterian Church, presided over by an energetic young divine named George W. Gale. Gale was three years Finney's senior, a graduate of Union College and Princeton Theological Seminary, eventually to become a rather remarkable

educator and the founder of Knox College in Illinois.⁴ His mind
was good enough to strike sparks out of the young lawyer.

The two men had argued over theology. Finney was unim-
pressed by Gale's sermons. Frankly, he said, he found official Calvinistic theory wanting when weighed in the balance of his legal
mind. Just what did the confession mean by "repentance," "faith"
and "regeneration"? What was the purpose of prayer? The Bible
said, "Ask, and it shall be given you; seek, and ye shall find," but
the Presbyterians of Adams attended prayer meeting without
any real conviction that their supplications would be answered.
Finney was a practical man; all of this made no sense to him. Gale
responded, fruitlessly and unhappily, with arguments from his
Princeton reading. He wanted badly to convince Mr. Finney, for
he was so popular that while he remained a skeptic, the whole
church choir was likely to stay out of the kingdom with him.⁵
Then the matter of conviction was taken out of Gale's hands.

Sometime during his legal training, Finney bought a Bible to
check on certain allusions to the Mosaic code. He had read it
only perfunctorily up to then; now he settled down to it, and
it began to simmer in his mind. After two or three years he
reached the conclusion that "whatever mystification there might
be . . . in the mind of the church," the Bible was "the true word
of God." Would he, then, "accept Christ as presented in the
Gospel"? One October day in 1821, mulling the matter over
while walking to the office, he suddenly got a dazzling insight.
What was holding him back? Gospel salvation was full and complete. All that was needed to receive it was "my own consent to
give up my sins, and accept Christ." *My own consent!* No waiting
for the regenerative power of the Spirit to descend, and no pro-
bationary good works! It was a matter of simple decision. The
thought was literally arresting. Finney stopped dead in the middle
of the street, he remembered, and said to himself, "I will accept it
to-day, or I will die in the attempt." Charles Finney had decided
in that moment that salvation was up to him. He was now going
to pound at the gate of heaven until he gained admittance.

His will was energized, but the way was not altogether easy.
Behind his practical self-assurance lay uptapped reservoirs of

powerful emotions, held in check by self-denial. The strange
Yankee mixture of realism and mysticism was in him, ready to
explode, but not yet heated to the critical temperature. Finney
turned away from the village, found a clearing in the woods,
and knelt to pray. But his lips were locked; he was in an agony of
apprehension that some neighbor might stumble on his devotions.
Was his pride, then, an insurmountable obstacle? He was de-
pressed, but he remembered a scriptural verse: "Then shall ye
go and pray unto me, and I will hearken unto you." Here was
a plain promise — a contract. Lawyer Finney knew what a contract was. "I told the Lord that I should take him at his word;
that he could not lie, and that therefore I was sure that he heard
my prayer, and that he would be found of me." With a lighter
heart, he went back to town.

He went into the office and tried to play some sacred music,
but the emotions were close to the surface now. He began to cry,
and gave it up. Judge Wright came in and they spent the afternoon moving furniture into a new office. As the early darkness
fell, Wright left for home. Finney saw him out the door,
turned and in a sudden electric moment his feelings seemed to rise
and flow out. His heart was "liquid." He rushed into a darkened
back room. It appeared brilliantly lit to him, and there he seemed
to meet the Lord Jesus Christ "face to face." The man of law
fell at His feet, wept aloud and confessed to Him. His sense of
time vanished. When he finally got to his feet and staggered
back into the front office, the fire he had kindled was burned out.
He turned to sit by the embers, and a "mighty baptism of the
Holy Ghost" overwhelmed him. It was a searing, stabbing experience. Writing about it a lifetime later, the words poured white-
hot from his pen.

> The Holy Spirit descended upon me in a manner that seemed
> to go through me, body and soul. I could feel the impression,
> like a wave of electricity, going through and through me. In-
> deed it seemed to come in waves and waves of liquid love . . .
> It seemed like the very breath of God. I can recollect distinctly
> that it seemed to fan me, like immense wings. . . .
> I wept aloud with joy and love; and I do not know but I

should say, I literally bellowed out the unutterable gushings of my heart. These waves came over me, and over me, and over me, one after the other, until I recollect I cried out, "I shall die if these waves continue to pass over me." I said, "Lord, I cannot bear any more"; yet I had no fear of death.[6]

So it was that Charles Grandison Finney met his God. Somehow he got home and tumbled into a dazed sleep. The next morning he awoke on the crest of an upsurge of confidence and euphoria. Heaven, he knew, had given him a mandate by this experience to preach the gospel as a full-time project. He went to the office, and waited. Presently Benjamin Wright came in and was startled to have his tough-minded young partner greet him with inquiries about the state of his soul. Wright gazed at him without saying a word, and went out to digest this new state of affairs. The next caller was a deacon of the church who came in with a reminder of a case in court set for ten o'clock.

Finney's answer was immediate, decisive and permanent. "Deacon," he replied, "I have a retainer from the Lord Jesus Christ to plead his cause, and I cannot plead yours." [7]

At first, Finney rushed about in a jubilant frenzy, in a fever to test his powers in carrying out the Almighty's commission. According to his own memories, the warrant proved good. On the first day of his "new" life he met a Universalist in a shoemaker's shop and took only a moment to "blow his argument to the wind." Next he stopped for tea at the house of a friend where a young man dwelt who was not only a Universalist, but a whiskey distiller. At the table Finney began to say grace, and burst into tears. The whiskey maker fled to his room, locked himself in and came out the next morning "expressing a blessed hope in the gospel."

The townsfolk soon got the exciting news that high-flying young Finney was brought under the power. Finney got them together at a meetinghouse, exhorted them, set future meetings and gave them no rest until he had converted all but one. There was no boggling at the word, either; no "entertaining of hopes," or "professing a change." "One after another," Finney noted with simple satisfaction, "they were converted."

But at the end of a week, he was on the verge of nervous prostration from lack of sleep and food. His feelings were still raw; his heart, liquid. One morning, meeting Gale at the church door, an "ineffable" light flooded his soul, and he found himself sobbing hysterically. He went in for private fasts, and felt as if the Lord were still physically near. Once, on his knees, when he was praying for the salvation of a local woman fallen into Universalism, "the whole subject opened to my mind; and as soon as I plead [*sic*] for her God said to me, 'Yes! Yes!' If he had spoken with an audible voice, it would not have been more distinctly understood."

So he wandered, a prophet in a business suit, up and down the streets of Adams, seeking recruits for the company of saints. He was apparently on the way to becoming a first-class mystic, complete with visions and trances.[8]

But this was a passing phase. Finney's true mission was to forge a popular Christianity that took full advantage of the practical and self-reliant character of his upstate New York environment. To the work he brought oratorical gifts, blazing conviction, and a reasoning and hopeful intellect which could grapple with "high tone" predestinarian Calvinism. Soon after his conversion he settled down to serious theological education. Once again, mind took over.

He was a unique candidate in divinity, a grown man, furiously independent, and already trained in another discipline. As he went from his Bible to conferences with Gale and back again, one by one he hammered out the practices and habits of mind which would mark his kind of evangelism — eventually, America's kind of successful evangelism. First, he broke with formal ministerial training. Finney was an ordained layman, and after him there would be no popular evangelist who was a graduate of a first-class university or seminary. The reign of Yale in the field was ending. Secondly, Finney leaned more and more heavily on the Bible as he interpreted it. He worked his way towards a revivalism that rested on a doggedly literal reading of the Scriptures, flung into the teeth of textual criticism. Thirdly, Finney's gospel swept into the discard the strict Calvinistic idea that man was utterly dependent on God for the mere ability to repent. Such a notion encouraged passivity, Finney thought — a frame of mind as alien to his Yankee personality as boosterism would be to a Hindu. Finney believed that the sinner *was* able to repent — indeed, had a duty to repent immediately. Armed with this doctrine, he could cast his net for sinners and expect it to return full every time. As Lyman Beecher said of himself, Finney was "made for action."

Finney rode hard over Gale's insistence that salvation was only for the elect. It was made for all men, he insisted, although not all of them would take advantage of it, as God knew beforehand. How did Finney know? "I had read nothing on the subject except my Bible, and what I had there found . . . I had interpreted *as I would have understood the same or like passages in a law book*." [9] And from this position, the ultimate in Protestantism, Finney would not budge. Others might have diplomas, but he had God's word. He applied to the local presbytery for a license to preach. The ministers urged him to go to Princeton, and even offered to pay his expenses. Finney curtly refused. "I plainly told them that I would not put myself under such an influence as they had been under; that I was confident that they had been wrongly educated, and they were not ministers that met my ideal of what a minister of Christ should be." [10]

They might have washed their hands of him then and there. But the clergymen of the St. Lawrence Presbytery were confronted by popular revivalism. Finney did not and would not submit to their yoke. Yet he had already made numerous converts in Adams, and it was obvious that he had wondrous ability to interest men and women in Christ. The choice was either orthodoxy and empty churches, or compromise and full ones. The pastors of the St. Lawrence Presbytery took the course of those who followed after; they sighed privately, but allowed Finney to go on. In 1823, the licensing board examined him.

When asked if he received the Presbyterian confession of faith, he answered stoutly that he had not examined it, but received it so far as he understood it.[11] The board passed him, but Gale sadly said a little later that he would be embarrassed to have it known publicly that Finney was his student. Gale had no need to worry. Finney was Finney's student. Accustomed as he was to "the close and logical reasonings of the judges," the tomes in Gale's library had not affected him. For enlightenment on hard questions, the aggressive soul-winner said, he could go "directly to the Bible, and to the philosophy or workings of my own mind, as revealed in consciousness." [12]

The exact shape of what was revealed to his consciousness became clear when he began to preach, for his doctrine and technique were inseparably welded. His chance to practice technique came early in the year 1824, when the Female Missionary Society of the Western District in New York commissioned him to work for three months in the northern part of Jefferson County. He was not perturbed by the missing links in his training. He went out to carry the good news of salvation, confident "that when the time came for action I should know what to preach." [13]

So began the first phase of his career, in the farming hamlets of the Ontario frontier where, as often as not, the "church" was a schoolhouse during the week, used on alternate Sundays by the Baptists and Congregationalists. The early Finney was a suitable revivalist for the frontier. Except for his superior education, he might have been a transplant from the Kentucky of 1800. He scalded the congregations, flailed unbelievers, and if he did not encourage the transports of the "jerks," he permitted agonies and hysterics which were certainly violent demonstrations of the Lord's redeeming power.

He began with a meeting in the little clusters of houses and stores known as Evans Mills and Antwerp. After a brief introduction, he shot the question bluntly at the congregation. Would they make up their minds to become Christians? Those ready to do so would please rise; those determined "not to accept Christ" would remain seated. The audience remained on the benches, puzzled by the sudden attack. "Then," snapped the missionary, "you are committed. You have rejected Christ and his gospel;

and ye are witnesses one against the other, and God is witness against you all." With a perfect dramatic sense, he stopped speaking. The crowd finally got the point and moved out the door.

Finney knew his townsfolk perfectly. He had an appointment for the next night, and the curiosity aroused by this beginning crammed the meetinghouse. He stood up and opened the batteries of his vocabulary on the audience. A woman slumped into the arms of two friends, unconscious. For sixteen hours she lay speechless, until she found voice to announce that her feet were set on a rock. It was a beginning. Later meetings brought more to admit conviction. There was a local "infidel" who was talking against the revival. One morning he dropped dead of apoplexy, gasping, "Don't let Finney pray over my corpse." That opened the gates further. A Universalist, enraged when his wife became one of the converts, came to a meeting with a pistol in his pocket. In the middle of the sermon he sank to the floor, shrieking that he was descending into hell. The next day he met Finney on the street and gave him a grateful hug for leading him to the Lord. A tavern keeper rose to make a "heart-broken" confession, and inaugurated nightly prayer meetings in his barroom. By July, 1824, the presbytery which had licensed Finney to preach had no hesitation about ordaining him.[14]

At Antwerp, he soon converted "the great mass of the population." One Sunday an old man asked him to preach in a nearby neighborhood. Finney got there and found the meeting trying to sing, each one with his own tune and meter. He was still a musician; the bawling and howling drove him distracted. He quieted them down and began to preach on the text: "Up, get you out of this place; for the Lord will destroy this city."

He did not know that the district was called Sodom. The residents at first suspected a practical joke; but as they listened to the blazing words of the preacher, they saw the hand of the Lord. Suddenly, men and women began to topple from their seats and cry for mercy. "If I had had a sword in my hand," Finney recalled, "I could not have cut them off . . . as fast as they fell." Inside of two minutes the air was filled with howls and shrieks. Finney had to bellow at the top of his lungs. "You are not in hell yet; and now let me direct you to Christ." Gradually he restored order.[15] He moved on to a Universalist neighborhood, let them have "Ye serpents, ye generation of vipers, how can ye escape the damnation of hell," and upturned their foundations. Next, he gave attention to the Methodists. Someone was spreading the rumor that Finney was masking his colors and avoiding the Calvinistic doctrine of election, which Methodists rejected, in order to beguile them. Finney took up the challenge and preached election to them — but in his own version. He said that election opposed "no obstacle to the salvation of the non-elect," and what was more, it was "not inconsistent with free agency." God knew in advance who would obey Him, but the duty of obedience remained, nonetheless. The elect were bellwethers of the flock, with greater responsibilities and obligations, but the nonelect were in no way relieved of their debts to God. All, in short, still had to flee from the wrath to come. At least one Methodist sister, presented with this novel view of the case, was willing to join a church which believed in "election."[16]

Six months after he had begun, he was already an evangelist of notable achievements. Yet the more he tasted, the harder he was driven. The Lord's work was crying to be done in Jefferson and St. Lawrence counties, and nothing must interrupt it. In October of 1824, Finney went down to Whitestown, in Oneida County, to marry Lydia Andrews. A day or so after the wedding, he went back to Evans Mills to arrange for moving household goods there. He was supposed to be back in a week, but conviction was striking sinners in little settlements all around Evans Mills, and requests for him to preach were waiting. So preach he did, all through the winter months, while Lydia Finney pondered alone the duties of a marriage to the chosen of God. It was not gallant, but what could a man do when, as he put it, "God revealed to me, all at once . . . the fact that he was going to pour out his Spirit at Gouverneur, and that I must go there and preach"? [17]

So to Gouverneur he went, reaping, threshing, winnowing the harvest — the sickle and flail and wind of the Lord. Each town presented its special problems. In Le Rayville a young woman

affronted heaven by coming to the service in a hat with grace-
fully waving plumes. She arrived early and sat down next to
Finney, whom she did not know by sight. "Did you come here
. . . to make people worship you?" he hissed at her, and rose
to pour out the sermon. At the end, he called on those who
would "give their hearts to God" to come forward and take the
front seat. The plumed young woman stumbled forward and fell
in the aisle, where she "shrieked with agony." [18]

At Gouverneur, as Finney's meetings aroused more and more
sinners to a sense of their lost estate, both the Baptist and Methodist churches hungered to make a call for members and pluck the
earliest fruits. Finally the Baptists went ahead, combing the town
for the "anxious" and leading singing processions to the waters
of immersion, whereupon the "grieved" Presbyterians cooled off,
and for six weeks the revival languished. Finney had to hold two
special lectures, giving the Baptist and Presbyterian views of
baptism as fairly as he could, in order to restart the machinery.
And thus a point of doctrine about which New England had
struggled for two centuries was hurried over in order to guarantee the revival's priority. The revivalistic harmony among Baptists, Presbyterians and Methodists was beginning to sound.[19]

In De Kalb, Presbyterians had long looked down their noses
at the enthusiastic religion of Methodism, which countenanced
"falling under the power." But the first man to fall from his seat
under Finney's spell was a Presbyterian, as were several who
followed him. Red-faced, the Puritans took counsel with the
Wesleyans on this mystery, and mutual "confessions and explana-
tions" reconciled the two groups.[20]

"Broken down, broken down" runs like a refrain through the
memoirs of this period, as Finney harrowed his way through the
townships. "The sword . . . slew them on the right hand and on
the left" at Evans Mills. At Gouverneur, when a Universalist
got in the way, God gave the preacher a chance to "use him
entirely up." At De Kalb a dissenting elder was "thoroughly
broken up and broken down"; in other places congregations
"wept, and confessed, and broke their hearts before God. . . . a
more thorough breaking down . . . I have seldom witnessed."

Sometimes this warrior against the unconverted seemed to demand the ultimate of God Himself. At the end of a year and a half, Finny was "alarmed" by his own fury.

> A spirit of importunity sometimes came upon me so that I would say to God that he had made a promise to answer prayer, and I could not and would not be denied. I felt so certain . . . that frequently I found myself saying to him, "I hope thou dost not think that I can be denied. I come with thy faithful promises in my hand, and I cannot be denied." I cannot tell how . . . certain it was, in my mind, that God would answer prayer. . . . I . . . put on the harness for a mighty conflict with the powers of darkness, and expected soon to see a far more powerful outpouring of the Spirit of God, in that new country where I had been laboring.[21]

As autumn of 1825 came on, he went to a meeting of the Central New York Synod, where he was no doubt well received, since the presbytery of St. Lawrence had joyfully written of his work, in 1824, "Verily, 'the day-spring from on high hath visited us,' and the sun of righteousness has poured upon us the light and glory of his beams." [22] On the way back from the session, he stopped at Western, where his old mentor, Gale, was mending his health. For Finney, this visit was a milepost. He conducted a revival in Western, and during its course, met the Reverend Moses Gillett, of the Congregational Church in Rome, New York. Gillett invited him to Rome. And Rome was on the banks of the newly completed Erie Canal, a region of challenging potentiality for growth. Moving into it, Finney was entering a better-publicized sphere of activity. He now began the "Oneida County" revivals, which culminated in the summer of 1827. The next year and a half made Finney notorious, and cut his ties to the crossroads village forever.

Why did his star blaze so brightly? To the grateful ministers, it was merely the Lord's work. But Finney himself would have been first to declare that the Lord worked through "means." The first of those means was the personality of Charles Grandison Finney.

His six-foot-two, long-armed figure was magnetic and compelling. When preaching, he whirled his arms about; at Troy, a
colleague on the platform spent a nervous five minutes of ducking
as Finney, describing the Creation, flung world after world into
space. In Rochester, in 1831, he was depicting the fall of the sinner to hell. His index finger stabbed at the ceiling, then curved
downward, downward, and the back benches rustled as the crowd
rose involuntarily to its feet to see the final disappearance.[23]

His eyes, staring at a sinner, had uncanny hypnotic power. One
of his converts, remembering those "great" eyes, said that no
man's soul ever gazed out so through his face. Opponents charged
that he would collect inquirers in a circle and demoralize them by
solemn stares. When a woman on one such occassion laughed
nervously, he asked, "Do you laugh God in the face?"[24] And
Finney himself told of being shown through a textile factory by
his brother-in-law at a little place not far from Utica, when he
noticed two of the girls at a machine, pointing to him, the mill
town's local sensation, and giggling. Finney turned and advanced
with a majestic glare upon them. One girl burst into tears at once,
and a general outburst of weeping took place. The pious owner
had the wheels stopped, a meeting took place in one of the unused
machinery rooms, and nearly the whole force was converted.[25]

Then there was his great voice, used by Finney to provide
the theatrical quality in religion which nonliturgical churches
so sadly lacked. Henry Ware, the Boston Unitarian, watching
the revivalist's "abject groanings, his writhing of his body," came
away convinced that he had seen a man calculatedly acting a
part.[26] At Rochester, in 1830, his sermons were "dramatically de-
nunciatory," sputtering with such phrases as "blistered," "broken
down" and "crushed."[27] Theodore Weld, the antislavery evangel,
was converted by such a "dramatic denunciation" at Utica in
1826. Weld's aunt had informed Finney that her skeptical young
nephew would be in the congregation on a certain day, and, said
Weld, "he just held me up on his toasting-fork." Weld's doubts
were toasted away. In New York City Finney would roar at a
hypothetical rum seller, "For shame, thou hypocrite! thou wretch!
thou enemy of God and man! thou wolf in the clothing of a

sheep! Lay aside your mask and write your name Satan on your sign-board!" [28]

At Andover, one theology student remembered how Finney sounded in a sermon against the "restorationists" — those who believed that men might go to hell for their sins, but after serving enough time to satisfy "justice," would be saved. Finney, insisting that all men deserved eternal punishment, put his argument in the form of a tableau, depicting "the *jar* which the songs of the saints would receive if any intruder should claim that he had already endured the penalty of the divine law."

> The tones of the preacher . . . became sweet and musical, as he repeated . . . "Worthy is the Lamb that hath been slain to receive the power, and riches, and wisdom, and might, and honor, and glory, and blessing." No sooner had he uttered the word "blessing" than he started back, turned his face . . . fixed his glaring eyes upon the gallery at his right hand, and gave all the signs of a man who was frightened by a sudden interruption of the divine worship. With a stentorian voice he cried out: "*What* is this I see? What means that *rabble-rout* of men coming up here? Hark! Hear them shout! . . . 'Thanks to hell-fire! We have served out our time. Thanks! Thanks! WE HAVE SERVED OUT OUR TIME. THANKS TO HELL-FIRE.'" Then . . . after a lengthened pause, during which a fearful stillness pervaded the house, he said in gentle tones: "Is this the spirit of the saints? Is this the music of the upper world?" [29]

But Finney knew how to persuade as well as thunder in his rich tones. His legal training weighed heavily in his preparation. In Rochester he triumphed among members of the bar with sermons designed so that "lawyers accustomed to listen to argument should feel the weight of logically presented truth." [30] He sounded, in fact, as if he were "arguing a case before a court and jury," which made even more striking his feat of holding an audience for an hour or two without the stirring of a hand or foot.[31]

Nor was this accidental. In his use of language, he was deliberately trying to "avoid what was vulgar," and yet employ "the greatest simplicity." He borrowed illustrations from the varied tasks of farmers and mechanics, and chose forms of address used by "the common people." He jarred cautious pastors by saying "you," and not "they," when talking of the wicked, and he bore down heavily on the monosyllable "hell."

He was looking for effects with every word. The gospel truths must be presented in forthright manner, with an eye to the single point of bringing about conviction, and literary graces could take the hindmost. A lawyer haranguing a jury aimed at getting a verdict then and there, not at sending listeners away to ponder. And as Finney recalled, "I was bred a lawyer. I came right forth from a law office to the pulpit, and talked to the people as I would have talked to a jury." The better the system worked, the deeper grew Finney's assurance that God had led and taught him. Even after he became a college president, Finney distrusted formal education and written preparation in the pulpit. A man could "never learn to preach except by preaching." He could preach best if emancipated from a written text. A sermon composed at ease before a writing desk had too much style and not enough content.

Finney, in short, recognized the pervasive influence of democracy in homiletics. McGready, Cartwright and the circuit riders had used great plainness of speech because it was in their fiber. Lyman Beecher had discovered that extemporaneousness made theology live. "Young men," he told students at Lane Theological Seminary, "pump yourselves brim full of your subject till you can't hold another drop, and then knock out the bung and let nature caper." The lawyer-evangelist built on these foundations, and perhaps his greatest accolade came from an Englishman who heard him once during a trip abroad and went home to tell his wife excitedly, "I have been to Mr. Finney's meeting. He don't preach; he only explains what other people preach."[32]

Finney made converts by what he was, as well as by what he said. He did not have to grope for the ear of rural Americans. His instinctive prejudices were theirs. Like them, he recognized only two classes — "common people" (by whom he meant the farmers, small businessmen and "mechanics" of the small towns) and "educated men," mostly lawyers. He felt that he was a bridge between these two groups, and as they made up the bulk of his world, his appeal was almost universal.

But this very parochialism was a badge of middle-class self-pride. Finney had little to say of other kinds of commoners, such as the Irish Paddies working along the canals, the Canadian mill hands, or the squatters of the more primitive frontier. They were Papists and rum drinkers and blasphemers, beneath his mention. And for the fashionable rich he had suspicion and contempt. He enjoyed "breaking down" the girl in the plumed hat. It obviously pleased him when the Reverend Dirck Lansing, at Auburn, was rebuked by a church member for the sin of coming to services with a ruffled shirt and a gold ring. In his eyes, the ideal convert was the Philadelphia lady who burned her artificial flowers and ornaments. "I wished," Finney sighed, "all Christians were as faithful as she." [33] Plain-talking, respectful of solid rural achievement, but distrustful of ostentation, he belonged entirely to the people who made him his reputation.

The folkways of the frontier lingered in him. Underneath his respectability were the dark emotional depths that were churned and tossed in his conversion, and through the lawyer's rational outlook ran veins of plain superstition. God was still near, and still vengeful. During a convention of the Oneida Presbytery, a clergyman rose to make a violent speech against revivals. The next morning, the man was found dead in his bed. To Finney, that was judgment underlined. And if God was real and close, so was Satan. Offered a buggy ride from New Lebanon to Stephentown in 1827, the preacher questioned the driver about the gentleness of his horse, explaining that "if the Lord wants me to go to Stephentown, the devil will prevent it if he can; and if you have not a steady horse, he will try to make him kill me." And sure enough, Finney remembered, the horse did bolt twice and "came near killing us." [34]

So Finney, the man, was tailored perfectly to become Finney, the soul gatherer. Who could better "revive" the New York of the eighteen-twenties, halfway between wilderness and industrial commonwealth, than a man who was himself halfway between circuit rider and seminary-educated pastor?

Yet all the credit does not go to Finney, no matter how fitted he was to be an instrument of redemption. He came into a world which was already well "revivalized," a champion whose hosts were already armed. His milieu prepared his victories. For one thing, there was a corps of zestful young evangelistic ministers taking station in the Presbyterian-Congregational churchdom of New York State. Many of them were graduates of the colleges and divinity schools founded in the revivals of the century's beginning. These plantings were now bearing fruit. Thus George Gale, pastor at Adams, was a graduate of Union College (established in 1795 at Schenectady) and had absorbed much of the godly drive of those who had been *his* teachers. Samuel C. Aiken, of Utica, and John Frost, of Whitesboro, had both gone to Middlebury, sown in the impious "wilderness" of Vermont in 1800, and then to Andover Theological Seminary, begun in 1808 to train orthodox ministers in opposition to "Jews, Mahometans, Arians, Pelagians, Antinomians, Arminians, Socinians, Unitarians and Universalists." Frost traveled for the foreign missionary society of the Presbyterian Church for two years before settling in Whitesboro. Between 1813 and 1819 he added 195 converts to his church, no mean total in a small town. Moses Gillett, of Rome, and the "electrically eloquent" Dutchman, Dirck Lansing, at Auburn, were Yale graduates of that day when, under Timothy Dwight, a "new era of revivals" was dawning. Under such leadership there had been a steady simmer of "awakenings" in New York even before Finney.[35]

Waiting for Finney in 1824 was another strange soldier of God, the Reverend Daniel Nash, a man of fifty when he and Finney first met at a meeting of a presbytery. Nash, a self-educated Yankee carpenter, was licensed to preach, but did not find his destiny until his encounter with the younger man, with whom he remained in close contact until Finney moved out of upstate New York. Nash had startling evangelical ideas. He believed that he could convert individuals by interceding with heaven for them specifically and by name. He therefore kept a secret "praying list" of people in need of regeneration, and would seek out private places to pray for them. Unfortunately, he had a voice which carried for half a mile — he could pray a horse from one pasture into the next, someone said — and a number of village citizens found their shortcomings publicly advertised.[36]

The revivalistic atmosphere pervaded the entire Northeast. Nettleton had done stout work in Connecticut, and Edward D. Griffin in New Jersey. Lyman Beecher was successfully entrenched in Boston, that fortress of Unitarianism, by 1823.[37] Vigorous evangelistic effort had accounted for steady gains in membership by the Presbyterians and the Baptists throughout the country.[38] Meanwhile the Methodists, with their permanently "built-in" camp-meeting revivalism, were being fruitful and multiplying, in New York State as elsewhere. In Troy in 1816, for example, a single eight-week revival brought 107 new Methodists into the ranks.[39] Methodist preachers seemed perennially to be rejoicing over mass salvation which descended "like dew upon the hills of Zion." [40] By 1824 a worker in New York State advised his brethren in the *Methodist Magazine* that it was "no new thing at this day, to hear of revivals." [41] The Wesleyans did not always get the publicity for their efforts which attended the Presbyterian campaigns of Finney, but the men of the eighteen-twenties knew the facts. Lyman Beecher had no use for the theology of John R. Maffitt, the Methodist evangelist from Ireland, but he was delighted when one of his own meetings was "crammed as much as if Maffitt had preached." [42] And in 1832, when revivalism was at high tide, a newspaper examined accounts of awakenings for the single month of January in about half of the country's religious journals. Some 12,640 converts were claimed. Such statistics were invariably inaccurate, but the notable fact was that the Methodists counted 5757 and the Baptists 2809. In short, some 8500, or about 68 per cent, of the newly saved souls were in these two churches. Presbyterianism and Congregationalism furnished the leadership for the mass revival movement, but the rank and file of the convert armies were Baptists and Methodists.[43]

Thus, even before Finney's time, the foundations of "successful soul-winning" were laid among the common folk. For plain men and women, in fact, the hopes of mansions bright and blessed and crowns of glory were the stellar consolations of hard-driven lives of work. Yet revivalism was no mere quirk of the uneducated. Shades of eternity also surrounded the growing boy being prepared for leadership at college. Joshua Leavitt, the antislavery and temperance editor, was typical in the affectionate advice he offered to a younger brother at Yale. "You may die . . . & may be immediately deprived of your reason . . . without any opportunity to examine whether you are prepared to meet Him who will judge both young and old," he wrote.[44] Beecher advised his son Edward to "agonize" to enter into the kingdom of heaven, for no "learning and human estimation" could balance one hour "of that miserable eternity in which all is lost!" [45]

The hapless collegian, in fact, was relentlessly prodded to add up his spiritual account. At Union College, when one student died, his classmates were gathered in a professor's study around the body and treated to a solemn discourse on their preparation for the grave.[46] Union's president, Eliphalet Nott, was an ardent revival supporter. Edward Dorr Griffin, who became president of Williams, lost no chance to arouse his students, even when it meant bursting into a prayer meeting with the breathless cry: "The Lord is in Williamstown!" [47] Heman Humphrey, president of Amherst, also encouraged revivals. At Yale there were eighteen "awakenings" between 1782 and 1838, an average of one every three and a half years.[48] Such treatment made some of the boys painfully serious — like the young Joel Hawes, later a Hartford minister, who wrote ardently to his fiancée, "I have lately purchased Dr. Witherspoon's works, two volumes of which I wish you to read when you have time. . . . I have also 'Watts on the Mind' — an invaluable book. Do you want it?" [49] But even those who skylarked through four years of lecture and chapel were insensibly prepared to accept the revival message. The old-time college president laid much of the groundwork for popular evangelism.

Once graduated and settled in a small town, the young man of Finney's day could not escape the revival contagion. In towns of one church and one hundred families the conversion of individuals was a theme of absorbing magnitude. In fact, revivalism was transplanted to large cities only when the press and publicity mechanisms made it possible to duplicate there the village grape-vine. In a society "near to a common level" where "every body knows every body," the awakening of one sinner would naturally "be the means of awakening others." [50] The tyranny of the majority, which de Tocqueville would capture in his notebooks in Jackson's day, was another help to the spread of revival piety.

The whole atmosphere of upstate New York thus worked on Finney's side. As he moved into Oneida County in 1826, there were certain added advantages for a revivalist. For Oneida County, bisected by the Erie Canal, completed in 1825, was part of a region primed to explode socially, and thereby to afford a place for enthusiastic religion. Hundreds of thousands of migrants floated along the canal, many of them bound for the golden pastures of Michigan, Illinois and Wisconsin, but many others settling on the canal banks. Cities grew within sight of the water-way, as flour mills, distilleries and packing houses prepared the grain and meat of the region for shipment to a hungry world. Farmers sweated to raise bumper crops now that a way to market was assured — and then groaned as the canal brought in pork and oats, corn and wheat from the virgin lands of the new Western states, underselling them and driving them into bankruptcy. Suddenly there was a new wealthy class, composed of successful commission merchants and jobbers, bankers, and owners of the textile, leather and glass factories springing into life. And just as suddenly there was a new group at the bottom of society, too, of pick swingers and mill hands.

New York State was shaken by the revolution in farming habits that went with opening the West, and at the same time was fac-ing the industrial revolution breaking up the fountains of the great deep in New England. Steadily, upstate New Yorkers watched the crumbling of certain eternal verities — fixed land tenure, a stable populace, small class distinctions, isolation for the outside world. They sought strange light from heaven to illumi-nate the meaning of it all. Many men believed that the unquiet times indicated the imminence of some great revolution, some overturn exceeding all that had come as yet. And so, in twenty-five years after the completion of the Erie Canal, western New York produced Mormonism, spiritualism, millennialism, perfectionism and the anti-Masonic, Liberty and Free Soil parties. No wonder that it was called a "burnt-over" land! [51] Yet this was grist to the mill of the revivalist. Some men, uneasy on such a rocking and heaving earth, thought longingly of the eternal and changeless peace of the New Jerusalem. Others wanted to recast the world in heaven's image at once and at whatever cost, because the times plainly demanded it. Together, they formed an audience ready to listen to God's word — an audience far enough from the raw frontier to have time for religion, and far enough from urban sophistication to want it sizzling!

Finney, stepping into this scene, filled all of Moses Gillett's expectations at Rome. In twenty days he had accounted for several hundred conversions, including "nearly every one of the lawyers, merchants and physicians, and almost all the principal men" of the town. In the spring of 1826, he went to Utica, and for the balance of the year to Auburn. The report of the Oneida Presbytery for the year was ecstatic about the results.[52] Finney was now winning continual victories. But having emerged from the obscurity of the St. Lawrence-fronting counties, he was provoking sharp controversy, too. An era of criticism was opening. Attacks on him highlighted the middle-ground position of revivalism. Conservative Presbyterians stood aghast at his "radical" measures, and religious liberals condemned his "fanaticism." By the end of 1826, disagreement split the camp of revivalism itself, when Asahel Nettleton became numbered among Finney's enemies.

Most of the complaints centered on Finney's use — or, at least, the use by youthful converts of Finney — of certain vigorous "new measures" to speed the redemptive work. For one thing, meetings were held almost daily, and prolonged until the small hours of the morning, so that the ordinary business of life virtually came to a standstill and whole communities were groggy with a mixture of exaltation and sleeplessness. In those meetings, individual sinners were "prayed for" by name, and thus put under devastating social pressure to "find" conviction in their hearts. And then, women were permitted to pray in public. Not only

did this affront conservative readers of Saint Paul, but it was for
some reason thought to be grossly indelicate. It seemed to be a
kind of spiritual undressing in front of the worshipers, and in any
case it encouraged girls to be "forward." Lastly, Finney and his
disciples were accused of making attacks on "unconverted"
ministers and rousing their flocks against them. The ghost of
Davenport seemed to be walking again.[53]

The conservative attack came from such men as the Reverend
William R. Weeks of the Congregational Church at Paris Hill,
New York. From the secure refuge of a Princeton education,
Weeks blistered Finneyism in a series of pamphlets later bound
into a book.[54] Liberal critics rested their case on a scorching
account of the Utica revival by Ephraim Perkins, a Unitarian
layman of nearby Trenton.[55] Perkins claimed that Finney was followed by a retinue of young theological students whom he had
converted, and that his corps of assistants, in Trenton and Utica,
had used such language in prayer to the Lord for sinners as "Smite
them this night," "Shake them," "Take off the blanket and show
them hell," and the like. They had also publicly proclaimed Unitarians to be "heirs of hell, children of the devil . . . and opposers of God." [56]

Finney himself appeared as a man distinctly short of Christian
humility. He was supposed to have told one group of assistants,
"God's eyes are upon you, my eyes are upon you, the eyes of the
Angels of Heaven are upon you." Perkins charged him with snap-
ping at someone who wished to borrow his horse, "That is Jesus
Christ's horse. If you are going on Jesus Christ's errand, take him;
if not, let him alone." A handbill was circulated to advertise a
Finney appearance in Utica, with the flamboyant heading BY
COMMAND OF THE KING OF KINGS. The assistants in his "holy band"
were anything but reverent. Father Nash was said to have named
God Almighty sixty-three times in one public prayer, and a
"Reverend Norton" to have shouted in a sermon delivered at
Trenton, "You Unitarians in that gallery, do you hear me? . . .
Christ will put you down." [57]

At the inquiry meetings, Perkins declared, Finney bullied the
anxious. When some of them lagged about "giving their hearts to

God," the preacher announced that he "beheld the angels of God sealing their eternal doom." [58] These sessions were held at night, in unlighted rooms, where an occasional muffled groan in the darkness heightened the awesomeness of the proceedings. Leaders tiptoed solemnly about, half whispering, "Don't you think this is a solemn place?" "Don't you think God is here?" One "inquirer" who retorted, "God knows my thoughts," got the answer, "So do I." A boy who was too frightened to answer questions was horrified to hear the minister call loudly for prayers to cure him of a "dumb devil." [59]

Finney never formally replied to such charges, and in a time when religious arguments were superheated, some were bound to be exaggerated or entirely false. Yet on the other hand, they were not wholly outrageous, and they probably gave some hint of the revivalist's methods. For one thing, Finney's version of Presbyterianism could easily take in violent attacks on the sinner. Man's depravity, to him, was a "voluntary attitude of mind." Man persisted in sin *by choice;* in Finney's phrase, the sinner's *"cannot* is a *will not."* God offered the means of overcoming this resistance by explaining the terms of redemption in the Bible. His influence was "persuasive." Ministers were supposed to enlighten the sinner's intelligence and confront him with the "unreasonableness of moral depravity." This was branded clearly enough with the mark of Nathaniel Taylor's New Haven theology, but Finney put a rod of iron into it. When the job of explanation was done, he said, *"we had a right to expect the Holy Spirit to cooperate with us."* If God was willing to save, and the clergy did its job, then only a hard and wretched heart stood in the way of conversion. A good tongue-lashing might be just what the sinner needed to bring him up to the mark.[60]

In addition, a revival that was "fanatical" to someone not bred in the Western school of religious ecstasy might well seem "orderly" to Finney. He himself wrote that "men are naturally mad on the subject of religion," [61] and he blended horse sense and wild pietism incongruously in his own personality. The core of the revivalistic belief was that a person on the brink of religious hysteria could, upon conversion, be changed *instantly* into an orderly and peaceable Christian. Finney wrote with pride of one of his conversions in Philadelphia. The subject was a burly man who objected to his wife's attendance at a revival meeting. He locked himself in the house with her, went into a furniture-smashing rage, and finally drew a dagger to stab her. At the last second he was suddenly overcome with revulsion and dropped the weapon in a storm of tears. He was then converted and made an "earnest Christian." [62] To the practiced evangelical preacher, such insane outbursts by the "convicted" were mere clinical de-tails — symptoms like pain or bleeding, bound to disappear when a cure was reached.[63] Yet it seems clear to more sophisticated eyes that men and women under such extravagant psychological pres-sures were capable of behaving with wild and weird abandon in religious gatherings.

Undoubtedly, some of Finney's disciples were carried away by enthusiasm. His correspondence is proof of that. "Our minis-ters in Shenectady [*sic*] are apparently asleep," wrote William F. Hurd from Union College in 1828. "I want to see them come down at the feet of Jesus and beg." [64] John P. Cushman urged Theodore Weld in 1830 to get right into preaching without go-ing to theological school. "The time is gone by when this trash can influence," he said.[65] One letter to Finney complained of a sermon "by a young man just from a theological seminary — or the moon — or some other cold climate." [66] And there was the incredible descent of Luther Myrick, a Finney convert, on Au-gusta, New York. The Presbyterian minister there, a Mr. Spauld-ing, had invited Myrick, recently licensed, to aid him one Sunday. After Spaulding had closed a prayer meeting, Myrick fell to his knees and told God loudly that if Christians left the house then, sinners would be "sealed over to damnation." Then Myrick called an evening meeting for later in the week. Spaulding came into this meeting at 11 P.M. to find some sinners groaning on the floor, while others were shouting and praying at the top of their lungs, in a performance which went on until two in the morning. The next day the minister of Augusta suggested that Myrick had better leave, as they did not work well together. Myrick coolly replied that he had been invited and would stay, and Spaulding distractedly wrote to Finney for advice.[67] In fairness, Myrick was too zealous even for Finney's band, and he later drifted entirely out of Presbyterianism and into perfectionist utopian schemes. But his "protracted meeting" could not have been entirely unique, for J. P. Cushman, in 1828, wrote enthusiastically of one which lasted the night through.[68]

All in all, while Finney's enemies were prepared to believe lies and misrepresentations about him, there was some fire behind the smoke.

The smoke drifted into the nostrils of Asahel Nettleton when chance threw him into sudden proximity with Finney. In the autumn of 1826, Nettleton was assisting in a revival at Albany when the younger evangelist appeared in Troy, a stone's throw away. During Finney's summer at Auburn, a number of parishioners had become so irritated that they withdrew and formed their own congregation.[69] Unperturbed, he now accepted an invitation from Nathaniel Sydney Smith Beman of Troy's First Presbyterian Church. Beman was a Middlebury graduate who had worked as a "home missionary" in Georgia and come back to a Northern pulpit after taking to wife a widowed Southern lady. He was a "new school" Presbyterian of liberal views — that is, favoring revivals and the so-called new measures — and his publication of his opinions already had landed him in trouble. As 1827 drew near, he had pending a trial for heresy before the presbytery[70] and was conducting a revival in which he begged Finney's help with the cry, "I hope we look to God, but we must have means." [71] Finney did come. He provided Troy with the two or three liveliest months in its religious history. He also helped to split Beman's congregation.

Conservative members were already unhappy with their pastor's doctrines, and some disliked Mrs. Beman. But that was not the worst. Beman was also charged with originating a new technique, the "prayer of faith." The idea of this was that if Christians prayed in good faith for a spiritual blessing, such as the conversion of a sinner, God would at once grant it. To doubt this was to insult Him. The prayer must name specific individuals, and be offered with "perseverance." Thus, according to Beman's critics, the minister would name a woman sitting in the church, and then say:

> "O Lord! thou seest this hardened enemy of thine! . . . Thou seest how she is . . . stretching out her puny female hands to lay hold of Thee, and pull Thee from thy throne. . . . Thou knowest how black her heart is, and how her enmity to Thee rankles and burns with all the malice of a demon. . . . Now, Lord God Almighty! come down upon this enemy of thine; break in upon her; break her down, O Lord, break her down! . . . Break her down; crush her at thy feet; slay her before Thee!"

A man who was singled out for the prayer of faith might hear Beman say:

> "O Lord! Thou knowest he is a hardened wretch; thou seest how he has raised his crest against Thee. . . . Now, Lord, don't let him boast himself against Thee; but draw thy sword and come down upon him; drive it through his heart, and let him bleed at thy feet."

Of ministers who disagreed with him, the Trojan divine was supposed to have said:

> "Lord, have mercy on these blind leaders of the blind; Thou knowest they have been blind long enough. . . . Lord, wake up these stupid sleeping ministers; for, Thou knowest, if they do not wake soon, they will wake in hell."

These prayers, sometimes forty-five minutes long, were made complete by the accompaniment of "loud groans." [72] It is not surprising that Beman was brought before the presbytery for trial. They cleared him, amid the grumbling of dissidents that he had played thimblerig with the session. In his enforced absence from his duties, he looked for continued leadership in the revival to Finney, whom he introduced to his congregation with the recommendation, it was averred, "Now, I want you all to listen to what God says." [73]

An impression of a camp meeting. The tents and rather formal clothes worn suggest that this meeting came much later than the Kentucky revival of 1800, but there is plenty of emotional potency left.

Timothy Dwight. As president of Yale from 1795 to 1817, he trained a tough-minded generation of revival ministers in the work of adapting ortho-doxy to changing conditions.

Lyman Beecher surveys the world with typical self-confidence and a forgotten pair of spectacles pushed up on his head. The Lord's business left little time for doubts or worries over small details.

Even in 1850, twenty years after his major revival campaigns, the piercing eyes of Charles G. Finney show the power that brought sinners to their knees before him.

Dwight L. Moody as he looked to a *Harper's Weekly*
cover artist when he brought the gospel to wicked New
York, early in 1876.

The "big-time" flavor of mass evangelism under Moody and Sankey is expressed in these *Harper's Weekly* sketches of the spacious auditorium which they used in Brooklyn in 1875.

Photo by the Detroit News

In his sixties, Billy Sunday could still strike the peppy
pose which made him famous on hundreds of revival
platforms in his 1909–1919 heyday.

Like Billy Sunday himself, the homely tabernacles of unpainted lumber which housed his crowds carried a lingering memory of the frontier into the busiest districts of the big cities.

Photo by the Detroit News

Inside a Sunday tabernacle the surroundings had the aroma of the circus tent, but the audience was obviously dressed in its Sunday-morning middle-class best. The contrast was a key to Sunday's success.

The enemies of Beman insisted that Finney was just as bad. One, Josephus Brockway, a mettlesome anti-Bemanite, published a short history of the revival which Finney's friends considered "a miserable attempt to propagate untruths." [74] In it, Finney was scolded for enacting a scene in the pulpit in which "restorationists," who had paid the exact penalty of the law, came "smoking and fuming out of hell" and to the gates of pearl, crying, "Stand away, you old saints of God! . . . And you too, Jesus Christ, stand one side! Get out of our way! No thanks to you, our being here: we came here on our merits." To some invisible enemy, Finney cried:

> "Why, sinner, I tell you, if you could climb to heaven, you would hurl God from his throne! Yes, hurl God from his throne! Oh, yes, if you could but get there, you would cut God's throat! Yes, you would cut God's throat!" [75]

Finney was also made responsible for a description of hell which added new dimensions to Jonathan Edwards.

> "Look! Look! . . . see the millions of wretches, biting and gnawing their tongues, as they lift their scalding heads from the burning lake! . . . See! see! how they are tossed, and how they howl. . . . Hear them groan, amidst the fiery billows, as they *Lash!* and *Lash!* and *Lash!* their burning shores." [76]

Even more disturbing was an undue zeal in "inquiries." Brockway said that on October 3, 1826, Beman and Finney called on a Mrs. Weatherby, in the home of her sister-in-law. The two men had been insisting that the lady pray for the immediate conversion of her family, and they came to press the point a little. Finney asked the sister-in-law if she loved God. When she said yes, he allegedly shook his fist under her nose and cried, "You lie! What reason have you to think you love God?" Next he asked if she would repent. Being a conservative Calvinist, she believed, and said, that she could not (without a special divine gift). Again, Finney's fist supposedly shook before her face. "You lie! You can repent and be converted immediately!" The upshot of the story was that *Mr.* Weatherby later accosted Beman and asked for an explanation. Beman told him he would go to hell. Weatherby lost his temper and threw the pastor on his back, but Beman continued doggedly to shout, "You will go to hell!" until released.[77]

Stories such as these were horrifying to Nettleton, a sworn apostle of prudence and veneration for the regular ministry. To his surprise, Finney came to see him at Troy. Finney, writing about it later, chose to make it a visit of youthful respect to an honored pioneer, and he said that the older man gave no indication of disagreement with his methods.[78] Finney's entire attitude towards the storms he raised, in fact, was one of wounded innocence. According to Nettleton's recollections, however, he asked Finney to give up certain "calamitous" measures and was rebuffed. In either case, it is clear that Nettleton refused to let Finney appear with him in public. He claimed that it would "sanction" the work of "disorganizers" in the churches. Perhaps it was only a sign of fading self-confidence. Aging and weakened by a bout of typhus, Nettleton evidently feared the aggressive young lawyer-evangelist. He accepted the darkest tales of Finney's virulence at full face value, and in something of a panic he wrote to Lyman Beecher and asked if someone in New England would say a word against the new measures. If not, he would speak up himself.

Beecher was unhappy. He regarded himself as a captain of the forces of revival, and this was war in the ranks. What he heard of Finney was a little unsettling, perhaps, but he was more concerned with his own continuing battle against the Unitarians, who would make much of any division amongst the orthodox. He was entirely right in this estimate of the tactical situation. The *Christian Examiner*, a Boston Unitarian paper, took note of the Utica and Troy revivals with a long review of five books on the subject, including those of Perkins and Brockway. It concluded that they were evidence of "extravagances committed of late, in various parts of our country, under the abused names of Revivals of Religion."

Although his temperament hardly suited him for it, Beecher

decided that he would have to play the role of peacemaker. After consultation, he dispatched a joint letter to Beman and Finney, with a copy for Nettleton. He referred as delicately as he could to rumored "irregularities" in the New York revivals, and asked if a few changes could be made which would preserve their essential "ardor, and boldness, and moral momentum." For, he said, it is *"necessary that Brother Finney should come upon ground on which we can sustain him, for we cannot justify his. faults for the sake of his excellencies."* [79]

It is clear that Beecher had no intention of allying with Nettleton to destroy Finney. To pacify his older friend, however, he enclosed a private note to Nettleton with the copy of the letter to Beman and Finney. In it he attacked the new measures more unguardedly than he had done in public. And this turned out to be one of Beecher's mistakes, for Nettleton was determined to upset the apple cart. He wrote to Samuel Aiken, at Utica, in January of 1827, raging against Finney for the alleged abuses of the new measures.[80] The next month he particularized his charges to John Frost at Whitesboro.

> The great secret is, to get females to pray in school houses and circles where men and *ministers especially* are present to see and hear them pray for them and others by name. . . . In this manner the spirit of a revival has been *destroyed* in many places. . . . And what is worse than all the rest, those ministers and Christians who do not fall in to defend these men and their *measures,* are denounced as *cold* and *stupid* and *dead* and *enemies to revivals.*[81]

Then, worst of all, Nettleton showed Beecher's private note to him to a number of his clerical brethren, thus landing Beecher in the controversy, where he did not want to be, and in the anti-Finney camp, where he did not genuinely belong. It was no wonder that Beecher's oldest son accused Nettleton of losing his head! [82]

Finney did not formally enter into the battle, but on March 4, 1827, he preached a sermon at Troy on the text from Amos 3:3, "Can two walk together except they be agreed?" The gist of it was that two individuals had to be on the same emotional plane in order to perceive an identical truth. Just as a man in a melancholy mood might be irritated by lively band music which someone feeling rather brisk might welcome, so in religion, a heart that was cold to the truths of the gospel would be offended by the zeal of one warmed by holy fire. In every congregation were "lukewarm Christians" whose torpid feelings accepted "dull preaching or praying," but were disturbed by the "fire and spirit" of revivals. If one part of a church was "spiritual and active," while another part remained "carnal and earthly," there might be a secession movement amongst the carnal. Finney named no names, but it was clear that he meant to say that the objectors to "new measures" simply did not understand real holiness.[83] It was rather deftly done, with something of an air of charitable regret for the critics about it.

Nettleton responded in a review of the sermon in the Presbyterian *New York Observer*, with a somber prophecy that those who did not distinguish between "true and false zeal" would be "traitors" to the revival cause. Another New York clergyman wrote to second this position. It was clear that Presbyterian churchmen would soon be trading blows under the interested gaze of the newspaper-reading public, and Lyman Beecher knew that the time had come to summon the fire brigade. He wrote to Beman and asked him to help arrange a conference of a "few Christian brethren" to bring matters into a condition "in which we can all act as one." [84]

This informal peace convention met for about a week on July 18, 1827, in the little New York town of New Lebanon, just west of the Massachusetts line. New Lebanon had a Shaker community, a store, a tavern, and a Presbyterian church under Silas Churchill. Churchill played host to seventeen other ministers, participants in what was frankly called by Beman "the Nettletonian war." [85] Finney, Beman, Beecher and Nettleton were on hand. So were the "Westerners," or New York defenders of the new measures — Gillett, Lansing, Frost and Aiken. There were four additional New Englanders — Caleb Tenney of Weathersfield, Connecticut, Joel Hawes of Hartford, Heman Humphrey, the president of

Amherst, and Justin Edwards, who was to become president of Andover Seminary. All of them were revival men, but supposedly of a "conservative" kind. There were six other preachers from New York, either opposed to new measures or uncommitted. They included William R. Weeks, who had assailed overardent revivals in print, and Finney's teacher, Gale.

The atmosphere of the session was strained and curious. Finney kept a certain aloofness, anxious to avoid any impression that this was an ecclesiastical trial in which he was the defendant.[86] On the other side sulked Nettleton, the aging chief, as he erroneously thought himself, waiting for the elders to rebuke the brash young warrior who had spoken out of turn. The other sixteen men were divided and unhappy. They were involved in a quarrel resting on unproved accusations and threatening to blow up an "awakening" whose success cheered them all, whatever they thought about techniques for achieving it. They never even tried to prove or disprove the charges against Finney. In fact, the convention merely introduced "resolutions" to be voted on. Everyone hurried to agree to inoffensive generalities. Revivals were God's work; they were carried out by human "instrumentalities"; ministers ought not to be called "stupid"; care should be taken not to exaggerate accounts of revivals.

The New Englanders then got down to business and proposed censure of the so-called "abuses," such as audible groaning and public female prayer. Some of the "Westerners" went along with these motions, and some abstained. Then the "Finneyites" moved to condemn believers in unfounded rumors, and "lukewarm professors," and in turn many of the "conservatives" refused to vote. After a final day or so of prayer, which was abundant, adjournment was reached. All parties had blown off some steam. Nobody had yielded anything, and the argument was to continue on about the same terms as before, but in much softer tones among the evangelical clergy. As they were to do many times later, churchmen had failed to agree on a definite statement of what measures were scriptural or sound or reverent in a revival. The field of revivalism remained, as always, wide open to individual innovation.

In spite of this apparent lack of consequence, the convention was a victory for Finney. The conservatives had let him escape unrebuked and an acknowledged leader of the revival men. Beecher had had a look at him, and emerged with a respectful evaluation. In his memoirs, nearly forty years later, he said that he cried, "Finney, I know your plan . . . you mean to come to Connecticut, and carry a streak of fire to Boston. But if you attempt it, as the Lord liveth, I'll meet you at the state line, and call out all the artillerymen, and fight every inch of the way to Boston, and then I'll fight you there." In *his* memoirs, Finney said he remembered no such thing. But if the remark was actually made, he should have treasured it, for no one else ever heard Lyman Beecher admit that he would retreat *before* a battle started! Beecher saw the situation realistically, however. Finney was too good a revivalist to be lost to the cause. Four years after the convention, he *did* come to Boston, and he did not fight his way through artillerymen, either. He had an express invitation from Beecher.[87]

On the other hand, the real loser at New Lebanon was Nettleton, whose little candle guttered dimly between the blazing lights of Finney and Beecher. He came to the conference expecting vindication against the interloper, and he found his brethren treating Finney as a sovereign and plenipotentiary power. After the adjournment, he continued to press Beecher for support, but Beecher had another idea in mind. In May of 1828, the Presbyterian Church held its General Assembly in Philadelphia. At that time, Finney was holding revival meetings in the city, and Beecher also was there, substituting in the pulpit of a colleague. Beecher took advantage of the presence of all parties to the dispute in the city of brotherly love. He got them to sign a statement promising that they all would cease thereafter from "publications, correspondences, conversations, and conduct designed . . . to keep those subjects before the public mind." With the peace treaty signed, he sat down to write a tactful letter to Nettleton. It would serve no purpose to agitate these questions further. Perhaps brother Nettleton could do most good by traveling to theological schools to "imbue the young men with correct views."

Nettleton was feeble in body, but not necessarily in mind. He realized that this was a way to ease him off the stage, but he could do little about it. All his potential supporters among the defenders of revivalism had agreed to the truce. It was natural for him, then, to drift further away from Beecher and the revival itself. When a battle began to rage between strict Calvinists, still insisting on man's inability to repent, and the proponents of the New Haven theology, he took the conservative side. He passed sorrowfully into outer darkness and a part-time chair at the ultraorthodox seminary in East Windsor, Connecticut. His kind of revival, in which the sinner was urged to pray that God would, in good time, perhaps, *permit* him to repent, was defunct.[88]

Meanwhile, Finney and Beecher drew closer together. The New Haven doctrines of Beecher and Taylor held that man was a reasoning moral agent, able to understand and act upon the threats and promises of the gospel. That was not so different from what Finney himself preached, except that he added certain fireworks. Charles Finney had left Connecticut in 1794 as an infant. In one sense he now came home.[89]

The New Lebanon conference, however, was more than a mere triumph for Finney. It was another major turning point in his career. He now had a choice between continuing his itinerant ways in the rural counties of New York, or moving into the more challenging realm of the city. He chose the path of prominence, the road to the metropolis.

As he lingered in the vicinity of New Lebanon during the balance of 1827, his mail was flooded with invitations which were a tribute to his reputation. For more than a year, in fact, local ministers, impressed with the good tidings, had been crying for help. "Brother Finney . . . the precious servants of Jesus are in the dark. . . . I cannot rest until you come." "We do not see how we can do without you." "Brother . . . our petition . . . comes from a few, in behalf of a town containing more than 6,000 inhabitants, who are . . . crying 'peace,' when there is no peace." "A great anxiety . . . prevails, of hearing *you* sound the

Gospel trumpet among this people."[90] These appeals were from towns in the countryside of New York and Pennsylvania. It was clear to Finney that in all those towns he could make hundreds of converts as adoring as the woman who wrote to him, "My dear Spiritual Father . . . Thou, dear servant of Jesus — I owe thee much for your intercession on my behalf."[91]

But calls of another kind were coming, too. There was a Presbyterian preacher of Wilmington, Delaware, who had met Finney at New Lebanon and asked him to preach in his church. Wilmington was a short trip down the Delaware from Philadelphia, heart and center of the Presbyterianism of the mid-Atlantic states. Sometime in the fall of 1827, Finney elected to go to Wilmington. Twice a week he would slip up to Philadelphia to speak in the pulpit of the Reverend James Patterson, carrying his kind of awakening into "old school" territory in Princeton's shadow. There was so much of this work that in the middle of 1828 he moved to Philadelphia to stay for a solid year. Here it soon was clear that he could work best by preaching steadily in one place, in a "central position." Such a place was found in a German church on Race Street which held three thousand people. So now Charles G. Finney remained in one spot, each night addressing as many souls as were contained in two or three of the little villages where he had made his start.[92] He was still a countryman, a little wide-eyed at the wickedness of Babylon, writing to Theodore Weld to pray for him in the city of "almost solid darkness." Even the relatively smaller city of Reading, where he labored for a time, seemed to him a place of "wealth and pride and abominations." [93]

Still, it was stimulating to meet a larger audience and expand the scope of one's work. Therefore, he began to listen to words from an even greater city, New York, where a band of pious businessmen were planning to bring Finney to their doors. At first, the prospects did not seem good. Zephaniah Platt and Anson Phelps, both natives of upstate New York, wanted Finney in their town, but Platt wrote to him in 1827 that conservative Presbyterians in New York might object. "Providence," said Platt, "does not seem yet to open the door for your labours among us." [94]

Almost at the same time, however, David L. Dodge, a dry-goods merchant, told Finney that at least four ministers would give him "the right hand of fellowship" provided he would not "introduce some things that has been such an occasion of handle to opposers [*sic*]." [95] The city was his, if he would let himself be tempered a little.

At that time Finney did not care to go. Instead, he went to Philadelphia, and when it became apparent that his meetings there did not result in "outbursts" and "crushed" ministers, things began to change. Wealthy and influential Presbyterians and Congregationalists saw him operating in an urban setting without applying a torch anywhere. By March of 1828, Platt could record "a very general change of sentiment here in regard to yourself." Soon thereafter Phelps, whose successful importing business had not dulled the edge of his piety, got Finney to spend the month of August, 1828, filling a vacant pulpit in what Phelps called "our Stupid, Poluted and Perishing City." [96]

That month in New York apparently satisfied all parties. In the spring of 1830, the revivalist came to New York again for a longer stay. He preached for some time in a former Universalist church near Niblo's Gardens, bought by Phelps for this orthodox purpose.[97] That summer, Finney rested at his wife's home and weighed offers to continue in New York or to go to Rochester. His upstate roots were not yet cut. He chose Rochester and spent six months there. Yet even Rochester was not De Kalb, or Evans Mills, or Antwerp, or Adams. It was a rapidly growing place, then of about ten thousand souls, with three Presbyterian churches. Moreover, in this revival, most of Finney's converts came from a class which he proudly described as "the leading men and women in the city" — lawyers, judges, doctors, tradesmen, bankers and master mechanics.[98] When he finished at Rochester, he made his last really protracted swing through the region of his beginnings. He held meetings at Auburn and Buffalo, and moved at last into New England, as Beecher had foreseen at New Lebanon, though without the predicted "streak of fire." He worked in Providence, and finally, with Beecher, in Boston. He was there in the winter of 1831-1832, noting carefully that even "professed Christians" of the city lacked the "spirit of prayer" which he was used to in New York.[99]

By the beginning of 1832, it had been four years since Charles Finney had held a revival in any really small place. His old associates were worried. They warned him, in their letters, that the countryside was his Jerusalem, and if he forgot it, his right hand would lose its cunning. Gale wrote to him after the New Lebanon convention, "These things have set you upon a hill which if you are prudent, humble and holy will greatly extend your usefulness, but which if you are not, will only publish your faults and indiscretions the wider." [100] There were pathetic letters from Father Nash, who could no longer follow him in the role of a combined fond retainer and parent.

> The truth is, my dear Brother, I am willing to pray for you all I can, go where you will. . . . But, I could do you much more good if I could see you and see what you do. . . . I wish I could see you one hour — then pray with you another. . . . Situated as I am I have neither guide nor assistant, this side of heaven. That, however, is sometimes much nearer to me than Philadelphia.

Theodore Weld, too, fretted over the temptations of his spiritual awakener in Philadelphia. "My dear father in Jesus," he wrote, "you are in such a maddening whirl of care, responsibility and toil, I do dreadfully fear that you neglect the culture of personal holiness." He begged Finney to remain on the old battleground. "I don't believe, I can't and I will not, that you had better go to New York City *now*," he appealed, and pointed to still fertile fields in the towns between Buffalo and Rochester. "Once get that region thoroughly soaked and all hell can't wring it dry, you know." [101]

Yet there were other letters to balance against these. Now it was the New York merchant prince and financial "angel" of reform causes, Lewis Tappan, who was writing him: "I do not think a powerful revival will take place here unless you do come." Skillfully, he dangled before Finney the clinching argument of enlarged usefulness.

Do what may be done elsewhere, and leave this city the headquarters of Satan, and the nation is not saved. . . . A blow
struck here reverberates to the extremities of the republic.[102]

Moreover, Tappan offered to buy a theater in Chatham Street
and to provide a regular haven there for Finney. He could be
pastor of the Second Free Presbyterian Church, with pews open
to "the poor," and continued association with those men who
supported benevolent efforts, reforms — and revivals!

In 1832, the citadel fell. Finney moved to New York, to accept
a settled pastorate. He stayed there, with some interruptions, for
three years, until he left for another field in the West. When he
came to the Chatham Street church, he brought as assistants not
only Dirck Lansing, Joel Parker, Herman Norton and John Ingersoll, but one Thomas Hastings.[103] It was the job of Hastings to
take over the musical directorship of the Second Free Presbyterian Church. He was one of the first of a long line of specialists
in church music who worked with revivalists. Some churches had
come a long way from the days of their founding by Puritans
who would sing nothing but unaccompanied selections from the
Book of Psalms.

Finney, too, had come a long way from the Adams law office
where, on an October night in 1821, the wind of God's wings had
fanned him. Certain things went with revivals in Philadelphia,
Boston and New York that were not true of the Lord's work in
De Kalb or Stephentown. There were always new faces — too
many to remember, as one remembered the same faces seen for
four or five weeks in the little hamlet. Much more had to be left
to assistants in the inquiry meetings. The enemies of revivals, too,
were apt to be more formidable than the village infidel or Universalist. They would have newspapers and men of learning to
fight their battles. The conditions of life were changed. No longer
did the revivalist board with the faithful minister who had lived
a dozen years among the townsfolk and knew their crotchets,
their standing, their gossip and their failings fully as well as their
spiritual estates. Now there would be a permanent home, servants
and trips out of the city to recuperate. The laymen of the con-

gregation were different, too. They were men in flowered silk vests and high hats who talked with a certain confidence of doing work to build God's kingdom, knowing as they did that spinning wheels and straining canvas were piling up, in their names, the dollars so indispensable to good works.

Did working in this new world affect Finney? Was it an accident that the dedication of the Chatham Street Chapel took place at five-thirty on the twenty-third of April, 1832, so as to avoid conflicting with business hours? Was it only touchiness in a colleague that made him write to Finney the next month, "I do not mean that you have essentially changed your stile [*sic*] of preaching but . . . you reason more than formerly"? Was it mere jealousy that spoke between the lines in a letter which came to New York from someone who had known him in the old days?

> I fear that the peculiar circumstances in which you have been placed have led you rather to a discussion . . . of abstract theological subjects than to those soul-stirring appeals to the heart and the conscience by which you once brought so many sinners to the feet of Jesus.[104]

Such questions could not easily be answered. The mind of Charles Finney was not open to be read except on such terms as he himself chose. But it was certain that he had taken revivalism on an eventful journey in ten years. He had led it from the still raw frontier of western New York, through the prospering towns of the Erie Canal's banks, and into the country's most booming great city. Now, as an urban thing, it had new adventures and new problems in store for it.

CHAPTER V

And a Great Number Believed

B RETHREN," wrote Saint Paul in the sixth chapter of the
epistle to the Galatians, "if a man be overtaken in a fault, ye
which are spiritual, restore such an one in the spirit of meekness."
Nineteenth-century reformers took delight in applying this verse
to each other, and the spirit of meekness was not always outstandingly evident. Hence, Charles G. Finney was probably not
surprised to receive an anxious note, one spring day in 1828, from
his convert, friend and co-worker, Theodore Weld. Finney was
then holding a revival in Philadelphia, and Weld was concerned
for him.

> Now brother beloved how is it with your own soul? Has *no*
> *sin* any dominion over you? . . . Are you digging your way
> *deeper* and *deeper* into the dust? Do you feel the power of sin
> waxing weaker and weaker? Are you remembering the com-
> mand which claimed the *whole* heart and soul and mind and
> strength, *all the time?* . . . My dear father in Jesus, you are
> in such a maddening whirl of care, responsibility and toil, I do
> dreadfully fear that you neglect the culture of personal holiness.
> . . . In my estimation your *theory* is in the main faultless "with-
> out spot or wrinkle" but the warm vitality of *practicals* where
> is it? And Echo answers where is it? I thought I saw when at
> Stephentown — and I have more clearly discerned it in your
> letters this winter — (unless I strongly mistake) that *revivals*
> have become with you matters of such every day commonness
> as scarcely to throw over you the least tinge of solemnity. I fear
> they are fast becoming with you a sort of trade, to be worked at
> so many hours every day and then laid aside. Dear brother do
> you not find yourself running into *formality*, a round of for-
> mality in the management of revivals? I mean of feeling. The

machinery all moves on, every wheel and spring and chord in
its place; but isn't the *main spring* waxing weaker? [1]

Weld was sounding a lonely alarm. He himself was a unique
kind of reformer, shunning publicity, brightly lit platforms and
the hubbub of conventions until the end of his days. He distrusted
the impact of popularity on reform, and he was in effect letting
Finney know that he doubted if revivalism could stand transplantation to the cities.

Such fears might have seemed groundless as the fourth decade
of the century opened. Revivalism, roused in 1800 from its sleep
after the Revolution, had gone from victory to victory, until, in
1832, a newspaper founded almost exclusively to chronicle these
"awakenings" could exult:

> The last year was undoubtedly distinguished above all that
> preceded it, since the formation of the Christian church. Never
> before has the Holy Spirit been poured out in so many places
> at once; never before has the Lord Jesus gathered so many into
> his churches . . .[2]

Moreover, the nineteenth-century revival, having won early
victories in the West, was sweeping into another frontier, the
city. In 1832 Lyman Beecher had been gathering fruits in Boston,
the very front yard of Unitarianism. New York City, that worldly
mart of nations, was making room for Charles Finney. Philadelphia had heard the voice of a revival party in the Presbyterian
Church ringing loud and clear when the General Assembly of
that body met there.

Yet Weld may have had a keener instinct than others for an
impending crisis. Great changes were about to overtake the revival movement. By 1835, both Beecher and Finney would abandon their urban outposts and take up academic chairs in colleges
in the West. There were other revivalists to take their places and
to harvest in countryside and city, but they were second-rate men,
lacking the crude zeal of the Kentucky revivalists, the deep humility of Nettleton, the relentless grasp of political and theological
issues which belonged to Beecher, the flaming tongue of Finney.

They were not breaking ground but consolidating, and while they were personally dedicated to the cause, revivalism was indeed for them a trade to be worked at so many hours a day.

Moreover, the energy of revivalism was now to spill over into reform crusades. Weld himself, turning from revivals into full-time work as an antislavery lecturer and writer, was a perfect example of the transition. These great drives to purge the world of such sins as rum drinking and slaveholding took their tone from revivalism, it was true. Yet they could not escape the effects of a change of focus. Managers and pamphlet writers for reform associations and parties might be warmed with the zeal of God's anointed, but their commissions were not so plainly stamped with the seal of heaven.

For when the revival movement successfully "rebuked infidelism" and began to seek new enemies, it changed somehow. It had to develop a particular logic and speech and set of attitudes. It had ripened for a quarter of a century along with the democratic spirit. When it stepped forward to contribute something particular to the issues agitating democracy, it was subjected to certain unlooked-for effects. Revivalism was cradled in a grass-roots revolt against formalism in religion, but in organizing itself to reach great masses of people, it developed forms of its own. That was one change. Another came about as a surprising fruit of victory. The truly major reform of the revivalists had been the breaking down of the ancient and exclusive doctrine of limited election. Yet by 1830, that battle was so thoroughly won that it no longer had much meaning either for "Calvinistic" or "Arminian" groups. Thus, one "main spring" waxed weaker through lack of action. Then, in addition, when the moral fervor of the revival was aimed at the evils of the world, something new happened. In order to be effective, that fervor had to operate in the fields of propaganda and politics, and those fields were managed and operated by laymen. Even the task of educating men as to their lost condition was in the process of being taken over by a growing system of popular schools.

In a sense, revivalism was delivered of various reforms and then left barren. It faced the perennial problem of religious movements.

What is conceived in ecstasy must be reduced to form, doctrine, ritual and organization in order to perpetuate itself. The tension between organization and inspiration — between priest and prophet — lasts throughout the life of a religion. Up to 1830, revivalism had known an era of prophets. As it became accepted and urbanized, it entered an age of priests.

Certainly some kind of high tide had been reached in 1831. Awakenings proliferated strangely and wonderfully throughout the land. A Baptist publication joyfully traced a string of them from western New England and New York, through Philadelphia, the District of Columbia, Cincinnati, and onward towards the West and South. Perhaps as many as a thousand congregations had been "visited." [3] In New York City there was a brand-new four-page journal, the *New York Evangelist,* whose duty it was to give weekly news of revivals, along with advice upon their management, testimonies of their converts, and reports of the missionary efforts which sprang from them.[4] The editors noted, in the spring of 1831, that revivals were multiplying in an "extraordinary manner." [5] So they were, and, as always, in the little villages — in Lime and Kingston, New Hampshire, in Orleans, Camden and Waterloo, New York, in Four Mile Creek and Bear Swamp, Virginia, and in Ahaskey, North Carolina.[6] Yet the lightnings struck in the great cities, too. In the "Revival Intelligence" for a week in April, 1832, Boston and Philadelphia took their places humbly alongside Ipswich, Connecticut, Clarksville, Georgia, and Gallatin, Tennessee.[7] Ambition suddenly burned feverishly in the minds of the godly. Might it not be, asked one minister in little Penn Yan, New York, that these showers of mercy would increase "until the *knowledge of the Lord shall fill the earth as the waters fill the seas; until the kingdom of Christ shall come, and his will be done on earth, as it is in heaven*"? [8] Why not? God's grace was clearly so abundant, the *Evangelist* pointed out, that it was "the privilege and duty of every church to enjoy a *constant* revival." In fact, protracted prayer meetings were so "highly in favor with the Lord Jesus Christ," said one correspondent of the paper, that only "a careless, slovenly, inefficient . . . mode of conducting them, can prevent them from receiving a blessing." [9]

If, however, God stood ready to "revive" any church which made an honest request, then a question was posed. Where would it end? Was there any limit to how many might be saved? To such a query there was but one answer from a populace which was fearfully growing, and hurling itself with reckless disregard for leisure or conservation upon a virgin continent. No limit! If human beings did their part, God would not allow the revival pace to slacken. And perhaps the furious increase in the number of those saved portended something. Were not the hosts being gathered in for the millennium? In the early eighteen-forties, a Vermont Baptist minister named William Miller was to send thousands into shivering fits of anticipation with his prediction that the end of the world was set for 1843. He was dismissed by many as an eccentric and fanatic. Yet in 1832, eleven years before that date, Calvin Colton, a respectable journalistic supporter of the conservative Whig Party and a Presbyterian minister so "unfanatical" that he would later turn Episcopalian, looked about him and discerned handwriting on the wall.

> God has been "overturning and overturning," until the great centres of political sway and social influence upon the earth are ready to shake off the abuse of power with the abuse of religion. And when this crisis shall have come, we may hope that the "redemption of the world draweth nigh." [10]

When a conservative could thus see the end approaching fast in the second administration of Andrew Jackson, portended perhaps by liberal revolts in Europe and Spanish America (those scenes of the "abuse of power"), true evangelicals were stirred into furious calculation. A Vermont newspaper computed that since the Reformation, one eightieth of the world's population had been converted to Christianity. At that rate, the rising birth curve would easily outstrip the pace of conversions. The editor set a goal of two hundred years for piety to become "universal," and estimated that the work of salvation must go on one hundred twenty times as fast as in the days of Luther in order to make the earth fully ready for judgment.[11] The *Evangelist,* too, thought it heard the trumpet of Gabriel tuning up. One of its staff writers called for an increase in revivals. Without such an increase, he could not "perceive how it is possible that 800,000,000 of souls . . . can be washed from their sins, within the most distant time to which the millennium can be deferred according to prediction." [12] A race to convert the entire world before the deadline of the last trump was an awe-inspiring assignment, but Americans were apt to believe that they had a head start. Had not Jonathan Edwards himself, minister of a tiny New England town in a remote colony, opined that the "latter-day glory is probably to begin in America"? [13] American churchmen, too, dreamed robustly.

Yet in this triumphant moment the men of revivalism's first generation were dying or leaving the field. The leaders of the 1800 meetings in the West had ceased from troubling, or were at rest among the Shakers or Campbellites. After 1831, Nettleton retired to a part-time professorship. As for those magnificently alive salvationists, Beecher and Finney, after carrying the war into Boston and New York, they retreated from the cities. Beecher left Boston in 1832, Finney departed from New York in 1835, and their lives were curiously connected in the manner of their going.

For Beecher, things had not gone as bouncingly as he wished in Boston. He had bad luck in the burning of his church on Hanover Street in 1830. Moreover, the fight between revivalists and conservative Calvinists was now blazing openly. Beecher begged his fellow Presbyterians and Congregationalists to compose the argument. He quoted the wise words of an associate: "We have Unitarians in all our societies; the moment we open on one another they will clap their hands for joy." But the battle went on, and Beecher disliked the sight of Calvinists warring with each other, instead of tackling Unitarians.

Besides, Lyman Beecher never accepted the fact that Boston's upper classes snubbed him. In Litchfield, he was a kingpin in the best society. In Boston, he was the slightly comic generalissimo of the unfashionable, countrified orthodox. Therefore, when he was offered a chair in theology and the presidency of a new seminary, Lane, in Cincinnati, he gave an attentive ear. The proposal came late in 1830. After a year and a half of hesitation, he accepted. He had plenty of reasons. He addressed a written prayer to God, pledging to help raise the foundations of His kingdom in the West. He announced his fear that without a good Presbyterian seminary there, "Catholics and infidels" would "get the start of us," and he was on solid ground in declaring that the "moral destiny" of the nation would turn on the character of the trans-Allegheny region. Still, there were plenty of infidels and Catholics in Boston, a place which also said a good deal about the national moral destiny. Beecher was simply looking for a new field.[14]

Finney, too, found the city hard going. Evans Mills, and even Utica or Rochester, might ring with the name of Finney after six weeks of revival, but in New York he was one excitement among many. Like Beecher, he had a stroke of bad luck. He contracted cholera and could not settle down to his duties as pastor of the Second Free Presbyterian Church until early in 1833. Then he found that the Presbyterian organization cramped him, so the Tappans put up a new Congregational church for him on lower Broadway. Early in 1834, however, he left the Broadway Tabernacle for a cruise in the Mediterranean, to solidify his still shaky health. On his return, he flung himself into giving a series of lectures on revivals — and to step from *conducting* revivals to lecturing on *how* to have them was stepping from inspiration into methodology. Within a year of concluding these talks, he left New York.

The occasion of his leaving had to do with enterprises of great pith and moment taking place at Beecher's Lane Seminary. Many of its students were interested in the cause of emancipation, and none more so than Finney's spiritual son, Theodore Weld. They soon had the school halls reverberating with debates on the practicability of immediately freeing the slaves, and they were organizing charitable and educational missions among the free

Negroes of Cincinnati. The conservative Presbyterians of the partly Southern town were properly scandalized. The trustees (while Beecher was away raising money) forbade further discussion of the question. Thereupon some three dozen students, late in 1834, withdrew from the school and began working under tutors in a private home.

Meanwhile, a group of pious New Englanders had founded a colony and a college at Oberlin, in Ohio's Western Reserve. Towards the end of 1834, one of their leaders started on a trip eastward, to raise money and to find a president for the new school. Through a coincidence, he learned of affairs at Lane. He also learned that one Lane trustee had sided with the students, and that this man, Asa Mahan, if chosen for the presidency of Oberlin, would not only bring the seceding students with him, but could attract some philanthropic backing from antislavery friends. Negotiations were opened, and Mahan was secured for the new office. The students also suggested that their leader, Theodore Weld, be appointed to a chair in theology — an important one, for Oberlin's function was largely to prepare ministers for the West. Weld declined, but suggested Finney. The upshot of it all was that Finney was offered the teaching post and accepted. The Tappans and others pledged a generous sum to the new school, and almost all the Lane "rebels" transferred there. (Weld himself, however, left school to give all his energies to antislavery.) Oberlin was launched on twin waves of reform and holiness; its doors were opened to women and to Negro students, and one of Finney's first acts was to have a large circular tent put up for prayer meetings, with a banner streaming from its peak, inscribed HOLINESS TO THE LORD.[15]

So in July, 1835, after three years in New York, of which time one third was taken up with illness and travel, Charles Finney went west. He remained to become Oberlin's president and to flirt with a new and "ultraist" theological doctrine of perfectibility. It is hard to avoid the conclusion that he left gladly. His memoirs devote only a dozen and a half pages to New York. In recalling his days of glory, he did not dwell long on those in the great city. He went out gladly to teach the young men whom

Beecher had infused with a touch too much of his own stubbornness.

It is true that Finney insisted on being allowed to spend half his time conducting revivals away from Oberlin. He preached vigorously in the town, and always felt that he was a minister before everything.[16] Periodically, he traveled on campaigns — visiting Boston, Rochester, Hartford, and even his old scenes of victory, Rome and Western. He visited England twice.[17] But fundamentally, he was now a college professor and administrator. He, who had scorned the coldness of "educated" Presbyterians in 1824 and believed in the Bible and legal common sense as sure guides to truth, was himself an educator. As for Beecher, nearing sixty, he was past the peak of his career. Taking the advice he gave Nettleton after the New Lebanon convention, he prepared young men to follow him. Education became an increasingly heavy responsibility to those innovators of revivalism who remained on the scene. The territory won must be held and built up.

A fresh band of revival men now took the stage. The Presbyterians had such new workers in the fold as Albert Barnes. Mostly an intellectual defender of revivalistic doctrines, his published sermons played an important part in splitting Presbyterianism, in 1837, into two distinct bodies — a "New School," ardently revivalistic, and an "Old School," more conservative about changing the established order, both in theology and in society.[18]

Another Presbyterian thunderer was Jedediah Burchard, who swept upstate New York in the thirties, working in many places still glowing with the fires kindled by Finney. His language was marked by picturesque imagery that was nothing if it was not bold and plain. "Do you know what hell is?" he asked a Rochester audience.

> "Well, I'll tell you; and I tell you, too, it's real. An ocean of liquid burning brimstone, that is daily replenished. It is walled in by great walls guarded by devils armed with pitchforks. High on the crest of the waves of fire, the damned soul is swept toward this wall, where the sinner thinks he may find at least temporary rest, but when at last he has managed to climb part

way out of this sea of fire he suddenly finds himself pitchforked
back and swept out by the receding tide." [19]

Less colorful, perhaps, was the Southern Presbyterian Daniel
Baker. Baker found his destiny in the religiously barren Southwest.
For years he traveled and held revival meetings in Texas. But he,
too, was finally drawn into education, and at last became the
president of Austin College.[20]

The Congregationalists had an entry in the field in Princeton-
trained Edward Norris Kirk. In a career that spanned the years
from 1826 to 1874, he led "protracted meetings" in many large
cities, but his most outstanding contribution to revivalism probably lay in arousing the religious interest, in 1857, of a hulking
young Boston shoe clerk named Dwight L. Moody.[21] The Congregationalists, nevertheless, no longer led the way and were overshadowed in revivalism by the swiftly multiplying Baptists, whose
champion conductor of awakenings was the Reverend Jacob
Knapp.

For twenty-five years Knapp held revivals in such diverse places
as New Haven, Providence, Boston, Washington, Chicago, Wilmington and St. Louis. He was a man of forthright opinions, and
he made enemies easily. There were charges that in order to attract gifts to him, he harped unduly on the poverty of his calling.
In New Haven, Yale students (he said) attempted to kidnap him,
though whether for a prank or in some kind of rebellion against
his theology is not clear. In Boston he was mobbed; in Providence
he was arrested; and in New York, in 1840, James Gordon Bennett sent a *New York Herald* reporter to his meetings to do a
series of lampoons on him. It was clear that the evangelist no
longer commanded respect merely by the awesome nature of his
message.[22]

Another active Baptist revivalist, a solid countryman with the
tang of new cheese about him, was Jabez Swan, born in Stonington, Connecticut, in 1800. Beginning in 1830, he mostly sought
out the waste places of Zion in New York and Connecticut.
Swan's recollections were dotted with traditional works and wonders, for he was much closer than many of his educated con-

temporaries to the folkways of the frontier. In Norwich, he cured a lady of a "dumb devil." He saw a man in Owego struck blind in the throes of conviction. Once, in Voluntown, Connecticut, the Lord broke the shaft of the water wheel which ran the machinery in the local factory, and the workers, involuntarily freed, came in great numbers to hear the word. Swan estimated that he had baptized nearly eight thousand people himself.[23]

The Methodists, of course, were forward in supplying revivalists. They had John Newland Maffitt, who in 1841 was made chaplain of the House of Representatives, a tribute both to the full-grown respectability of Methodism and to the influence of Western and Southern Congressmen. His presence in a given place never failed "to bring, as a necessary consequence, an accompanying 'revival.'" [24] They boasted also of men like James Caughey and John S. Inskip, who worked effectively in large and middle-sized cities as the diminishing frontier gradually eliminated the circuit riders.[25]

All these men, "spreading their nets," as they liked to say, were the forerunners of a group which, by the time of the Civil War, had made revivalism not merely a full-time profession, but a rather common one. Their names sound strange to modern ears, but in their time they filled the columns of the still popular religious weeklies, and they left volumes of little homilies and anecdotes which lay on parlor tables in many a Christian home. Among them were Absalom Earle and Emerson Andrews, Edward P. Hammond and Orson Parker, and Maggie Van Newton Cott — for by the sixties there was already an appetite for novelty in evangelism which she, as a woman revivalist, could satisfy.[26]

They were workers of the city. Revivals went on in the countryside without them, to be sure. A random look at the religious press for any week in the forties, the fifties, or the sixties would reveal news of grace abounding from East Troy, Wisconsin, to Parsippany, New Jersey.[27] The "local" revival was in some cases an annual phenomenon, with the townsfolk anticipating its excitement, its change of pace and its encouragement to gossip as one or another of them went forward to the anxious bench.

The Caugheys and Knapps and Kirks held forth in the few great towns, like New York or Philadelphia, and the hundreds of places halfway to urbanism — Hartford, Syracuse, Providence, Buffalo, Columbus, Indianapolis, Nashville. They announced their meetings and lectured nightly, each time to a changing audience. They called for hymns and they called for mourners, and on the appointed day they struck their tents figuratively and moved on by rail. They were locomotive-borne home missionaries. And in spite of the fact that they worked in well-publicized surroundings, they left almost no trace behind them. It was not really any wonder. They had nothing new to say, no enemies in the church to dislodge, no students to direct in unaccustomed but challenging paths. They themselves worked in established patterns, varying only in their personal characteristics or their selection of anecdote. They were men of technique.

In contrast, the frontier revivals of 1800 had been spontaneous religious explosions, welling out of the emotional needs of the people and couched in their earthy terms. Beecher, Nettleton, Griffin, Finney and their like had been genuine leaders — men important in their churches and in the political and social life of the day, equipped with vigorous minds and pens. They would have denied it, but they *made* the revival an instrument to achieve their end, the salvation of their brand of Protestantism in a changing world.

It was not entirely the fault of the second-line evangelists that they held a lesser place. In 1815, a Lyman Beecher could live in Litchfield, Connecticut, and be an important national figure in Presbyterianism. A Finney could shake the church from Rome, New York. By the eighteen-fifties it was harder to get a pamphlet published, and it was almost impossible to found a newspaper, as Beecher, say, had led in founding the Boston *Spirit of the Pilgrims* in the twenties. The reason lay in rising costs and in the growth of the nation. The revival was one of many political and social excitements. The voice of the revivalist was lost in the din of political conventions, theatrical amusements and assorted journalistic enterprises. No longer did the revival alone fill an aching need for emotional release, for entertainment, for social contact.

No longer did the revival alone offer consolation and assurance to the ordinary man. Democracy and popular culture had other agencies for their work.

Therefore, by 1850, there was a paradox. The evangelist was an accepted part of the national scene, and the anxious bench, protracted meeting, and prayer of faith were integral elements in the religious life of millions. And yet revivalism *as it existed from 1800 to about 1835* was dead.[28]

The friends of the revival knew that something had been lost. They knew it because almost immediately after the surging millennial hopes of 1831, the pace of conversion suddenly subsided. North, South and West, the murmur of concern was heard. In 1835, Presbyterians were deploring "spiritual lukewarmness," the "low state of religion" and the absence of any "outpouring of the Holy Spirit." Connecticut's Congregational General Association was equally disturbed.[29] The thinning out of revival news made one writer wonder whether a "pall of moral death" was overspreading the churches.[30] By the mid-forties, the situation seemed to be worse. The Presbyterian *New York Observer* in 1844 was running lead articles which asked why revivals were so few. The next year it was begging, "Dear Christian brethren, we *must* have revivals . . . or we are undone." By 1848 it still found the look of affairs "not encouraging." [31] In 1851 the *Independent*, then a relatively new Congregationalist journal in New York, found reason to "mourn over the desolations of Zion, and to hang our harps upon the willows." A letter in its columns feared that the extinction of revivals might be at hand, in which case, the writer mysteriously suggested, the nation would witness "scenes of excitement which no remonstrance can check." [32] Periodically in most religious papers, it seemed, someone was sure to remember the golden age of 1800 — how remote and antique it already seemed! — and to hope for a renewal "of those 'seasons of refreshing' which . . . in past days blessed the church." [33] It was a recurrent keynote in religious thought. A certain stage of maturity had been reached, it was clear, when there was yearning for the good old days.

Not every clergyman, of course, sensed moral darkness in the declining number of revivals. Denominations composed largely of foreign-born members, like the Lutherans at that time, had never taken the revival virus to any great extent. Catholicism had no room for the revival, and Episcopalianism little, if any. Those groups which did not make man's depravity and regeneration the core of their faith — Quakers and Unitarians, for example — had not danced when the revivalists piped. Opposition to the entire revival scheme had flickered and sometimes blazed in these quarters. Among ministers of the churches most thoroughly "revived," the Baptists, Methodists, Congregationalists and Presbyterians, there was dissent, most strongly amid the last named. For conservative Calvinists, a dwindling but often learned band, the revivalists put too much emphasis on states of feeling. There was a free-wheeling, exciting and rather democratic character to the revival message, which opened the gates of salvation wide, washed the underpinnings of doctrine loose in a torrent of groaning or hand clapping, and blew away the glooms of predestination. Old-fashioned Presbyterians disliked it.

And so a curious alliance — unrecognized but real — existed among certain enemies of "extraordinary awakenings." Many challenges to these outbursts came from Unitarians, apostles of a religion of enlightenment, benevolence and rationality, in their own view at least. Other rebukes were voiced by the so-called "Old School" men, the "consistent Calvinists." Between them they illuminate the middle-ground nature of the revivalists' achievement by 1830. The revival men had tried to save "old" Calvinism by blending it with some of the equalitarian, humanitarian and romantic ebullience of the nineteenth century. They *had* managed a blend of the two which won the loyalty of thousands. But they were still too warm for some old-line believers in man's utterly fallen estate, and they still had too much of a brimstone smell for some liberals.

The enemies of the revival, then, included both those liberals styled by Finney and others "infidels," and those Calvinistic churchmen who rejected "every revival measure, which they consider new." [34] They had some telling points to make, too.

The first one was that emotional zeal was not necessarily true religious feeling. The Unitarian Orville Dewey warned against mistaking "phrensy for inspiration," and quoted John Calvin himself to the effect that regeneration was "not accomplished in a single moment, or day, or year; but by continual, and sometimes even tardy advances." [35] Not much could be expected from a piety which was all "glooms and raptures." [36] Such a viewpoint was echoed by Edward Griffin, himself an original, or "conservative," revival man, who believed that sinners could do very little towards sanctifying themselves. He was fearful of "onsets upon the passions with but sparsely scattered rays of divine truth." [37]

Cautious Presbyterians were gnawed by a reasonable suspicion that converts swept into the church on a tidal wave of revival emotion would be washed back out in an ebb of backsliding. One of them at the General Assembly of Presbyterianism in 1832 said that he dreaded for the purity of the faith "from this hurrying people into the church, as soon as they give any tokens of conversion, dragging them sometimes from the table of the drunkard one day, to the table of the Lord the next." Another conservative remembered that it was Universalism which credited God with a desire to save "every individual," but now "we hear such doctrines preached by ministers claiming the sanction of the Presbyterian church." [38] Some "Old School" Presbyterians accepted the idea of a revival, but they still distrusted it. They wanted an awakening "gradual in its progress, without noise or commotion, and entirely free from a whirlwind of passion." [39] As late as the eighteen-seventies, a Presbyterian scholar, reviewing the work of Nettleton, Baker, Beecher and Finney, said that they "fixed the attention of preachers and hearers too much upon the subjective exercises of the sinner in conversion" — that is, too much upon how the convert *felt* and not enough upon the role of Christ in making his redemption possible.[40]

The antirevival forces bore heavily on the fact that there was something manufactured about a campaign of salvation. Once, said an anonymous pamphlet in 1827, revivals were considered the "extraordinary interposition of God," but they had come to be matters of "human agency and contrivance." [41] Orville Dewey

claimed that revivalists with a reputation for getting results automatically became irresistible. If their efforts supposedly had a
divine blessing, who dared to withstand them? "The people
among whom they come would account themselves guilty of the
most awful obduracy, and ready to be forsaken of heaven, if they
should refuse to be aroused." Hence, certain itinerant awakeners
could offer a virtually guaranteed performance.[42] Some of these
men, in the words of a Unitarian magazine, had "their full share
of vanity and ambition, neither of which . . . can be gratified
without keeping up what is termed the Revival System." [43]

From the wing of Protestantism at the opposite extreme to
Unitarianism came a series of similar taunts. Nathaniel Emmons,
a long-lived relic of the eighteenth century (who was born in
1745 and did not die until 1840), grumbled in his old age about
the "undue excitements" of "modern" awakenings.[44] Nettleton,
who had helped to set revivalism on its feet, worried about what
"the imprudence of a few zealous individuals" might do to it. He
objected to such devices as the anxious bench, to which those
"convicted" of sin came forward to be made the subject of public
prayer. In England, he discovered during a trip there, that was
used "only among the Methodists and ranters." [45] A conservative
Baptist newspaper in the thirties denied "fellowship with certain
professed revival makers" who went here and there with the
"avowed intention of 'getting up a revival.' " [46] A Presbyterian
journal in Philadelphia sneered at those "New School" men who
boasted of "their *revivals*." They had a right to boast, the editor
said sourly, "*of their own work;* the revivals which they can at
any time produce . . . are, in truth, their revivals." [47] By 1842
one New York presbytery was worried because ministers were
convinced that a specialist was needed to spark a congregation
into repentance. It deplored the "absurd notion that you cannot
expect a revival without calling in aid from abroad." [48]

As the middle of the century approached, stirrings of another
kind were felt. A slightly more sophisticated psychology and an
awareness of mounting social problems were cooling breezes
which blew on the quick heat of revivalism. It was in 1847 that
Horace Bushnell brought out *Christian Nurture*. He was himself

an ordained Congregational minister in Hartford, and he did not entirely discount revivals. But he declared in his book that too much emphasis might be placed on the actual experience of conversion, and not enough on the formation of a Christian *character*. It might well be, he thought, that a properly reared Christian child could grow to maturity without ever feeling that he was anything *but* a Christian — without needing a shuddering, passionate rebirth.[49] Whether he liked it or not, this put him in some kind of company with Theodore Parker, the vigorous Unitarian reformer. In 1858 Parker, in his Boston church, delivered three sermons on "A False and True Revival of Religion." He blistered revivals which ignored genuine problems of morality and social conscience in favor of dramatic conversions. A real revival of Christian charity and mercy and justice was needed, he said, but if one began, the ministers of orthodoxy would "turn it into a revival of ecclesiastical theology — the doctrine of the dark ages." [50]

Verbal as they were, the revival practitioners were ready with defense. They reminded the world of the original purpose of prayer for revival — to rejuvenate the church in a time of rising worldliness and "infidelity." The revival captured attention for the beleaguered religion of Christ.[51] It counteracted "criminal unbelief . . . cold reserve, and chilling apathy"; it offset "the corrupting influence of a pre-eminent national prosperity" and of an increase in intellectual power without corresponding moral restraint, which threatened to "turn . . . the whole family of human animals into one common field of unbridled appetite and lust." [52] The church depended on revivals for "its hopes of future prosperity."[53]

The friends of the "special awakening" had other good things to say about it. By 1831, a vast network of "benevolent" organizations existed in the churches, although much of the "benevolence" was aimed only at putting the means of salvation within the reach of all. (This was logical to the revivalists, however. It was more benevolent to help a downtrodden man to eternal bliss than to shelter him for a night or to fill his stomach for a day. They made sense on their own terms.) "Benevolent" societies existed, then, to send missionaries to the heathen, to distribute tracts and Bibles to the destitute, to forbid employers to demand work on Sunday and to provide Sunday schools for everyman. All of this, the *New York Evangelist*, naturally, claimed as the fruit of revivals.

> They have provided the hearts, and hands, and means, to superintend the manifold ministrations required to organize infant and Sabbath schools and all our benevolent voluntary associations. . . . And it may be truly said, that almost the entire moral energy by which the cause of Christ now moves on from conquering to conquer, is the result of those revivals of religion which for thirty years have been enrolling, augmenting, and disciplining the sacramental host.[54]

The revival inspired "works of justice, truth and mercy."[55] It was instrumental in "quickening and directing the moral energies of the church."[56] In crass terms, it got the Christian convert to pay. He could be seen "casting liberally his silver and his gold into the treasury of the Lord. The Bible, the missionary, the tract, the education cause participate in his bounty." Giving was, in fact, frankly labeled as "a test of genuine conversion."[57] There was an unspoken hint that the revival was worthy exactly *because* it won over those who could amply endow the Lord's treasury. In the early part of the century, conservatives had lampooned revival furor as the work of untutored and unpropertied Methodists and Baptists. But an editor of the *Independent*, looking over Finney's Philadelphia revival in 1829, took comfortable note of the fact that the converts included "merchants that honor God with their substance, lawyers that adorn the bar with their Christian integrity, physicians that minister grace to the soul as well as health to the body."[58] In short, property and professional respectability entered the church at the evangelists' bidding. If they were not evident before conversion, they were apt to be visible afterwards. Families which, before a revival, were "idle and improvident," said one Connecticut editor, "are now diligent, *thriving* and peaceful."[59]

Since most of the formal apologists for revivals were educated men, they were apt to overlook one more important value of the awakening. It brought a down-to-earth, a warm, believable kind of Christ to humble folk who could not read the dissertations written at ministerial study tables. A spontaneous but almost unanswerable tribute to the revival was written in 1837 in a small newspaper of the Christian denomination, which grew out of the frontier revivals of 1800.

> I know nothing about making calculations to get up a *revival*, other than frequent prayer, deep humility and faithful labor, waiting upon the Lord, until he shall pour out his spirit. No doubt much fanaticism at times in real *revivals* of God's work, has mingled STRANGE FIRE; yes I have seen it to my sorrow. But this is no strange thing. . . . I am a thousand times more afraid of lukewarmness and cold apathy than I am of the consequences of excitements and revivals. . . . Nothing gives me more pain and distress, than to see a minister standing almost motionless, coldly plodding on as a mathematician, would calculate the distance of the Moon from the Earth, with his words freezing upon his own lips, falling upon his congregation like frozen drops of rain; "from which may the good Lord deliver us." [60]

In words like these, a man who was spiritually descended from those humble souls who forsook their "motionless" ministers and flocked to hear George Whitefield gave the original revival its most genuine justification.

Still, in all the attack and defense of revivalism, men only skirted the real explanation for its decline in the forties and fifties. Those who criticized the "man-made" revivals were on the track, but they did not realize how far the engineers of the revival would go in reducing it to a simple matter of management. Those who, on the other hand, cheered the connection between revivals and reform never quite suspected the extent to which "benevolent enterprises" would kidnap the best talent and energies of the parent movement. Just how did these things come to pass? The evangelists of the twenties did everything they could, unwittingly, to render their own achievements a commonplace. The pioneer revivals were supposedly miracles. All "truly gracious affections," Jonathan Edwards wrote, "arise from the *special and peculiar influences of the Holy Spirit.*" They were "altogether supernatural." [61] The pioneer awakenings had enjoyed something of a supernatural flavor, too. They arose out of the felt necessities of the frontier — the urgent cravings of simple men for a faith that would warm their lives and promise them that heaven was individually concerned with their souls. When the awakenings came, they were such tremendous emotional explosions that they had about them some Pentecostal impact, and they did indeed seem like miraculous works of God.

Yet as the Beechers and Finneys came to believe that the revival was a necessity, they began to insist more loudly that it was *not* necessary merely to wait God's time. Even if they did not say so themselves, others were ready to go on from there and say that a given investment of "means" was sure to yield a profit in souls. Presently, a regular literature which frankly explained how to bring on a revival was emerging. In the autumn of 1831, the *New York Evangelist* carried notice of a series of lectures on revivals by thirteen ministers in sequence. The same paper warned readers that where "revivals are not enjoyed, Christians are not using in a humble and faithful manner those means . . . which God has appointed, and is ready to bless." In 1832, the editors ran a series of articles entitled "Revival Measures," containing solid and practical advice on how many meetings to hold, when to use the anxious bench, what to say to "inquirers," and how to deal with various classes of skeptics.[62] A correspondent drew the logical inference, that such "means" were necessary because God would work *only* through them. "As in the natural world he governs through the medium of second causes, so in the moral world." [63]

It was Finney who, as usual, put it in plain terms. In the winter of 1834-1835, he too gave a series of revival lectures in New York. Less than halfway through the first of them, he bluntly revised Edwards. "A revival of religion is not a miracle," he said. "There is nothing in religion beyond the ordinary powers of nature."

This was put so simply that its real significance was half buried. Finney went on to say that the means employed in a revival must have God's blessing. "No more will grain, when it is sowed, produce a crop without the blessing of God." [64] That might well be true, but farmers did not (even if they ought to, in the eyes of the pious) regard each annual harvest as a special gift, to be greeted with shouts of glory, or prayers of thanksgiving in the churches, or reports to the newspapers. Thanksgiving Day was only a ritual, celebrated in good years and bad. What was more, good farming was a matter of doing the right things, and the divine blessing was apt to light on a man who plowed and fertilized well, even if he skipped a sermon on Sunday now and then.

Nevertheless, Finney called the tune correctly. During the twenty years after his lectures, a number of manuals on revival technique came off the presses. By 1854, a correspondent of the *Independent* could write jovially, "Brethren, if you will follow the above directions for *two months*, and do not enjoy a revival of religion of the *old stamp*, you may tell me and the public, that I am no prophet." [65] A revival was now a "good old-fashioned" sort of thing, like a husking bee or a cabin raising, a friendly reminder of simpler days. It was not a suspension of the laws of nature which brought the awesome presence of Jehovah into the meetinghouse. It could be brought off any time, if the right tricks were used.

As the trappings of the miraculous fell from the revivalist, his language grew more colloquial and folksy. The original Western evangelists had spoken a down-to-earth tongue, but their speech was part of the life pattern of country people. Now the necessity was less pressing. Universal education was claiming the illiterate. Even the Methodists prescribed reading courses for their ministry — courses which included Morse's *Geography* and Rollins's *Ancient History*.[66] The "simple style" was more a matter of art than need. Moreover, as it became less mandatory to make a theological defense of the awakenings, eschatology began to fade away. The Kentucky revivalists spoke of the millennium, Beecher preached election, and Finney quoted the Westminster Confession in his battle with conservative Calvinists. But a typical sermon of Jacob Knapp, on the text "The ox knoweth his owner, and the ass his master's crib," was full of little tales about stubborn animals and children.[67] Revival preaching took on some of the style of popular journalism. It reached more people and created sensations, but it did so, in fact, by avoiding serious questions.

The fathers of mass salvation had done their best to make the gospel message live by emancipating its presentation from formalism. Finney boasted that he had helped to bring the common touch into church services in the shape of plain dress for ministers, the use of choirs, and prayers led by laymen. But a price was paid for this. The evangelist made himself commonplace. Jonathan Edwards, in wig and gown, thundering of God's anger, was an awesome ambassador of the heavenly powers. So was James McGready, addressing a jerking, shrieking multitude in the red light of the campfires. Unless he had unusual gifts, a man speaking in a suit of plain cut, from a platform in a rented hall, was something far less inspiring. In the transition stage from original to professional evangelism, from about 1830 to 1870, no man of unusual gifts was yet in sight.

In fact, just as the first revivalists had, to some extent, shouldered aside regular ministers, so they were now diminished by some of their own creations. There was the matter of hymns, for instance. Collections of revival hymns dropped from the presses in steadily increasing numbers. They were important, for their simple words and images offered a key to the longings of the crowds which sang them, and their simple tunes and meters required no skill and therefore invited everyone to participate in the service.[68] Yet precisely for this reason, they furnished a backbone to a revival meeting, and sometimes they were almost the meat of an entire revival in themselves. In 1856, for example, when Orson Parker conducted a meeting in Burns, New York, he gave a sermon, called for a "season of prayer" and then led in singing. Finally, the verse "Welcome, welcome, dear Redeemer" was sung, and those who felt "that they [could] adopt its sentiments" rose. That was all that was left of the tears and terrors of Cane Ridge.[69]

There was an unconsciously ironic demonstration of what things had come to in 1857 and 1858 when a revival took place which was led almost entirely by laymen. The commercial crash and panic of 1857 touched it off. A number of New York City businessmen began noontime assemblies for prayer meetings in a Fulton Street church. Soon the gatherings overflowed into other buildings, and "by the Spring of 1858, twenty daily union prayer meetings were being held in different parts of the city." The movement spread, and soon every large town had its prayer meetings, its special services, and its columns of newsprint dedicated to the awakening born in the countinghouse. Defenders of the revival were elated that in a time of crisis men would turn from their ledgers to God. They missed a significant fact, however. There was also a grasping for something familiar, established — something which could be managed without special guidance. The technique was so stabilized that there could be a revival without revivalists.[70]

As for the other problem of the revival, its gradual yoking of itself with reform, the portents of trouble dawned slowly. The early revival-inspired crusades were clearly linked to church matters. They took the form of work to distribute tracts and Bibles, send out missionaries and promote religious education. Their only potential threat was that with the multiplication of societies to plant and nourish, ministers of the gospel were sometimes under pressure to spend more time as board members than as pastors of God.[71]

But the revivalists branched out into movements designed to improve a fallen world — particularly to purge it of the use of tobacco, the drinking of rum, the pursuit of Sunday amusements and, ultimately, the employment of slave labor. The purpose was to "save" mankind by "giving universal and saving empire to the kingdom of Christ." [72] The trouble was that unconverted men might well learn and apply the propaganda methods of these secular missions. When reform journals and reform political parties were born, they could and did fall into the hands of editors and bosses who were richer in skill than in evangelical impulses. Besides this, reform as an organized affair took money to pay for agents and presses, and it was therefore at the mercy of the business system. Its backers could be suddenly ruined — could experience the embarrassment of Lewis Tappan when, in the depression of 1837, he had to default on promises of support to Oberlin College.[73] A bad business season might incline the mind of man towards religion, but it was only in good times that godly thoughts could be spread abroad.

So the revival impulse was dissipated in the political excitements to which it gave birth. What was more typical than Theodore Weld, the pupil of Finney, becoming so absorbed in the abolition movement that he gave it all his time after 1832? And the money to send a Weld on the lecture circuit might become an end in itself. Some of those converts whose "improvidence" was replaced by thrift and industry after the revival merely "bowed and lingered at the shrine of Mammon." [74] Wealth and political power could become absorbing goals in themselves. In a sense, the antislavery movement, which ultimately became a political force that split the nation, "carried with it the men interested in the revival movement." [75] It was a Presbyterian paper which noted with angry irony in 1844:

> There *are* REVIVALS, many of them and mighty, and *in* them we may find a reason why there are so few manifestations of the Holy Spirit's presence.
> First, there is a *revival of business*. Within the last year or two, there have been most evident tokens of another general rush toward riches. Almost every department of enterprise has gathered new life and energy. The minds of men have been startled with the prospect of returning prosperity, after years of depression . . .
> There is also, just now, a great *revival* in politics. . . . We are in the midst of one of those struggles now; in some respects as fierce a struggle as we have ever passed through. Certainly we have never known the minds of men to be more *infatuated* with party zeal than they are at this moment. Even Christians persuade themselves that, *for the present*, politics have claims superior to *religion*.[76]

So revivalism, having in a sense brought religious enthusiasm to confront the abuses of the world, had to step back and take a spectator's seat as they grappled. The world was too big to be overcome exclusively by sermons.[77]

How did the balance sheet of revivalism stand, then, as it clearly came to the end of one great phase? To what extent were its ministers entitled to their crowns of glory?

They had certainly aided in building up the number of believers. Although church statistics are far from accurate in many cases, there was no question that by 1840 great numbers had been won. The Presbyterians boasted of a fourfold increase; seven Methodists prayed in 1840 where one had existed in 1800; the Baptists said their membership had tripled. It was a relative as well as an absolute growth — one church organization for every 1740 inhabitants in 1800, and one for every 895 in 1850.[78] Beyond question, much of the credit went to "extraordinary visitations of grace," no matter how many relapses thinned the ranks of the converted.[79]

Moreover, the revivalists recruited exactly among those pushing Americans of the middle class who were not held to the church by love of tradition or fear of the state, but by loyalty — who could be won, but not frightened, into religion. The revival *did* win these energetic Yankees. It furnished them with an emotional drive, a hope of heaven, a sense of communion with the Almighty, and a quickening of the sensibilities: And precisely because it did these things, it exercised a saving effect. In the restless thirties, forties and fifties, many new ways to heaven were pointed out. Mormonism waxed fat. The Shakers reaped a harvest. William Miller's followers, waiting for an imminent judgment day and living each moment with the same intensity as if it were their last, numbered thousands. Some men and women sought sanctification in "perfect" communities like that established in Oneida by John Humphrey Noyes.[80] Perhaps thousands more would have joined these movements if a compromise had not been offered to them by revivals. They could remain faithful to the churches of their fathers and yet fill their lives with hope, excitement and useful works. There must be some "give" to a religion which aims to survive in a changing world. The revival furnished that "give" to American eighteenth-century Calvinism. A third gift of revivalism to the nation was its influence on reform. There is no minimizing the genuine contribution which it made. Revivalists hoped to scour and purify the earth against the coming of the Messiah, and there was a thrilling urgency about the job. "The emancipation of man — the intellectual, political and moral emancipation of the world," said the *New York Evangelist*, "must engross the desires . . . and the enterprize of the world itself." The paper's own masthead was evidence of how the evangelical impulse broadened out. In 1831, it announced that the paper was "Devoted to Revivals, Doctrinal Discussion, and Religious Intelligence Generally." In 1835, it added "Practical Godliness." In 1837, it further added "Human Rights." [81]

It was a double blessing which the Beechers and Finneys gave to reform. They energized the crusaders by making them feel that they were part of a universal plan of salvation — that there was a mighty goal to be reached by their efforts on behalf of the temperance cause, antislavery, or the antidueling law. Under such a divine blessing, reformers could withstand discomforts and heartbreak with iron will. Even the smallest action had meaning. When a member of the Oberlin faculty was urging a friend to come and take a teaching post at the school, he made it far more than a question of a job.

> And when you decide the question of coming here I wish you to do it in the fear of God, and consider that we are not our own, but that we are bought with a price. . . . Consider, my dear brother, that when we became christians [*sic*] — we became members of Christs Kingdom, which is not of this world. If Jesus Christ, the Eternal Son of God is calling you to come here, and to take one of the most important trusts on yourself, that he has to give to any man, in educating ministers to preach his gospel, will you not do it? And if you will not serve him in his kingdom on earth, acceding to his directions, will he take you to heaven and try if you will serve him there? [82]

In addition to this desperate intensity, the reformer borrowed another notion from the revival. *Immediate* change was possible.

If the vile sinner could rise from the mourner's bench, washed white as snow, then a reformer need not quail at the thought that it would take time to subdue the devil. Certain texts remained in his mind. One was, "Behold, I come quickly." Another was, "Behold, I make all things new." And a third was, "With God nothing shall be impossible." The man whe believed these things and went out to battle unrighteousness was a formidable contender.[83]

It was no wonder, then, that Mormonism sprang from upstate New York soil scorched by revivals — that John Humphrey Noyes was a Finney convert — that the "Lane rebels" carried the antislavery reform through the West with a toughness unexpected in ministerial candidates — that Miller, the end-of-the-world harbinger, was turned to the Bible by a Vermont revival. No wonder that the frontier Methodists and Lyman Beecher, each in a different way, gave the temperance movement a mighty fillip.[84] And no wonder that revivalism helped to found colleges all across settled America before the middle of the century.[85] They were intended to be the hatcheries of reform.

There was a happy result. More Christians than ever worked side by side in these efforts. Nineteenth-century Protestantism left behind it gowns and bands, established churches, and infant damnation. It also left behind it a good deal of interdenominational warfare. "Father Abraham," George Whitefield had roared in Philadelphia in 1739, "whom have you in heaven? Any Episcopalians? No. Any Presbyterians? No. Any Independents or Methodists? No, no, no. Whom have you there? . . . All who here are Christians." [86] That was a new sound in religion after a century of whipping Quakers and fining Baptists. By 1832 it had taken good hold among revival-minded preachers. Flocks were warned against that great "hinderance [*sic*] and . . . quencher of revivals . . . the spirit of *Sectarianism*." [87] Revival reports all through the thirties emphasized the joint work of Presbyterian, Baptist, Methodist and Dutch Reformed ministers, in some cases.[88] By 1842 Lyman Beecher, who had battled Episcopalians when they worked for disestablishment in Connecticut, joyfully reported that Cincinnati buzzed with revivals and that "Methodists, Baptists, Presbyterians, and Episcopalians share[d] in them." [89] In 1863 the *Independent*, borrowing the then fashionable military terminology of wartime, said that in the campaign against Satan, the "Commander-in-Chief allowed each people to fight under its own colors." [90]

The messengers of salvation, then, could claim partial credit for a Protestantism which was healthy, stable, socially alive and partly unified. On the other hand, they bore some responsibility for less admirable developments.

For one thing, revivalism could divide as well as unify. In the Presbyterian Church, the rift between "new measures" men and their slower-moving opponents blazed higher and higher. Finally, in 1837, the church broke apart, into two distinct bodies, which were not reunited until 1869. There were many reasons for the break, but the fight over the how and wherefore of revivals was a key issue.[91] So one of the oldest and most powerful of American Protestant bodies was fragmented once again — just as it had been split into Old Side and New Side groups in the Great Awakening, and into "regular" Presbyterians, Cumberland Presbyterians and "New Lights" shortly after 1800. Lyman Beecher, himself involved in a heresy trial in 1835 for espousing the "New Haven theology," must have wondered glumly how the infidels would clap their hands at *that* development. The whole revival movement always carried the dangerous potentiality of showing up a church in its most argumentatively unchristian light.

Then, too, the revival might work admirably in smoothing religious dissension, but it aided in reducing real differences to the point of unrecognizability. In 1845 the British geologist Charles Lyell, on an American tour, was told by a friend that about one fifth of New Englanders were "Nothingarians," indifferent whether they "attended a Baptist, Methodist, Presbyterian, or Congregationalist church, and . . . often equally inclined to contribute money liberally to any one or all of them." [92] It was well for Calvinist and Arminian to join hands, but would Calvin or, say, Wesley have recognized their children? Was it an unmixed blessing that genuinely serious discussion of real religious problems retreated to the seminaries? Just as the majestic ministry of the seventeenth century was reduced to plain clothes by democracy, so were the awesome doctrines of that age shrunken to inoffensive popularization. Was this a cheapening process? Were issues solved, or merely avoided? And was this a high price to pay for peace among Christians? To this question few men, and especially few revivalists, had even a tentative answer.

There was this, too, to be said. On closer examination, the contribution of revivalism to democracy was not entirely a blessing. Evangelical zeal did not always dovetail smoothly with democratic politics, the politics of compromise. The book of Revelation dwelt colorfully on the rewards of the saints, but it reminded many reformers that "without are dogs, and sorcerers, and whoremongers, and murderers, and idolaters, and whosoever loveth and maketh a lie." Too many crusaders remembered that fifteenth verse of Revelation 22. The man who did not see the need for reform was a *sinner*, to be won over if possible, but until he was won over, a subject for scorn, contumely and castigation. A "revivalized" reformer thought only in terms of "black-and-white," of "either-or," and above all of "now, at-once." This made havoc of the democratic process when issues were moralized. John Brown, after all, was a child of the revival age. His last written words to his countrymen were: "I, John Brown, am now quite *certain* that the crimes of this *guilty land: will* never be purged *away:* but with Blood." For whatever John Brown meant, good or bad, the revivalists bore much of the responsibility.

When all was said and done, too, the leaders of the movement to awaken thousands at once were interested only in certain kinds of social transformation. They insisted on their right to criticize politicians, but their interest in the working mechanics of political life was slim. "I looked forward to the election day with considerable solicitude," Finney recalled of one year in upstate New York, "fearing that the excitement of that day would greatly retard the work." [93] Few of the apostles actually entered politics themselves. Moreover, they would not likely have joined the more democratically based parties if they had. Reared largely in a countryside where most people were of English or Scotch-Irish descent, they distrusted or ignored foreigners, and especially

Catholics. Many furnished fuel for the anti-Catholic Know-Nothing Party of the fifties. A leading anti-Catholic writer, in fact, was Herman Norton, one of Finney's New York City assistants.[94] Christian collaboration was all very well, but excluded Catholics and Unitarians — interestingly enough, Christians drawn largely from the ranks of the very poor and the notably rich in those days. But this was natural for these solidly middle-class ministers who, when they thought of economic theory at all, were apt to follow the classical school with its stern rules. In political thinking they were distrustful of Locke and the antitraditional implications of his philosophy.[95] For all these reasons, revivalists who openly announced a political preference did not usually favor the Democratic Party, the home of reform in the Jacksonian era. They preferred to cast their lot with the more conservative Whigs. They were anything but "reform politicians."

Indeed, the list of reforms for which they battled is limited. The evils they fought against were all individual vices of character, and not always the worst ones. They objected to infidelity, drunkenness, gambling, dancing, the theater, Sabbath breaking and profanity. The reformation of the world, for them, began with the conversion of the infidel. Even the antislavery movement was not an effort to solve a national social problem, but a holy war against the idle slaveholder, who earned his bread by the sweat of another's brow. Some abolitionists were men of broad and humane vision, but facts are facts, and many of them would, beyond any reasonable doubt, have been witch burners in the seventeenth century and Prohibitionists in the twentieth.

The revivalists ignored crusades which were primarily *social* movements. Of the utopian communities founded in the yeasty decades of reform, many, like the Amana colony in Iowa, the Rappite group at New Harmony, Indiana, or the Separatists at Zoar, Ohio, originated with German sects whose "revivalism," if any, was a thing apart. The communities at Brook Farm and at Hopedale, Massachusetts, as well as Bronson Alcott's Fruitlands, owed their impetus to Universalism and Unitarianism as much as anything. Shakerism was an English transplantation. The colonies of Frances Wright at Nashoba, Tennessee, and of Robert Dale Owen on the site of the Rappite community at New Harmony were founded by rationalists and anticlericals.[96] Nor do the names of Beecher, Finney, Knapp, Burchard, Swan or the others appear high on the lists of such "radical" movements as those favoring the rights of women or the reform of prison conditions. Revivalists simply were not interested. The millennium would begin by the conversion of each individual. And, in fact, they were not always specific about the meaning of conversion in terms of character. Few revival tracts specifically said that a good convert ought *not* to be autocratic with his family, quarrelsome with his neighbors and close-fisted in his business. It was assumed that conversion automatically cured these social defects.

So, as the world got more complicated, it went past them. Some dabbled with the problems of the city and of labor. The editor of the *New York Evangelist* once superintended a seamen's bethel, a haven for out-of-work sailors. Lewis Tappan experimented unsuccessfully with a Magdalen Society, to reclaim prostitutes from their shame. But neither movement worked much at improving laws governing the merchant marine or clearing the slums where vice bred. In 1854, Charles Loring Brace, a minister who *was* concerned with exactly such problems, wrote:

> Mr. Finney, Mr. Kirk, or any other minister distinguished in revivals, might preach at the Broadway Tabernacle all winter; and his labors might be blessed in a genuine, and powerful revival of religion, and yet hardly a wave of that "religious excitement" would reach the Five Points, which is within a stone's-throw of the building, or the large population of French, Germans and Italians, living in its vicinity.[97]

Why would revivalists care about such problems? They aimed to bring "the greatest weight of character in the community" to the communion table,[98] and they knew only communities divided into respectable professional men, tradespeople and farmers, on the one hand, and on the other, those whom Lyman Beecher styled "ruff-scuff."

Therefore, as reformers, the revivalists became obsolescent. The job of bringing on the millennium fell to the politicians. But if the inner spark was gone, the outer husk of professionalism remained, apparently, vigorous. More and more it was ceasing to be a reproach that men "got up" a revival. "They are made matters of human calculation, by the arithmetic of faith in God's engagements," Calvin Colton observed in 1832.[99] It was put more neatly by a religious paper, reviewing Finney's revival lectures.

> We have no doubt that Mr. Finney is essentially right in his notions of revivals, technically speaking. They belong to no particular set of opinions, but to a system of operations set in motion by human contrivance. Consequently, the most modern and approved practice has been to make use of particular persons, who have acquired practical skill in the art of bringing about an excitement, *on the principle, we suppose, of the perfection in art, which is compassed by division of labor, and of a particular adaptation to a particular branch of professional work.*[100]

That was exactly the case. And if so, some Christians were beginning to think, why not recognize facts? Why not accept the notion of the ministry as a special agency within the church, whose labors were capable of division into preaching, pastoral visits, charitable work, organization, writing — each a task for an expert? Why not, in short, call outright, as was suggested in 1851, for "an order of evangelism"? [101]

It seemed to make sense, but there was an admission involved. A professional school of evangelists was a confession that religious emotion could be awakened and channeled and stereotyped by skilled practitioners. It meant that the age of propaganda was dawning on another horizon. A revival managed by technicians — who, like all technicians, were not complete men — was to the camp meeting what the political convention was to the town meeting, or the printed newspaper to the town gossip. It was a planned assault on the emotions, designed to produce predictable results. Such revivals would be truly modern affairs.

The church was not ready to make such admissions in 1851.

But then things happened. First, there was a twenty-year crisis in organized religion, which called for unprecedented efforts and readjustments. Secondly, a man would emerge who could, by force of his own personality, reveal unsuspected power in the "professional" revival and breathe into it some of the spirit of its beginnings even while he tailored it to fit industrial America. The "new" evangelism faced an uncertain fate in the eighteen-fifties. Across its future loomed the shadows of urbanism and science. But within those shadows bulked the figure of Dwight L. Moody.

CHAPTER VI

Troubled on Every Side

THE Civil War came and the Civil War ended and then, for thirty or forty desperate years or more, the Protestant churches in America reverberated to the sound of alarms. At the mid-point of the nineteenth century, some evangelical Christians triumphantly awaited the beginning of the millennium on United States soil. Yet by 1900, the "orthodox" religion of the eighteen-fifties was battling for its life. Irresistible forces were twisting its universe out of shape.

First, the spearhead of Darwinism plowed through the foundations of belief. The world had been a solid and everlasting place for the men of Charles Finney's day, and humankind only a little lower than the angels. Now, evolution seemed to be saying that the earth itself was in constant, if barely visible, flux, and man was only one of the many forms of life which it supported. The work of justifying God's ways to man had to be commenced again, on new and difficult terms.

The Holy Scriptures were under siege as well. It was impossible to reconcile Genesis as a literal historical record with anything taught by evolutionists. Now, to vex things further, "higher criticism" began to render its testimony. Under the light of archaeology, mythology, history and anthropology, the Bible stood out clearly as the product of many men and centuries. The shock was of earthquake force for some Protestant denominations — particularly those which were revivalistic. They had long been accustomed to prove their propositions by references to both Testaments, where God's very words were to be found, unshakable and eternal. Towering structures of doctrine were likely to come crashing down if the foundation of "the gospel" crumbled.

Lastly, a great tidal wave of migration was sweeping millions into the cities. The whole center of gravity of American life moved with those millions. The cities were alien. They dissolved roots and connections. They swarmed with newly arrived "foreigners," the great majority of them belonging to the Catholic Church, an institution still surrounded by mystery and fear for many rural Americans. The cities were full of new temptations — snares for the feet of those reared in simple folkways. The major American denominations — the Baptists, Congregationalists, Episcopalians, Methodists and Presbyterians — had drawn their strength from the countryside. Their congregations were fairly homogeneous — mostly made up of Americans who traced their ancestry to the British Isles. From them came the molders of America — the majority of the republic's politicians, poets, journalists, preachers, traders, builders and warriors.

Now the intellectual and social status of this community was threatened by urbanism. The Protestantism of the older America, "the product of a rural, middle-class society, faced a range of problems for which it had neither experience nor aptitude." [1] There is an old Greek myth, concerning the giant Antaeus, who gained fresh power whenever he touched the earth. Hercules overcame him by holding him in the air and strangling him. Was the city Hercules? And were the most representative American churches in the position of Antaeus?

There was no one reply to all these problems. The answers were fragmentary, as befitted a fragmented and complicated world. The responses varied from church to church, and even from congregation to congregation. In some "liberal" circles, like those of the Unitarians, the ground was always fallow for new ideas. In other church bodies, a loose kind of organization allowed individual ministers and believers to find their own paths of reconciliation. Wealthy congregations took to innovation with some of the tolerance of the already arrived. The pattern of church history became complex and stippled, and generalizations shallower and patchier.

Some Christians accepted a so-called "Christian evolution," in which God unfolded the Creation bit by bit through time. Thus, the gospels of Saint Matthew and comparative zoology might be harmonized. Some were content with allegorical and poetic interpretations of the Bible, which conserved the vitality of faith for them, even though kings, judges and prophets no longer seemed as "real." Others tried to meet the city on its own ground; they reached out for the new urban masses through "institutions" offering recreation, support and employment to the lost souls of the metropolitan darkness. And still others began to work out new ideas of Christian duty and salvation, and busied their minds with the problem of justice in the economic system, forging a "social gospel" that wanted to reinforce the obligations of individual sinners with new tasks for employers and governors.

Yet when all was said and done, millions were untouched by these "new" religious movements — particularly those recent migrants from the country, held fast in the faith of their fathers. Not yet at ease in Zion, they were still respectable — and so the soup kitchens and "rescue missions" of the Salvation Army and the Y.M.C.A. were not for them. Nor did the "social gospel" make much appeal. This class was still on the make; it might be well enough for some to fear that wealth was accumulating and men decaying in the new America, but youngsters who had "come to town" to seek their fortunes were concerned with the immediate rewards of the competitive system, not with its long-range problems. Nor was there much comfort for them in the newer "intellectual" views of religion. Their down-to-earth minds revolted at the idea of the Bible as a great and inspirational treasury of legends and parables. They wanted a Bible that could be taken in the same way as a *real* document — a will, a contract, an almanac! They needed a religion that a plain man could understand on sight. And the need was all the more acute because of the frustrations and upheavals of their new life. They wanted reassurance that God was concerned with individual souls; that hard work would be rewarded; that personal obedience to plain rules of good conduct was a sign that eternal bliss awaited in the land beyond the sky. They wanted a solid, simple, tangible, "old-time" faith.

For them, there was always the revival. It was not meant to reach the "masses," whatever its sponsors might say. Its real power was in the strength it gave to the hearts of those already sure of calling and election, but anxious for reassurance in a world largely indifferent. Yet the revival itself could not remain entirely unchanged. Its message had always been couched in the language of everyman. So it would have to develop a new vocabulary, as natural and comfortable to readers of the daily press as the language of Peter Cartwright had been to bear hunters. Moreover, it would have to develop new emphases which more directly answered the heresies in the air. In attempting to rescue "true" religion from a damned world, as always, it would be forced to carry some of the imprint of that world.

The first earmark of a "new" revivalism would be defensive. More than ever, the revivalist would trumpet the importance and utter truthfulness and undiminished glories of the Bible. There had always been a "back to the Scriptures" flavor about the movement, and Finney had been explicit in rejecting all confessions and doctrines and resting his "case" with the audience upon the Old and New Testaments. Now, with the volumes undergoing the dissection of scientific and literary and historical critics, the rally was even more ardent. The *Origin of Species* might win adherents at Harvard, or even at Oberlin,[2] but the answer of orthodoxy was that "evolution and the scriptural account of man" were "irreconcilable," and those who claimed anything else were men who "[knew] not God and obey[ed] not the gospel of His son."[3] "Higher critics" might pour dictionaries of Greek and Hebrew scholarship into the presses, and even find a wide sale for such a presumptuous effort as a "Revised Version" of God's word in 1881.[4] But conservatives could strike back with heresy trials of Biblical scholars — the Presbyterians alone had three such courts as late as the eighteen-nineties[5] — and with rancorous criticism. There was a sting of bitterness in words like those of Thomas De Witt Talmage, the popular, conservative minister of Brooklyn's Central Presbyterian Church.

The heinousness of finding fault with the Bible at this time by a Christian minister is most evident. In our day the Bible is assailed by scurrility, by misrepresentation . . . and all the venom of perdition, and at this particular time ministers of religion fall into line of criticism of the Word of God. Why, it makes me think of a ship in a September equinox [*sic*], the waves dashing to the top of the smoke-stack . . . and many prophesying the foundering of the steamer, and at that time some of the crew with axes and saws . . . try to saw off some of the planks and pry out some of the timbers because the timber did not come from the right forest![6]

Many a pastor, like Theodore Cuyler of Brooklyn, sighed for his student days, when preachers "were not hamstrung by any doubt of the divine inspiration or infallibility of the Book that lay before them on their pulpits." [7] Revivalists worked hard to restore that infallibility.

The excellency of merely belonging to a church was another new note sounded in revival preaching which owed something to the restless times. The goal of the evangelist seemed narrower. At times it seemed as if the whole duty of an "awakening" was only to add members to the churches. In the early part of the century, when at least nominal adherence to a church was the rule, the thunders of condemnation were aimed mostly at the unsaved within the circle of worship. After 1865, it was more common to urge the audience to join and attend a church, with an unspoken suggestion that faithful performance of those duties was in itself a reasonable sign of salvation achieved. Simple membership in a congregation became a more highly praised virtue. This was a far cry from the exhorters who had once condemned "deadness" among churchgoers in the days of the Half-Way Covenant. Yet the change in appeal had to come, because the bare necessity of getting members — any kind of members — into Protestant bodies became yearly more urgent. An ebb tide was setting in, as established Presbyterian, Congregational, Episcopalian, Baptist, Methodist and Reformed congregations eddied out towards more attractive sections of the growing cities. Behind them they left religious wastelands. In the twenty years before 1888, seventeen

Protestant churches moved out of the district below New York's Fourteenth Street, while two hundred thousand people crowded into it. In Boston, whole wards existed without a Protestant church; in Chicago at one time there was an island of sixty thousand souls without *any* church.[8] Yet the ministers had to follow those worshipers who could support their work. Theodore Cuyler sketched in his autobiography the saga of many a Protestant body in those years. In 1854 he took over the Market Street Dutch Reformed Church, within walking distance of the New York City Hall. Six years later he discovered that "rapid migration up town would soon leave our congregation too feeble for self-support." Cuyler began urging the construction of a new "edifice" on Murray Hill, then well north of town. He himself, however, moved to another church, and the uptown trek was never completed. The church itself in a short while, "bleeding at every pore, from the fatal up-town migration . . . peacefully disbanded." Its building fell to a missionary group which made it a "light-house amid a dense tenement-house foreign population." [9] Multiplied a thousandfold, it was not a heartening story.

The older churches seemed to be losing their hold on the plain people who had once been the foundation stone of American religion. The newcomers who moved into the heart of the city had no money to build their souls more stately mansions. Clergymen of what were now the "uptown" churches were slow to recognize the needs or existence of a new kind of "common man." They preached a gospel of individual responsibility for charitable works and clean living, which comforted their well-fed upper-class flocks. Some critics were unkind enough to say that a pewholder in a successful church was merely a "stockholder in a wealthy and flourishing corporation." [10] Ordinary citizens were apt to lose interest in such churches.

In addition, the very composition of the population was changing, and in a way that robbed Protestant denominations of adherents. Most of the new immigrants were bound to the faith of Rome and Byzantium, or worshiped in the synagogue. In 1890 New York had half as many Italians in its populace as Naples, twice as many Irish as Dublin, and two and one half times as many Jews as Warsaw. Only two cities in the German Empire — Berlin and Hamburg — had more Germans than Chicago.[11] Greeks and Poles, Ukrainians and Hungarians moved by the million into the city, to take up new lives. Soon "the Catholics greatly outnumbered any Protestant group."[12] Notes of alarm passed among some evangelists. "Did you see the item about the attendance in fifteen *of the largest protestant [sic] Churches on the South Side* in Chicago *all combined* not being as large on a recent Sunday as the attendance in *one* Catholic Church?"[13] It appeared as if the immigrant ships were working a kind of counter-Reformation, a prospect which brought shudders to some Americans who were brought up faithfully believing that all things good in modern life began with Luther. The attitude might be narrow and illiberal from a later era's viewpoint.[14] Nevertheless, it existed, and it seemed to sharpen the demand for some dramatic movement to recapture mass loyalties for Protestantism. So it was that when the cry for new Christians went up from the evangelistic pulpit, it would be less insistent than of yore on differentiating between those who merely paid pew rents and those who were bona fide "saints."

And then "modernists" began to take places alongside sinners and infidels in the rogues' gallery of revivalism. It pained the revivalists to see the new heresies gaining ground, but they were. Science and progress walked hand in hand in nineteenth-century America, and progress was a faith for American churchmen as well as for their flocks. The seminaries training young ministers, moreover, stood only a short distance along tree-shaded walks from the growing laboratories on university campuses. So it was not long before peace was made with science. By the eighties, Henry Ward Beecher, the son of Lyman Beecher himself, could state his belief that man "as to his physical being evolved from the animal race below him."[15] Other Congregationalists, like Lyman Abbott, who succeeded Beecher in Brooklyn's Plymouth Church, were now ready to see the omnipotent God as the "one Great Cause from whom all forms of nature and of life continuously proceed."[16] That simple word, "continuously," did away with an entire chapter of Genesis! Phillips Brooks said, on behalf of many Episcopalians in 1882, that Darwin's "doctrine of development" was but "the continual indwelling and action of creative power." [17] Here and there, spokesmen for other faiths signed their own treaties. To genuine evangelical believers of an older mold, this was treason.

The "orthodox" were equally unhappy when "up-to-date" churches reached out for "the masses" with new institutions. Close by the gray, moss-covered walls of the old church buildings, a network of social clubs, nurseries for working mothers, special classrooms and play areas grew up — the earmarks of the "institutional church." [18] A few well-established congregations seriously indulged in "self-denying labor for the masses of poor and outcast." [19] Sometimes, indeed, the religious core of a church was wrapped in many layers of social activity. Under Lyman Abbott, Plymouth Church had "reading rooms, penny provident banks, boys' clubs, two gymnasiums . . . lodging-house visitation, organized aid to the unemployed, and work among the sailors on the docks and on ships in port." [20] Revivalistic pastors could not see that such activities had much to do with the real business of Christianity, which was, in their view, to lead sinners to find atonement in the blood of Jesus. Reluctantly, they took part in some "social service" work in the slums, for sinners had to be tracked down in their haunts. The Y.M.C.A. and above all the American branch of the Salvation Army were evangelistic organizations undertaking social work as a means of spreading the gospel of redemption.[21] But there was always a fear that "slum brigades," rescue missions and soup kitchens would distract attention from the evangelical message. They might even lead to a new heresy, namely, that Christianity should be more concerned with reforming society at large than with converting individuals.

Such ideas did, in fact, flourish among a few "liberal" Christians. Loosely defined as the "social gospel," they ranged from a mere gentlemanly concern with physical care of the needy, to outright rejection of the capitalistic system and demands for a "Christian Socialism." They were given form and content by men of diverse training and temperament — Darwinists and mystics, imperialists and pacifists, practitioners of "simplicity" in thought and sophisticated intellectuals. Washington Gladden and George D. Herron, William D. P. Bliss and Josiah Strong, and dozens of cohorts fought against the social conservatism of the church in post-Civil War America, urging a Christianity which should "concern itself with the ills of the new industrial civilization that the conflict had helped bring to birth." [22] They believed that they were making honest efforts to keep abreast of the exacting times. Revivalists, however, were either wary of their doctrines or venomously opposed to them. In this opposition to ungodly and even unpatriotic "liberalism," they were to find a great source of strength.

For the "social gospel" and "Christian Socialism" were failing to reach a vast, undigested middle class transplanted from the farm. The flight to the metropolis did not take place entirely on the immigrant steamers. Daily, trains delivered thousands of farm boys and girls, with carefully brushed clothes and cheap suitcases, into the maw of one Babylon or another. In 1890, twelve of the nation's principal cities were in the Midwest, drawing their vast increases in population from the countryside around them. More than half the townships in Ohio and Illinois declined in population between 1880 and 1890. Great portions of Pennsylvania, New York and New Jersey were reduced in numbers. In New England, land of Pilgrim and patriot heroes, rank fields and abandoned farm buildings greeted visitors. Elsewhere, too, the countryside was denuded. The city was taking from the agricultural world its more independent and aggressive younger men and women.[23]

For these Ebens and Enochs, Prudences and Rebeccas, clerking in offices, mending machinery, struggling to establish small shops and raise families, or painfully acquiring professional skills in part-time schools, the social gospel meant little. Theirs, rather, was the gospel of Horatio Alger. William Dean Howells caught the likeness of many of them — and whether they were honest souls like Silas Lapham, or scoundrels like Bartley Hubbard of *A Modern Instance,* who lived on the unethical fringe of the new journalism, they were united by a desire to "get on." Goodhearted though they were, it meant nothing to them if a preacher talked of social responsibility, or the mutual duties of classes, or the uselessness of the struggle for gain. They wanted to hear, rather, that the ancient virtues still paid. They wanted to be told that the only obstacles in their way were those of character — that a few selfish men, perhaps, were monopolizing the chances of success, or that the great mass of city folks who never seemed to rise above the level of struggling for subsistence were not kept down by the system, but by their own indulgence in drink or amusement. They did not need to be brought back to church by mission workers. They might well go to church on Sundays. Perhaps they had already been "saved" in a revival back home. Yet they desired a renewal of the promise that with God's help and a change of heart, the gates of the kingdoms of heaven and earth would be open to them. They were ready for reassurance, for a *nostalgic* revival.

In these ways, the revival after mid-century was shaped negatively. In reacting against "science" and "materialism" and "radical" social ideas, it clung more closely to the Bible, stressed the value of church affiliation and reaffirmed the notion that the "saved" sinner was bound to become a success in the world. Yet other changes took place along more positive lines. Revivalism was willing — or compelled — to borrow certain attitudes and devices from the distrusted modern world. It was shaped not only by resisting, but by adjusting. Even the very faithful believers felt new influences. Except for the most pious, a Sunday paper or a lending-library book might be waiting at home for the conclusion of the services. Not everything from the pulpit would be taken at face value. Nor would those ordained of God furnish the only available standard of oratory and persuasion. So changes needed to be, and were, made.

One of the most important of these accommodations was in the field of theology itself. The harsh doctrines of primal Calvinism, already shaken, were losing even their final power to terrify. In the crossroads hamlet, it was true, the old ways might hold.

My grandmother told me of Old Peter Cartwright
Who preached hell-fire
And the worm that never dies.

And here's a young preacher at the New Hope Meeting house,
And every one allows, he has old Peter's brows,
And flaming of the eyes,
And the very same way, they say.[24]

In the city, however, one might pick up the Monday paper and read the sermons of those popular ministers who fed the large and successful city congregations. These men were saying something rather different. The flames of hell were cooling in their discourses. Though they spoke of the old cycle of sin-to-salvation, they put more emphasis on the salvation. Spectacular evidence of that was to be found in the writings of Henry Ward Beecher. Beecher's father had preached thousands of words on the doctrine of election, that forbidding concept which consigned millions irretrievably to hell from the day wherein they were born. But to Henry Ward, large, florid, deeply emotional, loving flowers and uncut jewels (of which he liked to carry a handful in his pocket), such notions were abhorrent.[25] He "made conscience and fear secondary";[26] and it was his belief that Christ would throw about him the shield of His righteousness, "not because I am not a sinner, but because I am a sinner, loved and shielded of Christ."[27] Hundreds of listeners and thousands of readers were stirred when Henry proclaimed:

> When I come before the Eternal Judge and say, all aglow: "My Lord and God!" will He turn to me and say . . . "You did not come up the right road. Go down!" I to the face of Jehovah will stand and say: "God! I won't go to hell! I will go to heaven! I love Thee. Now damn me if Thou canst. I love Thee!" And God shall say, and the heavens flame with double and triple rainbows, and echo with joy: "Dost thou love? Enter in and be forever blessed." [28]

Nor was this idea unique with Beecher, even if the lush style was peculiarly his own. One by one, the ancient and craggy doctrines of seventeenth-century Christianity were veiled with optimism, and even cordiality. Lyman Abbott was proud that he himself had always avoided "what a friend called 'the *patois* of

Canaan' — such words as Trinity, Atonement, Vicarious Sacrifice, Regeneration, Decrees, Foreordination, Plenary Inspiration, and the like." That enabled him to "preach Divine Sovereignty to Methodists, Orthodoxy to Unitarians, the Civil Rights of the Negroes to Southerners, Industrial Democracy to capitalists, and the leadership of Jesus Christ to Jews," and always to get a hearing if not to be sure of convincing his audience.[29] All of this was superb for ending interdenominational warfare. It meant that for educated churchmen, the intellectual concepts underlying those words were no longer as relevant to modern life as more pressing social issues. But it meant also that when such notions filtered down to more popular and less learned levels, they would result in a preaching style stripped of some of the terror which had once lent it a certain frightening excitement. There had been a kind of drama, for example, in the older theory of conversion, by which a leprous and sin-spotted wretch was turned, in a twinkling, into an angel of God. To take away that drama was to change old-fashioned evangelism almost beyond recognition.

In the eighteen-twenties, Finney had filled New York meetinghouses with crying, groaning sinners, so distraught that he had to shout at them, "You are not in hell yet." But in 1873, a minor revivalist named George F. Pentecost told of a woman who came to him after a sermon and said, "I have no deep feeling of repentance. I have not shed a tear over my sins; have had no fear or dread of God's wrath. I just seem to know that I am a sinner and want to be a Christian." Forty years before, those would have been, in revivalistic eyes, the words of a "cold and stupid professor." But Pentecost's comment was, "Thank God!" "*I assured her that faith in Christ was the only preparation required, and that she need not be anxious about her feeling.*" [30]

Thus was the pathway to salvation made less rocky. There was a second adjustment of the revival to the then contemporary world. The gospel was presented to the light of reason in ever more genial terms. The preaching of the eighteenth century had been severely intellectual, rich in the "*patois* of Canaan," uncompromisingly didactic. The preaching of Nettleton, Beecher and Finney had edged towards the more purely exhortatory, aimed at bringing the sinner to immediate decision. Now preaching began to sound more simply anecdotal. The transformation came slowly. The religious press was gradually filled with stories of brave little boys who did not swear, wicked little boys who played with hoops on Sunday, and noble savages who, happy in the assurance of a home in the skies, laid down their lives for the sake of devoted missionaries.[31]

Why were these changes taking place? Partly because of a vast revolution in the secular press. Popular newspapers and cheap magazines multiplied everywhere. Their easily disgestible stories, rich in sentiment and suspense, were making a revolution in popular taste. Even the godly, who once despised fiction as a diversion from serious thoughts about eternity, had to trim sail to the prevailing breezes.[32] Some ministers caught on quickly. One vastly popular preacher of the day was the Reverend Thomas De Witt Talmage, of Brooklyn. Whereas a century before, sermons had dealt with foreordination, spiritual work and gracious affections, his widely circulated pulpit talks bore such titles as "The Ferry Boat Over the Jordan," "The Gospel Looking Glass," and "Religion an Antiseptic." In them, flowers of religious rhetoric such as these bloomed:

> Religion is sweetness, and perfume, and spikenard, and saffron, and cinnamon, and cassia, and frankincense, and all sweet spices together. . . .
> It counteracts all trouble. Just put it on the stand beside the pillow of sickness. It catches in the curtains, and perfumes the stifling air. It sweetens the cup of bitter medicine, and throws a glow on the gloom of the turned lattice. It is a balm for the aching side, and a soft bandage for the temple stung with pain. . . . And it is good for rheumatism, and for neuralgia, and for low spirits, and for consumption; it is *the catholicon for all disorders.* Yes, it will heal all your sorrows.[33]

How surprised Jonathan Edwards would have been to learn that this was what was meant by the indwelling beauty and joy of holiness! Nevertheless, it was necessary to speak in these terms to reach the general ear. The taste for sentiment and for make-believe was deeply rooted by the middle of the nineteenth century, and it demanded gratification. It was significant that the most spectacular best-seller of the century was a novel basically evangelical, yet centered on the characters of a simple Negro and a good little girl. Eventually, Little Eva, and even Little Nell, left an indelible mark on popular religion in America.

Therefore, the revivalist who would rekindle the loyalties of millions would have to speak the new commoner's tongue. He would have to command the language of popular culture as it existed in the seventies. And, he would have to succeed in the cities. The country towns still had their revivals, now an annual religious festival in some cases. Particularly was this true in the South, which had not yet yielded to the city. Reports in the Southern religious press were couched in the old terms. "The fire ran through the audience like an electric shock. Tears, shouts, and sobs were strangely intermingled," ran a Methodist report from Knoxville, Tennessee, in 1866. Elsewhere, altars were depicted, "thronged with weeping penitents," from Columbus, Georgia, to Howard County, Missouri.[34] The older orthodoxy lingered in the South. Its embattled armies had taken time out for revivals in the ranks. Its typical hero, in some ways, was not Lee, the cavalier, but Stonewall Jackson, the praying warrior who came straight from Cromwell's army of Roundheads. Yet even in the South, after 1865 the Methodists spent much more time than before in educational and social work.[35]

And as it was in the South, so it was elsewhere among those still tied to the earth — in the middle border of Hamlin Garland's youth, the Kansas of Ed Howe, the Maine of Mary Ellen Chase's childhood.[36] This kind of revival was a continuous undertone to religious news. It was this kind of meeting that made the columns of the *Independent* year in and year out, with good news of salvation in towns that were hardly flyspecks on the map.[37]

But these revivals were now side-show affairs. The main tent was in the city. It was there that the flame lit in the village must be kept burning for the transplanted farm folk. It was there that religion must challenge the theater and the cheap press, those children of Satan. Or, if it could not challenge them, then it must convert them to the uses of God. A man or men must be found who could achieve the task of translating the revival into big-city terms — a man strong in faith, winning in speech, masterful in using the publicity weapons of the industrial age against the age itself. No such man existed among the professional revivalists in 1873. Hammond was not qualified, nor Parker, nor any of their cohorts. George Pentecost was not, and he knew it. Commenting sadly in March of 1873 on the fact that there had been no "general" revival since 1857, he wished that he could "see another race of Edwardses and Finneys raised up to bless the Church." [38]

Even as Pentecost was writing, a man who would answer his prayers was preparing for a visit to England, where he would ready himself to become the most successful revivalist in post-Reconstruction America. The era of Moody was about to begin. It was a Massachusetts farm boy, grown into a successful Chicago businessman, who was to be the Edwards and the Finney of the eighteen-seventies.

CHAPTER VII

Words Easy to Be Understood

NEW YEAR'S EVE of 1876 brought its special quota of associations to millions of Americans. For some ten thousand residents of Philadelphia it was a night of memories which they would long carry — memories of wooden chairs, and gaslight falling on their upturned faces, and on the bare walls of a boxlike wooden building at Thirteenth and Market streets which only a few weeks before had been a railroad freight depot. There, as the hours of 1875 ticked away, they sat before a raised wooden platform, big enough for a huge choir and several hundred ministers. At the very front of it, in a small, railed enclosure, a man waved a limp-covered Bible over his head and shouted to them that life eternal was theirs for the asking; that to achieve it, they had only to come forward and t-a-k-e, TAKE!

He was a big man — over two hundred pounds, and in his fortieth year. His voice filled the auditorium without strain. Words poured swiftly from his bearded lips, and those words carried the colloquial tang of the New England back country. As he spoke, the characters in his gesticulating Bible came to large and sudden life. Zaccheus and David, Paul and Noah, Lazarus and Daniel walked before the audience, as palpable, and big, and brimful of energy as Commodore Vanderbilt or Phineas T. Barnum. From time to time the speaker paused, and another portly man, seated at a small organ on one side of the platform, took over. Touching a few chords, he sang plainly worded ballads, about lost sheep, and erring children, and a place called Heaven that was, put simply, a home — spacious, sheltering and forgiving, full of the suggested but unseen presence of a benign, but exacting, Father. Plaintively, the singer asked the audience to come home.

The speaker was Dwight L. Moody, and the singer Ira Sankey, together conducting a religious service which might have puzzled Jonathan Edwards, but which had a well-nigh universal appeal in the eighteen-seventies. They had recently returned from a triumphal two-year tour of England, where they had spoken literally to millions. Since then, they had faced auditoriums crowded to suffocation in Brooklyn and Philadelphia itself, and they were about to go on to further packed houses, and the front pages, in New York, Chicago and Boston. The seats in the "tabernacles" were jammed (by their choice) with plain folk, but the guest platforms glittered with respectability. At one of the Philadelphia meetings, President Grant himself was there, along with a Supreme Court justice, the governor of Pennsylvania, and a sprinkling of senators and representatives.[1] Finney himself had not achieved nearly so much, working as he had in the era when railroads and newspapers were primitive. It had taken Moody, the driving force and organizer of the campaigns, to give mass evangelism a spectacular rebirth.

Moody had brought his life to a climax in these meetings. Born in Northfield, Massachusetts, in 1837, he had gone to Chicago at the age of nineteen to work as a shoe salesman. He belonged to the generation of country boys who made good in the turbulent America of post-Civil War days. He was one with Rockefeller and Armour, Leland Stanford and Mark Hanna. Like them, he sensed the country's extravagant potentialities for a man of energy. Had he stayed in business, he would almost certainly have built some kind of empire, like those in oil, timber, steel, meat, rails or grain which rose around him. But in his youth, religion had laid its hand on him. *His* business was souls. And therefore, he found himself confronting a market even more dazzling than an imperialist of the countinghouse could conceive. For any product, no matter how cheap, there was a point of market saturation. But every human being on earth was a customer for salvation. There was a campaign to challenge a *big* man!

So Moody made it his mission to put the presentation of the gospel on a basis suitable to an age of telegraph wires, railroads, blast furnaces and dynamos. He sought for money to be used in

"Christian work" on a massive scale, and he spent it as lavishly in the Lord's service. He used the whole panoply of modern persuasion — publicity, organization and advertising — to win audiences. Then he gauged to a T the temperament of those audiences, mostly suspended between a rural past and an urban present, their childhood tastes in process of remolding by popular journalism. He cast his message in terms suited to those tastes, warmed it with his indestructible energy and honesty, and made "converts" in uncounted droves. He belonged in an age in which, as one observer said, men talked as confidently of millions as they once had of thousands.

Yet in this fulfillment, there was an unsuspected note of sadness. Moody completed the reduction of evangelism to a matter of technique and personality. He harrowed the ground so thoroughly that others, borrowing his skills and innovations, could reap where he sowed, without radiating his warmhearted goodness. Moreover, Moody was outdated. In technique, he was a creature of his age, but in faith he belonged to the half century which preceded him. Unshakable in his confidence that the Bible was literally inspired, he preached a gospel of individual salvation which took little heed of the fierce complexities of an industrialized world. So compelling was his personality that he won the love of men gifted with genuine perception. They warmed to him even though they knew him to be a child in scientific intelligence. Yet "his" gospel could easily become the property of bigots, and when he died in 1899, there were plenty of them on hand to claim his mantle in their holy wars on "modernists," "foreigners," and "booze."

Paradoxically, Moody's very success may have helped to retard a realistic fusing of the democratic and humanitarian elements of rural Protestantism with the scientific enlightenment underlying the progressive movements of the early twentieth century. His charitable soul abhorred strife in the churches, but his enormous triumphs among the middle class helped to perpetuate the division between "modern," or "social," Christianity and the dogged proponents of "old-time religion." In bringing the revival up to date with the billboard and the trust, he hindered the re-examination of its theological core, on a popular level. His preaching froze a part of American Christianity into nostalgia and created a ready-made body of listeners for some men who, without his charity, were as sounding brass and a tinkling cymbal.

He came by his countryman's religion honestly, being born in Northfield in the Connecticut River's valley, not too far from the seedbeds of revivalism in New York and Vermont.[2] His father dropped dead when the boy was four, leaving a wife and seven children. Betsy Moody kept the household together by an iron will and by giving her children a baptism of grinding work. A steady diet of plowing, chopping, hauling and gathering did nothing to harm Dwight Lyman Ryther Moody physically or emotionally. He grew into a strapping boy, outgoing and lively. Lorenzo Dow, as a child, fell into religious trances. Asahel Nettleton wept over sunsets. Moody, on the other hand, showed no evidence that his future delight would be in the law of the Lord. The tolling of the church bell for a funeral would make him "very solemn," but that was hardly strange.[3] His schoolmates at the local grammar school, where he unenthusiastically picked up a few scraps of education, were less likely to remember him for piety than for pranks, often of considerable ingenuity. It was Moody who, at the annual elocution exercises, chose to deliver Marc Antony's oration and had "Caesar's coffin" brought in before him. When he lifted the lid to gaze on the remains of the noblest Roman, a tomcat jumped out, by prearrangement.[4] Life eternal did not weigh heavily on his mind.

Life temporal, however, did. Moody was not soured by what amounted to life on a poor farm, but he had too much energy to stay put. His eighteen-year-old bones soon were telling him what his mature mind would later articulate: "Cities are the centers of influence. Water runs downhill, and the highest hills in America are the great cities." [5] So he looked with longing at the Yankee's mecca, Boston. Two of his maternal uncles had a boot and shoe business there, and he asked to be admitted to it. After some hesitation — caused in part by an older brother's advice that Dwight would soon want to run the store — Uncle Samuel, the elder, gave in. Dwight might come to Boston, but care was taken to screen him from the temptations of the wicked city. He would have to promise not to drink or gamble, to board at a place chosen for him and to attend Sunday school regularly.[6]

Moody made the bargain gladly, was introduced to the world of business and fell lustily in love with it. On slack days he stationed himself in front of the store to beckon passing Bostonians in. Soon he induced his uncle to let him keep the store open on holidays and split any accruing profits. If wealth did not exactly flow in as a result of this, he was happy enough, with practical jokes to play on fellow clerks, walks on the common, and abolitionist lectures to attend in nearby Faneuil Hall. The city was not disappointing in its opportunities for fun, at least.[7]

Meantime he took to religious life unspectacularly. He joined the new Boston Y.M.C.A., enthusing over the fact that for a dollar a year he could read all the books in the library for nothing. There is no evidence that he read any of them. He joined the Mount Vernon Congregational Church, presided over by Edward N. Kirk. But Kirk's oratory wove no spell for a hard-working young shoe clerk who, according to rumor, slept through the sermons in the gallery. Nor did Sunday school begin very auspiciously. On his first day there, the class was asked to turn to the Gospel of John. Moody, perspiring, fumbled the Bible in his big hands, desperately looking for it in the Old Testament, amid snickers. Healthy as he was, those snickers must have cut deep. Perhaps he remembered them in later life, when, no matter how busy the schedule, he arose at 4 A.M. and studied the Scriptures until he knew them virtually by heart.

Then one day something akin to a miracle happened. The Sunday-school teacher, a young and forgotten man named Edward Kimball, was lecturing on Moses, praising his statesmanlike qualities. Suddenly, from the rawboned teen-ager Dwight Moody burst the highest praise in the New England vocabulary. "That Moses must have been *smart!*"[8] The class howled; this was not sacred rhetoric as practiced in Boston. But Moody did not care. A world had suddenly been opened to him. For when it came to the Bible, Moody was a true believer. Moses was not an ancient

Jewish lawgiver, or yet a shadowy figure through whom Jehovah had spoken. He was real. The boy did not imagine him; he *knew* him, as he knew Uncle Samuel, or the owner of the neighboring farm. There was direct contact between the mind of Moses and that of Moody. And this passionate, ingrained acceptance of the Bible was to become his great strength. Its characters were so alive for him that while he might respect them, he did not corrupt his style with the stereotypes of false reverence. On the other hand, "higher criticism" could not dent him. He was intellectually and emotionally incapable of absorbing it. He no more doubted the Bible than his own senses, and in some way, he could communicate this passion to others, even when they did not share his faith.

This was Moody's true conversion, and it only needed to be followed up. Kimball was a perceptive man. He dropped in on his young scholar one afternoon and found him wrapping shoes in the back of the store. There, amid half-opened boxes, the smell of leather, the murmur of retail transaction, Moody experienced his "rebirth." It gave him his own idea of what the experience should be like. There were no "jerks," and he did not, like Finney, bellow out the unutterable gushings of his heart. A quiet conversation, hand on shoulder, and a simple decision, and that was everything. He felt inwardly lifted — he remembered falling in love with the birds as he walked, later, on the common.[9] To souls of a neurotic bent, conversion is a searing fire. To those of an open and healthy temperament, it is supreme joy.[10] This very sense of the elation in religious life saved Moody from bigotry and contentiousness in his later years. Yet it also led him to preach a conversion by decision which had less meaning for others, perhaps, than it did for him.

For Moody, in "accepting Christ," had dedicated all of himself. It did not show auspiciously at first. He was still ignorant of doctrine, and the committee which examined him for admission to the church was not impressed by his answer to the question, "What has Jesus Christ done for you?" Moody, always straightforward, answered that He had done a great deal for everyone, but "I don't think of anything He has done in particular as I know of." [11] On this basis, to their later embarrassment, they made him wait nearly a year before taking him in. It did not matter, anyway. Moody had found business and found religion, and thus he had used up Boston. In 1856, prompted by instinct, he moved into a larger and more active sphere. In September of that year, he went out to Chicago, to begin a new phase of his education.

Chicago and Moody were made for each other. The prairie city was already pulsing with its gathered energies. Moody came to work for a shoe store owned by a Mr. Wiswall, on Lake Street, then a long dirt strip flanked by raised wooden sidewalks.[12] Chicago hustled! Lake steamers and schooners poured the iron, grain and timber of the Great Lakes onto its wharves; railroads brought it the meat and cereal of the rapidly opening plains to be processed; the smoke of its foundries, machine shops, factories and slaughterhouses eddied into the sky; and the Chicago River was already choked with sewage. The town had a jerry-built look. Its wealth outran its refinement. In such a grabby milieu, Moody was at home. He slept in the back of the store, and in dull times he roamed hotels and depots, looking for out-of-town buyers. Lingering in front of the show window, he looked like an overgrown spider, waiting for flies.[13] Quickly his energy was put into demand. He branched out into jobbing and wholesaling, then began making collections, for a commission, from country merchants.[14] Long trips in smoky railroad coaches and jolting wagon rides over unbroken prairie to wrest five dollars from a country grocer were wine to him. Speculation simmered in his bones. He enthusiastically reported home that he had averaged thirty dollars a week; that he had made twenty-five per cent on a land speculation; that once he had lent a hundred dollars for *seventeen per cent a day!* "I am collecting for a house in Chicago," he wrote to the family. "I like it better than anything I have ever done. It is nothing but excitement all the time." By the time he had been there five years, he was making a respectable annual five thousand dollars, with fifteen thousand dollars laid away to gather interest.[15] Chicago, which in those years was making the fortunes of the Fields, McCormicks and Armours, to name only a handful, seemed on the way to producing another millionaire in Moody. But Moody was a religious man, too, and the peculiar conditions of church life in brawling Chicago dictated another result.

The city's churches were already suffering the major wounds of urbanization. Some were large and successful and ensconced in goodly dwelling places in fashionable neighborhoods. But others were languishing in the portions of the town already abandoned to poverty. Chicago had its human refuse, too — its more poorly paid laborers, its transient tramps, its lake sailors on the beach — all those who were churned to the bottom by the wheels of progress, and those who lived by selling these outcasts cheap food and clothes, bad living quarters, whiskey and diversion. These were the "unchurched," and the godly leaders of the city's congregations wondered how to bring religion to them. It was under the prodding of this problem that city missions, "lighthouses," "bethels" and "rescue stations" began to grow in slum streets. The continuance of these demanded money and a special breed of men, neither theologians, nor speakers, nor writers, but relentless workers, unafraid of dirt. It was at this point that God gave Moody and the Chicago churches to each other.

Moody had joined the Plymouth Congregational Church on his arrival in the city. His fractured grammar inhibited him from taking much part in the social affairs of the congregation, but he was incapable of belonging to an organization without doing something. So he framed his own solution. Out of his pocket, he rented four pews, and on Sunday mornings he wandered into boardinghouses singling out visiting commercial travelers and inviting them to services as his guests. In a small way, this began his work of collecting souls. But this hardly accounted for more than a few hours of his day of so-called "rest." He then joined the Young Men's Mission Band of the First Methodist Church — quite unconcerned about denominational tags — and walked the streets distributing tracts and invitations to prayer meetings. Still, filling a Congregational and a Methodist church did not fill up the void in Moody. Prowling unfamiliar districts, he found a small, out-of-the-way "mission" Sunday school at Chicago and Wells streets. Assuming that his command of English would at least match that of street-Arab pupils, he asked for a class. The superintendent said that he had enough teachers, but if Moody would recruit a class, he was welcome to instruct it. The following Sunday, Moody showed up with eighteen ragged and filthy urchins, collected somehow on street corners. He had made his first conquest for God.[16]

He had also, unknowingly, begun his career by choosing to fight on what was then the major battlefront of the churches. Not only had he chosen the city as his theater, by instinct, but he had chosen the job of reconciling the city and the old-time religion to each other. For the next several years, Moody would hunt for lost sheep susceptible of a Christian education in Chicago's rougher districts — particularly in "The Sands," a stretch just north of the Chicago River, described by one observer as a "moral lazaretto." [17] Among its shanties, bordellos and saloons he moved tirelessly, as a Sunday-school recruiter and organizer first, and as a Y.M.C.A. agent and church deacon later, carrying the good news of salvation. It was superb experience. It gave him a chance to test his enormous energies, for one thing. For another, it gave him a wide scope of acquaintance in church circles, because of the urgency and publicity of "rescue" work. In the course of the work, too, he discovered a new talent for cultivating money and bringing it down in showers on thirsty city missionary fields. Moving from the parlors of rich contributors to the shabby garrets of poor beneficiaries, Moody served an apprenticeship in human relations which paid well. He was attending a unique theological seminary. If a whaling ship was Herman Melville's Yale and his Harvard, as he said, then "The Sands" was Moody's divinity school. There were no professional talkers there and no smell of sanctity; no teacups in the study or contests in rhetoric. But there were plain people and quantities of work to do for them, and Moody's nature widened as he came to know them; "the vast humanity which was born in him and was the secret of his power was released and trained and deepened by his contact with all these lives." [18]

Moody's first class delighted his soul. As he put it, "I had found out what my mission was." [19] He was so enthused that he went out collecting again, and within a short time, he had more salvageable guttersnipes on his hands than one classroom could hold. Undaunted, he conceived the idea of setting up an undenominational mission Sunday school on his own. Acting on the impulse, he found and rented out of his own pocket an empty saloon to accommodate his scholars. He found a helper in J. B. Stillson, a visitor from Rochester, whom he met one morning when they were both tramping the lakeside piers looking for sailors to bring to church. Before long, the two of them had gathered enough children to overflow the new quarters. An empty hall over a city-owned market was found and leased, and the North Market Sabbath School was under way. The undiscriminating municipal fathers rented the hall out for dances and parties on Saturday nights, so Moody's Sunday began at 6 A.M. when he swept cigar butts and wrestled empty beer kegs out of his house of learning. Then, with Stillson and one other man to lead the singing,[20] he took over the teaching of the boys, of all ages and sizes, at first lumped higgledy-piggledy in one classroom.

Moody kept them coming in, by means that were to be characteristic later. He would try anything, he spared himself nothing, and he never let up. He was not exactly orthodox in his ways. He kept his pockets full of maple sugar on his excursions into the alleys, and when the word got out, children gravitated to him, after which it was an easy matter to get them into the school. It was not always so simple to get the consent of their parents. Many of the fathers were burly loafers with a wholesome distrust of slumming Christians bringing gifts and respectability. A good many, too, were Irish Catholics, who were all too willing to strike a blow for the faith by pummeling a Protestant heretic looking for converts among them. Now, Moody himself was a figure to command respect, with the physique of a logger or stevedore, but fighting was against his Christian principles. Sometimes a mere look at Moody discouraged a potential attacker, but more than once he went sprinting through back streets, dodging barrels, carts and boxes, with a bellowing Irishman in pursuit. "If they persecute you in one place, flee into another," was a favorite text with him.

Parents who threatened Moody away, however, made a discovery that surprised them. Moody was irresistible. He would not give up. He would be back — again, and again, and again — frequently answering a curse with a prayer, and never relaxing his hold. Finally, in sheer amazement that any man could be so passionately concerned about them, families would give up and allow the enrollment of their children. What could a mother do with a man who chased her daughter half a mile over wooden sidewalks and through saloons merely for the purpose of getting her into school on Sunday morning? What could a father do when he came home unexpectedly to find Moody pouring a jug of his best whiskey down the sink? He could roll up his sleeves for battle, as one did, but then what if Moody promptly began to pray for him — not in the conventional cant phrases, but with an unmistakable and plain-spoken earnestness? What was there to do then except shake hands sheepishly and wish the missionary good luck? Moody's sincerity was so transparent that Pharisees as well as publicans and sinners were helpless before it.

Nor was Moody above using a little Yankee sharpness when it was convenient. Once, when certain Irish boys were hindering the work, Moody went to Chicago's Bishop Duggan and asked if he would use his influence to restrain them. Delicately, the Bishop suggested that it would be easier if Moody himself were a Catholic. A look of innocence undoubtedly crossed Moody's face, as he explained that his conversion to Rome might hamper his work among Protestants. Not at all, demurred the other. Did the Bishop mean, then, asked the shoe salesman in surprise, that Catholics could pray together with Protestants? Yes, such was the case. Well, said the Sunday-school organizer, that was splendid. Would the Bishop kneel and pray with him then and there for guidance in this matter? Bishop Duggan's reaction is not a matter of record, though there must have been some amusement in it. But he did kneel and pray, if the story is true, and what was more, he did intervene with his parishioners on behalf of Moody, who remained a Protestant. Another ten minutes, and the Bishop might have found himself teaching in the Sunday school.

The students themselves were equally spellbound by Moody, who took control of a roomful of "toughs" with names like Madden the Butcher and Darby the Cobbler as if he had been born to it. He would try any honest method of winning support. To one class of boys wrapped in dirty and oversized coats foraged from their parents, he promised new suits if they attended regularly for a year. Others he delighted by taking them on picnics in the woods south of the city and running foot races with them. When rocketing enrollments — inside of a year there were over a thousand students — forced a division into classes, he let the youngsters pick their own teachers, a guarantee of a popular faculty. When all else failed, he could be direct. Once he singled out a fractious adolescent and led him into a clothes closet, while directing an assistant to lead a hymn, fortissimo. The sacred strains muffled sounds of combat. Presently, master and disciple emerged, red-faced and sweating. The boy was thereafter an exemplary scholar. Candy, spankings, romps and bribes — it was all one to Moody. What did it matter if "undignified" allurements were used, provided they were legitimate? If the boys and girls, given a taste of the gospel, were converted, they would need no bribes to be good thereafter, which was the thing that counted, the result. Thirty-five years later, Moody would use exactly the same logic to justify the holding of gospel meetings in a circus tent on the Chicago World's Fair grounds and the advertising of prayer meetings on the theatrical pages of the papers.

Moody's persuasive gifts were put to another test when it came to raising money for his mushrooming school. Early in its life, he looked up John V. Farwell, then beginning a great commercial career in Chicago, and invited him to a session. At its end, Farwell, to his astonishment, heard himself nominated for superintendent and elected with a roar of acclamation from the children. He gallantly accepted, however, and supported the school liberally. Moreover, he got many of his millionaire friends to do the same. In the meantime, Moody was not neglecting the smaller donors, who deserved their chance to do something for God. Needing ten thousand dollars to put up a new building, he issued forty thousand shares in the North Market Sabbath School at a quarter apiece, and sold them with ease. By 1860, the school was a Chicago institution. Lincoln visited it on his last trip to the city, shortly after the election.[21] Moody himself was almost as much of an institution. He even had a special pass on the Chicago, Burlington and Quincy Railroad, so that he could always get back from his out-of-town business junkets for his Sunday work.[22]

Meanwhile, he had opened up another front. Moody was almost a charter member of the Chicago branch of the Y.M.C.A. An organization of laymen which put the emphasis on Christianity in practical work was virtually invented for men like him. He began by regular attendance at noonday prayer meetings, unmercifully interrupting speakers who ran over the allotted speaking time of three minutes.[23] Then, just as he had stood in front of the shoe store casting for customers, he went down to the entrance of the meeting hall and brought in Chicagoans hurrying about their lunchtime affairs.[24] Then he was made head of the Visitation Committee, in charge of seeking out households which needed both charity and enlightenment in the gospel. It was a great opportunity to continue his pursuit of potential Bible students. He wound up and down rickety staircases, into roach-ridden kitchens, through alleyways clogged with offal, past saloons, gambling dives and amusement halls, steadily pressing his query to all: "Are you a Christian?" In one year he visited over six hundred families. He got a pony, to cover more ground, and thus he rode, the new-model circuit rider, through the urban wilderness.[25]

Four or five years of this apprenticeship went by, and then he reached another major turning point. Sometime in 1861, he gave the truest evidence of his conversion. He abandoned business. It was, unknown to them, a joyful day for any competitors who might one day have crossed his path. It was a black one for Satan.

In part, the decision came about because the pace was killing even for Moody. Every evening saw a meeting, a series of visits, a fund-raising conference or the like, and Sundays were evenings multiplied half a dozen times. More than this, however, religious work was Moody's passion, and he could not do things by halves. He could have stuck to business, become a fleshy deacon, taken his Sunday-school classes and poured money into the collection basket, making the best of both worlds. There would have been no conflict in his mind between Christian and business principles, for he saw none. But when he gave, he gave all of himself (and demanded as much from others). So, in spite of his engagement to Emma Revell, he left his employer and set out to live on savings and whatever donations came his way.[26] Moody had grown in five years. Money had meant a great deal to a hard-driven farm boy. Now, however, he was sublimely unconcerned with money for himself. Actually, in later life, he was a "millionaire" many times over. He had only to conceive of a religious institution or program, and he had the pick of a dozen private fortunes at his command to make it a reality. But the early days were hard. For a time, as his savings disappeared into his various enterprises, he slept in the prayer-meeting room of the Y. and lived on cheap restaurant food. He depended for a personal income on whatever the financial sponsors of his work chose to give him, and his fortunes fluctuated wildly. Once, for conducting an out-of-town Bible-study meeting, he got a cheap, gold-headed cane, which he wryly put away, as he said, until he should become a D.D.[27] About 1868, his business friends, on the other hand, gave him a free lease on a completely furnished home.[28] Yet, two years later, he turned up in a rare mood of discouragement in the wholesale grocery house of B. F. Jacobs, in a threadbare coat, confessing that he had left the house without a bite of food in it, and would perhaps have to "give it up" after all. (Jacobs came to the rescue with a ham, flour, butter and potatoes.) [29] Even on the verge of an evangelistic tour of England, in 1873, which made his national reputation, he was dead broke. A surprise last-minute gift of five hundred dollars was all that made it possible for him to sail.[30]

Despite all these ups and downs, however, Moody felt an enormous freedom once he had given up business, and his efforts redoubled. The outbreak of the Civil War opened a new avenue of effort. Various church agencies joined to form the United States Christian Commission. It was a mobile combination of Y.M.C.A., Red Cross and canteen. Its activities ranged from first aid in the front lines to providing Christmas dinner for shattered men in the hospitals. Moody became a delegate and shortly made it known that he regarded the commission's job as one of saving souls, first and foremost. Holding tent prayer meetings and distributing pocket Bibles were of more importance to him than writing letters of condolence or washing sick men's faces. The justification for care of the wounded was evangelistic — to get a soldier's ear for the time it took to bring the message of salvation. Once, aboard a Tennessee river steamer, splashing up to the field of Shiloh with a load of food and medicines to relieve the casualties who swamped the pitiful army medical facilities, Moody shocked some of his fellow delegates. He said that if he found a dying man already "saved," he would leave him to go on to another who needed to be kept alive while there was a chance of his conversion.[31] This apparent hardness was a paradox in Moody, and at the same time a key to his strength.

Moody's statement was revealing because, in a sense, some of his Y.M.C.A. activity, too, had been a kind of first-aid service consisting in binding up the wounds of those who had fallen in the economic battle. In that, too, his philosophy had been the same. Charitable work was not an end in itself, but one more means of reaching men to prepare them, one at a time, for final judgment. Free groceries were calling cards by which the missionary got an introduction to sinners who had strayed from the church. Once a charity case became a "child of God," Moody was completely convinced that his economic problems would solve themselves, for it was impossible that a righteous man should beg for his bread in an America of limitless opportunity. Moody had no concern with any supposed responsibility of Christians to revamp the social order. So, in a sense, just as he would pass by a dying soldier already "saved," he would ignore the economic hardships of the already converted. "Seek ye first the kingdom of God," said the New Testament, "and all things shall be added unto you." Moody was not a callous man, but he believed this with all his heart.

Yet he had to take his converts where he found them, and finding them in Chicago slums or in army hospitals, he was working elbow to elbow with other Christians, some of whom were more concerned with a general reform of the ethics of competition. Evangelism among the hungry could also prove to be a training ground for Christian social work, or even Christian socialism. It did not prove so for Moody, but the work undoubtedly broadened his toleration of other viewpoints. Later on, he would draw added power from his ability to work with churchmen of almost any persuasion. The Christian Commission was one more force shaping him towards this end.

So, in camps around Chicago, and in half a dozen or more visits to the front, Moody continued his pursuit of cardplayers, drinkers, and lost souls in uniform.[32] Sometimes he got help from unexpected quarters. There was one Indiana colonel who hated to have his regiment outdistanced in any kind of competition. Hearing one day that there had been twenty conversions in a neighboring regiment, he bellowed for his adjutant and ordered him to detail the same number of his men for baptism immediately! [33]

The war drew to a close, but Moody's pace was hardly slackened. By 1864, the North Market Sabbath School was plucking brands from the burning at a lively annual rate. The school made efforts to distribute its graduates among the local churches, but many of them had no church background and no interest in Christian comfort except when it was dispensed by their big and bearded superintendent. Finally, a church was organized, technically under the Congregationalists, but actually independent and interdenominational. Moody was its "unordained" minister. Other divines occasionally were called in to administer the sacraments, but otherwise Moody was the pastor. From his headquarters in a new building on Illinois Street he organized prayer meetings, Bible-study groups, missions and services, and made flying visits to his down-at-heels congregation.[34] In a sense, Moody as a lay pastor was a city equivalent of the "uneducated" ministers of the backwoods, half a century before. Freed from technically "sacred" responsibilities, he could pour more of his energy into "secular" ones. As always, those energies were immense. An officer of the church remembered a breathless New Year's Day when he followed Moody on no fewer than *two hundred* calls. The pastor would burst into a room and blurt out in one breath, "I am Moody; this is Deacon DeGolyer; this is Deacon Thane; this is Brother Hitchcock. Are you well? Do you all come to church and Sunday-school? Have you all the coal you need for the winter? Let us pray." He would drop to his knees, utter twenty words of prayer, and then his bulky form would be clattering down the staircase to the next call.[35]

In the meantime, the vigorously growing Y.M.C.A. was spilling out of its rented quarters. While prayers were going up from leased auditoriums and vacant social halls for more seemly quarters, some members thought of the expedient of choosing Moody as president of the organization. This was done, and immediately Moody took hold of the problem in a way that made it clear that in abandoning business, he had not forgotten business methods. He organized a stock company with twelve trustees, chosen from the blue book of Chicago's wealth, and including B. F. Jacobs, George Armour, Cyrus McCormick and John Farwell. One hundred thousand dollars' worth of stock was issued. The trustees were to hold the building, rent portions of it out when they were not needed by the Y., and use the proceeds to retire the stock gradually. On September 29, 1867, the building stood finished in the heart of the business district, on Madison Street — complete . with auditorium for three thousand, offices, living quarters for transients, a library and prayer-meeting rooms. They named it after Farwell, but it was Moody's, and he made a speech of dedication which showed why he was called "the lightning Christian."

> When we stop trying to enlarge our work for the Lord and raise more money for it, we shall become stale and stupid, like some of the rich institutions of the Old World, which are set-

tling down into indolence and dying of dry rot, because they are "full and have need of nothing." We must ask for money, *money*, MORE MONEY at every meeting; not for the support of the Association — as it now is — but to enlarge its operations.[36]

These words could have been a credo for any businesslike American Christian in 1867. Moody had an unexpected opportunity to test them shortly. Farwell Hall burned down in the following year, and the ashes were hardly cold before he was out collecting subscriptions for its replacement. It went up in the following year — only to become a victim, like the Illinois Street church, of the great Chicago fire of 1871.

At the end of twelve years in Chicago, Moody had plenty of cause for pride. Having arrived with empty pockets and a stumbling tongue, he had become a one-man civic showpiece. On his own he had built a thriving Sunday school; he was the drive wheel of the city's Y.M.C.A.; he had his own church, to all intents and purposes, which he ran without restraint from any synod, conference or association. He moved freely and easily among the wealthy residents of the town, and he had a vast and loyal following among its commoners. He could rest now, but it was not in him to rest. A new vision had been opened to him, and he was ready for another change — this time, as he had gone from business to religious organization before, he would enter the field of evangelism.

Just when this goal took possession of Moody's mind is not clear. The one certain thing was that each year in Chicago brought new self-discovery and increasing confidence. Moody's work with the Y.M.C.A. and the Sunday-school movement involved him in dozens of conventions annually, as county, state and national organizations met to ponder new ways of serving the Lord. Somehow he found at these that despite his lack of formal education he could speak crisply and with results, prodding a meeting towards a goal, whereas others were apt to let it ramble. While this apprenticeship in administration was going on, his duties at the Illinois Street church plunged him further and further into lay preaching. There were Bible lessons to be gone over with the Sunday-school teachers and students, lectures at innumerable prayer meetings, and conversations at all hours with those whom he had aroused to self-examination with his repeated question, "Are you a Christian?" which he put indiscriminately to friends and strangers alike, until it was a trademark. (One story had it that a man snapped in response, "It's none of your business." "Oh, yes it is," was the reply. "Then you must be D. L. Moody," said the other.) In order to find material for these efforts, Moody plunged into the study of the Bible — not commentaries, or exegeses, but the unadorned testimony of the hallowed chapters themselves. He had no time for any other reading, but he poured himself so furiously into this one task that he knew the Bible — in his own interpretation, at least — as he knew the cow paths of Northfield. He was a one-book man, but of that one book he was absolute master and servant.[37]

Slowly his skill grew, until other ministers of Chicago swallowed their distrust of his clipped speech and his occasional "aint's" and his slurred "Dan'ls" and "Sam'ls" and invited him to their pulpits occasionally for a Bible lecture.[38] Facing an audience from the front of the room, he became more and more the victim of what he called his "passion for souls." [39] In return, he invited other preachers to speak in his own church, and without their knowledge, allowed them to conduct a seminar in homiletics. Sitting on a front bench himself, apparently sunk in concentration, Moody watched and listened to them all — the long-winded ones, the unctuous ones, the essayists who paraded their knowledge, the thunderers who shook their fists and slammed the pulpit rail, those who spoke meltingly and wooed the congregation, and those who aimed their eyes and words at an invisible spot on the ceiling. He learned what he wanted to avoid, and what he liked, and he tested his lessons when his own turn to speak came. Little record remains of his early preaching efforts.[40] As a convention speaker, however, he was growing more formidable. He turned one Illinois Sunday-school convention into a revival. At another, he was accused of dominating the proceedings, and it was said that he reduced the delegates to tears by his defense. He per-

suaded one assembly of Y.M.C.A. workers in Boston to reverse
a decision they had adopted by a large majority only that morning, and at a Christian convention in Missouri, he was chosen to
be chairman, as the only man acceptable to both ex-Confederate
and ex-Union sympathizers.[41]

By 1867, he was still little more than a layman of unusual vim.
Within the next five years, however, three portentous things
happened. His preaching style was revolutionized, he found a perfect musical collaborator, and he experienced a rather dramatic
second conversion, pressing him overwhelmingly forward to seek
for souls. After these three events, he was fully ready to impress
himself on American church history.

In the first of those turning-point years, 1867, he made a trip
to England, mostly to see how Sunday schools and Y.M.C.A.
branches were operated on the other side of the Atlantic. But,
in addition, he wanted to learn something about the Plymouth
Brethren. The Brethren were Englishmen who had withdrawn
from the Church of England in 1830, offended by its "formalism
and worldliness." They had no ordained preachers, they expected
the millennium shortly, and they took all their ordinances from
the New Testament, which they interpreted literally.[42] Obviously
a religious movement resting on a lay ministry and a Bible taken
in its plainest meaning had a great appeal to him. Later, he would
make special trips to Philadelphia and New York to talk with
Brethren who had emigrated to America.[43] There was a strange
need in Moody, suddenly, to find others like himself — perhaps
to reassure himself that he was not some uncouth freak in the
world of professional men of God. He spoke to Charles Haddon
Spurgeon, a Baptist whose plain-spoken evangelistic sermons year
after year jammed the Metropolitan Tabernacle in London. He
looked up the gigantic orphanage created by George Müller, a
Prussian-born English preacher who, like Moody, took no salary
from his congregation and lived on donations.

It was not Moody's way to toady to the English, however.
He was American to the core. To Farwell, he wrote in complaint
of the poor management of English Sunday schools, which were
"very slow and behind the times." Even Spurgeon's school, with-

out heat and with unpainted rooms, struck him as deficient. "We are one hundred years ahead of them, at least," was his opinion. His idea of an exceptional Englishman was the Liverpool business-man who went to "the circuses," hired a hall at his own expense every Sunday and preached to the "low and vicious crowds."[44] And if Moody found the English slow, they must have felt that he himself was a little breath-taking. At a London meeting of the Sabbath-school Union, he was invited to speak. The custom was to get a speaker onto the floor by having him move or second a formal resolve. Moody was chosen to move a formal vote of thanks to the Earl of Shaftesbury, who was presiding, and was introduced as an "American cousin, the Reverend Mr. Moody, of Chicago." Up rose a confirmed Yankee to jar the hall.

> The chairman has made two mistakes. To begin with I'm not the "Reverend Mr. Moody" at all. I'm plain Dwight L. Moody, a Sabbath school worker. And then I'm not your "American cousin." By the grace of God I'm your brother. . . .
>
> And now about this vote of thanks to the "noble Earl" for being our chairman this evening. I don't see why we should thank him any more than he should thank us. When at one time they offered to thank our Mr. Lincoln for presiding over a meeting in Illinois, he stopped it. He said he'd tried to do his duty and they tried to do theirs. He thought it was an even thing all around.[45]

Under the circumstances, it would have appeared that England left little impression on Moody. But a decisive influence was to follow him back across the ocean. Among the Plymouth Brethren was an English evangelist named Harry Moorehouse whom Moody had met briefly. He was not impressed with the youth-ful-looking Moorehouse, who was known as the "Boy Preacher." Shortly after Moody got back to Chicago, he received a note from Moorehouse, saying that he was in America and would like to preach in Moody's church when he got to Chicago. The idea was not appealing to Moody, but he planned to be out of town during the week end of Moorehouse's arrival, and so he told his deacons to call a Thursday night meeting and give Moorehouse the pulpit. If he did well, he might have Friday, too.

On Saturday morning, Moody bounced back into town and asked how things had gone. He learned that Moorehouse had preached both evenings on the same text, John 3:16: "For God so loved the world, that He gave His only begotten Son, that whosoever believeth in Him should not perish, but have everlasting life." Most likely with a New England "humph" of reserved judgment, Moody asked what Moorehouse had said. "Well," was the reply, "he tells the worst sinners that God loves them." Moody was triumphant. "Then he is wrong," he snapped.

That was a natural answer for him to make. Moody was fundamentally a humane man, but almost all his religious associations had been with churches and ministers whose main concern was pointing out the wages of sin. A certain Puritan grimness had lingered over his Northfield boyhood (though his mother's church was, on paper at least, Unitarian). The new evangelistic emphasis on God's love and His anxiety to redeem the fallen, as it was creeping into the sermons of someone like Henry Ward Beecher, had not yet touched the founder of the North Market Sabbath School.

Now, however, he went to hear Moorehouse, whom the deacons had asked again for Sunday night. To Moody's surprise, he chose the same text. What was more, he had asked the audience to bring Bibles with them and follow the sermon. Wide-eyed, Moody listened as he "just took that whole verse, and then went through the Bible from Genesis to Revelation to prove that in all ages God loved the world. God had sent prophets and patriarchs to warn us, and then He sent His Son, and after they killed Him, He sent the Holy Ghost. I never knew up to that time that God loved us so much. This heart of mine began to thaw out; I could not keep back the tears. It was like news from a far country."

For three succeeding nights, Moorehouse preached on that same text. "He just beat that truth down into my heart," Moody later remembered. "I used to preach that God was behind the sinner with a double-edged sword. . . . I preach now that God is behind him with love, and he is running away from the God of Love." [46] Moody thus made a complete break with any lingering remnants of predestination. The result was significant, for it led him to tell his listeners that conversion was not hard, but easy. Why should one agonize over his sins, when forgiveness was full, free and waiting? The hell-fire had been slowly simmering out of evangelism — at least out of successful popular evangelism — since frontier days. Moody could now take full advantage of the change.

The second step in Moody's final polishing for his life work came in 1870. It was even more of a dividing line for Ira D. Sankey, whose life up to that year was exemplary only in its normality. Born of a Methodist family which moved to Newcastle, Pennsylvania, when he was a boy, he had enjoyed an up- bringing both pious and satisfying. In the Methodist Sunday school it had been discovered that he had a pleasant and winning voice for singing hymns. He got some elementary training in piano and organ at home and sang in various local choirs. During the Civil War he served with a three-months regiment in Maryland, organized a soldiers' gospel-singing group, and returned home to take a job as a collector of revenue for the Federal Government. Sankey was basically a conventional man, the kind given in later life to wearing mutton-chop whiskers, silk vests and high hats, and to patting small boys on the head. In 1870 he was thirty years of age, properly married and on the way to honorable and pensioned retirement. But he was also a member of the Newcastle Y.M.C.A., and in June of that year, he went as a delegate to a convention of Y. workers in Indianapolis.[47]

Sankey came late to a morning meeting and found it somewhat dispiritedly dragging through a hymn. A minister present who knew him asked if he would sing the next one. Obligingly, Sankey rose and delivered "There Is a Fountain Filled with Blood." A few moments later a broad-chested man pushed over to his side as the session closed. Sankey recognized him as "Mr. Moody," the well-known Chicago Y.M.C.A. president. Without wasting time on formalities, the Chicagoan shot questions at Sankey. Where did he live? Was he married? What did he do for a living? Sankey told him. The response came like a lightning bolt. "Well, you will have to give that up; I have been looking for you for eight years." Briefly he explained that he needed a singer in his church and possibly for traveling work, to fill intervals in his talks. Sankey was the best he had heard and he wanted him. Feebly, the Pennsylvanian asked for time to consider.

The next morning there was a note for him, asking if he would meet Moody at a certain street corner at six that evening. Sankey showed up, curious and uncertain. Moody was on hand to greet him briskly, and then he disappeared into a nearby store and came out dragging a dry-goods box. Keeping one eye on the crowds of workmen straggling home to supper, he climbed on it and began to address the crowd. In a few minutes, he had a knot of spectators at his feet. It was old, familiar work to him. Sankey was a little less sure of himself, but remorselessly, Moody announced that they would now have a hymn, and pushed his brand-new acquaintance up onto the box. Sankey opened his mouth and sang. In another moment or so, a sidewalk service was in full blossom. Moody then, in a few barking sentences, adjourned it to the nearby Academy of Music, where the convention of Y. workers was in session. Seizing the arm of Sankey, he began to sing, and they marched up the street, two portly Pied Pipers, with a crowd tagging at their heels, while above the rattle of wagons rose the strains:

> Shall we gather at the river
> Where bright angel feet have trod;
> With its crystal tide forever
> Flowing by the throne of God? [48]

Sankey might as well have given up then and there. He was up against the demon persuader of his century, and he never had any real chance to say no. He managed to escape back to Newcastle, but it took Moody only six months, in his own phrase, to "pray him out of business." By the following winter, he and his family were living in Chicago, and he was alternating songs with Moody's anecdotes in the church on Illinois Street. [49]

Finding a gospel singer was not a stroke of innovation. More than one revivalist had already discovered that it was easier to sow the seed when the emotions were harrowed by music. A singing audience was less bored and critical, too. This was a matter of common knowledge. Moody might have been influenced by an example in his own Chicago, where D. W. Whittle, of the First Congregational Church, was holding successful sidewalk meetings with Paul P. Bliss, a Pennsylvanian with a homely genius for creating sentimental religious ballads. Whittle, like Moody, was a businessman, the superintendent of the Elgin watch works. They were the best of friends, and in due time, Whittle, like Moody, went into full-time evangelism.[50] But if Moody borrowed the idea of a "service of song," he was unusually lucky in the results, for Sankey was enormously affecting and effective. With him at his side, Moody was even more confident about venturing with the gospel message outside of Chicago, where he was known.

Events now hurried Moody towards a final decision. The Chicago fire burned out his church and school in 1871, and he hurried to New York to raise some money for their restoration. While there, he had some kind of reconsecration experience. Unlike earlier revivalists who kept minute clinical records of their souls' health, he was disinclined to speak of his feelings. For Moody, it was "almost too sacred an experience to name." He could only say, "God revealed Himself to me, and I had such an experience of His love that I had to ask Him to stay His hand." Once again he began his preaching, interrupted by the fire, and found that "hundreds were converted." Something had given him an enormous sense of power and finally overcome his reluctance to make a frankly evangelistic appeal — a reluctance born of self-consciousness over his poor schooling. In the spring of 1872, he made another trip to England. While there, he was invited to substitute in a London pulpit. He concluded with an invitation to all those who wished to "become Christians" to rise. Benches creaked and heads popped up throughout the church. Ultimately, four hundred new members were gathered in.[51]

This was the third sign from heaven. Moody was ready. The long training period in the back rooms of saloons, in basements and attics, and the days of sticking up posters and drumming funds were fulfilled. Three of Moody's ministerial friends in England invited him back the next year to hold evangelistic services. In June of 1873, he went, with Sankey. In two years, he was famous in two countries. The Lord had begun to use him to full capacity.

Nobody could have guessed, at the beginning of the trip, that it would be a success.[52] The Americans arrived to learn that two of the preachers who had invited them were dead. A tiny crack in the door was ajar, for Moody had in his pocket an old bid from the secretary of the Y.M.C.A. in York to speak to the young Christians of the city if he should happen to be in England again. Into this opening, Moody shoved a square foot. He and Sankey showed up in York and faced a skeptical crowd of young men who had come to see the Yankees perform.

At York they attracted an invitation from nearby Sunderland, and during a few weeks there the ball, amazingly, began to roll. Word filtered through evangelical circles of the two American gentlemen, the one with the Bible and the other with a small organ, who had a rather unique grasp on audiences. From Sunderland they went to Newcastle, where they worked like beavers to make themselves better known, holding as many as thirty-four meetings in one week. If the meetings fell dead on the market of public awareness, it would not be for lack of trying!

But they did not fall dead. By November, they had an invitation to Edinburgh, and two thousand listeners were showing up each night, struggling through bleak winter fogs to the various halls in the city which housed the meetings. The next spring, in Dundee, the weather allowed them to have outdoor meetings, where the audiences were double and triple those indoors. In the fall of 1874, they moved on Dublin. In the city's Exhibition Palace they drew as many as ten thousand nightly, in a city whose Protestant population was only forty thousand.

The winter of 1874-1875 saw them move into England. In the Free Trade Hall at Manchester, as many as fifteen thousand listened every night while Moody waved his Bible and told them that whosoever believed should have life eternal. In eight days in Birmingham, one hundred fifty-six thousand industrious Victorians heard Sankey, eyes closed and head leaning to one side as he played, sing the news that Jesus of Nazareth was passing by. By the time the evangelists reached Liverpool, they were in the wake of a tidal wave of press notices. It was easy to fill Victoria Hall with six thousand people for a noonday prayer meeting, the same number for an afternoon Bible lecture, and ten thousand at night.

On the ninth of March, 1875, they arrived triumphantly in London, where they remained for four months. The city had to be divided into districts and assaulted piecemeal. In south London's Camberwell Hall and in the Agricultural Hall in the north, ordinarily used for cattle shows, they filled acres of floor space with expectant sinners. They spoke and sang in Bow Road Hall in the Cockney neighborhoods of the East End, and in the fashionable West End nothing less than the Royal Opera House was at their disposal. The attendance figures were not exactly marvels of statistical accuracy. Often they were arrived at merely by multiplying the capacity of the hall by the number of meetings, and they took no account of the fact that thousands were repeaters, coming again and again to hear the two. Nevertheless, they must have reached a million and a half Londoners.[53] When they prepared to sail home in July, the naked fact was that in a day before radio, Moody and Sankey had reached some three or four million Scots and Britons, with no more sensational attractions than Bible stories and hymns easy enough to be memorized in two or three singings. It was an amazing demonstration of the part religion could play in popular culture.

The victory came in the teeth of wide-ranging opposition, from fundamentalist Scots who thought of Sankey's portable organ as an invention of the Deil, to the Marquis of Bath, who objected formally in the House of Lords when the rumor reached his ears that Moody was about to take his vernacular preaching into the guarded precincts of Eton.[54] (Eventually, a meeting was held, not in Eton, but nearby.) Nor did Moody's brusque ways always prove charming. One Y.M.C.A. delegation, calling upon him to invite him for a talk, was offended when he bustled in and asked their business without offering them seats.[55] Another time, a group of clergymen from the tony West End of London approached Moody and asked if, in view of their knowledge of conditions, he would let them arrange his schedule there. Pensively, Moody sucked the handle of his umbrella, and replied, "I wun't. No. I wun't leave myself in the hands of . . . no committee." [56]

It was no wonder, then, that some newspapers condemned Moody as a "ranter of the most vulgar type." Even the *New York Times* fired a shot from the rear, when it announced that it had credible information that Phineas T. Barnum had sent the evangelists to England, presumably as a sideline to his circus attractions. A criticism of this sort could be blunted by an action like that of thirty-six Chicago Christians who mailed an affidavit vouching for Moody to British church officialdom.[57] On the other hand, the recommendation of ministers was not enough to forestall the complaints of Marxists. Friedrich Engels, whose eye did not miss the fall of a single capitalist sparrow, later explained that the British *bourgeoisie* had imported the evangelists to increase the native supply of opium for the people. "Not content with his own native religious machinery," he said, John Bull "appealed to brother Jonathan, the greatest organiser in existence of religion as a trade, and imported from America revivalism, Moody and Sankey, and the like."[58]

By the end of the campaign, however, such criticisms could be safely ignored. The testimony of those thousands in exhibition halls and auditoriums all over the country was enough to bring the clergy over; after all, they remembered, it was a Christian duty to bring the good news of salvation to all men. Pious leaders like the Earl of Shaftesbury and William E. Gladstone lent their dignity to the cause, and by the time London was reached, respectability overflowed the meetings. The lights of the Royal Opera House gleamed on the shirt fronts and gowns of dukes and duchesses, and the Countess of Gainsborough went so far as to suggest that Queen Victoria herself attend. The reply was a frosty letter, declaring that "it is not the *sort* of religious performance which I like." [59] But if the Queen was not amused or impressed, her church was. At a farewell meeting, nearly two hundred ministers of the Church of England sat among Congregationalists, Baptists, Presbyterians, Methodists and clergymen of other denominations to give Moody and Sankey a homeward-bound blessing. Meanwhile, the hymns played by Sankey were issued by a British publisher, and the royalties amounted to thirty-five thousand dollars by the end of the tour. Moody and Sankey gave evidence of their good faith by signing the money over to a committee consisting of John Farwell, William E. Dodge and George Stuart. The revivalists never saw a cent of the proceeds from the hymnbooks, which eventually totaled more than a million dollars. The money went to the empire of Christian training schools and missions which Moody built up later in his life.[60]

Then it was the turn of America. Moody and Sankey returned in the summer of 1875, to find invitations pouring in, but their first need was rest. Moody came back to his mother's home in Northfield. Soon he bought an adjoining farm and made the little town his permanent base. He was modest, but he could enjoy the savor of coming to rest, as a national religious folk hero, among the townspeople who had known him as an undistinguished boy. He held some revival meetings in Northfield, and the neighbors delighted in finding themselves on the front pages of the New York press.[61] In October, he sallied forth to hold his first series of meetings in Brooklyn.

It was a big challenge. Brooklyn was a formidably churched city. On Sundays, its avenues were crowded with handsome rigs, carrying well-dressed parishioners to hear the amply rewarded sermons of Cuyler, Beecher and Talmage. Moody had no need to worry, though. The arrangements committee rented the Rink, a five-thousand-seat auditorium on Clermont and Vanderbilt avenues. For days before the opening on October 24, streetcar-company crews laid extra tracks to the doors. Special police were held in reserve, and *Harper's Weekly* saved an inside double page for a drawing. At 6 A.M. of the first day, the crowds were lined up for blocks. For the afternoon session, fifteen thousand were on hand, and when the doors swung open, an irresistible crush surged inward; women screamed, fainted, and grappled with their clothes torn; families were separated; and the straining policemen were lifted off their feet.[62] It was a great beginning for a city already accustomed to wonders. In the succeeding weeks, the mobs did not stop flocking to the Rink. Some of the New York papers sneered that this was "merely . . . entertainment." Even the *Independent*, the leading church paper in New York, was unhappy with Moody's grammatical stumbles and the fierce, rapid flow of his diction. He lacked, they said, "the mighty, convincing strength of Mr. Finney," and had "vastly less mental power." [63] But to masses of New Yorkers Finney was a long-forgotten name. He had been in New York forty years ago, and the age of journalism had gotten them accustomed to new sensations taking the place of old ones at a regular rate. There was, to be sure, one flaw. Moody wanted to reach the "unchurched," and the thousands who filled the Rink were for the most part members of congregations already. In vain Moody asked them to make room for the wayward and lost; in vain the committee gave tickets only to those who swore that they belonged to no church; in vain the press scolded "conscience-hardened professors" who would "rob their unconverted neighbors of their tickets." [64] The flocks of Brooklyn wanted to hear the new shepherd, and they came in headline-creating numbers until the end of his stay.

Philadelphia was next on the list. John Wanamaker, the department-store colossus of the city, had given the money to fit out a Pennsylvania Railroad freight warehouse for the occasion. It was jammed with chairs and fitted with lights; around its walls were hung banners with Scripture texts; extra doors in its bare wooden walls were cut to move the crowds in and out. The opening Sunday was one of pouring rain, but the faithful stood and shivered in Market Street and had the hall filled half an hour before the time to begin. For two months Moody drove himself at the usual pace. In one three-week stretch he spoke to thirty-eight meetings, with audiences totaling over one hundred fifty thousand. He lived, meanwhile, what would have been to others a double life — first addressing prayer meetings for the "fallen" and seeking out the eyes of shabby drunkards when he could find one who had crept into the back rows, and then retiring to the home of millionaire Wanamaker, whose personal guest he was. It should be noted that Wanamaker and John Keene, another wealthy Philadelphian, handled all the personal expenses of Moody and Sankey during those weeks.[65]

Then it was New York (after a day-long stopover at Princeton[66]) and the Hippodrome on Fourth Avenue and Twenty-sixth Street, a huge shed, once used by Barnum for his show, with a lingering atmosphere of sawdust and animal smells. Night after night, Moody and Sankey filled it with eleven thousand people for four months, until more than a half million had received the good news. And in New York, Moody stayed at the uptown Madison Avenue residence of Morris K. Jesup, a banker who was later to shower down two millions of his fortune on schools, orphanages, hospitals, settlement houses and museums.[67] There was no question about it. Evangelists might quote with approval those parables about the sins of great wealth. They might even say, with James, "Go to now, ye rich men, weep and howl for your miseries which will come upon ye." Nevertheless, successful revivalism rested squarely on the support of a part, at least, of the new class of postwar millionaires.

Moody took a breathing space once again in the summer of 1876, and moved back for a second triumphal homecoming to Chicago — this time to a special, barnlike wooden tabernacle built at Franklin and Monroe streets. The scenes were photographic copies of those in the East. Half an hour before meeting time, seats disappeared "like a field of wheat under a visitation of locusts," and when overflow meetings were announced for neighboring churches and halls, they were filled in minutes.[68]

In the spring of 1877, as he had gone back to Northfield and to Chicago with heralds to run before his chariot, he returned to Boston. There he was lampooned by one newspaper as badly as he ever got lampooned anywhere, but despite this, he had success enough to make the ghost of Lyman Beecher intensely happy. Henry F. Durant, the founder and treasurer of Wellesley College, led in marshaling financial support. The Boston pulpit stood behind him for the most part, and even Phillips Brooks, the Episcopalian minister of the ultrafashionable Trinity Church, labeled him a "good healthy religious influence," and to prove his opinion, conducted a service in Moody's absence one night.[69]

After Boston no great centers of influence were left to conquer. For a year after the campaign there, Moody worked in smaller New England cities — Burlington, Manchester, Concord, Providence, Springfield, Hartford and New Haven. In the fall of 1878, he began a six months' series of meetings in Baltimore. The succeeding winter saw another protracted effort in St. Louis. A year later, winter found Moody and Sankey touring the Pacific Coast, with a major stopover in San Francisco. Finally, in the spring of 1881, they sailed on a second two-year trip to Great Britain.[70]

In eight years, Moody had accomplished the rejuvenation of the revival. He had spoken to millions. His converts were as the stars of heaven for multitude, though he sensibly refused to count them. Any American who read a newspaper was likely to be, at the very least, familiar with his name. Few Americans, church-going or otherwise, could fail to identify at least the opening stanzas of the hymns most frequently used by Sankey in the meetings. The names of Moody and Sankey, joined indissolubly together, were a kind of public trademark for a certain type of religious performance.

All this was achieved in the midst of the urban and scientific upheavals which were proving so unsettling to the churches of the seventies. Moody brought millions out to listen to religious messages untouched by any revelations from the laboratory. Even more impressively, he transferred the excitement of the still lingering small-town revival to the metropolis. New Yorkers and Chicagoans jammed the streetcars to hear him, in preference to other sensations, just as if they had been villagers, starved for any kind of novelty, in Finney's day. Moody made clear what he had known all along: the American-born, middle-class urbanite of his day was still a villager under the skin. The genius of Moody lay in the way in which he took advantage of the fact.

Moody did not invent the professional revival. Men like Caughey, Hammond, Parker and Knapp had done that. But

Moody adapted it to contemporary America. He had a feel for
the gigantic and, above all, for the newly found power of mass
communication. (How his eyes would have sparkled at a television set!) He could organize and consolidate like a superman-
ager. He could present his message in the brisk and simple terms
of a salesman who trusted his product and knew his customer —
and was, in fact, a replica of him. He crossed an old institution
with new techniques and produced a spectacular hybrid. He
never knew that it contained its own self-destroying flaws.

Moody's campaigns were heroically drilled, financed and organized. Although he himself did not make the preliminary arrangements in the cities he visited, his spirit dominated the preparations. The campaign in Philadelphia in 1875 was a good example. To begin with, he refused to come until all the ministers
in the city's evangelical churches invited him. That laid the basis
for a unified effort. Some weeks before the opening date, the
co-operating clergy met to draft the invitation and to put a sub-
committee to work on a variety of business preparations. The hall
had to be found and rented, advertisements placed, announce-
ments made, and posters and tickets printed.[71] William G. Fischer,
a piano dealer, gathered a volunteer choir of three hundred voices
and drilled them like a righteous army in selections from the
hymnbook compiled by Sankey. Ushers were chosen and trained,
along with a new breed of Christian helpers called "inquiry room
workers." In the simpler days of Nettleton, the revivalist had
followed conscience-stricken members of the audience to their
homes, in company with their pastor, for private conversation
and prayer. Now it was necessary for listeners concerned with
their souls to move into smaller quarters, after a mass meeting,
where individual ministers, and sometimes laymen, could answer
questions, quote texts, and guide them gently but unerringly
towards union with a church. The inquiry room was not Moody's
invention. Finney had used something like it long before, when
he was in New York. But Moody made it a characteristic feature
of all his campaigns, and the inquiry workers, like the choir and

ushers, became part of a smoothly operating team which, from beginning to end, never allowed the audience a moment of confusion or distraction.[72] All of this took money — thirty thousand dollars went into the eight weeks' work in Philadelphia.[73] Moody needed Wanamakers and Jesups to finance him. He took no collections at meetings, and his personal compensation was given to him by the sponsors of a campaign.

During a campaign, however, Moody himself took charge of conventions for "Christian workers," which were in effect workshops in organized revivalism. The topics were crisp and practical — "How to Conduct Prayer Meetings," "How to Expound and Illustrate the Scriptures," "The Training of Young Converts" or "How Should the Music Be Conducted in the Lord's Work?"[74] Over these, the evangelist presided like a good-humored professor among excitable freshmen, spraying pungent bits of tactical advice in every direction. His eye for detail was inescapable. He told his disciples to keep windows open and the mouths of long-winded brethren closed. Controversial questions were to be side-stepped or settled by reference to the Bible, and never anything else. Meetings getting out of hand should be broken into with a hymn. For hecklers and bores, for drunks and crying children, for every kind of contingency he had some remedy. Above all, things must be kept *moving* — talks short, songs frequent and adjournments punctual. It was ideal advice for church workers in cities which no longer had time for leisurely two- and three-day camp meetings, and where souls had to be saved for God on schedule, like everything else.[75] A perceptive newspaperman caught the idea as he watched Moody run through a service in New York.

> The meetings are opened and closed promptly at the preappointed hour; there is not even a minute of time lost during the meeting by delays; his own prayers are brief, very earnest, and directly to the point. . . . Indeed . . . Mr. Moody . . . opens a meeting as though the audience were the stockholders of a bank to whom he was about to make a report. He has the air of a businessman to whom time is extremely valuable, and slow and tedious people are evidently a trial to him.[76]

An evangelistic sermon delivered like a stockholders' report was not a handicap in an America whose business was business. Moody was also a businessman who knew the uses of publicity. Among the hundreds of letters which he scrawled off in a large, energetic hand — letters misspelled half in ignorance and half in haste — were directives to his Chicago church and Sunday-school lieutenants, warning them to keep their lectures and meetings in plain sight of busy men and women.

> I would not spend mony on the St Cars but if you can get Posters up on the Churches & in shop windows it will be a good thing & get people to send stamped envelopes & use the press you will get out your tickets in that way & 90/c will use them if they send for them & then get as many as you can to push them in their churches Prayer meeting nights & Saturday noon at the Y.M.C.A. &c.[77]

So the news of salvation was posted everywhere, even on the amusement pages and on billboards where Satan flaunted the attractions of the world. What did it matter where a sinner's eye caught the message, once he was converted.

When the curious had been brought into the hall, Moody was doggedly insistent that already-saved Christians present to them a united front. The audiences might be divided for special meetings, of young and old, or men and women, in order to intensify or adapt the message here and there and create a fellow feeling among listeners. But if the armies of the unconverted were to be divided and attacked in detail, the Lord's battalions must be concentrated. It was true that his advice to converts never varied from "Join some church at once." [78] He was not particular, however, about which church. He kept his own theology simple enough to embrace almost any evangelical viewpoint and drew his examples exclusively from the Bible, deftly avoiding any entanglement in creeds and platforms. Even his techniques were adapted to this end. The inquiry room was substituted for the old-fashioned "anxious bench," where the awakened sat in public view, mainly because some denominations disliked the bench. Once a minister got a convert into his own church he might indoctrinate as he pleased, but Moody believed his own statement: "Evangelists are just to proclaim the gospel." [79]

Above all, the churches were to work. "Now's the time to be doers of the word," he shouted to a Chicago audience. "Let Christians wake up and go to work." [80] His own schedule during a revival was a fearful thing to contemplate — up before dawn for study, two or three prayer meetings, lectures, or training sessions with workers, the large evening meeting, and often as not a talk in the inquiry room afterwards. Every odd moment was crammed with correspondence and interviews. In spite of summer rests at Northfield, even Moody's enormous physique was eventually burned out. His heart failed at sixty-two. But, as he put it himself, his gift was "to get things in motion." [81] He fought Satan as a railroad builder of his generation would have fought cautious bankers, slow-moving engineers and competitors.

The Moody pattern was a new one for some church organizers. It was to sweep all details into the field of observation, divide the job, unify the forces, and drive and drive and drive inexorably towards the goal. It was no wonder that the lords of industry listened to Moody and subsidized him. When a wealthy donor once was asked why he saw Moody freely, while other petitioners faced an impassable wall of secretaries and assistants, his answer was short and informative. "He is one of us." [82]

In gathering his crowds, then, Moody was "one of them" — a businessman in method, realistic to the core. His second contribution to revivalism was to simplify its exhortations. He reduced the warnings and invitations of his predecessors of a century to a few simple propositions that could be driven home with all the repetitive urgency given to advertising slogans and political catchwords. "Oh, I'm sick and tired of this essay preaching!" he snapped at a meeting near the end of his life.[83] Essay preaching was the fruit of theorizers and thinkers, those whom he could not abide as churchmen, though he might make room for them under his roof at Northfield as a host. What need was there for "essays," who had time to listen to essays, when no man knew how near the world was to final judgment? The up-to-date methods of the evangelist drew attention away from his thoroughly old-fashioned belief that the things of the world lasted for only a moment and were hardly worth considering. "We are strangers and pilgrims here, in this world," he cried to packed houses. "It is the height of madness to . . . run the risk of being called by God and have to answer without Him." [84] What point was there in fine-spun discussion of social and individual morals? Why should he, as a Philadelphia reporter said, "try to tell people how to live, when the important thing is to prepare them for death and the last judgment"? [85]

No, there was only one thing for an evangelist to say. There was Harry Moorehouse's old text, burned into Moody's heart. He that believed should have eternal life. It was single-minded, it was simple, and therefore it was infinitely marketable.

If it was simple for the preacher to say, was it difficult for the sinner to accept? Here again, Moody moved away from the revival's past, in a direction already marked out in the fifties and sixties. It was an easy thing to accept Christ, easier than the way of the transgressor. There was no need of anguish, suffering, or torments of introspection. "The way to be saved is not to delay, but to come and take — t-a-k-e, TAKE." Salvation was universally offered for the asking, and every man had his chance to ask, if he would only make up his mind. In London one night, Moody leaned over the platform railing and asked the crowd which among them would accept the promises of the New Testament. A jeering voice rang through the room: "I won't." The revivalist was not disconcerted, but triumphant. "It is 'I will' or 'I won't' for every man in this hall tonight. . . . *The battle is on the will, and only there.*" [86]

So a trail of progress culminated in Moody. Seventeeth-century Calvinism had taught in the strictest sense that man could not repent without God's special intervention. The frontier evangelists and Beecher and Taylor and Finney had said, in their different ways, that he could, if given a proper view of the gospel. Yet all of them had to fight the old system in its own language. They hurled words like "foreordination," "sanctification," "justification" and "election" at their congregations, like red-hot missiles.

And some of them had thought of conversion as the climax of a bitter struggle between terror and hope, rending the nervous system until shrieking or fainting brought precious relief.

Moody was under no such handicap. There was no intellectual barrier, raised by Calvin, to overcome. That was long since swept away. Preaching was not an exercise of mind, but an arrow of common sense shot to the heart, through pride, false sophistication, reluctance, or shame. No theology was needed, only a direct and straightforward appeal. So Moody, at an inquiry meeting, could, with consistency, climb on a chair and say:

"Who'll take Christ now? That's all you want. With Christ you have eternal life and everything else you need. Without Him you must perish. He offers Himself to you. Who'll take Him?"

Did it sound unfortunately like a salesman's final, jabbing thrusts against crumbling consumer resistance? Did Moody have a brisk air of getting the signature on the contract as he pressed on?

"Now let all inquirers and all who now will take Christ as their own for the first time, kneel down and take Him." [87]

If it did have a bargain-counter flavor, that was no handicap among the kind of men and women whom he wanted to reach. Moreover, Moody himself was too patently sincere, too dedicated, too big in every sense to carry any taint of cheapness. Yet somehow a change had come over popular religion. The preachers of the turn of the century had been spokesmen of a fearful God, holding the universe in the palm of His hand, and making the mountains skip like rams when He chose. It was hard to say whom Moody represented when he stood on a stool and waved his Bible, in perilous resemblance to a carnival hawker with a patent can opener.

The very largeness of Moody disguised some of the impact. Men of every hue of belief were drawn to him — Phillips Brooks, Lyman Abbott, Henry Drummond, a brilliant Scottish evolutionist, George Adam Smith, the Hebraist and Biblical scholar, Washington Gladden, an uncompromising fighter for social reform under Christian leadership. They filled pulpits for him, and he in turn allowed them to address crowds gathered by the magic of his name.[88] "Liberals" and "fundamentalists" could both claim him after his death.[89] He did not waste time in attacking critics. His own enormous faith insulated him from doubts, and his man-killing labors kept him too busy to speculate with his limited intellectual equipment. "If God says it, faith says, I believe it," was his talisman against skepticism.[90] But all of this disguised, rather than narrowed, the gulf between what he preached and genuine religious *thought*.

Ironically, his simple appeal was best adapted to modern "merchandising," and that was a part of his triumph. Yet the simpler he made the content of the revival, the further it got from the complexities with which his "modernist" friends were honestly grappling. Perhaps the millions who heard him gladly did so because they yearned for an echo of that simplicity which was disappearing with agrarian America. Neither he nor they liked to face the irony.

One other gift he had, that of language. The circuit riders of earlier times had translated the theology of Princeton, Yale and Harvard into the language of keelboat men and trappers. Moody, whose camp meetings had been held on street corners and in empty saloons, brought religion down to the level of those who read the popular magazines and the penny dailies, with their growing columns of jokes, their pen-and-ink sketches, and their interminable, serialized, tearful novels. The sermons of Moody were free of cant, of mustiness, of stilted archaisms wrenched from the context of the King James Version, and of pulpit archness. His specialty was vividness, directness and brevity. A Moody talk, rarely more than twenty minutes long, rested on two sets of props. First there were "Bible stories" — lively and vernacular, and sometimes barely saved from irreverence by the big man's instinctive taste. Then there were "illustrative anecdotes" which were often mawkish vignettes straight from the cheap literature of an extravagantly sentimental age.

The men and women of Moody's Bible were west Massachusetts farmers, speaking dialects that had a country sharpness. Some of them wandered to Jerusalem or Tarshish or Antioch, cities not easily distinguishable from Boston and Chicago. Every character whom Moody summoned from either Testament was life-size and American. Moody gave them movement and being with small touches that showed nothing less than untutored genius. When he spoke of Jews slaying the lambs on the eve of Passover, he wondered what the Egyptians thought "when they heard the bleating of the lambs — there must have been over two hundred thousand." Those lambs were real; the audience could hear them bleating; and two hundred thousand was a concrete number to get hold of with the imagination. What did it matter if the number was not in the Bible? Far from being a "literalist," Moody was impatient with the lack of detail in the work of the scribes and prophets, and glad to furnish information they had overlooked. What did a little invention matter, anyway, when "the whole teaching of this book is of one story, and this is that Christ came into the world, and died for our sins." [91] Unperturbedly Moody proceeded to give a matchless pungency and intimacy to the story. Christ, in forgiving those who persecuted him, said:

> "Yes . . . go, hunt up that man that spat in my face, tell him he may have a seat in my kingdom yet. Yes, Peter, go find that man that made that cruel crown of thorns and placed it on my brow, and tell him I will have a crown ready for him when he comes into my kingdom, and there will be no thorns in it. . . . Search for the man that drove the spear into my side, and tell him there is a nearer way to my heart than that." [92]

Belshazzar's feast was a vivid scene.

> As they were drinking out of those vessels of gold and silver . . . I don't know but what it was at the midnight hour, all at once came forth the fingers of a man's hand and began to write upon the wall . . . The king turns deathly pale, his knees shake together, and he trembles from head to foot. . . . That very night the army of Darius came tearing down the streets, and you might have . . . seen the king's blood mingling with the wine in that banquet hall. [93]

The casual reference to the midnight hour, the Persian army "tearing down the streets" like a village fire brigade, and the brilliant touch of the mingled blood and wine are the effects of a man with a natural gift. Moody was full of unexpected surprises. When Jesus called, "Lazarus, come forth," to the man in the grave, Moody pointed out, "it was a good thing He called him by name, for if He hadn't, all the dead men in that yard would have leaped up." [94] What combination of artistry and conviction could think of a detail like that? When Moody came to scenes which were even more susceptible to "translation," he could hold an audience breathless. The prodigal son became nothing more nor less than a farmer's boy who had gone to the city, as millions were doing in Moody's day, and gotten into trouble. He had wandered through "the billiard hall and the drinking saloon."

> At last his money is gone, and now his friends begin to drop off, one after another. He is not quite so popular as he was when he had plenty of money. He is getting a little shabby; his clothes are not so good as they were. He had a good wardrobe; but now he goes to the pawn-shop and he pawns his overcoat. I have seen a good many such young men in Philadelphia.[95]

Saint Paul, coming to Corinth, was a traveling evangelist, as Moody himself had been in more obscure days. "He had no influential committee to meet him on his arrival at the station, and conduct him to a fine hotel," Moody said. He had to "find cheap lodgings in some alley," and after all his pains, a group deliciously described as a committee "took him down to a cross street and gave him thirty-nine stripes." [96] And the crowds winced as they saw the apostle ducking under the blows at the intersection nearest to Moody's tabernacle.

Story by story, Moody worked his way through from Genesis to Revelation, turning the gospel which was the core of Protestantism into popular drama. It was a Bunyanesque performance, but this was a Yankee Bunyan, and he preached, not to seventeenth-century English weavers and tinkers, but to American clerks and railroad conductors and farmhands of the seven-

ties. They understood him, and even those better educated caught
something of his magic, as a New York editor did in 1876.

> We think delicious his "had ought to have done," and his
> "they come and said"; his "you was there" . . . his "meracles"
> and his "heavun"; his "Ja-eye-rus's" daughter, and his "Ca-eye-
> phas" the high priest. We have come to desire his frequent
> "thank Gods," his oft-recurring "but thens"; his interlocutory
> ejaculations, and his boxing gesticulations. . . . And we shall
> not soon forget his incomparable frankness, his broad undenom-
> inationalism, his sledge-hammer gestures, his profuse diction,
> which stops neither for colons nor commas; his trueness, which
> never becomes conventional; his naturalness, which never
> whines; his abhorrence of Phariseeism . . . his mastery of his
> subject, his glorious self-confidence, his blameless life, and his
> unswerving fealty to his conscience and to his work.[97]

So he passed his test with at least some of the literati. What was
more important to him, he succeeded with his great middle-class
listening body. Moody's audiences were his absolutely. He knew
them and he controlled them. He could and did reduce them
to tears, over and over again, by drawing on the great reservoir
of family sentiment in America's late Victorian period. God, the
all-patient, if all-powerful, Father, wanted nothing so much as to
forgive his erring children before welcoming them home. The
theme lent itself to infinite variations, all of them irresistible.

What mother could withstand the story of the Englishwoman
who found her lost son working as a chimney sweep and took
him to her arms, all black and sooty as he was, covering his
little head with kisses? Through the sobs, a woman could hardly
hear the voice of the evangelist explaining that God welcomed
sinners even blacker with equal warmth. What father could not
put himself in the position of the aging man who said to a wayward youth, "My boy, you are just killing me, as you have killed
your mother. These hairs are growing whiter, and you are sending me, too, to the grave"? What hardened sinner wanted to
flout the love of God as that young man was scorning his
father's? [98] What parent of either sex did not melt, in an age

when few families did not lose one or two children to disease, when Moody's voice took on the tones of a little boy on his deathbed, telling a sorrowful father, "When I go to heaven, I will go right straight to Jesus, and tell Him that ever since I can remember, you have tried to lead me to Him"? [99] Even a strong man was permitted to blow his nose loudly at the tale of the mortally wounded soldier gasping, "Here. Here. Here," in an effort to answer to his name when the roll was called up yonder.[100]

Parting and death were real terrors to that generation. The sentimentality which overflowed in the short stories of both the popular and religious presses,[101] however mawkish it might be, had a foundation in real anguish. The prospect of a family reunion in heaven was more tempting than anything held out by the prophets of "realism." Since only the "saved" would meet on that beautiful shore, there was a genuine incentive to believe and to be converted. Moody knew this; he believed it himself. He knew the evangelist's prize secret, which was that the gospel must be presented in the terms and images of the widest popular currency. What the fear of hell-fire had been in an earlier day, bathos and nostalgia were to Moody's. Without thinking too much about it, he made the most of them. His choice of Sankey was enlightened, for the religious ballads which Sankey intoned were mostly about wandering sheep and the perils of the darkness and a bright land of happiness far away.[102] Their simple words and melodies were of the music-hall variety, and their wistfulness set the proper melting mood for the surrender to Christ.

Moody was himself something of an ideal Victorian father image. His own sentimental stories could bring tears to his eyes, but a moment later he was the brisk man of affairs, standing for no nonsense. Long-winded guest speakers found themselves interrupted in mid-flight by a call for a hymn. Ushers were briskly directed to remove a hysterical woman, while Sankey was summoned to distract attention with a solo. An inattentive listener was likely to hear Moody suddenly announce that salvation was offered to all — even to the young man chattering and disturbing others in the third row. Once a six-year-old girl in Richmond, to her horror, heard the preacher announce that "the little girl in blue in the front bench" would start the hymn "Rescue the Perishing" for them all. Stiffly, she sat mute while Moody turned a kind, but unrelenting, gaze on her and said, "Now, little girl. Now!" And somehow, because it was unthinkable that this man should not have his way, Ellen Glasgow found herself shrilling out the first verse of the hymn. She went on in unsanctified ways, but she never forgot the experience.[103] Moody practiced the perfect democracy. He would give a command to a prelate of the Church of England and to a Bowery derelict in the same tone, and would expect the same obedience. He got it, too. Oxford dons and country schoolma'ams, Princeton professors and street sweepers listened to him, and each felt that Moody was addressing him individually. To thousands of his converts, God must have looked uncannily like Dwight L. Moody.

In a sense, this was the fatal weakness. For more and more, evangelism came to center on Moody's stout and dominating figure. There was no one of equal stature to share the work, and as the eighteen-eighties succeeded the seventies, more and more of Moody's time went into efforts to consolidate the gains — to build up organizations and training schools which would carry on where he left off. Between 1880 and 1890 he became the driving force in three annual religious conferences on Christian work held at Northfield; he founded two preparatory schools and a Bible school; and his help was called for in a number of movements which others were struggling to launch. The Y.M.C.A. in Chicago still leaned heavily on him, and so did the successive pastors whom he brought to his church. His life revolved around letters and appeals for funds. He was actually going backwards from evangelism — back into Christian organizational labor, this time on a vaster scale. He was now the "lightning Christian" of the United States, as once he had been of Chicago. There was no longer time for the lengthy campaigns of the seventies. Once again, the original dynamic energy of the revival was absorbed into the less spectacular work of perpetuating its results.

So Moody's very strength was a handicap. In another way, too, the greatness of Moody had postponed certain problems, not solved them. His energy had breathed new vigor into revivalism, but his own refusal to recognize that Christianity had any broad social problems was pushing his followers further away each year from the main preoccupations of American thought. In the year of the 1877 railroad strikes, perhaps one could still believe that the questions involved would solve themselves if the owners and the trainmen both "found Jesus." By the time of the Haymarket affair, in 1886, it was harder to accept this as the *only* answer. In the days when slavery and intemperance and Sunday mails alone seemed to stand in the way of universal salvation, revivalism and reform had walked hand in hand. Now they were drifting apart, and Moody could not reconcile them.

Even this, however, was not the worst problem of all. What would happen when smaller men than Moody tried on his armor? With his breadth of spirit taken away, what was to prevent his vernacular presentation of the Bible from lapsing into vulgarity? What was to keep his use of anecdotes, in other hands, from turning into mere entertainment? Without his personal warmth, what could keep his distrust of scientific criticism of the Bible from decaying into bigotry? These things were to happen after his departure from the scene. Revivalism had been born in the marriage of Calvinism and the American frontier, introduced to the city by Finney, and nourished to gigantic growth by Moody. Now it was about to put on the trappings of vaudeville.

CHAPTER VIII

Yea, What Indignation . . .
Yea, What Zeal

THE students at the Moody Bible Institute looked expectantly at the speaker before them. It was the sixth of February, 1911 — just twenty-five years since Dwight Moody had conceived the notion of founding a school in Chicago to train lay evangelists and Christian workers in his image. Now, on this anniversary, they were to hear a talk by John M. Hitchcock, who had supervised the Sunday school of Moody's Chicago Avenue church and known him in the "old" days. To the young men and women of the institute, the founder was already a shadowy figure. It was nearly forty years since he had left Chicago for world-wide fame, and for a decade he had slept in death atop his favorite hill at Northfield. They were curious to know what stories they would hear of the great chief, father and counselor who was already on the way to becoming a legend.

Hitchcock did not disappoint them. He *did* tell stories of Moody's early days. And one of them contained a warning to fledgling followers of the revivalist. It concerned a time when Moody had helped in a series of "special meetings" in an Illinois town. His compensation for two weeks of driving work was a silver watch, worth about twenty dollars. Hitchcock looked steadily at the youthful faces before him.

> "I have, at the risk of wearying my hearers, told the story of the open face silver watch for the benefit of the Institute students, who are preparing for the evangelistic field, that they may not set their hearts too much upon the 'Almighty dollar'; and that when they hear of an evangelist visiting a place for

three or five or eight weeks and leaving with as many thousand dollars . . . or̲ of others who make it a condition that the money must be raised and in the bank subject to call before they will begin a work of evangelism, that the students may then recall the story of the 'open face silver watch.' . . .

"Mr. Chairman: Personally, I have grave fears that our modern evangelism is in peril. I fear it is imperiled from becoming commercialized, compromised, businessized, formalized, materialized, machineryized, and so systematized as to have reached the danger verge of becoming demoralized." [1]

What the students made of this is not recorded. Few seemed to be aware of the problem which Hitchcock had thrust out, and even this group was unlikely to suspect that Hitchcock's "grave fears" were not new in the institute. Seven years before, Reuben A. Torrey, the school's first superintendent, had complained in a letter about a "good deal of commercialism . . . creeping into our work and more and more machinery, and I fear, less dependence upon God." [2]

Yet even such men as Torrey and Hitchcock might have recoiled from the full impact of the truth. Once the idea had been accepted, in Finney's day, that the revival was something to be worked for, an inexorable march was under way towards business and formality and machinery in winning souls. Moody had hurried it along. In the twentieth century, the march led into a frightening landscape of commercialism. Year by year, as the "old-time" evangelical beliefs lost contact with contemporary reality, they needed a more lavish use of the "machinery" of modern persuasion to remain alive in the public mind. In 1911, in the world of popular ideas, the race went not only to the swift, but to the loud and aggressive. Popular religion had to make its own conspicuous way in a nation that began to look like a gigantic market place. It was not a pleasant picture for thoughtful men of God to consider.

More agonizing yet, the "commercialized" revival was not a sign of health in the churches, but rather an aggravated symptom of a crisis that hung stubbornly on. The cleavage between "modernists" and "fundamentalists" did not close with the swift-running decades, but instead grew wider. Before the Civil War, "orthodox" and "liberal" Christians had been able to make common cause in several reform drives. They shared certain beliefs about a man-centered universe, an eternal law, the powers of the individual and the bright prospects of American life. Outside of purely theological matters, they could talk a common language. But by the eighteen-nineties, the distance was measureless between strict defenders of a "revealed" and "other-worldly" religion and the champions of "scientific" and "socially conscious" faith. The battle grew even more bitter as the machine crunched away at the rural foundations of American society. The most publicized battle of "fundamentalism" was not to take place until the Scopes trial in the nineteen-twenties in which a Tennessee schoolteacher was tried and fined for teaching the theory of evolution in his classroom.

Precisely *because* of this rift, some religious leaders felt that it was all the more important to show the world a united front. A quarreling Protestantism could not keep its grip on the masses of solid, respectable, hopeful Americans who wanted the light of Christianity thrown on their bewilderment. Repeating the fundamentals in a revival seemed, on the surface, to bring that precious unity. For dogged believers in the ancient orthodoxies, it was a defense against modern, "destructive" criticism — against the whole order which threatened the position of the farming and shopkeeping and professional classes that once had dominated a pious and homogeneous and wide-open America. Meanwhile, for those who would go part way in accepting the new scheme of things, and who were not so sure of simple solutions, evangelistic work was, if nothing else, a worthwhile expedient. It got people into the churches of Christ, and that was at least a beginning, because one thing was certain — the religious world was not going to make a successful adjustment to the modern tempo without worshipers. So within the evangelical denominations, men of many temperaments could abate their quarrels for the length of time it took for a revival campaign to succeed.

But there were costs. No one knew the price, in the long run, of postponing the search for a real match between what was good in both the "old" and the "new" approaches to Christian duty. The immediate concessions to "commercialism," however, were soon distressingly plain. For if the aim of the revival was to get people through the doors of the churches, then the most numerically "successful" soul winners held a trump hand. If the skilled users of religious "machinery" put God consistently on the front pages, was there any reasonable limit to what they could say in the way of self-advertisement? Or to the charges they might make for their services? What could the churches afford to sacrifice in the way of doctrine and dignity in order to maintain some show of their former universal appeal?

These questions, nagging in 1911, became searing in the next half dozen years, when the Reverend William A. Sunday forged a national reputation as an evangelist. "Billy" brought millions to hear him call for a "return" to God. Acting as if he were something of a right-hand man to Jesus, he vied for attention with kings and soldiers, politicians and desperadoes, baseball players and movie heroes. Hundreds of thousands shook his hand as a token that they accepted Christ as their Saviour, and busy reporters recorded those handshakes with the same prominence that they gave to the presidential addresses of Woodrow Wilson, the battles of the First World War and the scores of World Series games.

"Billy" symbolized the price of popularizing religion and burying its discords and problems in a rush to enroll new church members. Only a handful of ministers was ready to claim that he was too expensive. His career came to a sudden downfall in 1920, not because the church assessed his worth and decided to do without him, but because life in America abruptly turned a new corner. Revivalism had reached another ebb.

Sunday appeared as a final unlikely product of a system set on foot by Dwight Moody. For a time, Moody appeared to solve the crisis of evangelical religion by revitalizing it. But he could not stave off a decline forever. When his power began to slip, he unwittingly showed others an apparent way out in the superdevelopment of his "machine-made" revival.

Moody had fought hard to avoid "strife" in the churches. The conflict between science and religion he brushed aside. What could a botanist tell the world about the Rose of Sharon? A geologist about the Rock of Ages? An astronomer about the "bright and morning star"? [3] He would not grapple with what he considered to be abstractions. Moreover, he preached so incessantly of God's love, and demanded so little anxiety from his listeners, that it was easy to believe that he had reconciled "orthodoxy" and "liberalism."

Yet a closer reading of the sermons showed that he was a thoroughgoing conservative. He might strip the conversion process of its agonies, but he still insisted that it was indispensable to good works. Men were unable "to serve God with the old Adam nature." "You are not to try to serve God," he warned, "until you are born of God, until you are born again, born from above . . . born of the spirit." [4] No "Old School" Presbyterian could have put it more crisply. The task of the church was not to reform society, but to save individuals, and so organized efforts to purify the world were useless. "A heart that is right with God and man," Moody declared, "seldom constitutes a social problem, and by seeking first the kingdom of God and His righteousness, nine-tenths of social betterment is effected by the convert himself and the other tenth by Christian sympathy." [5]

How could Moody believe that Christianity must help to improve the social order? The order was perfect, and those who failed in it only failed to use its opportunities. The gospel of Horatio Alger had no better prophet than Moody. He told a Boston audience that a man who really wanted work would work for anything — twenty-five cents a week and board, if necessary. If he served faithfully enough, he would become indispensable to his employer, and then his star would rise. The man who worked diligently and honestly for three dollars a week would soon have six, then ten, and then more. Only those who would not work would starve. [6]

Sin was still largely a personal matter to him. He blamed France's loss of the Franco-Prussian War partly on French neglect of the Sabbath, and he expressed the usual horror of the "atheism" of the French Revolution. He had no use for "smoking, chewing, drinking, horse-racing, dancing, card-playing Christians"; only the fact that redemption interested him more than sin kept his talks from becoming burdened with conventional fulminations against these habits.[7]

In short, Moody contributed nothing towards shaping the faith of preindustrial America around a new core. He merely made his own common sense and friendliness a bridge between conflicting camps in the church. But by the eighties, Moody was withdrawing into other works and the bridge went with him. He founded the Bible Institute in Chicago and private secondary schools for poor but pious boys and girls at Northfield, and then he launched a whole series of summer institutes at his Massachusetts home. College students aiming at "Christian work" and men and women already *in* the work gathered to exchange notes on technique during hayrides and to listen to the cream of the country's ministers in the delicious atmosphere of a New England country summer.[8] Over it all, Moody presided like a large genial seigneur, taking visitors about in his buggy, bringing baskets of apples to the schools and dropping in for a few inspiring words at meetings here and there. A meeting with him became an "audience" for a lucky few. Northfield was a kind of "spiritual spa, a religious Chautauqua."[9]

All this cost Moody something. He was constantly absorbed in raising money for "his" institutions. Letters streamed out in a never-ending current to subordinates and to wealthy friends like Potter Palmer, Marshall Field, Nelson Armour, John Rockefeller, Gustavus Swift and Cyrus McCormick. Business details cumbered his instructions to the superintendents of the schools. Sometimes, when the drain got heavy, he wistfully looked back on his early years of Sunday-school work.[10] Gradually, he had less time for protracted meetings, or for the kind of attention which made them crowd catchers. In his meetings on the West Coast in 1880 and 1881, audiences were falling off. A second visit to England in the following year no longer brought the converts stampeding in. A campaign in New York failed to fill even a small building.[11] The great surge of revivalistic energy of the seventies was obviously receding. And Moody had given conservatives in the church nothing to take its place except himself and his methods. Now he himself was not so readily available. Only the methods were left.

There was a turning point here for orthodox ministers of the revivalistic church communities. They could pick up the Moody technique and refashion it to keep abreast of changing times, pushing hard, at whatever cost, to raise evangelistic activity to a new peak. Or they could look for new ways to "reach the masses" and let the big-city revival settle into the past. (In the rural towns it would go on, from habit, indefinitely.) There were good reasons for adopting the second course.

Revivalism no longer had the role it had played in the republic early in the nineteenth century. In those days, for one thing, the revivals had softened the hostility of educated, "conservative" Calvinists to democratizing change. The untrained preachers of the frontier had led multitudes of the plain people defiantly towards heaven, over the barriers of "election." Now the situation was reversed. In the better-known seminaries, efforts were afoot to fit together old theologies and new discoveries about man, society and the universe. The "learned" ministers were now more often the "liberals," tending towards humane and flexible interpretations of religion, and it was among the less well-educated clergy that men talked stubbornly of holiness in the next world instead of justice in this.[12]

In Finney's day, revivalism had lent a certain passion and vision to reform movements. This was no longer true. In a sense, the evangelical impulse still burned in American betterment groups even in the progressive era that lasted from the eighteen-nineties until the United States entered the First World War. The dream that men could be made perfect and the kingdom of God realized on earth was still there. But year by year, even the most idealistic Americans were realizing that the problems of modern life were stubbornly tangled, inseparable from each other and from the world of city and factory which produced them. The revivalistic prescription for saving the world by converting individuals, one at a time, was clearly less adequate than it once had seemed. The "old" evangelical crusades — against tobacco, rum and gambling — had enjoyed a certain nobility in the eighteen-forties, perhaps, when they were part of a general scheme of improving all human institutions and bringing on a reign of millennial righteousness — when it appeared that the perplexities of humankind might all be unlocked with a few simple keys. In 1900, however, something like the antisaloon war, prosecuted independently in a world beset by strikes, monopoly, depression and urban decay, was dwarfed and shrunken. Reform of personal habits was a beginning, but not, as many Americans still believed and hoped, a cure-all. The revival was lagging well behind the impulses towards betterment which it had once set in motion. And even those impulses were given voice most widely by editors and political leaders, not ministers.[13]

There were clergymen who felt, as early as the seventies and eighties, that the revival was aging. Even ministers of revival-minded churches were discouraged by the transience and the blare of the "modern" methods of arousing sinners. Some objected that the religious excitement puffed into flame by the evangelist "died out when he left." [14] A Southern editor complained:

> We have no idea that the Pentecostal season was preceded by flaming handbills announcing to Jerusalem that Peter would preach on such a day . . . or that the apostles took lessons in advertising themselves and their mighty work from some Jewish Barnum; or that the number of conversions day by day was heralded by Roman couriers . . . through the length and breadth of the land.[15]

And more than one man wondered, with a New England Baptist, if the converts of a revival were not more interested in "novelty" than in the "sincere milk of the word." [16]

If these were the qualms of evangelicals, the objections of "liberal" church leaders were even more cutting. A Unitarian pastor in Moody's own home town of Northfield condemned the habit of many congregations, which slept nine months a year, "because those months are not revival months." He continued:

I think there is almost nothing that stands so much in the way of earnest and intelligent work on the part of the churches in the direction of sanitary reform, and social reform, and educational reform, and setting in operation and carrying forward the thousand agencies that might be employed to improve the physical and social and mental and through these the moral and spiritual condition of the masses of the people as the excitement and sentimentalism and "other-worldliness" of revivals.[17]

The liberal case against the revival was thus almost unchanged since the time of Theodore Parker, but it had new power in the turbulent seventies and eighties, full of social restlessness. What with the increasing need of social reform, and objections to the machinery of mass salvation, there was no lack of argument for the churches to deny the large-scale revival the support without which it could not live. The slowing of the wheels allowed time to consider that alternative.

But the revival did not die. For every argument against it, a dozen were spoken on its side. Most of them were unaltered in terminology from Beecher's day. Revivals were an antidote to formalism, to what was "perfunctory or mechanical" in religion.[18] They were part of the plan of "divine action." [19] They were a "spiritual shower" on a "thirsty Church," bringing "vigor, zeal, faith, numbers and general prosperity," and if they were a little raucous, it was better to save men from hell by any means, than to wait for their redemption in the most "orderly, tasteful and approved style."[20]

But the defenders of mass evangelism had one clinching persuasion. Towering over all other problems was the failure of the churches to attract membership. Protestant denominations increased their numbers, but they barely kept abreast of the soaring population curve, and sometimes they lagged behind it. It was a far cry from the days when the conversion of the world seemed a reasonable target. With millions of Catholic immigrants arriving every decade, the tingling fear remained that Protestantism might become a minority religion in the United States.[21]

The special evangelistic campaign might do little to make

Christianity relevant to the world of steam and steel. But it did
get the sheep back into the fold, and for at least some believers it
was answer enough merely to be there. The revival kept religion
in competition with worldliness for the prize of men's attention.
From a practical viewpoint, too, an enlarged membership brought
in more money, and that money went into the "institutions" —
the missions and welfare centers and recreational programs which,
in turn, beckoned in and kept new parishioners. The revival was
itself an institution; it had its own logic and its own momentum,
and was an ever-present refuge in time of trouble.

Above all, the revival still had a vital function for great multitudes of middle-class American Protestants, lost in the complicated world which they had made. It gave them, as always, an
emotional outlet, and it furnished some of the missing poetry of
ritual. More than this, it still offered them identification and
comfort. They longed to believe that the "old-time religion"
was true in every particular — that opportunity still knocked for
the hard-working and morally upright, that nagging economic
questions of the day would disappear if everyone "found Jesus,"
and that despite the "foreign" criticisms of "Socialists" and
"anarchists" they were still the salt of the earth. As they listened
to a revivalistic tirade against the sins of contemporary life, they
felt warmly at home. The world was out of joint, but sin was at
the root of it all. The old, competitive ways were still and eternally good. The revival advertised itself as a way to reach "the
masses," but its real appeal was to the small businessman, the
farmer, or the white-collar worker of "native" stock. These were
the people who needed to be "reclaimed" from indifference to
church work and membership. These were the men and women
whom the revival could bring "home." Time and again, evangelists would ask "those already saved" in the audience to rise, and
most listeners would spring to their feet. The revival was a
dramatic means of rewarming the loyalties of these already
baptized believers. As they formed the backbone of the church,
it was a means which the ministers could not deny themselves.

So in the end of the nineties, the big-city revival felt stirrings
of rebirth. Once the unspoken decision to continue with pro-

fessional evangelism was made, however, certain demands had to be met. The only way to beat the world in winning men was to meet it head-on, on its own terms. If "sin" advertised itself in sensational terms, then God must be advertised still more colorfully. If the Devil offered amusement, so must the angels. If the humming bazaar afforded little time for reflection and penitence, then the church must not ask for them, or it would ask in vain.

Bit by bit, certain new trends crept into the American revival as it entered its fourth half century since the Great Awakening. It became more frankly entertaining, even folksy, apparently getting back to some of the audience participation that had marked the camp meeting — except that now the participation was artfully managed and directed by the evangelist, who was professionally versed in the work. In actual fact, the revivalist was now competing with other specialists in mass persuasion. The audience was no longer his by right or default. He had to win it over.

At the same time, even Moody's efforts in organization were outstripped. Any pretense that a revival was a special act of God had been hollow by Finney's time, but ministers still insisted that human means were unavailing to bring one about without a blessing from above. Now, enormous and expensive publicity campaigns and elaborate networks of organizing committees made sure that the blessing would not be held back because some detail had been overlooked. The machinery of a "season of mercy" no longer clattered in the background; it roared.

Conversion itself ceased to be a mighty leap out of the abyss of condemnation onto the firm shore of assurance. The new-model evangelist asked of the penitents nothing more than a statement of their *intention* to live decently, to join a church, or to work harder in a church to which they already belonged. The decision itself was the outward token of God's inward work of transformation, and it was so simple to make that no anxious bench was needed — not even the inquiry rooms of Moody's day. No emotional outcry was needed or wanted to interrupt a smooth-running performance.

Last of all, something else showed itself. The organizers of revivalism were now defending a way of life that was under attack. And so something strident and bitter crept into the gospel message. Less was said about forgiveness and more about the blackness and wickedness of "modernism," "radicalism," "fashionable" vices or "alien ideas." Increasing numbers of "enemies" were flung into hell, not to frighten listeners, but to allow them the satisfaction of applauding the downfall of the wicked.

All these changes had been implicit in Moody's work — in his little anecdotes, his businesslike ways, his ultrasimplified appeals and his innate hostility to "this world." Moody, however, had kept the more sensational possibilities of his technique under control. Gradually, the controls were slipping away. Paradoxically, the revival was moving backwards, too, towards its cruder frontier origins, in a tangled syntax and plenteous doses of hellfire, but what was natural in 1800 was studied in 1900. The audiences of the twentieth-century city revival would experience the hell-fire, the crudely worded aspirations and even the physical transports of the backwoods awakening *vicariously*, as the evangelist calculatedly acted them out.

The climax of these developments came in the new century's second decade. Out of the Midwest, about 1910, Billy Sunday came raging. He synthesized and magnified to the hundredth degree the tendencies towards big-time religious showmanship begun by those before him. He gave the revival its most spectacular turn, up to then, on the brightly illuminated stage of public notice, before the spotlights finally swung in other directions. Nobody was, or ever would be, exactly like him. For all his novelty, though, the foundations of his work had been well laid.

First came a drift towards sardonic humor. Moody's anointed successors had nothing to do with that. The master of Northfield, though he never officially threw his mantle on any single evangelist, spoke warmly of J. Wilbur Chapman and made Reuben A. Torrey the first superintendent of the Moody Bible Institute. Both these men conducted large revivals in such major cities as Boston, New York and Philadelphia in the ten years after Moody

died. Both made evangelistic speaking trips around the world.
And both were basically conservative. Chapman was a graduate
of Lake Forest College and Lane Seminary, a veteran of regular
pastorates when be began to hold revivals — a severe-looking,
thin-lipped man whose dignity was enhanced by eyeglasses.[22]
Torrey was a rarity in the evangelistic world. His faith had
survived a season of study in Yale's divinity school and another
in Germany, home of the high priests of historical Biblical
criticism.[23] Neither man gave any hint that the revival pulpit
was moving towards liveliness. The two of them, however, offset
their reserve by working with Charles Alexander, who was in
turn the musical partner of each. Alexander, in contrast to
Chapman and Torrey, was cordiality personified.

But other less austere revivalists were in the field, working out
their own "improvements" — such men as Earle and Hammond
and Pentecost. The homey gospel songs of P. P. Bliss had more
of a flavor of the fireside or the parlor than of the cathedral.[24]
His music, which sounded so very much like the ballads of the
music-hall stage, normally forbidden to the pious, spelled the
beginning of a relaxation. By the mid-seventies, one now-for-
gotten laborer named Knowles Shaw had made startling additions
to the evangelistic service. Possibly he was driven to adopt them
as marginal "extras" to outstrip competition in what was becoming a crowded field. Whatever the reason, Shaw took the
little stories which were a staple of Moody's kind of sermon
and began to.act them out in his presentation. A reporter noted
the results.

> He can support the character, in the same scene, of clergy-
> man and clown, actor and ape, nightingale and parrot. During
> his discourse you may see him pacing the platform singing some
> thrilling song of Zion, or seated by the organ playing some
> touching sentimental ballad. You may behold him on bended
> knee, before some cruel king, in tender tones imploring mercy;
> or perched upon the end of a bench . . . stiff as a poker and
> cold as a midnight spook, burlesquing the lukewarm Christian.
> . . . You may behold the audience baptized in tears, while he
> stands in memory by the bedside of a beautiful dying daughter

. . . or you may see them convulsed with laughter, as he portrays, in pantomime, with walled eyes and distorted countenance, gestures and grips, grimaces and grins, a balky horse or a bad boy.[25]

Clowns and apes, sentimental ballads, and audiences "convulsed with laughter" were something new. It was not always easy to tell, apparently, where piety left off and worldly amusement began. There were, after all, no formal requirements that Christianity be solemnly presented. The lack of official definition that always surrounded the revival also smoothed the way for Milan B. Williams, another relatively unknown preacher who conducted gospel awakenings in the Midwest in the eighties and nineties. Williams specialized in robust, often condemnatory language. He would tell an audience that listening to an "infidel" made him feel like a woman who had swallowed a fly. He spoke of Cain choosing a wife from among numerous "buxom damsels," and he emptied vials of wrath on "fat, red-nosed" bartenders, with "stinking whiskey breath." [26] Off the platform, Williams was a stylishly dressed and comfortably living man who appeared to symbolize a new approach to the "profession." A touch of novelty in language or dress or manner was now a distinct asset. The preacher no longer got attention merely by the importance of his work. Part of the appeal of Rodney Smith, an English-born evangelist who made numerous trips to the United States, beginning in 1889 and continuing beyond the First World War, lay in the fact that he was born a gipsy. His dark shock of hair, broad cheekbones and swarthy skin helped to focus attention on him, and he did not hesitate to advertise himself as "Gipsy" Smith or in later years to have his daughter Zillah appear with him, as a singer, dressed in "native" costume.[27]

Better known than Shaw or Williams was Samuel P. Jones, who successfully spanned the distance between two revivalistic traditions. He was a Georgian, and in the South, the annual village ingathering of souls still went on with much of the informality of the camp meeting, unmarked except in denominational journals. After a wild and liquorous youth, Jones was

converted and became a preacher of the Methodist Church
South.[28] His zeal got him a widespread reputation and invitations
to the larger cities of the Ohio and lower Mississippi valleys —
Memphis, Cincinnati, Louisville, Nashville and Indianapolis —
and even to Northern centers like Brooklyn and Chicago. Jones
carried the camp meeting with him. He brought the rustic and
earthy qualities of religion in the Southern hill country to the
other revival world, the urban one, with its filled auditoriums,
careful schedules and squadrons of trained assistants.

Jones's technique consisted in speaking to a Chicago or Cincinnati crowd as if it were gathered from the shanties of a
dirt-farming Georgia county. Homely little aphorisms studded
a drawling delivery, which emerged from behind long mustaches.
Prayer, he said, was like fuel for the locomotives which chugged
in and out of ramshackle depots. "I will tell you, brethren, when
you run up to God Almighty's coal and water station, you
must take on enough for your needs. That is it. That is the way
to get steam to make the trip. That is the meaning of prayer." [29]
If prayer sometimes seemed unavailing, the answer was simple.
"Many a fellow is praying for rain with his tub the wrong side
up. . . . Turn them up . . . for the shower is coming."
Humility was necessary, too. "The Lord fishes on the bottom, and
if you want to get to his bait and hook, you've got to get right
on the bottom, brother." As for the obligation of a Christian to
be heedless of the demands of the world, Jones put it this way:

> "Mamma, if you don't take these red flannels off of us we'll
> quit school." "What's the matter?" said the mother. "Well," said
> her children, "all the other children laugh about wearing red
> flannels, as they're out of fashion." . . . "Now, look here, chil-
> dren, you mustn't come here and complain about the fashions,
> because I set the fashions here, myself." [30]

Red flannels and fishing poles were relatively new things in a
big-city sermon. And Jones went further. To make the point that
any sinner was worthy of salvation, the Southern preacher drew
a caricature of a hungry man who was offered a meal.

He says, "Ugh, ugh!" I say, "Why?" He says, "My hands ain't
fitten." "Well," I reply, "there is soap and water and a towel.
Wash your hands." "Ugh, ugh! I ain't fitten to wash." So he just
stands there and starves to death. . . . There you are, friend.
Give yourself to God and his Church. "Ugh, ugh!" "Why?" "I
ain't fitten." Well, come up here and seek to be saved and . . .
to be made fit. "Ugh, ugh! I ain't fitten to get fitten." [31]

The miracle of the sun's halting for the Israelites, as Jones
described it, had little in common with the King James Version.

Old Joshua went out one day and fought all day long. He was
crowding the enemy, when he looked up and saw the sun going
down. He said: "Lord, if you will just give me three or four
more hours of sunshine, I'll clean those fellows up off the face
of the earth." And the Lord just made that old sun rack back on
the dial; and Joshua won a victory the fame of which has lasted
until this day.[32]

Many years before Jones, Lorenzo Dow had satirized the
Calvinistic belief that the "elect" could not backslide by describing a redeemed saint as "safe as a codfish, pickled, packed and in
port." [33] Moody, too, had translated the gospels into the vernacular, though it would have been unthinkable for him to refer
to "Old Joshua." But Sam Jones was after something different.
He was a widely read man, unlike Dow or Moody, and his avoid-
ance of the rules of grammar was "always obviously studied." He
consciously aimed, as he said, to "scatter the fodder on the
ground," where all could reach it.[34] But for whom was he scattering? The audiences in places like Nashville and Chicago were
not illiterate; at the very least they read the daily press. What
Jones knew was that they welcomed a *deliberate* change from the
stilted pulpit style of the "regular" clergy. In effect, he gave them
the accustomed sermons in the form of a dramatic monologue —
and at a time when the comic "hayseed" was a stock stage figure.
Jones got other evangelists to thinking about popular taste, as a
catalogue of religious books in a Moody Bible Institute publication of 1898 made clear:

The following selection of 50 books includes numbers that are suitable for distribution among all classes of readers. Stories for those who don't like sermons, and sermons for those who don't like stories. Doctrines popularly treated. All thoroughly evangelistic, unsectarian.[35]

The change was inevitable. The revivalist had always spoken the popular language; when the theater and the newspaper were framing that language, he had to follow suit. The revival monologue — for it was now hardly describable as a sermon or lecture — was hammered into shape by dozens of minor professionals of whom no fewer than six hundred and fifty were roaming the land by 1911.[36]

Meanwhile, a change was stealing over the musical service as well. If the preacher was sometimes frankly funny, there was a reason for it. A laughing audience was a responsive audience. A new generation of song leaders also began to work at the job of putting the crowd into a good humor. Charles Alexander was their acknowledged forerunner.

Ira Sankey had been a large and dignified man, anxious to prove, by stately clothes and manners, that he was something more than a "mere" musician. By contrast, "Charlie" Alexander had no fear of appearing lightweight. His very nickname spoke volumes. Moody's musical co-worker was always "Mr. Sankey." But Alexander, born in Tennessee and trained at the Moody Bible Institute, was a jovial first-name type. He made church music a joyful noise.

Bald-headed and smooth-shaven, Alexander dressed quietly in a long coat and high collar, but there was nothing high-collared about his manners. Bouncing onto the platform to rehearse a choir before a service, he would call for a song while discarding his overcoat and beamingly announce, "I like you!" A brisk hour or two would follow, punctuated by cries of "Bless your old hearts." "Catch that phrasing? Just like that," he would shout as a soloist demonstrated a number. Sopranos were told to wait for the cue, and then "GRAB IT!" Still jaunty at the end of the session, he would disappear like some dematerializing sprite.

Alexander's specialty was "warming up" an audience before

Torrey or Chapman appeared. "Get ready for a long, hard, delightful evening," he would cry, as he walked onto the platform. "Have you all got books? Every man and woman, every silk hat and busted shoe, has got to sing tonight!" A wave of chuckles put the hall in the palm of his hand and there he held it for half an hour or more — smiling, cajoling, offering gifts of a free Bible to volunteers who would lead a chorus, chatting delightfully, until every soul in the auditorium overflowed with mellowness and good temper and nostalgia. A smoothly fused, co-operative mass was created, ready to listen acceptingly to the revival speaker. "There is not a single Gospel singer on this continent," Torrey said, "who hasn't modelled his work on the lines first laid down by Charlie Alexander." [37] It was quite true. Alexander's winning ways and his selection of simple, singable tunes made it possible for a group to have a good time in the process of being saved. No successful "chorister" afterwards could forget that.

Meanwhile, the Moody touch in organization was growing steadily, until the meetings themselves represented only the pinnacle of a towering mountain of preparatory labor. One notable bellwether in this movement was Benjamin Fay Mills, a popular evangelistic leader of the early nineties. Mills did not move on a city until the ministers inviting him had established a labyrinth of committees — to secure and train ushers and musicians, to raise funds, to rent space, to spread publicity through the newspapers, to organize prayer-meeting groups, to bring guest preachers in for invocations and benedictions and, in short, to do all those things embraced in Mills's advice for a successful campaign: "Get to work, pray and plan." Mills recognized a new problem of the work in the sprawling growth of cities — that no single auditorium could be entirely accessible or hold more than a tiny fraction of the population. So he worked out a "District Combination Plan" under which he scattered his meetings through different parts of a metropolitan area and settled for a culminating week or so in the largest and most central hall which he could get.[38]

Chapman went even further in putting the Lord's work on the organizational footing of monster corporations. In 1901 he was made the head of a special committee in the Presbyterian Church to stimulate evangelistic work in the country. He immediately set up a national network of revivalism. Ten field secretaries supervised the reclaiming work of local presbyteries, prodded backward churches into organizing campaigns, funneled information on costs and arrangements, co-ordinated schedules and made money available for small-scale meetings in barren districts. Chapman himself ground out a widely distributed book on the ways and means of "awakening" churches. He oversaw the mailing of fully ten thousand letters, and he managed a staff of fifty-six revivalists, singers and "other helpers" who soon were carrying on the work in more than a dozen states.[39]

Braced by this success, Chapman worked out a variant of the Mills plan for big-city revivals and gave it the name of "Simultaneous Evangelism." He used it himself in Boston in 1909. The metropolis was divided into twenty-seven districts, and while Chapman and Alexander worked in a spacious midtown arena, a team consisting of an evangelist and a singer held forth in some church in each of the other twenty-six zones. Thousands of workers and singers were selected, the mails crowded with distributions, and billboards blazoned by the hundreds with notices. On the Sunday before the campaign began, every co-operating minister preached on the same topic, and every Sunday school taught the same lesson. An executive committee kept its finger on the twenty-seven separate pulse beats, and with the smoothness of an automatic belt line bagging feed or bottling milk, a great "return to Christ" was set on foot.[40]

The success of such an effort was measured in the number of converts, and what with the voracious demand of such an apparatus for money, a "failure" was not only a religious but a financial disaster. So a new and desperate need arose to make converts in massive numbers. The aim of any revival, of course, had always been to bring men into the fold, but now a growing urgency about quantity was felt. Yet it was inevitable. Conversions en masse justified the enormous expense and labor that went into a revival. Suddenly, a passion for statistics inflamed the evangelistic churches. The business of being born anew somehow came down to a matter of signing a card which could later be shuffled, indexed and, above all, counted. The effect was to mechanize the conversion process itself as much as possible. The miracle of regeneration, in order to be mass produced, had to be simplified in design.

In the pristine days of the revival, preachers often avoided the word *convert*. Only heaven could be sure of final results. Finney had no such hesitation, but he expected some testimony of a sincere redeeming struggle. His awakened "sinners" had to show repentance by enduring public scrutiny as they huddled on the anxious bench. Moody allowed penitents the relative privacy of inquiry rooms, but even there, long and searching conversations took place between "sinners" and Bible-quoting workers, often with both on their knees and in tears. A sensitive or doubtful soul might well be reluctant to take the plunge of declaring "anxiety."

By 1875, such barriers were breaking down, as prorevival men reduced conversion to an act of will. They left a little room for the supernatural, but not much for earthly visions, raptures, transports or soul searching. They said that a mind breaking free of the bondage of sin was still getting help from divine grace. But the convert was not to expect "ecstasies"; his immediate blessing was only to be "made strong against temptation and sin." [41] This was logical and even scriptural, for the Bible contained authoritative examples of quiet conversions. The effect in practice, however, was to make some simple word or gesture the token of a "baptism of the Holy Spirit" and a guarantee of robes and crowns above. Moody himself asked for no more than a final "I will." A revivalist named Thomas Harrison, who preached in Baltimore in the very same year as Moody, simply requested those who had "a desire to be saved" to stand up, and that was all.[42] Harrison's way came to be the dominant one, with a refinement added. In case some sinners should prove reluctant to advertise their fallen state, listeners were even told to bow their heads and close their eyes, so that the upraised hands should be visible only to the revivalist and his assistants. "Now, while your heads are bowed, and your eyes closed (please don't look around), who of you will cease sowing to the flesh and begin sowing to the Spirit?" So spoke Gipsy Smith in Boston, in 1906, and even added, coaxingly, a plea to put up a hand for Jesus, because "He put up two for you." [43]

From that point the next step was to register the great decision for the information of pastors. The "decision card" was produced and given to the new-born men and women. The converts of Mills signed their name, address and preferred church under the statement: "I have an honest desire henceforth to lead a Christian life." Chapman asked for a more elaborate statement: "Turning from all past sins, and trusting in the Lord Jesus Christ for salvation, I do hereby decide, God helping me, to henceforth lead a Christian life. This I do, freely, fully, and forever." Thoughtfully, Chapman warned ushers to provide themselves not only with packets of these cards, but with sheaves of sharpened pencils for distribution.[44] The final triumph was in counting the cards. Moody had dispensed with any pretense of estimating numbers; he had no wish to "keep the Lamb's book of life." [45] But when Gipsy Smith was responsible for 2550 "decisions" in Boston in 1906, seven years after Moody's death, the figure was a proudly reported news item.

At last, the "success" of a revival could be assessed in bookkeeping terms, for the cost of a campaign could be divided by the number of converts and a figure called the "cost per convert" arrived at, which was an index of revival efficiency. Some sort of ultimate was reached when an evangelist wrote to ministers in one city with a clear-cut proposition. He had estimated Moody's total number of conversions during a campaign in the same place, and also the expense, and had come to the conclusion that Moody's converts had cost $7.43 apiece. He guaranteed, in his circular letter, to produce reborn souls for $4.92 each.[46] He apparently did not say what share God would receive for His part. Yet vulgar as they were, such figures were crucial to already debt-burdened churches when they debated whether or not to assume the vast extra expenses of a revival.

One other change in the revival would have especially saddened Moody. It soured. Speakers lashed out with increasing viciousness at critics, at "society," at "modernist" clergymen, at drinkers and at a host of other often nameless foes. Verbally they pounded away, using the second person, at an individual sinner, who was everyone, and yet no one. It was backtracking, in a sense. Under Beman and Finney, the unconverted had been "blistered," and "crushed," but with a difference. Then the enemy had been luke-warmness, unbelief, or false doctrine. Even the individuals singled out for attack were only particular examples of a fallen race of man. Now the victims of attack were more palpably identifiable with all the forces of modern life which were closing in on the "native" American. There was more anger, a sharper cutting edge, to the tirades. Ministers themselves, if they did not show enough zeal for the revival, were not spared. In some ways the revivalist in his towering indignation seemed to be seeking an outlet for frustrations; sometimes, in the name of Christ, he invoked feelings dangerously close to hate.

Jones was the early master of the medium. "I photograph your ugliness," he would tell no one in particular in the crowd, "and you sit there and laugh at it. You ought to be ashamed." Hard words flew like shot from his lips. "You are not fooling anybody, you great big old fool, you." "You lie from head to heel!" One by one, he singled out categories of sinners. A dancing master? "I would not wipe my feet on the rotten rascal." A preacher who did not support revivals, but advocated "the effeminate Christianity of the present day"? He was fit only "to marry the living and bury the dead." Society? A "heartless old wretch that is cursing every city in America." One who cursed? "You ought to have been in hell, sir, before you had a child born to you!" Cardplayers? "You old cymling [squash] headed goose, you never read five hundred pages of a solid book in your life and here you are playing cards." Drinkers? "I would rather associate with a hog." The performance was vigorous, and had very little to do with turning the other cheek.

Home, God and Mother now became the eternal verities, and there was no quarter for their enemies. "One of the things you will reap at harvest time will be the murder — I say it deliberately — the *murder* of your mothers," Gipsy Smith warned. "You are . . . hastening her gray head to the grave by your wayward, willful, wicked ways." The gaze of the audience was turned not so much to the eternal future as to the golden and pious past romantically and inaccurately symbolized by the Scripture reading at Mother's knee. Yesterday was hallowed, and tomorrow in the heavenly mansions was blissful, but nothing was too hard to say about the present, for which old-fashioned Americans had lost stomach. "It takes grace, grit and greenbacks to run a meeting," Jones observed accurately. God would furnish the grace; donations would provide the greenbacks; and the revivalist, twenty-five years after Moody and Sankey first toured England, was not backward about furnishing the grit.[47] And this, too, fitted the pattern of the revival meeting as a planned attack on the feelings. From the warm and sentimental good humor of the music master to the blazing fury of the sermon, the evangelist carried the audience along the entire gamut of emotion, building up to a bandwagon rush to sign cards.

By 1910, the situation was ripe for the master touch. The revival had come far from the "surprising work of God" in Jonathan Edwards's Northampton church in 1734. Its fame was in the cities, where it was invited by united bodies of evangelical clergymen who had long since forgotten denominational differences. A professional bringer of salvation rolled into town on a wave of organization and advertising. He had a corps of aides to help in the work, and the star among them was the "chorister," usually a lively and ingratiating master of ceremonies. The culminating address was a spirited monologue, made up in equal parts of denunciation of the world, half-humorous stories and "spiritual" exhortation. The grand climax was the "conversion call," a matter of inducing people to stand, to raise their hands, to march up an aisle, but above all, to sign cards with their names and habitations for distribution to the churches. So much had the industrial revolution done to one particular slice of American life!

Then out of the corn belt came Sunday to trumpet the badgered glories of grass-roots "Americanism" and self-reliant individualism; to lash out at "the booze crowd" and the "skeptics" as the "hell-bound gang" which corrupted national life; and to lead those who had kept the faith back to the old-time righteousness. By turns truculent and comical, coarse and conciliatory, naïve and shrewd, he was a gifted combination of showman and businessman. Religion had no spokesman more clearly cut out for popularity and wealth in the dawning age of ballyhoo.

Sunday was born in Iowa, in 1862, the orphaned son of a Union soldier.[48] Like most successful men of the city, he liked to claim, from a safe distance, that he was "a rube of the rubes." The widow Sunday was desperately poor, so the future revivalist got plenty of the supposedly improving taste of youthful adversity. He was sent to an orphanage, worked on his grandfather's farm and then ran off to Nevada, Iowa, where he worked his way through high school with the help of friends and a job as errand boy. Sunday was a mentally and physically agile youngster and, as it turned out, lucky, too. Playing amateur baseball in Marshalltown, he was noticed by "Cap" Anson, the manager of the Chicago "White-stockings," a championship team in those early and uncertain days of organized sport. Anson liked Sunday's looks and signed him up as an outfielder. For eight years, he played ball with distinction. Not a heavy hitter, he was nevertheless valuable as a fast man on the bases and usually led off. The diamond gave him a first, tingling taste of fame.[49]

Later, on the platform, Sunday would declaim against the stage with as much gusto as any fundamentalist, but paradoxically, he was now part of the rising empire of professional amusement. A prize fielder was a traveling showman. Baseball was not in the category of the theater, of course; it was then played by day, involved no women and underscored the manly arts. Yet America was moving from a day when men got their exercise by unremitting work, into one of throngs taking their sport vicariously as they watched specialists at play. Sunday was part of that change, and it left a mark on his career.

Baseball made him an urbanite. Off season, he lived in Chicago and supported himself by odd jobs. One day, in 1886, he met the religion of the city. He was sitting with several teammates on a curbstone by a vacant lot at State and Madison. In his own phrase, he was "tanked up." A wandering band, equipped with horns, flutes and trombones, came by, sent out by the Pacific Garden "rescue mission" to attract wayward souls to services. They approached Sunday's group with an interesting invitation to come and hear "girls tell how they have been saved from the red light district." Something stirred in Billy Sunday. His surroundings were hardly evangelical. Ball players were still considered roughnecks, and a good many handlebar-mustached hitters did their training in saloons. But the old-fashioned hymns emerging soulfully from the trombones reminded Sunday of something forgotten in his boyhood. He got up, left his companions and went to the mission. Shortly afterward, he painlessly "accepted Christ as his Saviour."

Nobody ever doubted the sincerity of Billy Sunday's conversion. He became a model athlete. He refused to play ball on Sunday; he forswore drinking, smoking, cards and the theater; and on his road trips he passed his free time giving talks at chapters of the Y.M.C.A., to the delight of directors who found it easy to get an audience for a baseball star's talk on "Earnestness in Christian Life." [50] He married Helen Thompson, a solid Presbyterian young woman of Chicago, and, moving steadily from sport to "Christian work," finally broke with baseball in 1891 and went into full-time work as an assistant secretary in the Chicago Y.

Sunday now began the respectable upward march of a clean-cut young man from the country. He was the mirror of white-collar ambition. Giving up the glamour and the high salaries of his past, he worked for $83 a month, leading prayer meetings,

finding work for new converts, passing handbills, securing halls
for prayer meetings and doing the undramatic pick-and-shovel
work of city evangelism. He walked to work to save fare, wore
celluloid collars and made-over clothes and skipped lunches
when the weekly budget went askew. He strove for self-im-
provement, taking a public-speaking course at Northwestern
University and practicing long declamations studded with gems
of "poesy," which he put to use in his Y.M.C.A. talks. The goal
of all this striving was not clear. The best that the future
seemed to offer was a painful and unspectacular rise to a high
position in the Y., which was no Parnassus for a man who had
already known the thrill of being applauded. Perhaps Sunday
momentarily lost his way upward in the faceless mass of humanity called Chicago. But in 1893, greatness was unexpectedly
thrust upon him, and after that his ambition was without rest.[51]

J. Wilbur Chapman came on the scene with a request for an
assistant in one of his campaigns. The Chicago Y.M.C.A. rec-
ommended Sunday, who went to work as Chapman's "advance
man," preceding him into towns to make local arrangements,
drill workers, choose choirs and put up tents. Sunday learned
the details of professional revivalism from the ground up. As
he pasted up posters, tightened guyropes and endorsed checks, he
educated himself in the mechanics of the meeting. And as he
stumped with Chapman through towns like Paris, Ottawa,
Peoria, Fort Wayne and Terre Haute, he learned still more.
From Chapman himself, from Milan Williams, whom he also
served for a time, and from the others encountered in the course
of the work, he absorbed all the facets of the "new" revivalism.
He buttressed his training with reading in the sermons of
Moody, Mills, Jones and others. By the time he had finished his
apprenticeship, he knew the trade thoroughly, and was ready to
make additions of his own.

Then, in 1895, the chance came to play an independent role.
Chapman suddenly decided to take a settled pastorate in Philadelphia, leaving Sunday teetering without support or prospects.
But the ministers of a little town named Garner, in Iowa, wrote
him, at Chapman's urging, and asked him to come and conduct

a one-week revival. Hesitantly, he went. Other invitations followed, and slowly Sunday worked his way into steady demand. With each new campaign came confidence; with renewed confidence, he dared to break away further from Chapman's own dignified ways and supply his own innovations; with the innovations came further demand. In ten years he was solidly established; in twenty, he had reached the top.

The mere details of the rise were, in the words of one biographer, "spectacular." Until 1900 he worked mostly in Iowa towns of under two thousand, usually in tents. Then he was able to hire a gospel singer, Fred Fischer. By 1901 he drew large enough crowds to insist on the building of a special wooden tabernacle wherever he went. In 1904 his staff included not only Fischer, but an advance man and a special architect for the "tabernacle," and he was demanding a choir of three hundred voices and careful preparation before he would take an invitation. Meanwhile, he had been ordained by the Presbyterian Church, but the title of "Reverend" sat grotesquely on him. He much preferred to be "just plain 'Billy' Sunday."

Costs rose, but so did the number of converts. Ministers found that a Sunday campaign was a steep but useful purchase, and larger and larger towns indicated a willingness to make the investment. Up to 1906 over half of the Sunday revivals were in towns with populations of fewer than two thousand five hundred. By 1908, however, he had been as far afield as Spokane, Washington. By 1910 Youngstown, Ohio, and Boulder, Colorado, had heard his voice. In 1911 he had graduated to Toledo. In 1913 he worked in Columbus, Wheeling and Wilkes-Barre. In the climactic years between 1914 and 1919 he preached in Pittsburgh, Philadelphia, Baltimore, Boston, Los Angeles, Dallas, Detroit, Washington and New York. There were nine revivals, in those years, in mammoth cities of more than half a million souls. Two hundred thousand dollars was thrown into the New York meetings, but a triumphant ninety-eight thousand "conversions" were claimed. Sunday averaged forty thousand "decisions" in his revivals of places with more than five hundred thousand residents.[52] It was the biggest kind of "big business

for the Lord." Sunday had multiplied the force of the new
methods in revivalism until he constituted a religious upheaval.

The overwhelming reason for Billy Sunday's success was his
own talent for dramatization. He acted out the homely little
stories and the Bible vignettes which had become a revivalist's
stock in trade, and he gave them a breath-taking vigor. Sunday
skipped, ran, walked, bounced, slid and gyrated on the platform.
He would pound the pulpit with his fist until nervous listeners
expected to hear crunching bone. He would, in a rage against
"the Devil," pick up the simple kitchen chair which stood behind the reading desk and smash it into kindling; once it slipped
away from him and nearly brained a few people in the front
rows. As he gesticulated and shook his head, drops of sweat
flew from him in a fine spray. Gradually, he would shed his
coat, then his vest, then his tie, and finally roll up his sleeves as
he whipped back and forth, crouching, shaking his fist, springing, leaping and falling in an endless series of imitations. He
would impersonate a sinner trying to reach heaven like a ball
player sliding for home — and illustrate by running and sliding
the length of the improvised tabernacle stage. Every story was
a pantomime performance. Naaman the leper, washing himself
in the Jordan to cleanse away his sores, was reproduced with
extravagant vitality by the evangelist, who would stand shivering
on the bank, stub his toe on a rock, slap sand fleas, shriek with
cold at the first plunge, and blow and sputter as he emerged
from each healing dip. Crowds guffawed as Sunday depicted a
society woman cuddling a pug dog, a staggering drunk weaving
into a saloon, or a mincing preacher ordering groceries in his
pulpit manner. Hurling some imprecation at a "boozer," the
ex-outfielder would leap to the edge of the platform, one leg
stretched out behind him, the other knee bent double, his arm
stabbing out ahead of him, his whole taut, tense body like a
javelin held in rest a few inches off the ground. Drama critics
who saw the performances in the tabernacle agreed that no
stage imitation of Sunday could begin to reflect the reality of
him. A dancing dervish, he reproduced the jerks of Cane Ridge

while the sinners, in this case, were transfixed merely by watching. At the end of a sermon he was drenched with perspiration. Sometimes he would pull a Thermos bottle from a hidden recess and splash water on his face, before plunging once again into gymnastics.[53]

While Sunday was leaping and twisting and pounding, his hoarse but resonant voice was never still. A torrent of words streamed from him at a rate that drove reporters into agonies of frustration. They were words unlike those ever heard from a Presbyterian minister in any previous era. Sunday borrowed heavily from Jones and Williams and dozens of other predecessors and then far outdid them. He had a retentive memory, and fragments of sentimental poetry, verses of Scripture, statistics and whole paragraphs of famous orations poured easily from his lips. He could preach conventionally when he chose. But he rarely made that choice. His greatest drawing card was his use of slangy invective. Where else could a Christian hear the story of the Devil's temptation of Jesus in these words: "Turn some of these stones into bread and get a square meal! Produce the goods!" In what church could the miracle of loaves and fishes be described in this way:

> But Jesus looked around and spied a little boy whose ma had given him five biscuits and a couple of sardines for his lunch, and said to him, "Come here, son, the Lord wants you." Then He told the lad what He wanted, and the boy said, "It isn't much, Jesus, but what there is you're mighty welcome to it."

No one, save Billy Sunday, could tell an audience that the church needed fighting men of God, and not "hog-jowled, weasel-eyed, sponge-columned, mushy-fisted, jelly-spined, pussy-footing, four-flushing, charlotte-russe Christians." No one, not even Jones, could put in the Lord's mouth such words as those allegedly spoken to the sun: "Stay there; don't move until my servant, Joshua, gives you the high-ball." Or describe the prophet Elisha as telling a messenger to "beat it, beat it, BEAT IT." Or tell women in his audience, "If . . . you . . . would spend less on dope, pazaza, and cold cream, and get down on your knees and pray, God would make you prettier." And above all, no one else could pray an auditorium into unrestrainable laughter by addressing the Saviour, "Oh, say, Jesus, save that man down at Heron Lake that wrote that dirty black lie about me! . . . Better take along a pair of rubber gloves and a bottle of disinfectant, but if you can save him, Lord, I'd like to have you do it." Or, "Lord, there are always people sitting in the grandstand and calling the batter a mutt. He can't hit a thing, or he can't get it over the bases [*sic*], or he's an ice wagon on the bases, they say. O Lord, give us some coachers out at this Tabernacle so that people can be brought home to you. Some of them are dying on second and third base, Lord, and we don't want that." [54]

Sunday was indescribable except in lengthy direct quotation. He made the "familiar style" of discourse — the shirt-sleeved talk, full of illustration from daily life — a superb and supple weapon for the control of a crowd, and he did it with full consciousness of its effects. The greatest of those effects came from his attacks upon the sins of the world — a damned world, incurably addicted to drink, amusement and flouting the word of God. Billy made every opponent's name a hissing and a reproach. He was a fighter without quarter against the foes of womanhood, cleanliness, God, motherhood, hard work and "America," and he built up time and again to rousing climaxes of pure hatred which wrung the emotions of the tabernacle crowds until they tossed on seas of irrational feeling. "The saloon is a liar," he screamed in his most famous sermon against the "booze traffic." "It cocks the highwayman's pistol. It puts the rope in the hands of the mob. It is the anarchist of the world and its dirty red flag is dyed with the blood of women and children. It sent the bullet through the body of Lincoln; it nerved the arm that sent the bullets through Garfield and William McKinley. Yes, it is a murderer. Every plot that was ever hatched against the government and law, was born and bred, and crawled out of the grogshop to damn this country." A man who drank was a "dirty, low-down, whisky-soaked, beer-guzzling, bull-necked, foul-mouthed hypocrite." A bloated beer drinker was "pussy . . . full of rotten tissue."

"The dance is the moral graveyard of many innocent girls," Sunday declaimed to women who associated the ballroom vaguely with "high life" in the city. Tobacco was the earmark of a "damnable, cigaret-smoking, cursing libertine." Lawmakers who failed to support crusades for Sunday laws or prohibition amendments were "pliable, plastic, stand-pat, free-lunch, pie-counter politicians." The new immigration had made America "the backyard in which Europe is dumping its paupers and criminals." Liberal preachers were often fools, "breaking their necks to please a lot of old society dames." Those who persisted in sin "ought to be hurled out of society; they ought to be kicked out of lodges; they ought to be kicked out of churches, and out of politics, and every other place where decent men live or associate." Intellect without faith was dismissed as "culchah." And patriotism went hand in hand with Christianity: "Thank God," said Billy, "I'm in good company, for the greatest men of my nation are on the side of Jesus Christ." [55] Inexorably, Sunday hammered home the fact that there were two worlds — one "hell-soaked" one, including those who drank, gambled, danced, read "skeptical" books, denied the use of their wealth to religious purposes, or harbored "foreign" ideas, and another, of decent Christian Americans. Yet the very terms of the invitation to repent were part of the act, and the most spleen-filled denunciations were broken by pauses for applause and laughter.

Sunday did not rely wholly on his spellbinding strength to achieve results. The organizational prelude to a campaign was fearful and wonderful. The Sunday party included "Ma" Sunday, who came to be a figure no less familiar than her husband. She acted as business manager, later assisted by one of her sons. By 1916 there were a musical director, two pianists (one of whom doubled as a secretary), a general assistant and specialists in work with business women, Sunday schools, high schools, children and commercial organizations. There were two helpers who did nothing but take care of the tabernacle — and every city which wanted Sunday had to build a huge wooden auditorium with a sawdust floor before it could expect to hear him. Sunday insisted on the sawdust to deaden the sound of shuffling feet. He wanted complete silence when he was at work. A campaign-organizing staff supervised the usual committees, but in addition, Sunday had a team drilled in what was called "extension work." This consisted of organizing lunches, dinners and meetings in shops and factories or places of business for weeks before and during a revival.[56] The whole group, numbering as many as twenty, was usually housed in some palatial private home during a visit. Thousands of prayer meetings were arranged; neatly printed cards had spaces for the block, district and section of the city, the leader's name, the attendance and the numbers of prayers and conversions. All these figures were tabulated as further evidence of a revival's success.[57]

Co-operating ministers were bluntly ordered to take direction from the Sunday workers, and to cancel all meetings, services and activities for the period of a campaign. Sunday insisted on absolute control of the religious life of a city while he worked in it, and the pattern of that life was minutely broken down and refashioned to suit his needs. There never was a machine better designed for publicizing "the Lord's work." Every day of a Sunday campaign saw meetings in schoolrooms and lunchrooms, in lofts and basements, in parlors and foundries, and in offices and church basements — every one planned and led by a Sunday worker or by someone under a Sunday worker's direction, and every one elaborately reported to the press. It was the Chapman method of "simultaneous evangelism," except that it was far more centralized and always pointed towards the center of the stage, the tabernacle itself.[58]

In the great, echoing, windowless shed the only person allowed to share Sunday's limelight (besides the hundreds of guests on the platform) was the "chorister." Sunday's first musical assistant, Fred Fischer, had blazed a trail by having Iowa audiences whistle and hum the choruses, clap their hands and vie with each other in groups to see who could sing the loudest. Sunday's song leader after 1909, Homer Rodeheaver, was even more of a genius in public relations. "Rody" himself played a trombone — an instrument more associated with circus bands than worship — but his talent was not primarily musical. His job was to emerge before the expectant throng, his face lit by a smile of greeting, and begin warming up the audience, which was already packed with special visiting delegations — a detail arranged by the staff.

"What hymn would *you* like?" the grinning Rody would ask a group. Never was a genial host so anxious to make the company feel at home. When college students came in a body, they were sure to hear their alma mater or football "fight" songs, and Rody might well have a pennant dangling from his trombone and call for a cheer. One by one, he would boom a greeting — to Elks and Rotarians, to aggregations of workers in different trades, to railroad men and subway guards, Irish firemen and Swedish benevolent societies, delegations from girls' schools and chambers of commerce from outlying towns. For every one there was a special song, and very often a joke. Rodeheaver's jollity came naturally and was heightened by the fact that as publisher of many of the Sunday hymns, he was making a tidy income. His well-fed contentment was genuine and infectious.

The trombone and piano background to the choir singing was far from unctuous; it approached the jazzy. Soon, Rodeheaver would have the audience playing musical games — the first rows antiphonally responding with alternate lines to the chorus being sung by those in the back, the sopranos singing wordless scales while the tenors boomed out the melody, the men imitating a steam whistle and the children repeating some phrase over and over with the rhythmic beat of horses' hoofs. The songs that rose up to shake the tabernacle rafters were a mixture of "good old" hymns, inspirational melodies like "Brighten the Corner," and such secular favorites as the "Battle Hymn of the Republic" or "I've Been Working on the Railroad" if the presence of some group made them appropriate to the occasion.[59] It was a performance that brought the revival solidly into the camp of the "pep" rally and the political convention, but, like the rallies and conventions of the day, its enthusiasm was the result of careful and crafty staging.

The Rodeheaver "singfest" was the prelude to the service. The finale, of course, was the call for converts, and this, too, climactic as it might appear, was the fruit of long practice. When Sunday finally concluded his oration with some rousing appeal to come forward and take a stand for God, Rodeheaver would, by arrangement, break into an appropriate tune — "Onward, Christian Soldiers," if the mood was martial, or "Softly and Tenderly Jesus Is Calling," if it was melting. Trained workers guided the stream of humanity into the aisles and up along the sawdust-covered dirt floor towards the speaker. Hence, making a decision in a Sunday revival came to be popularly known as "hitting the sawdust trail." [60] Sunday himself, meanwhile, had come down from the platform to a special wooden enclosure at floor level, and as the two lines of "trail-hitters" were shepherded up to him, he would shake each presented hand, smile, and murmur, "God bless you!" While this was going on, ushers briskly moved spectators out of the first few rows of seats, and the trail hitters were now shown into these and given their decision cards.

The decision was an easy one. Sunday himself did not object to emotion, provided it did not break out into demonstrations which distracted attention from him. But he saw no real reason for a struggle. Conversion was guaranteed and instant when a sinner rose to come forward. "The instant you yield," he said, "God's plan for salvation is thrown into gear." In token of this, the trail hitter, once he was seated, received a four-page tract bearing Billy's picture, a brief message and the promise that he was "NOW a child of God (John 1:12)" and had "NOW eternal life." That is to say, the printed statement continued, "if you have done *your* part (i.e., believe that Christ died in your place, and receive Him as your Saviour and Master) God has done HIS part and imparted to you His own nature (II Peter 1:4)." Two pages of advice followed on how to "make a success of the Christian life." The mandates given were to study the Bible, "pray much," win someone for Christ, shun evil companions, join some church and give to the support of the Lord's work.[61] But those who already belonged to a church could experience the thrill of Billy's handshake as well, for a blank square on the card bore the word "Reconsecration," to be checked when it fitted. One third to one half of the cards signed were of this category. What was more, not all of the trail hitters turned in cards, so that Sunday's "conversions" by no means were synonymous with new church members.

Nevertheless, the "altar call" was the ultimate goal of the revival, and Sunday let out all the stops in bringing his redeemed sinners forward. He would appeal to special groups by name, urging veterans, soldiers and sailors, students, visiting clubs from out of town, civic federations, benevolent associations and trade-union groups to come forward in blocs. "Come on, Boston and Maine," or, "Come on, Erie," he would cry, waving a green lantern, the signal of a clear track ahead. "Come on, Epworth Leaguers, Christian Endeavorers, everybody." He would wave an American flag from his pulpit, or if it was a night earmarked specially for an ethnic group, he would shout, "Come on, Scotchmen," and hold the streaming banner of Saint Andrew over his head, or, "Come on, Swedes. The Swedes have never been cowards yet." [62] He would bellow to members of a college Y.M.C.A. delegation that their manhood was at stake, or appeal to a lodge from a distant city not to let their town be outdone. In the heat and fury of the moment, directly religious appeals were forsaken, and the whole meeting seemed to resolve into a dramatic contest between the one small, gesticulating figure on the platform and the fifteen or twenty thousand listeners, as Sunday tried by sheer magnetic attraction to start a tidal wave of people rolling forward.

Every one of these coaxing and whipsawing methods had been tried in a dozen places and seasoned by repetition in the collections taken up to meet expenses. Much of the money required to put Sunday on the stage came from donations made in the churches and from the gifts presented by wealthy industrialists and businessmen, who found Sunday an enormous force for "sobriety" and good order and "Americanism" among the

"working classes." No campaign began without such pledges
and donations being gathered to create a guarantee that no debt
would be left behind. But every effort was made to raise money
to repay the guarantors in the meetings. Sunday's success at this
was enormous; his revivals almost always did raise their expenses,
and what was more, the offering of the final meeting, which
was a "freewill" gift to Sunday himself, grew in size from year
to year.

Sunday did not, of course, lead the demand for money at this
final gathering, but his assistants worked effectively in the tabernacle and in covering the city with a network of appeals for
checks to be mailed to the revival headquarters, earmarked for
Billy. Civic pride, church loyalty, group status and individual
reputation were played upon with consummate skill, and in the
end, Sunday left his "revived" cities with gifts amounting to
twenty, forty and fifty thousand dollars. His "freewill offerings" in his peak period averaged eighty thousand a year and
totaled a million by 1920. Though he was said to tithe this income, and though he paid one third of the salary of his staff
members out of his own pocket, he was still a wealthy man as
the result of his work.[63] Working in the Lord's vineyard, he was
vouchsafed his own generous share of the grapes.

Sunday's most spectacular campaign, held in New York between April and June of 1917, brought his work and his methods
to a colorful culmination. In the work there, everything about
him was summed up and thrown into high relief. Somehow, the
frenzy of the first weeks of American participation in the First
World War lent a garish, unbelievable aspect to the entire
spectacle. Sunday's power and his controversial nature rarely
were better illuminated.

He came into New York on the first of the month. The six-
teen-thousand-seat tabernacle on One Hundred Sixty-eighth
Street and Broadway had already been dedicated in a speech
by the governor of New York. The Sunday party moved into
a twenty-two-room home belonging to William Kingsley, the

chairman of the board of directors of the United States Trust Company. On the opening Sunday, Billy announced that he would donate his entire freewill offering, which would include all the collections of the closing week, to war charities, and he told the audience that an angel could not live in New York for a week and return to heaven without "being disinfected and fumigated and given a bath in lysol and formaldehyde." [64]

The day after the opening, Sunday lunched with John D. Rockefeller, Jr., and Leonard Wood, and received a call from Theodore Roosevelt. Thus refreshed, he went to a conference of eight hundred ministers and put them in their place. "I have a perfect right to expect your co-operation," he said. "Perhaps you won't agree with my methods. Well, I won't agree with yours. But I will have grace enough to keep my mouth shut." [65]

Then he began to give New York a hectic ten weeks. On the initial evening he urged the crowd to donate generously to meet the estimated expenses of one hundred fifty thousand dollars. "This country is lousy with money," he advised. "It would be a mere bagatelle for this community to toss it in, and I'm almost ashamed to ask you for it. However, ushers, go to it; get all they've got." Swinging into the sermon, he lost no time condemning "the latest scholarship" to hell. He also told of how God had flung a great revival in Wales "in the faces of the scoffers and said 'Take that, you mutts!' " [66]

On the fifth night, reporters watched Rody lead delegations from all the New York City high schools through their various cheers. One week after his arrival, Sunday was advising New York girls to marry men "manly enough to wear a forty-nine cent pair of overalls," and to avoid a "Cuthbert who can play ting-a-ling-ling on the mandolin and live on his old man's money." No dissent came from a pair of rich men's sons, John D. Rockefeller, Jr., and Vincent Astor, on the platform behind him. Nor was Sunday in danger of being taken for a "Cuthbert," even in a gray striped suit, patent-leather pumps and blue and red polka-dotted necktie. Sunday was, in fact, a smooth dresser who was not at all hesitant about wearing rings, stickpins and spats. It was a long time since Finney had rebuked fellow Christians for yielding to worldly fashion in the matter of ruffled shirts.[67]

By the nineteenth of April, Rodeheaver, at collection time, was warning that "you folks here in great big New York" were not "doing so well as they did in Detroit and Buffalo." Sunday, meanwhile, having worked himself into a fury at the "dirty, stinking," whiskey "bunch," was scolding the audience for coughing. By the twenty-first, he had made his second appeal for trail hitters, and one thousand six hundred had responded. On the following Thursday, with the mayor of New York and Elbert H. Gary on the platform, Billy said that the Kaiser could "go to hell with the rest of them," and the ushers collected nearly fourteen hundred dollars.[68]

On the last Friday in April, Sunday twice threatened to leave the platform, once when a baby cried and once when someone scraped a chair on the platform. He also confided that when he got to heaven, he was intending "to rush up first and shake hands with Jesus," and he hurled a bolt at women in society who were "fooling away . . . time hugging and kissing a poodle dog, or . . . drinking some society bran mash or a cocktail, or having some God-forsaken tango lizard squeezing the gizzard" out of them. But apparently not all society women came under the ban. The following Monday he spoke at the home of Mrs. William H. Woolverton to an audience of wealthy women, who walked across velvet carpets, not sawdust, to shake his hand later.[69]

In mid-May, he was in full stride, preaching one day to delegations of businessmen from the Standard Oil and Guaranty Trust companies, and on the next, asking the men of the audience if they would like Christ to find them "in a cabaret," with a "sissy" on their knees "without enough clothes on to make a pair of leggins for a humming bird." The following morning he spoke privately to Mrs. Andrew Carnegie, Mrs. Frederick Vanderbilt, Mrs. William Sloane, Mrs. Bayard Cutting and Mrs. Finley Shepard (the daughter of railroad millionaire Jay Gould), among two hundred ninety-six other society leaders. In these talks he used no slang and did not condemn "high fashion." [70] By the twentieth, he was growing nervous and irritable. "Ma" had been stricken with appendicitis and had had an emergency operation, and a luncheon with the Theodore Roosevelts had been canceled on that account. Morris Hillquit, a leader of the Socialist Party, had nettled Sunday by challenging him to a debate. Short-temperedly, he threatened once again to break up the meeting when attention was distracted by a woman who fainted in the overheated wooden building.[71]

As June approached, the patriotic note was sounding loud. "Say, Jesus," Sunday asked as he spoke of Germany, "damn a country like that." On the first Sunday of the month, with registration for the draft imminent, he again asked God to "strike down in his tracks" any man who failed to sign up and any woman who encouraged such a failure. "We ask this, Lord, because we love our country," he declared, as he looked approvingly at a special group of a thousand sailors from the Brooklyn Navy Yard who were present. On the evening of the appointed day for registration, he announced his own purchase of twenty-five thousand dollars' worth of Liberty Bonds, and told the world that if "hell could be turned upside down, you would find stamped on its bottom 'Made in Germany.' " [72]

The final week was hectic and historical. On Monday, June 11, Sunday, who always made Monday his day of rest, played golf with John D. Rockefeller, while the papers announced that some eighty thousand had "hit the trail," up to that date. Tuesday night, Sunday once more unwittingly revealed how small his appeal was to the "unchurched masses" by asking how many were already confessing Christians. "Instantly, more than half of his hearers were on their feet." On Thursday, Billy told of how, when he got to heaven, he would see a FOR RENT sign on one mansion and would learn that "it had been intended for a professor in Union Theological Seminary," but he had lost it "because he does not believe in your divinity, Jesus." On the final Sunday, the revivalist preached to seventy thousand people in three services. The announcement was made that collections in the final week's freewill offerings had already come to more than one hundred fourteen thousand dollars. In that single final

day, 7228 people hit the trail and presumably found eternal life.
And Sunday's parting words included the benediction: "Good-by,
preachers. I said some hard things about you — but maybe they
were true."

The preachers could afford to be indifferent to the slur. A
total of 98,264 "trail-hitters" had responded to the entire campaign, and as the younger Rockefeller pointed out in a newspaper article published the morning after Sunday left town,
"however crude or unusual or vulgar" the man had been, he had
emphatically reached "the masses whom the city churches have
failed to reach." [73] Nothing could better have summarized the
justification which the evangelical world offered for their acceptance of the strange works and ways of William A. Sunday.

Justification of some sort was needed. Billy Sunday was the
last and most phenomenal of a long line of revivalists who had
affronted men of quiet temper in the Christian world. From the
start, the professional awakeners had dealt roughly with doctrine, overshadowed ministers, exaggerated one function of pastoral work above all others and bidden the world defiance.
Criticism had been hurled at them from all quarters — from
those who rejected evangelical religion, as well as those who
claimed that it was presumptuous for mere men to take credit
for God's atoning work. Sunday was a target too big to miss.
His gaudiness and public ill will brought him inevitably into
the arena of wordy combat. The attacks on him varied from
pamphlets as sensational as his own sermons,[74] to sincere and
thoughtful evaluations by Christian leaders who wondered if
there was much of the revival or of the Christian religion left
in the skillfully engineered public-relations triumphs of the
dapper, well-dressed and wealthy ex-athlete who reveled in the
language of the sidewalks.

Ministers who weighed Sunday and found him wanting came
from various walks of church life. There were many evangelical
preachers who resented the machinery of the revival and who,
moreover, doubted that it was a genuinely effective instrument.

For, in the long run, Sunday's converts did not pour into the churches in anything like the numbers in which they thronged up the tabernacle aisles.

A vast percentage, amounting to more than half, of the decision-card signers rarely showed up on succeeding Sabbath mornings in houses of worship. Most of them had been swept along in the enthusiasm of the moment; the appeal was so general, so compelling, so deeply rooted in arousing general feelings of decency and patriotism, that thousands of men and women who did not at all belong in the Protestant churches moved up hypnotically to take the outstretched hand of Billy. Sunday always managed to bring some Catholics forward, although that was not his aim. At least one Catholic publication had to warn its readers away from Sunday's Protestant preaching. Yet despite this smattering of Catholic trail hitters, the "calliope of Zion" was no attraction to most members of the working class, simply because so many of them were not Protestants.[75]

Thousands of card signers were already church members. Of the remainder, some had given false or erroneous addresses, others turned out to be children, and in innumerable cases, the converts did not come from the city of the revival. It did a New York minister little good to be handed, for "follow-up" purposes, the consecration card of a resident of Poughkeepsie who had come to the metropolis to see Sunday.[76]

Other ministers objected to the excruciating pressure which was applied in order to get them to join in invitations to Sunday. Still others resented the obvious insistence of the Sunday party on monetary questions. Washington Gladden, the long-time champion of the "social gospel," was besought to join in inviting Sunday to Columbus in 1913. He refused, but decided merely to remain aloof from the movement rather than to attack it. He was finally brought to criticize Sunday vigorously, however, in a Congregationalist journal, first when he heard Sunday declare, "The Fatherhood of God and the Brotherhood of Man is the worst rot that ever was dug out of hell, and every minister who preaches it is a liar," and then above all when he learned that someone who he was certain was Sunday had claimed, "*I've got all those other fellows skinned a mile in the free-will offering."* [77]

Other clergymen found Sunday's language completely incompatible with any reasonable interpretation of what constituted reverence. John M. Mecklin, who began his life work as a Presbyterian minister and then turned to teaching philosophy, was driven into a final break with his church by Sunday. The revivalist came to Pittsburgh in 1915, and Mecklin bitterly watched guest ministers on the platform laugh as Billy paraphrased God's conversation, at the gate of paradise, with churchmen who did not co-operate in the campaign. "Are you from Pittsburgh?" "Yes, Lord." "Were you there when Bill was trying to save the city?" "Yes, Lord!" "Did you help him?" "No, Lord." "Beat it." When those who wore the cloth could laugh at such a dialogue, Mecklin decided, the "simple faith of Jesus was dead in Pittsburgh." [78] More than one minister winced along with Methodist Bishop Joseph Berry at the "grotesque, flamboyant, sensational" tactics of a man who claimed to be preaching the gospel of the Prince of Peace.[79] The Reverend John Haynes Holmes, when Sunday came to New York, noted that the people in Sunday's hell supposedly included those who refused to accept the idea of Christ's atonement. A list of such people, Holmes pointed out, would carry the names of Darwin, Lincoln, Tolstoy, Jefferson, John Marshall, Longfellow, Emerson, John Adams and Daniel Webster, among others.[80]

Outside of the church fold, Sunday was condemned for other reasons. His constant association with the wealthiest men of the day, his own private fortune, his condemnation of anyone who challenged the old belief in the perfection of the American economic pattern, and above all his open admission that his revivals worked on the side of political prohibitionism, all combined to make it clear that he was, in the words of one critic, the tool of "special privilege."

Sunday was not only the darling of the "drys," but his campaigns were unquestionably timed in some cases to coincide with statewide elections on the prohibition question. What was more, businessmen made no bones of the belief that Sunday was "good for the workingman" in diverting him not only from the saloon, but from the possible allurements of union or Socialist meetings.

And, in fact, workingmen were not often in evidence in the tabernacles. A few trade-union delegations appeared from time to time, but most of the visiting groups who filled the seats were recruited from suburban congregations, white-collar jobs, professional associations and dues-paying lodges. One supporter of the work in Philadelphia said plainly that businessmen considered Sunday a "good investment." Thousands would "turn their attention to Philadelphia as a good place for a home or an investment because of the meetings and publicity. These people will naturally be the *best class of people* — generally church folks." Nor could labor enthuse over Sunday when an official of the Cambria iron works applauded his work for prohibition in the Pittsburgh area as worth a quarter of a million to the concern. Asked why, he replied:

> Because of the increased efficiency of the men. They were steadier. . . . They produced enough extra steel to make their work worth the quarter million additional.

At no time did Billy Sunday suggest that the fruits of such "higher and steadier output" be passed on to labor in the form of pay raises. The money that the "workingman" saved by not buying liquor was apparently his recompense. It was no wonder that industrialists were glad to help in raising Sunday's guarantee funds and offerings.[81]

The charge was finally made openly that Sunday had been invited to Colorado deliberately to forestall a coal strike, and to Philadelphia to take attention from the grievances of workers in the Baldwin locomotive works. "Send for 'Billy' Sunday," mimicked George Creel in 1917. "He will pack people into a great amphitheatre, set their emotions to boiling with music and passionate oratory, and convince them that all poverty, all injustice, all starvation, is due to drinking, dancing, card playing and a refusal to say 'I am for Christ.' "[82] Other progressive critics saw in Sunday the final concession of the American churches to the worship of money and success.

The *Nation* observed:

> Success is the one touchstone for religion, too; and the only success worth having is shouting thousands. That old notion about the Lord being in the still, small voice is absurdly obsolete. How are you going to fill a church . . . without a brass band and a vaudeville performer? This is an intensely practical age, and it is not going to be too nice in criticising a man who can show "results."
>
> It is not really strange that religion should begin to turn sensational. What we cultivate or run after in every other walk of life, we cannot keep out of our churches. . . . The Rev. "Billy" Sunday is only a kind of prophet in the yellow wilderness. . . . He has the gaping crowd; therefore the Lord must be with him.[83]

Yet on the other side of the ledger was a mountain of testimony in Sunday's favor. From little New England Methodist ministers who applauded his "great work," all the way up to Lyman Abbott, a distinguished and aging Christian evolutionist and the editor of the cautious and thoroughly respectable *Outlook*, there were those who found "the net result . . . an ethical and spiritual benefit." [84]

In the long run, even with his claims halved, Sunday did have the talisman of sucesss, and in the long run, the churches could not afford to ignore success, measured in numbers, without cutting themselves off from the roots of the culture they served. "Why, my dear Sir," said an Iowa preacher who doubtless spoke for thousands of fellow ministers, "the man has trampled all over me and my theology. He has kicked my teachings up and down the platform like a football. He has outraged every idea that I have had regarding my sacred profession. But what does that count against the results he has accomplished? My congregation will be increased by hundreds. I didn't do it. Sunday did it. It is for me to humble myself and thank God for his help." [85]

The price of remaining contemporary, of going with the world, had turned out to be greater than a man like Reuben Torrey estimated in 1907. Billy Sunday did have the secret of the successful soul winner; he converted formal religion into the terminology and concepts which were most familiar to the widest middle-class audience. That had been true since the beginning of the nineteenth century. In the twentieth, popular culture was doing new things to that terminology. And people were ready to watch a revivalist portray the passions of religion in preference to a genuine experience of the same emotions themselves. It was no accident that Sunday was an ex-baseball player and that he talked slang and that he yet became a crowd-compelling minister. His pulpit fame was achieved *because* of, and not in spite of, these things. In 1916, at Sunday's peak, *You Know Me, Al* appeared. Billy Sunday was fully at home in the America that spoke — or at least laughed at — the language of Ring Lardner and George Ade, and paid to see George M. Cohan strut.

In the final analysis, that was Sunday's undoing. No voice in the church was powerful enough to deny him his place or his fortune. But the world war which began just as he reached New York, the largest and wickedest city of all, brought about his Waterloo. For the war was a sudden dividing line between two centuries. Within two years after the armistice, the automobile, the radio, Hollywood and the triumphant adman swept away most of whatever authority still lingered in the commandments of rural nineteenth-century folkways. Once more, a sinful world turned its back on the old-time religion.

A corner had been turned. Billy Sunday, nearing sixty years of age in 1920, could no longer find audiences which had learned their loyalties personally from fathers who broke the plains, built the factories and railroads and fought the Civil War. His crude but effective dirt-floored tabernacles of unpainted wood belonged to a day of independent simple living, hard work and sacrifice. For all his diamond stickpins, vaudeville patter and streamlined business organization, he conveyed something of the

lingering essence of the frontier. The frontier was now irrevo-
cably gone, and with it, the religious expression of the frontier
spirit. The revival had come to a sudden period of doldrums.
Had it reached an end? Or merely a temporary halting place
in the road?

All Things New

IN 1920, the gray light of an uncertain dawn played on the American scene. In the future lay the nervous extravagance of the jazz age, great tidal migrations of men and money within society, the sullen torment of the depression and the sharper agonies of new wars. The morning haze which hid these things was a twilight for Billy Sunday. He was the victim of his own success. From sinful New York, a revivalist could only go downwards.

The war hurt him, too. It put barriers in the way of building tabernacles and collecting crowds, but most of all it offered a more absorbing theme than regeneration. And then Billy grew dated. He had mastered a particular style of entertainment that was a kind of religion set to ragtime. But religion as a show was vulnerable. Styles in amusement have a short life cycle before they flutter into oblivion. At last, Sunday found out what a cruel mistress popularity could be. After 1918, no great cities called for him. His clippings in the national press dwindled to inches. He went on trying to recapture the old fire in the smaller population centers of the South and the Midwest. The famous voice became hoarser, the gyrations slower, the attacks on sin more querulous than funny. To the sophisticates of the twenties he was not even a formidable enemy, but a vaguely comic figure of the past. Even the final dignity of being hated was denied to him.

So the whirlwind passed, and once again there was time for the still, small voice. Just as the revival went into a diminuendo when Finney moved to Oberlin and when Moody's life settled more firmly around Northfield, so now it dwindled with Sunday's star. Hundreds of professional evangelists were still "booked" into tents and tabernacles in rural county seats, or into neighborhood churches whose influence radiated only over a few dozen metropolitan blocks. No city, however, was the scene of a supercampaign on the Chapman-Sunday model for at least thirty years after 1918. For years on end there were no front-page stories of expenses running into six figures and converts by the thousand; no evangelistic headquarters alive with typists and envelope addressers; no tabernacles full of delegates decked in badges and ribbons; no ministers with committee buttons; no file boxes bulging with decision cards; no hawkers doing a land-office business in the sheet music of the revival songs; no senators, mayors and governors appreciatively bowing to the crowd from the guest platform.

Once again there was a quiet time to weigh and measure. Once more the church could scrutinize the man-made urban revival, examine its accounts, sample its fruits for perishability and decide how well or poorly it answered the real needs of the hour. For a third time, there was a chance to see just how far the "extraordinary awakening" had traveled from its theological and social beginnings. It had gone a long way, from spontaneous outburst to managed ritual; from a pattern in which the goal of salvation was the only important thing, to one in which technique lorded it over all.

The trail behind the "professional" revival vanished into half-forgotten beginnings in a land not yet broken to the harness of tradition and giddy with promises of plenty. In such a world, old ways had to change or die. The early revivals were the lusty efforts of American Calvinism to change and stay alive.

The Puritan universe of the seventeenth century was a marvelous and solid thing, a mirror of Almighty God's unchanging will, with a set order beyond man's feeble control. Every human wretch wore Satan's collar, save where God's grace flicked out here and there, at His pleasure, to snatch a sinner from perdition as a token of heavenly love and power. Society needed tight rule, degrees, duties and stations, to mark the path for faltering human feet. Calvinism *did* give some freedom to man. The lowliest believer might be a potential saint, eligible to interpret Jehovah's dread purposes. But freedom was held within the looming walls of man's weakness and God's infinite power. The Puritans fixed a cold and realistic look on man's powers and infirmities and tried to work out a system that took stock of both. Their achievement was superb — and doomed just as America reached national independence.

For by then, wild forces surged against the Puritan barriers. God's acres lay for the taking before the westward-moving pioneers, and where land spelled social position, the ranks and orders of a settled community vanished in the vastness of the forest. Then the industrial revolution appeared, smoky and wheezing and mighty. Suddenly, man had a dizzy vision of himself as God's partner. God was willing to unlock the secrets of His pattern of behavior in the physical world. He had already given dominion over creeping, flying and swimming things to man; why not over seas and mountains and rivers and winds as well? Among countries touched by the hand of science and invention, optimism became a heady tonic to the intellect. In America, where land and resources were both limitless, faith in nature and the future grew into a national obsession. There were always new lands to break, new markets to conquer, new resources to be burrowed into; tomorrow was infinitely and forever promising.

The older Calvinism could not comfortably live with wealth, science, progress and democracy. It was too hard, too fearful and perhaps too realistic about Adam's children. Yet it was the bone and flesh of American life, with its heavenly vision and calls to duty. It could not die. Instead, it was transformed, and the revival was the agent of its metamorphosis. And that was the paradox at first. The revival was misnamed by its American founders. Its face was turned forward, not back. It did not really "revive" the faith of the Puritans, but it created a strange kind of progressive, democratic orthodoxy under old names.

After the Great Awakening, the first overflow of new impulses was in the West in 1800. The meaning of the mass meeting and mass salvation on the frontier was plain. The ax-swinging pioneers who claimed squatter's rights on every foot of God's earthly domain would not be shut out of heaven. They demanded and got assurance that although they were born in bondage to sin, redemption was theirs in the end for an honest effort. As they knew that in their lifetimes they would move from log cabin to frame house and full barns, so they insisted on knowing that in death they would pass over the banks to the land of corn and wine behind the gates of pearl.

Beecher, Taylor and Finney refined this wild leveling impulse for the benefit of the successful farming and trading and pro-fessional classes of the East. They wrought mighty changes in the old Calvinistic scheme. They declared that God still ruled the universe, but through moral law — as perceptible as the physical law which the universe unswervingly obeyed, but which knowledge could unravel. Man could obey the moral law, too, provided God gave him the power. *But God was willing if man played his part by repentance and service.* The revival's purpose was to stir sinners to accept the bargain and to do what the Lord their God required of them.

Standing out above this "new" theology were the twin towers of law and individual will. The revival, therefore, belonged in the economic and social setting of the eighteen-twenties and -thirties — that wide-open day of a self-sufficient and nearly equal-itarian country, of Andrew Jackson, of reform movements, of a time in which traditions of aristocracy were dead and the re-straints of industrialism had not yet hardened. "Revival Christi-anity" and progress could meet halfway.

But the revivalists did one other thing. They naturally gave man's will a greater share in affairs. That was the meaning of the age. They talked still of the revival as a "shower of grace," but it was no unexpected rain. It was sure to come if men did their part, just as the crops were sure to spring up if the farmer's toil was well done. Finney's generation opened the gates to human arrangement in the plan of salvation, and technique came in through the aperture. And technique was immortal, whereas the day that bred the revival was not.

Soon, the age of Grant swept away the Jacksonian order. The concentration of industry, the rise of the city, inundations of immigration, materialistic philosophies and vanishing free lands stripped some of the reality from the old assumptions. The world was no longer an oyster, certain to be pried open by any man who labored hard and kept his sensual appetites firmly reined in. Righteousness was not a matter of obeying simple maxims of individual decency. It was harder for religion to describe a way of life and duty that was realistic in society. In the eighteen-thirties, the churches had advised a behavior which made men hard-working, abstemious and forward-looking — precisely the qualities which an America building up a magnificent productive economy seemed to need. But it was impossible to say just what qualities were needed for salvation in the less rich in opportunity and more interdependent society of the eighteen-seventies. Churchmen, however, could not stand still to debate their problems. No one in America had time, it seemed, for discussions about values — and no one in America *had* to go to church. The only way for the clergymen to hold their own was to call more loudly for the "old" virtues, and for this task they had the machinery in the revival. What they needed was a man to modify the machinery to suit the age, and they found him in Moody.

Moody brought the old-time awakening up to date. He put it on a solid organizational basis, and he pared the last theological subtleties from it as he popularized its terminology. He made the bargain with God — eternal life in exchange for repentance and belief — a simple over-the-counter transaction. In fact, salvation was free, he declared, because the real price had been paid by Christ. Righteous living was involved, too, but that would come easily once the decision to "take" the gift was made. With infinite persuasiveness, he brought thousands back to the "old faith." But this time, the revival *was* looking backwards, to the confident piety of easier and more spacious times.

Moody hopelessly magnified the flaw in the system as it came from the hands of his predecessors. That flaw was in leaving too much to human work. His beautifully arranged campaigns were triumphs of skill. If salvation was available for the asking, then a revival was a matter of getting the greatest possible number to ask — a matter of salesmanship. As theology grew simpler, technique became predominant. And a technique which is repeated when the original goal has been submerged is a ritual, indefinitely surviving change because it has no connection with a shifting reality. The revival after Moody was a secular rite of the Protestant evangelical churches.

The next step was a rationalization of the rite. For the revival was an enormous and complicated ceremonical act. Following the lull that succeeded Moody's greatest period, the churches turned once again to the revival, but with a new aim. This time it was to involve the greatest possible number of people in the stylized performance of submission to God. And once the idea took hold that "bringing men to Christ" in droves was a task that justified the use of any means, there was no point at which ministers could say that the machinery was too formidable, too costly, too irreligious. The "modernization" of the revival went on to unrecognizability. Once, the salvation of a soul had been a miracle, recorded for certain only in God's book of life. Now, it was a nightly crowd performance, registered on cards. Once, the preacher had spoken of atonement and justification to an audience familiar with Bible and catechism, deeply concerned with eternal life and keenly aware that heavenly destiny might turn on minor points disputed between denominations. Now, the heirs to Edwards were colorful storytellers, for the most part, and utter strangers to theological dictionaries.

Once, in the little world of village and clearing, the coming of God's anointed winner of souls was a dash of heaven-sent excitement. Now, the excitement was manufactured by placards and posters. Once, the crowd had flung itself literally, body and soul, into the excitement of the struggle with the Devil, led on by ministers who lived among them for weeks or months and knew them as frail human brethren. Now, the audience, consisting mostly of church members who had learned to live vicariously in public amusements, sat passively while jovial and expensive choristers expertly wrung laughs and sobs. The revival at the last was not even so much of a ritual as a spectator sport with religious overtones.

There was good reason to cast a cold eye on the revival in the years that trod on the heels of the First World War. Stagy and money-conscious, it might well have outlived the charter of its usefulness. What was more, every passing year thrust the world in which the revival was conceived further into remoteness. The radio not only brought the city to the villager's doorstep, but it put something resembling the tabooed theater into his parlor. The automobile offered possibilities of recreation on Sunday that even the most pious found irresistible. The old staples of the sermon were changing, too. The attack on the saloon or the holy war on "radicalism" could be mounted with more skill and practice by politicians.

Some of the old enemies, then, could not be condemned with the same gusto as of yore. And many of the ancient acts of merit were now, somehow, less palpable tokens of righteousness. The age of advertising was not a time in which to praise abstemiousness. An attack on cigarettes or movie theaters was a threat to prosperity. Debt could hardly be condemned as a sin when installment buying turned the wheels of factories on which an entire nation depended for its wealth. The very meaning of opportunity was changing. The successful young man of popular fiction was apt to be a go-getting salesman, not a mechanic who opened his own shop, and the salesman was the enemy of thrift. Finally, when the great collapse of 1929 spread a pall over the country, it was no longer possible to pretend that only the idle or the dissolute knew the pinch of poverty. The entire core of the revival message was becoming obsolescent.

But there were still a few things which suggested that it might not yet be time to sing a final dirge over the revival. The crisis of the Protestant churches was still reflected in static or declining membership. The day arrived when the Catholics outnumbered any single Protestant denomination. Men of many shades of good will wondered uneasily about the shape of an American future in which Protestantism might be a minority religion. It was not easy to face a losing battle against Rome as well as time. There was still a temptation to make a beginning of recovery by bringing worshipers into the tabernacle, no matter how. Things might change, but the argument that a good end justifies desperate means remains seductive throughout the ages.

Moreover, the rhythm of ebb and flow is built into religious life, as prophets arise to found faiths and priests follow to organize them, and new prophets come in turn to condemn and denounce and apply the cleansing torch of purification in the name of the old and the true. The Protestant church in America, mostly without tradition and liturgy, rested heavily for support on the conscious decision of millions. And so it rose and fell on alternating waves of commitment and backsliding. The revival had been a steady recourse in the slack period. It was so much a part of the institutional life of the churches that it might well go on indefinitely on its own ritualistic momentum.

Moreover, the technique was still malleable. What if the revival of 1916 had shown no apparent identity with that of 1800? Had the revival of 1875, or even of 1828, borne any greater resemblance? Then why not change its dress once more? The radio, the television set, the movie screen could be instruments of its publicity. Intrinsically, they were no more hostile to religion than the newspaper column had been in Moody's day. The revivalist could adopt a public personality consonant with the new American image created by the advertising agencies. Moody had been the brisk man of affairs, and Sunday, the snappy but right-hearted "regular guy." Both had appealed to millions who identified themselves in these types. Certainly a new type could be created — sincere, modest, well-groomed and fit to trade places with an executive in any organization.

The organizational apparatus for a campaign needed almost no change from Sunday's day. And the content of the message? There were plenty of "enemies" left — "atheistic" dictatorships, alcoholism, marital infidelity, to name only a few. But enemies were no longer necessary in quantity. The approach would be more positive — more concerned with what "getting right with God" *offered*. Salvation might no longer be a guarantee of a spectacular rise from office boy to tycoon, but it could be the basis of group acceptance, or peace of mind, or some form of security. What opportunity was to the nineteenth century, security was to the twentieth — a fact for religion to ponder. The successful evangelist had always spoken in terms set by the forces which molded popular culture. It would not be insuperably hard to find a new language for the revival. If Moody could couch the message in the style of *Harper's Weekly*, if Sunday could state it in the vernacular of the baseball field and vaudeville stage, certainly someone could deck the faith of the fathers in the fashion set by Madison Avenue's "communicators."

Yet there was this question: Would the "new" revival really have any roots at all in the American past? If not, what would it "revive"? Would "modern" evangelism still be calling the hosts of the saved to be cleansed of their sins as they had been in the days of the frontier? Or had sinners met by the shore of eternity for a final time? Had the old-time revival ended with the innovations of Finney? Moody? Chapman? Sunday? Or not at all? Whose voice, if any, was the last to summon the faithful to gather by the banks of the shining river that flows past the throne of God?

Bibliographical Comment and Notes to Chapters

There are numerous histories of revivals in the United States written by devout ministers or worshipers in the evangelical denominations. They are, almost without exception, useless as history. Every successful revivalist is treated as an anointed prophet or apostle, and no attempt is made at further explanation of his victories. The sources of statements are uniformly omitted. Those written in the nineteenth century, however, have some value in giving a little of the flavor of the period, and they sometimes contain useful extracts from contemporary newspapers. Examples of this genre are Phineas C. Headley, *Evangelists in the Church from Philip, A.D. 35, to Moody and Sankey, A.D. 1875* (Boston, 1875); Charles L. Thompson, *Times of Refreshing: A History of American Revivals From 1740 to 1877* (Chicago, 1877); and Samuel B. Halliday and Daniel S. Gregory, *The Church in America and Its Baptisms of Fire* (New York, 1896). In 1904, Frank G. Beardsley published *A History of American Revivals*, subsequently revised and enlarged in a second edition (New York, 1912). It makes at least some attempt at scholarship and has clearly been the source of a good deal of the material written on revivals since 1912.

In 1928, Grover C. Loud's *Evangelized America* appeared. Loud's book was an attempt to put revivalism in America into a historical context, but it was uneven. For one thing, he indiscriminately included popular settled preachers, founders of new religions, and outright cranks, like the faith healer John A. Dowie, along with the full-time professional revivalists recognized by the churches, which blurred the line of his story. For another, he tended to lump all the orthodox ministers in American history together with twentieth-century fundamentalists, a common error of his day. The book lacks perspective, pace, sympathy and depth.

The best treatment of the subject by a historian to date — that is, the general subject of revivals and not particular episodes — is by William Warren Sweet in his *Revivalism in America, Its Origin, Growth and Decline* (New York, 1944). However, it is a series of interpretive lectures rather than a history, and it ends with 1844, omitting the development of professional evangelism altogether, a justifiable but disappointing decision by Sweet, since no one is better qualified to speak on American church history.

The reader who really cares to pursue the subject is best advised to do his own tunneling in the sources. Several bibliographical guides will be useful to him, all unfortunately quite old. (An up-to-date bibliography of American church history is a crying need.) In addition to the standard bibliographies of American history, listed in such a work as Handlin *et al., Harvard Guide to American History* (Cambridge, 1954), the following are useful and sometimes indispensable: Samuel M. Jackson, *A Bibliography of American Church History, 1820-1893* (New York, 1894), a later edition of which appeared in 1908; William H. Allison, *Inventory of Unpublished Material for American Religious History in Protestant Church Archives and Other Repositories* (Washington, 1911); Ernest C. Richardson, *An Alphabetical Subject Index . . . of Periodical Articles on Religion, 1890-99,* 2 vols. (New York, 1911); Peter G. Mode, *Source Book and Bibliographical Guide for American Church History* (Menasha, Wisc., 1921); and Shirley J. Case *et al., A Bibliographical Guide to the History of Christianity* (Chicago, 1931).

As for the many special works consulted in the making of this book, I have not compiled a formal bibliography, but have chosen instead to give the full data of publication for works cited in the footnotes whenever they appear in a chapter for the first time. Although this leads to repetition, it means that there is no need to look back further than the beginning of the notes for a chapter in order to get complete information on the source of any citation. Where several cities of publication are given for a book, I have used only the first, or left-hand, one. The date is always that of the edition which I used.

CHAPTER I   *Woe unto Thee, Chorazin*

Title is from Matthew 11:21.

1. William W. Sweet, *Religion on the American Frontier*, Vol. II, *The Presbyterians, 1783-1840* (New York, 1936), 55.

2. Charles R. Keller, *The Second Great Awakening in Connecticut* (New Haven, 1942), 5.

3. *Connecticut Evangelical Magazine*, II (1801-02), 24-27.

4. *Ibid.*, I (1800-01), 268-73.

5. *Ibid.*, IV (1803-04), 179-89.

6. *Ibid.*, I (1800-01), 136-42.

7. Charles C. Tiffany, *A History of the Protestant Episcopal Church in the United States of America* (New York, 1895), 387. This figure presumably leaves out Bishop Samuel Seabury, who had not yet patched up a quarrel with his American brethren respecting his Tory activities during the Revolution. See William W. Sweet, *Religion in the Development of American Culture, 1765-1840* (New York, 1952), 74-75.

8. William W. Sweet, *The Story of Religion in America*, 2d rev. ed. (New York, 1950), 38.

9. Tiffany, *op. cit.*, 389-90.

10. Sweet, *Story of Religion in America*, 224.

11. Lyman Beecher, *Autobiography, Correspondence, etc., of the Rev. Lyman Beecher, D.D.*, 2 vols. (New York, 1864), I, 43. At the same time William Ellery Channing, later a Unitarian opponent of Beecher, was also complaining of the worldliness of *his* fellow students at Harvard. See David P. Edgell, *William Ellery Channing: An Intellectual Portrait* (Boston, 1955), 11.

12. Beecher, *op. cit.*, I, 273.

13. Jane L. Mesick, *The English Traveller in America, 1785-1835* (New York, 1922), 249. Most modern historians of American religion have accepted all these glum estimates. Thus Thomas C. Hall, in *The Religious Background of American Culture* (Boston, 1930), simply entitles his chapter on post-Revolutionary developments "The Collapse of Organized Protestantism in the New Republic" (177-79). Andrew Drummond, an English observer, avers, in *The Story of American Protestantism* (Boston, 1951), that religion was in a low state in this period (171-73). Willard L. Sperry's *Religion in America* (New York, 1946), written by an American for the edification of the English, speaks of the period as a "moral and religious low water" (56-57). Sweet, in *Religion in the Development of American Culture*, calls the Revolution an "awful blight" on religious life, making a subsequent "revitalization" necessary (53). I do not think these judgments are altogether reasonable, as I point out in the text of this chapter, and in n. 38, *infra*.

14. The entire deistic movement is well described in G. Adolf Koch, *Republican Religion* (New York, 1933), and Herbert Morais, *Deism in America* (New York, 1934).

15. Koch, *op. cit.*, 231-33; Keller, *op. cit.*, 14.

16. Koch, *op. cit.*, 72-73; Merle Curti, *The Growth of American Thought* (New York, 1943), 159.

17. Koch, *op. cit.*, 83-84.

18. *Ibid.*, 77-113.

19. *The Theophilanthropist*, I (1810), 3-4.

20. Keller, *op. cit.*, 12, quoting a religious journal of 1833.

21. Harriet Beecher Stowe, *The Minister's Wooing* (Boston, 1866), 61. This entire book is a fine study of the late eighteenth-century New England divine in his local habitation.

22. John B. McMaster, *A History of the People of the United States from the Revolution to the Civil War*, Vol. I, 2d ed. (New York, 1883), 31-35.

23. Sweet, *Story of Religion in America*, 189. Anglicanism was established in Maryland, the two Carolinas, Virginia, Georgia and parts of New York. The Congregational Church was established in Connecticut, Massachusetts and New Hampshire.

24. Sweet, *Religion in the Development of American Culture*, 14-24. For the story of Yankee parsons and their part in the war with Britain, see Alice Baldwin, *The New England Clergy and the American Revolution* (Durham, N. C., 1930).

25. Sweet, *Story of Religion in America*, 189-93.

26. Beecher, *op. cit.*, I, 442-43; II, 23-24.

27. Peter Oliver, " 'Probationers for Eternity.' Notes on Religion in the United States in the Year 1800," *Harvard Theological Review*, XXXVII (1944), 219-35. This article, though a potpourri without much coherence, covers the entire subject rather acutely.

28. Hugh H. Brackenridge, *Adventures of Captain Farrago* (Philadelphia, 1856), 57.

29. Ray A. Billington, *Westward Expansion* (New York, 1949), 246. The literature of westward expansion is, of course, enormous. Billington's book, intended for use as a text, has a fine bibliography, up to the year of its publication. For the population drain on New England, of particular concern in this story, see an old but unsurpassed work, Lois K. Matthews's *The Expansion of New England* (Boston, 1909). Stewart Holbrook, in *Yankee Exodus* (New York, 1950), covers the same ground.

30. Billington, *op. cit.*, 308.

31. Henry Adams, *History of the United States of America During the First Administration of Thomas Jefferson*, 2 vols. (New York, 1921), I, 177.

32. Timothy Dwight, *Travels in New-England and New-York*, 4 vols. (London, 1823), II, 223.

33. Lorenzo Dow, *The Dealings of God, Man and the Devil; As Exemplified in the Life, Experience and Travels of Lorenzo Dow*, etc., 2 vols. in one (New York, 1844), I, 33-34.

34. Peter Cartwright, *Autobiography of Peter Cartwright*, ed. W. P. Strickland (New York, 1856), 24-25.

35. Sweet, *The Presbyterians*, 668-70.

36. Peter G. Mode, *Source Book and Bibliographical Guide for American Church History* (Menasha, Wisc., 1921), 430-32, quoting the Reverend Charles Hodge.

37. Alexis de Tocqueville, *Democracy in America*, tr. Henry Reeve, ed. Henry S. Commager (New York, 1947), 198.

38. I take issue, it will be seen here, with the scholars mentioned in n. 13, *supra*. It seems to me that they have not always allowed for human failings in the vast body of their primary material which comes from orthodox churchmen. The "decline" of a religon depends upon who is doing the looking.

39. Details are given in Sweet, *Religion in the Development of American Culture*, 54-84.

40. *Methodist Magazine*, I (1818), 75.

41. Sweet, *Religion in the Development of American Culture*, 174-76.

42. *The Theophilanthropist*, I (1810), 273-77.

43. Alvan B. Hyde, *The Story of Methodism: Tracing the Rise and Progress of That Wonderful Religious Movement, Which, Like the Gulf Stream, Has Given Warmth to Wide Waters and Verdure to Many Lands; and Giving an Account of Its Various Influences and Institutions of To-day* (Greenfield, Mass., 1887), 85-89.

44. Albert H. Newman, *A History of the Baptist Churches in the United States* (New York, 1894), 271, 283, 303, 332-38.

45. Sweet, *Story of Religion in America*, 75.

46. Curti, *op. cit.*, 161-62. There is a large body of literature on Unitarianism. Most recent is Earle M. Wilbur, *A History of Unitarianism in Transylvania, England and America*, 2 vols. (Cambridge, Mass., 1952). See particularly II, 401-34. Older, standard works are

listed in Wilbur's bibliography. Henry S. Commager's *Theodore Parker* (Boston, 1936) has interesting material on the intellectual influence of Unitarianism.

47. Mode, *op. cit.*, 402-03.

48. Williston Walker, *A History of the Congregational Churches in the United States*, 3d ed. (New York, 1898), 342-43. Unitarianism, of course, was not confined to Boston or New England. It even leaked through the mountain gaps and "infected" Kentucky before the orthodox got it under control. See Niels H. Sonne, *Liberal Kentucky, 1780-1828* (New York, 1939).

49. Mode, *op. cit.*, 367-68.

50. Keller, *op. cit.*, 72-94.

51. *Ibid.*, 201-08, 205-09.

52. Walker, *op. cit.*, 313-14. The entire home missionary story is told in Colin B. Goodykoontz, *Home Missions on the American Frontier* (Caldwell, Idaho, 1939). See particularly 115-64.

53. Beecher, *op. cit.*, I, 449.

54. *Ibid.*, 517-18.

55. *Ibid.*, II, 21, 77. Except for the words *"St-boy"* I have supplied the italics. See also a statement in *ibid.*, 110, to the effect that "all the literary men of Massachusetts were Unitarian. All the trustees and professors of Harvard College were Unitarians. All the elite of wealth and fashion crowded Unitarian churches." This statement is actually in a letter from Harriet Beecher Stowe to one of her brothers, reminiscing about the family's days in Boston. It is erroneously and almost universally attributed to Beecher himself. For other pot shots at the Unitarians, see *ibid.*, I, 389, 541-42; II, 144-45.

56. Sherwood Eddy, *The Kingdom of God and the American Dream* (New York, 1941), 255. For a good discussion of the difference between the meaning of the church in the American small town and the European village, see Oscar Handlin, *The Uprooted* (Boston, 1951), 117-23.

57. Beecher, *op. cit.*, I, 394. A footnote in which one of the Beecher children quotes H. B. Smith, *Tables of Church History*, is the source here.

58. *Ibid.*, I, 69.

CHAPTER II *Walking and Leaping and Praising God*

Title is from The Acts 3:8.

1. James B. Finley, *Autobiography of Rev. James B. Finley, or, Pioneer Life in the West*, ed. W. P. Strickland (Cincinnati, 1853), 83-84.

2. Peter Cartwright, *Autobiography of Peter Cartwright, the Backwoods Preacher*, ed. W. P. Strickland (New York, 1856), 7.

3. See Archibald T. Robertson, *That Old Time Religion* (Boston, 1950), for an interesting survey of such survivals nowadays among the Pentecostal groups, faith healers, snake handlers and speakers of strange tongues in out-of-the-way parts of the South.

4. Charles A. Johnson, *The Frontier Camp Meeting, Religion's Harvest Time* (Dallas, 1955), 3-7. I have used this book copiously in preparing this chapter, although I have gone directly to the sources for almost all of the information given. It is in no way to detract from Johnson's excellent book that I call attention to an earlier work of equal excellence, Catherine M. Cleveland, *The Great Revival in the West* (Chicago, 1916). Johnson feels that the yeastier portions of camp-meeting history have been overdone. He certainly proves that after 1810, at least, it was a much more decorous affair than people in the East supposed.

5. William Speer, *The Great Revival of 1800* (Philadelphia, 1872), 13-14.

6. Z. F. Smith, "The Great Revival of 1800. The First Camp Meeting," *Kentucky Historical Society Register*, VII (1909), 19-23.

7. William W. Sweet, *The Story of Religion in America*, 2d rev. ed. (New York, 1950), 144-45; Joseph Smith, *Old Redstone, or, Historical Sketches of Western Presbyterianism, Its Early Ministers, Its Perilous Times, and Its First Records* (Philadelphia, 1854), 166-79.

8. This sketch of McGready's early preaching days is based mainly on Smith, *Old Redstone*, 360-64, and William W. Sweet, *Religion on the American Frontier*, Vol. II, *The Presbyterians, 1783-1840* (New York, 1936), 84-85.

9. Benjamin W. McDonnold, *History of the Cumberland Presbyterian Church*, 2d ed. (Nashville, 1888), 39.

10. Cartwright, *op. cit.*, 24.

11. Franceway R. Cossitt, *The Life and Times of Rev. Finis*

Ewing, *One of the Fathers and Founders of the Cumberland Presby-terian Church* (Louisville, 1853), 44.

12. All of this is from McGready's own account — a fact for which due allowance must be made — in a letter to a friend, October 23, 1801, Cossitt, *op. cit.*, Appendix F, 494-99.

13. *Ibid.* McGready, in this letter at least, omits mention of the McGees. The history of the meeting is hard to unscramble. One of the McGee brothers, in a letter written twenty years later, placed the meeting in 1799, but Charles Johnson, who has consulted enough material to know what he is talking about, including another McGee version written in 1803 for the *New York Missionary Magazine*, says that the date was later corrected to 1800, which he accepts. See Johnson, *op. cit.*, 34-35 and 273-74. Z. F. Smith, in his article on the Kentucky revivals, *loc. cit.*, also says 1799 and provides the quotation in which John McGee exhorted with "all possible ecstacy." But Smith spells McGee "McGhee," and may have made other errors. McDonnold, *op. cit.*, 16-18, establishes the year as 1799. McDonnold is concerned with rebutting the notion that the revival technique was lifted from the Methodists, so he gives John McGee less credit than does McGee himself, but he does agree that the Methodist initiated the shouting, and he seems to base the story on interviews with contemporaries of McGready. Sweet, in *The Presbyterians*, 85, ignores the question. Incidentally, this writer wonders why, if the floor was "covered with the slain," the room filled with cries of distress, etc., there were only a few conversions. See also A. H. Redford, *The History of Methodism in Kentucky*, 3 vols. (Nashville, 1868-70), I, 264-72.

14. Redford, *op. cit.*, I, 266-70.

15. Johnson, *op. cit.*, 25-40, discusses camp-meeting beginnings and makes it clear that, while the term is hard to pin down, many earlier outdoor religious services of more than a day's duration had been held.

16. John 3:3.

17. See article "Conversion" in *Encyclopedia of Religion and Ethics*, ed. James Hastings, 12 vols. (New York, 1908-22), III, 104-11.

18. Peter G. Mode, *Source Book and Bibliographical Guide for American Church History* (Menasha, Wisc., 1921), 66.

19. Perry Miller, *The New England Mind; From Colony to Prov-ince* (Cambridge, 1953), 70.

20. William James, *The Varieties of Religious Experience*, Mod-

ern Library ed. (New York, n.d.), 224. The two lectures on conversion, 186-253, contain a brilliant discussion of the entire phenomenon. I have not included a bibliography of the psychological literature on conversion here, as it seems irrelevant. The reader can find lists of such works in a good encyclopedia of religion.

21. The physical phenomena of the frontier revival are discussed at some length in Frederick M. Davenport, *Primitive Traits in Religious Revivals* (New York, 1902). The book is an interesting relic of the early and hopeful days of "social science." It is full of quaint anthropological notions — for example, that the American Negro is a "primitive" — and it reflects the viewpoint that revivalism is dead (in 1900) because man is growing progressively more rational! It does, however, contain interesting material on religious transports. See also the appendixes in Cleveland, *op. cit.*

22. Johnson, *op. cit.*, 36.

23. McGready, *loc. cit.*

24. Speer, *op. cit.*, 40-43.

25. J. P. MacLean, "The Kentucky Revival and Its Influence on the Miami Valley," *Ohio Archaeological and Historical Society Publications*, XII (1903), 242-86.

26. Marguerite F. Melcher, *The Shaker Adventure* (Princeton, 1941), 268-69.

27. Ray A. Billington, *Westward Expansion* (New York, 1949), 250.

28. The figure of 147 wagons is from Angier March, *Increase of Piety, or the Revival of Religion in the United States of America*, quoted in Mode, *op. cit.*, 336-37. The guess of 25,000 present is from Finley, *Autobiography*, 166, although he gives the number as the "supposition" of others. The Methodist William Burke says that the *estimated* total by Sunday night was 20,000, and he does make a flat claim of preaching to some 10,000 himself, in James B. Finley, *Sketches of Western Methodism, Biographical, Historical and Miscellaneous, Illustrative of Pioneer Life* (Cincinnati, 1855), 77-79. The Reverend Archibald Alexander, president of Hampden-Sidney College, in Virginia, repeated the figure of 20,000 in a letter in the *Connecticut Evangelical Magazine*, II (1801-02), 354-60. Peter Cartwright, who was not there, gives a more realistic estimate of 12,000 to 20,000 people present "at times during the meeting," in Cartwright, *op. cit.*, 30-31. Obviously, some worshipers stayed on the ground for the entire week end, and others came and went. Richard

McNemar gives color to the more conservative estimates by his statement that 135 "carriages" — presumably wagons — were there. See Richard McNemar, *The Kentucky Revival, or, A Short History of the Late Outpouring of the Spirit of God in the Western States of America* (New York, 1846), 26.

29. Mode, *op. cit.*, 336-37.

30. Archibald Alexander, *loc. cit.*, says that the disorder was increased by crowds wandering from minister to minister.

31. Finley, *Autobiography*, 166.

32. The rain is attested to in the account given in Charles L. Thompson's *Times of Refreshing: A History of American Revivals From 1740 to 1877* (Chicago, 1877), 81-89. William Burke, *loc. cit.*, says that nobody had any tents.

33. Burke, *loc. cit.*

34. *Ibid.*

35. William H. Milburn, *The Pioneers, Preachers and People of the Mississippi Valley* (New York, 1860), 357-61; Finley, *Autobiography*, 364-65.

36. Mode, *op. cit.*, 336-37.

37. Finley, *Autobiography*, 15-16, 99-118, 147-70.

38. McNemar, *op. cit.*, 32-33. The journal of Benjamin Lakin, a Methodist itinerant preacher, refers, under date of March 14, 1802, to the case of a young woman "in the neighborhood of Caneridge" who did exactly this. Perhaps it was the same person. Lakin's comment was: "Shurely it is the Lord's doings and it is marvalous in our eyes." William W. Sweet, *Religion on the American Frontier*, Vol. IV, *The Methodists* (Chicago, 1946), 223.

39. Mode, *op. cit.*, 337.

40. Cartwright, *op. cit.*, 48-49.

41. Finley, *Autobiography*, 412.

42. Lorenzo Dow, *The Dealings of God, Man and the Devil; As Exemplified in the Life, Experience and Travels of Lorenzo Dow*, etc., 2 vols. in one (New York, 1844), I, 85-86, 99.

43. Jacob Young, *Autobiography of a Pioneer* (Cincinnati, 1857), 135-37.

44. Davenport, *op. cit.*, 74-81. Although some of the forms of excitement seem well vouched for, it must be noted that Davenport draws, for these pages, on Robert Davidson's *History of the Presbyterian Church in the State of Kentucky* (New York, 1847). Davidson was a "conservative" Presbyterian opponent of the revival, and

apparently was eager to cast ridicule on it. A rebuttal to him, for whatever it is worth, is to be found in Cossitt, *op. cit.*, 325-478. See Johnson, *op. cit.*, 57-62, for a good evaluation, and the appendixes to Cleveland, *op. cit.*

45. Alexander, *loc. cit.*

46. *Connecticut Evangelical Magazine*, II (1801-02), 392-94.

47. Sweet, *The Presbyterians*, 89.

48. Finley, *Autobiography*, 364.

49. Dow, *op. cit.*, I, 107-08.

50. Thompson, *op. cit.*, 84-85.

51. Speer, *op. cit.*, 24-49. These revivals are all Presbyterian. For a description of the work among the Baptists, see William W. Sweet, *Religion on the American Frontier*, Vol. I, *The Baptists, 1783-1830* (New York, 1931), 608-25.

52. Hebrews 4:12.

53. Cossitt, *op. cit.*, 35.

54. McDonnold, *op. cit.*, 8-9.

55. *Ibid.*, 41-47.

56. Sweet, *The Presbyterians*, 318-19.

57. This system is still retained in essentials. The modern organization of Presbyterianism is discussed in Frank S. Mead, *Handbook of Denominations in the United States*, rev. ed. (New York, 1956), 172-73.

58. The full story of the schism is contained in Sweet, *The Presbyterians*, 82-98. Pages 99-110 contain a selection of documents from the various trials and examinations. The Cumberlanders' side of the story is given in McDonnold, *op. cit.*, 48-81. The date of the return of most of the Cumberland Presbyterian churches to the fold is from Mead, *op. cit.*, 172.

59. The New Light secession is discussed in Sweet's volume cited in the footnote immediately preceding this one, on the pages indicated in that note. The rather celebrated document dissolving the Springfield Presbytery, the "Last Will and Testament of the Springfield Presbytery," is given in Mode, *op. cit.*, 342-43.

60. Melcher, *op. cit.*, 57-66.

61. See Mead, *op. cit.*, 76, for the early history of the Christians.

62. Sweet, *Story of Religion in America*, 235-38. The Disciples, still an active denomination, are described in Mead, *op. cit.*, 78-81. Many of the Christian churches continued independently until merged, in 1931, with the Congregationalists. See *ibid.*, 73-77.

63. Sweet, *The Presbyterians*, 224.

64. Cossitt, *op. cit.*, 486-88.

65. Benjamin Lakin, a Methodist, sums up these doctrines in his journal, quoted in Sweet, *The Methodists*, 257-58. Allowing for some partisan exaggeration in a time when denominational warfare was hot, they seem an adequate short summary.

66. *Ibid.* Italics mine. In this one selection, I have cleaned up Lakin's spelling, so as not to distract attention from the doctrine. Elsewhere, all quotations are left just as they appear. Lakin cited his source as *Bucks' Theological Dictionary*. A more modern discussion of Methodist Arminianism may be found in an article by Frederic Platt in the *Encyclopedia of Religion and Ethics*, I, 807-16.

67. Sweet, *The Presbyterians*, 60.

68. Sweet, *The Methodists*, 77.

69. *Ibid.*, 83, 117.

70. *Connecticut Evangelical Magazine*, II (1801-02), 392-94. For other examples of complaints about Methodist "ranting," taken from a copious supply, see Timothy Flint, *Recollections of the Last Ten Years* (New York, 1932), 75, *The Theophilanthropist*, I (1810), 273-77, and Charles G. Finney, *Memoirs of Rev. Charles G. Finney Written by Himself* (New York, 1876), 136-37. Finney does not exactly criticize Methodist enthusiasm, but he tells of how, during an upstate New York revival which he was conducting in the eighteen-twenties, a man toppled prostrate from his seat, leading Finney to the immediate deduction that he was a Methodist! As it later turned out, Finney was wrong, but the story is a fine reflection of the popular notion of Methodism at the time.

71. Sweet, *The Presbyterians*, 695-700.

72. Sweet, *The Methodists*, 38-47, 64-65; Johnson, *op. cit.*, 18-24.

73. Johnson, *op. cit.*, 19.

74. Sweet, *Story of Religion in America*, 220, 238. In 1792, James O'Kelley led a small group out of the church in protest against the creation of the episcopal system, and in 1830 a number of reformers who had been trying to curb the power of the bishops finally gave up, left, and set up as the Methodist Protestant Church.

75. Sweet, *The Methodists*, 51-65.

76. The all-too-brief group portrait of circuit riders in the next few pages is based largely on a close reading of six books of recollections — the autobiographies of Jacob Young, James Finley, Peter Cartwright and Lorenzo Dow, already cited earlier, plus Finley's

Sketches of Western Methodism and Henry Smith's *Reflections and Recollections of an Old Itinerant* (New York, 1848). If the reader wants to know more about these remarkable preachers, there is an ample literature, although no good, complete, modern account of their apostolic wanderings is available. See the bibliography in Mode, *op. cit.*, which is very full for its 1921 date, and in Sweet's *The Methodists*. There are a number of interesting sketches of the rise and progress of Methodist revivals in the West which appeared under the name of "Theophilus Arminius," a pseudonym for the Reverend Thomas Hinde, in the *Methodist Magazine*, II (1819), 184-87, 221-24, 272-74, 304-08, 349-53, 393-96 and 434-38.

77. There is an interesting discussion of the demonology of the Old West and particularly the Southwest in Bernard De Voto's *Mark Twain's America* (Boston, 1932).

78. Dow, *op. cit.*, I, 13-59. The best way to get the curious flavor of Dow is in his own journal, which appeared in several editions and under several titles. A reasonably good biography is Charles C. Sellers, *Lorenzo Dow, Bearer of the Word* (New York, 1928). A sketch in Herbert Asbury's *A Methodist Saint. The Life of Bishop Asbury* (New York, 1927) is interesting, but snide, although Dow is certainly vulnerable to such treatment. There is an article by Benjamin Brawley in the *Methodist Review*, XCVIII (1916), 535-43, and another by Emily Gilman in the *New England Magazine*, XX (1899), 411-17. (The Brawley article is reprinted in substance in the *Journal of Negro History*, I (1916), 265-75.) Neither of these two writers has anything much to add to Dow's own eccentric story.

79. Dow, *op. cit.*, I, 9-10.

80. *Ibid.*, 147, 150.

81. *Ibid.*, 113.

82. Cartwright, *op. cit.*, 35.

83. Finley, *Autobiography*, 191.

84. Young, *op. cit.*, 46-47.

85. Finley, *Autobiography*, 167-81.

86. Cartwright, *op. cit.*, 37-38.

87. Young, *op. cit.*, 41-43.

88. Dow, *op. cit.*, I, 125-26.

89. Finley, *Autobiography*, 171.

90. Cartwright, *op. cit.*, 80.

91. Johnson Hooper, *Simon Suggs' Adventures* (New York, 1928), 83-93.

92. The story may be found in *Four Great American Novels,* ed. Raymond W. Short (New York, 1946), 379-81.

Title is from Ephesians 4:11.

1. William B. Sprague, *Memoir of the Rev. Edward D. Griffin, D.D., Compiled Chiefly from His Own Writings* (New York, 1839), 2-8.

2. William Speer, *The Great Revival of 1800* (Philadelphia, 1872), 57.

3. William W. Sweet, *Religion in Colonial America* (New York, 1942), 273.

4. Peter G. Mode, *Source Book and Bibliographical Guide for American Church History* (Menasha, Wisc., 1921), 214-17, quoting Jonathan Edwards's *A Faithful Narrative of the Surprising Work of God . . . in Northampton,* etc., first published in 1736 and many times subsequently. The Great Awakening is a large subject, deeply involving the entire social history of the American colonies in the eighteenth century, and there is no pretense in the following paragraphs to anything but the most superficial treatment. I have relied mainly on the excerpts in Mode, *op. cit.,* and on the secondary treatments both in Sweet's *Religion in Colonial America,* 271-317, and his *The Story of Religion in America,* 2d rev. ed. (New York, 1950), 127-54. The reader who wishes to pursue the subject further will regret the lack of a recent, single comprehensive study of the entire movement. There is a good bibliography in Mode, but it naturally includes nothing written in the last thirty-six years. The bibliographical guides by Samuel Jackson and Shirley Case, mentioned in the bibliographical comment which introduces these notes, are also dated. The 1954 edition of the *Harvard Guide to American History* lists a few more recent interpretations. I have referred to works on special phases in the notes that follow. Perry Miller is the best student of the New England mind of this era. His *Jonathan Edwards* (New York, 1949) and *The New England Mind; From Colony to Province* (Cambridge, 1953) are the best studies available for the intellectual side of the Great Awakening in the Northeast. The absence of a modern book on the entire movement, however, still leaves a gap in our historical literature.

5. Sweet, *Religion in Colonial America,* 274-81, 291-311. Sweet

acknowledges the special help of two studies of the awakening in the Middle and Southern colonies, namely, Charles H. Maxson, *The Great Awakening in the Middle Colonies* (Chicago, 1920), and Wesley M. Gewehr, *The Great Awakening in Virginia* (Durham, 1930).

6. Benjamin Franklin, *Autobiography*, Pocket Books ed. (New York, 1940), 119-24.

7. Sweet, *Story of Religion in America*, 131-33.

8. Sweet, *Religion in Colonial America*, 284-87. The quotation concerning the "taste of the theatre" is from Ola E. Winslow, *Jonathan Edwards* (New York, 1940), 181.

9. Mode, *op. cit.*, quoting Reverend Thomas Prince, assistant pastor of the Old South Church, from Joseph Tracy's standard nineteenth-century history, *The Great Awakening, A History of the Revival of Religion in the Time of Edwards and Whitefield* (Boston, 1842).

10. Sweet, *Story of Religion in America*, 133. The complete sermon may be found in many anthologies; to name only one: Walter Blair, Theodore Hornberger and Randall Stewart, *The Literature of the United States* (Chicago, 1949). Incidentally, this sermon was still being used to terrify the unrepentant in frontier Iowa as late as the sixties. At least one local evangelist did so. See Cal Ogburn, "The Pioneer Religious Revival," *Annals of Iowa*, 3d ser., XV (1925-27), 483-506.

11. Sweet, *Religion in Colonial America*, 288.

12. Bennet Tyler, *Memoir of the Life and Character of Rev. Asahel Nettleton, D.D.* (Hartford, 1844), 52n. This lengthy footnote quotes an unnamed pamphlet containing "nine sermons by the Rev. Joseph Fish, pastor of a church in Stonington, preached in 1763."

13. Sweet, *Religion in Colonial America*, 289.

14. Mode, *op. cit.*, 222-23.

15. *Ibid.*, 225-26; Sweet, *Religion in Colonial America*, 114, 290-91.

16. Sweet, *Religion in Colonial America*, 289-90.

17. The issues in this warfare are ably discussed by Sidney Mead in *Nathaniel William Taylor, 1786-1858, A Connecticut Liberal* (Chicago, 1942), 12-23, 95-123.

18. See Edwin S. Gaustad, "The Theological Effects of the Great Awakening in New England," *Mississippi Valley Historical Review*, XL (1953-54), 681-706.

19. Sweet, *Story of Religion in America*, 133, and *Religion in Colonial America*, 291.

20. *Connecticut Evangelical Magazine,* I (1800-01), 1.
21. *Ibid.,* 19-21. Italics mine.
22. *Ibid.,* 21-30.
23. *Ibid.,* 268-73.
24. *Ibid.,* VI (1805-06), 65-71.
25. Sprague, *Memoir of Griffin,* 39. Accounts of all these small revivals under local pastors may be found in many places; a few
such sources are William Speer, *The Great Revival of 1800* (Philadelphia, 1872); Ebenezer Porter, *Letters on the Religious Revivals
Which Prevailed About the Beginning of the Present Century* (Boston, 1858); Bennet Tyler, *New England Revivals . . . at the Close
of the 18th and Beginning of the 19th Centuries* (Boston, 1846); William Woodward, *Increase of Piety, or, The Revival of Religion in the
United States of America,* etc. (Philadelphia, 1802). This last-named
work, with the identical title, was also published by Angier March,
under his own name, at Newburyport, Mass., in 1802. A modern summary is in Charles R. Keller, *The Second Great Awakening
in Connecticut* (New Haven, 1942), 36-49.
26. Keller, *op. cit.,* 40.
27. Mead, *op. cit.,* 42.
28. A full biography of Dwight is Charles E. Cunningham's *Timothy Dwight* (New York, 1942). There is a brief but highly satisfactory sketch in Constance Rourke, *Trumpets of Jubilee* (New
York, 1927), 11-13. Vernon L. Parrington has a few remarks and
selections in *The Connecticut Wits* (New York, 1926). Concerning
the question of whether or not Dwight was an Edwardean there is
debate. Keller, *op. cit.,* 35, says that Dwight's election "symbolized
the New Divinity victory in Connecticut." But the contention of
Sidney Mead throughout his book on Nathaniel Taylor is that
Dwight and his protégés, Beecher and Taylor, were more akin to
the "Old Calvinists" or pre-Edwards days. The reason is, he says,
that the *true* Edwardeans stressed the passive role of the sinner in
regeneration, and insisted that *until* conversion, all exercises of the
sinner, such as prayer, were basically sinful. The revivalists of
Dwight's generation, however, came to feel that even an unconverted
person might use the *means* of grace — that he had latent impulses
in his heart towards regeneration that might be awakened by these
means. Only thus could efforts to "get up" a revival be defended.
And, moreover, human reason might assist in apprehending God's
revelation even before conversion — an "old" Puritan position, ac-

cording to Mead. The error stems, Mead says, from the fact that Edwards conducted revivals and so did Dwight and his followers. But Edwards did not seek the revival; Dwight did. One way or the other, Dwight and his school perforce gave human effort a much greater role in securing conversion. Thus, these enemies of "democracy" wound up by democratizing Calvinism to some degree.

29. Tyler, *op. cit.*, vi, 54-55. There is no comprehensive biography of Nettleton, and I have had to rely on Tyler's laudatory work rather heavily. There is a sketch of his life and considerable discussion of his work in Charles C. Cole, Jr., *The Social Ideas of the Northern Evangelists, 1826-1860* (New York, 1954). Cole has used a manuscript study by George H. Birney, done in 1943, at the Hartford Theological Seminary.

30. *New York Observer*, May 25, 1844, "Death of Clergymen."

31. Tyler, *op. cit.*, 13. I have used Tyler freely in the following pages and thought it necessary to footnote only direct quotations or specific incidents.

32. *Ibid.*, 15, 17, 24.

33. Sweet, *Story of Religion in America*, 241, 247-48.

34. Tyler, *op. cit.*, 210.

35. *Ibid.*, 237.

36. *Ibid.*, 64.

37. Lyman Beecher, *Autobiography, Correspondence . . . of the Rev. Lyman Beecher, D.D.*, 2 vols. (New York, 1864), II, 483-84.

38. Tyler, *op. cit.*, 334.

39. *Ibid.*, 272.

40. *Ibid.*, 67, 69-70, 77, 87-89.

41. Nettleton's methods of personal work are discussed in Tyler, *op. cit.*, 203-32.

42. Keller, *op. cit.*, 4-7.

43. Mead, *op. cit.*, 96.

44. Tyler, *op. cit.*, 105-09.

45. Nettleton's work at Yale in 1820 is dealt with in Tyler, *op. cit.*, 125-29. I have taken the description of a Yale revival from Mode, *op. cit.*, 339-42, quoting the Reverend Ashbel Green, who was present during an awakening at the college in 1812. There seems no reason to assume that the pattern was much different eight years later. The comment on Connecticut as an "ecclesiastical state" is part of a Republican attack on Dwight quoted in Mead, *op. cit.*, 77.

46. Tyler, *op. cit.*, 153-202.

47. Beecher, *op. cit.*, II, 9. In the biographical material which follows I have leaned heavily on this work. Edited by Charles Beecher, it is a piecing together of Beecher's octogenarian recollections, supplemented by those of his children. It is altogether partisan on controversial matters and probably careless as to dates and events. But as it happens, it is also deliciously readable and lively, something not easily said for other clerical memoirs. And there is, unaccountably enough, no full-length biography of Lyman Beecher that I have been able to find except for a brief chronicle by Edward F. Hayward, *Lyman Beecher* (Boston, 1904). There are lively sketches in Rourke, *op. cit.*, in Lyman B. Stowe's *Saints, Sinners and Beechers* (Indianapolis, 1934) and in several biographies of his most famous children, Henry Ward Beecher and Harriet Beecher Stowe — notably, Paxton Hibben, *Henry Ward Beecher, An American Portrait* (New York, 1927), and Forrest Wilson, *Crusader in Crinoline: The Life of Harriet Beecher Stowe* (Philadelphia, 1941). All of these rely extensively on the *Autobiography*. I have footnoted only direct quotations from it. I indulge a hope that someone will yet properly "do" Beecher with the mixture of sympathetic understanding and judicious skepticism that is needed.

48. Beecher, *op. cit.*, I, 21.

49. *Ibid.*, 30-31.

50. *Ibid.*, 33-34. Italics mine.

51. *Ibid.*, II, 555.

52. *Ibid.*, I, 77-78.

53. *Ibid.*, 69-70.

54. *Ibid.*, 100-01.

55. *Ibid.*, 120-21.

56. The *Independent*, January 29, 1863, "Reminiscences of Dr. Beecher."

57. Beecher, *op. cit.*, I, 150-56.

58. *Ibid.*, 161-65.

59. *Ibid.*, 165-68.

60. *Ibid.*, 216.

61. For details, see Richard J. Purcell, *Connecticut in Transition* (Washington, 1918).

62. Beecher, *op. cit.*, I, 297, 337. For a good, understanding, general view of Beecher's activity in this period, see Mead, *op. cit.*, 76-93.

63. Beecher, *op. cit.*, I, 263.

64. Keller, *op. cit.*, 188-201.

65. Rourke, *op. cit.*, 28. See also Beecher, *op. cit.*, I, 344-45. Italics mine.

66. *Ibid.*

67. Beecher, *op. cit.*, I, 389.

68. *Ibid.*, 438-39.

69. *Ibid.*, 449.

70. *Ibid.*, II, 110.

71. *Ibid.*, 72-78.

72. Joshua Bradley, *Accounts of Religious Revivals in Many Parts of the United States from 1815 to 1818 Collected from Numerous Publications and Letters from Persons of Piety and Correct Information* (Albany, 1818).

73. See the *Methodist Magazine* (1815-26), *passim*, but especially I (1818), 154-59, 237-40, 356-60, and III (1820), 277-80.

74. See Cole, *op. cit.*, 18-58.

75. Beecher, *op. cit.*, II, 187; I, 329-30, 347.

76. The entire story of the development of "Taylorism" and the succeeding war over it is excellently told in Mead, *op. cit.*, particularly chapters VII, XIII and XIV.

77. Beecher, *op. cit.*, I, 37.

CHAPTER IV   *Out of His Mouth Goeth a Sharp Sword*

Title is from Revelation 15:19.

1. Charles G. Finney, *Memoirs of Rev. Charles G. Finney Written by Himself* (New York, 1876), 228. These memoirs, written without notes in his old age, give an excellent picture of the tough-grained evangelist himself, but are naturally disposed to present a one-dimensional view. They should be supplemented by George F. Wright, *Charles Grandison Finney* (New York, 1891), admiring, but grounded on careful investigation. Wright was one of Finney's faculty colleagues at Oberlin. There is a good "intellectual" biography in an unpublished piece of work, Roy A. Cheesebro's "The Preaching of Charles Grandison Finney" (Ph.D dissertation, Yale, 1948). There is no recent published biography worth consideration. A few uniformly unenlightened and uncritical "lives" have been put out by evangelical publishing houses. Examples of this class are Frank G. Beardsley, *A Mighty Winner of Souls, Charles G. Finney* (Des Moines, 1944); Richard E. Day, *Man of Like Passions . . . Charles Grandison Finney* (Grand Rapids, 1942); Victor R. Erdman,

Finney Lives On (New York, 1951); and Basil W. Miller, *Charles G. Finney. He Prayed Down Revivals* (Grand Rapids, 1941). Short sketches of Finney in other works will be referred to in the notes that follow.

2. Finney, *Memoirs*, 199-200.

3. Ray A. Billington, *Westward Expansion* (New York, 1950), 251-61.

4. Philemon H. Fowler, *Historical Sketch of Presbyterianism Within the . . . Synod of Central New York* (Utica, 1877), 552-53.

5. Synthesized from Finney, *Memoirs*, 4-17; Wright, *op. cit.*, 1-6; Robert S. Fletcher, *A History of Oberlin College From Its Foundation Through the Civil War*, 2 vols. (Oberlin, Ohio, 1943), I, 1-7; and Charles C. Cole, Jr., *The Social Ideas of the Northern Evangelists, 1826-1860* (New York, 1954), 58-59.

6. Finney, *Memoirs*, 18-21.

7. *Ibid.*, 24.

8. *Ibid.*, 25-41; Wright, *op. cit.*, 14-19.

9. Finney, *Memoirs*, 42. Italics mine.

10. *Ibid.*, 45-46.

11. Finney says that he was licensed in March, 1824, but Fowler, *op. cit.*, 258n., gives an earlier date.

12. Finney, *Memoirs*, 51-60; Wright, *op. cit.*, 20-25. Cheesebro, *op. cit.*, has the most thorough available discussion on Finney's religious education. See Part II especially.

13. Wright, *op. cit.*, 26; Fowler, *op. cit.*, 200; Finney, *Memoirs*, 65.

14. Finney, *Memoirs*, 60-83; Wright, *op. cit.*, 32-33.

15. Finney, *Memoirs*, 103-05.

16. *Ibid.*, 107-08. For Finney's notions of election, see his sermon, "Doctrine of Election," in *Sermons on Important Subjects* (New York, 1836), 209-20. Although the book was published twelve years after Finney began his preaching career, there is no good reason to believe that he had changed his views. These sermons were written hastily from short notes, and Cheesebro thinks they do a poor job of representing Finney's views. I suspect, however, that their casual nature in itself makes them more faithful to what Finney, always an extemporaneous speaker, said.

17. Finney, *Memoirs*, 11-13; Wright, *op. cit.*, 37-39.

18. *Ibid.*, 115-16. This reference to sinners' taking the front seat is interesting. Wright, *op. cit.*, 100, says that the "anxious bench" — the calling of those "convicted" to sit in a special (and visible)

location — was introduced by Finney in Rochester in 1831. It would appear that he overlooked this passage in the *Memoirs.*

19. *Ibid.,* 127-33.

20. *Ibid.,* 136-37.

21. *Ibid.,* 74, 120, 142-43, 147, 152.

22. Fowler, *op. cit.,* 198. Wright makes 1826 the date of the synod meeting which Finney attended just before the revival at Western, but internal evidence shows this to be an error.

23. Robert Aikman, "President Finney," *The Independent,* September 2, 1875; Henry B. Stanton, *Random Recollections* (New York, 1887), 42.

24. Ephraim Perkins, *A Bunker Hill Contest, A.D. 1826, Between the 'Holy Alliance' for the Establishment of Hierarchy, and Ecclesiastical Domination Over the Human Mind, on the One Side: and Asserters of Free Inquiry, Bible Religion, Christian Freedom and Civil Liberty on the Other. The Rev. Charles Finney, 'Home Missionary' and High Priest of the Expeditions of the Alliance in the Interior of New-York; Headquarters, County of Oneida* (Utica, 1826), 68-69.

25. Finney, *Memoirs,* 183-84.

26. Fletcher, *op. cit.,* 16.

27. H. Pomeroy Brewster, "The Magic of a Voice," *Rochester Historical Society Publication Fund Series,* IV (1925), 280.

28. Lyman Beecher, *Autobiography, Correspondence . . . of the Rev. Lyman Beecher, D.D.,* 2 vols. (New York, 1864), II, 311; Benjamin P. Thomas, *Theodore Weld, Crusader for Freedom* (New Brunswick, N. J., 1950), 15; Aikman, *loc. cit.*

29. Wright, *op. cit.,* 71-74.

30. Brewster, *op. cit.,* 283.

31. Stanton, *op. cit.,* 40-42.

32. I have synthesized this discussion of Finney's style from his own extended comments in his *Memoirs,* 80-96. The Beecher quotation about "knocking out the bung" is from Weld, *op. cit.,* 101-02. See also a letter of Beecher to daughter Catharine in 1819. "I am glad, my child, that you feel the difference between the gospel preached plainly and that despicable, pitiable stuff called, or meant to be called, fine writing." Beecher, *op. cit.,* I, 408-09.

33. Finney, *Memoirs,* 249-50.

34. *Ibid.,* 180, 193, 228.

35. Biographical information is in Fowler, *op. cit.*: Gale, 552-53,

Aiken, 209-10, Frost, 220-23, Gillett, 91, and Lansing, 86-88. The statement from the charter of Andover is in Peter G. Mode, *Source Book and Bibliographical Guide for American Church History* (Menasha, Wisc., 1921), 368-70. A description of revivals among New York State Presbyterians from 1800 to 1825 is in Fowler, *op. cit.*, 168-206.

36. William F. P. Noble, *God's Doings in Our Vineyard, Being a History of the Growth of Evangelical Religion in the United States*, etc. (Philadelphia, 1882), 412-16; Wright, *op. cit.*, 40-42; Finney, *Memoirs*, 52, 70-71, 134.

37. Parsons Cooke, *Recollections of Rev. E. D. Griffin, or, Incidents Illustrating His Character* (Boston, 1855). Griffin also held a pulpit in Boston for several years, and made a valiant attempt to evangelize that city. For a record of this attempt see *A Series of Lectures Delivered in Park Street Church in Boston* (Boston, 1813).

38. Fowler, *op. cit.*, 179. See also Robert E. Thompson, *A History of the Presbyterian Churches in the United States* (New York, 1895), 79-101, and especially 93, where Thompson claims that the Presbyterians had grown from 598 churches in 1807 to 2158 in 1830.

39. *Methodist Magazine*, I (1818), 152-55. For more on the Methodists in New York particularly, see George Peck, *Early Methodism Within the Bounds of the Old Genesee Conference* (New York, 1860).

40. *Ibid.*, II (1819), 75-76.

41. *Ibid.*, VII (1824), 435-36; VIII (1825), 158-61.

42. Beecher, *op. cit.*, II, 176-77.

43. *New York Evangelist*, April 14, 1832, "Revival Department."

44. Joshua Leavitt Papers, Library of Congress, Joshua to Roger Leavitt, February 28, 1819.

45. Beecher, *op. cit.*, I, 431, 460.

46. Bennet Tyler, *Memoir of the Life and Character of Rev. Asahel Nettleton, D.D.* (Hartford, 1844), 108-09.

47. Cooke, *op. cit.*, 146.

48. Mary Mitchell, *The Great Awakening and Other Revivals in Connecticut* (New Haven, 1936), 31.

49. Edward A. Lawrence, *The Life of Rev. Joel Hawes, D.D., Tenth Pastor of the First Church, Hartford, Conn.* (Hartford, 1871), 69.

50. Calvin Colton, *History and Character of American Revivals of Religion* (London, 1832), 17-19, 76-77.

51. See Whitney R. Cross, *The Burnt-Over District: The Social and Intellectual History of Enthusiastic Religion in Western New York 1825-50* (Ithaca, N. Y., 1950), a labored but exhaustive study of the religious rip tides of the period. It is interesting to note that Finney himself uses the term "burnt district" — i.e., one already burned over to clear it of stumps and underbrush before planting — to refer to St. Lawrence and Jefferson counties at the beginning of his work there. (*Memoirs*, 78.)

52. Finney, *Memoirs*, 144-201; Wright, *op. cit.*, 46-50, 62; Fowler, *op. cit.*, 184-226. Theodore Weld has an interesting description of his own conversion at Utica in Beecher, *op. cit.*, II, 310-12.

53. These practices are described in many places, but for a concise summary, see the chapter in Cross, *op. cit.*, entitled "New Measures." Also, Fowler, *op. cit.*, 257-77, for a defense of them.

54. William R. Weeks, *The Pilgrim's Progress in the Nineteenth Century* (New York, 1848); Wright, *op. cit.*, 66.

55. Perkins, *op. cit.* Wright refers to this pamphlet, *op. cit.*, 68, and attempts to refute it. Finney mentions it, too, not very charitably, in the *Memoirs*, 188. He erroneously labels the author a Unitarian minister, though the title page of the work carefully describes Perkins as "A Layman of Trenton."

56. Perkins, *op. cit.*, 6, 61.

57. *Ibid.*, 64-67. But in fairness it should be stated that Perkins, who seems to have been a man with some respect for facts, says that the story of "Jesus Christ's horse" is stated on "good authority" only, and that Finney's name was not connected with the "King of Kings" handbill, a point which Wright underlines, *op. cit.*, 68. In addition, Finney says that Lewis Tappan much later wrote Perkins and offered five hundred dollars for proof of some of these charges, which Perkins was unable to furnish. See the *Memoirs*, 281-82. The term "holy band" is widely used for Finney's disciples — see, for example, Thomas's book on Weld, 16 — but I have not been able to run down its origin. The "Reverend Norton" is most likely Herman Norton. A store clerk, converted in Auburn in 1817, he attended Hamilton College and Auburn Theological Seminary, and was working in upstate New York as an evangelist from about 1826 to 1830. See Fowler, *op. cit.*, 615-16.

58. Perkins, *op. cit.*, 68-69.

59. *Ibid.*, 56-60.

60. Finney, *Memoirs*, 154-55. See also the sermon "Sinners Bound

to Change Their Own Hearts," *Sermons on Important Subjects,* 1-42, especially 29-30. The italics in the last sentence are mine.

61. Finney, *Memoirs*, 110.

62. *Ibid.*, 242-44.

63. It is interesting to note that Lyman Beecher took exactly this view once when being shown around a hospital by a Boston doctor. Beecher observed that a notebook was kept which recorded the patients' histories. "Why," he said, "it's almost an exact image of my inquiry meeting. I have my book, where I note down my cases and their symptoms, just as you do." Beecher, *op. cit.*, II, 77.

64. Charles G. Finney Papers, Oberlin College Library, Oberlin, Ohio, W. F. Hurd to Finney, February 10, 1828.

65. Gilbert H. Barnes and Dwight L. Dumond, eds., *Letters of Theodore Weld, Angelina Grimké Weld and Sarah Grimké, 1822-1844*, 2 vols. (New York, 1934), I, 33-35.

66. Finney Papers, N. S. S. Beman to Finney, September 25, 1826.

67. Finney Papers, G. Spaulding to Finney, February 16, 1827. There is a sketch of Myrick in Cross, *op. cit.*, 151-97, and one in Fowler, *op. cit.*, 278.

68. Finney Papers, J. P. Cushman to Finney, February 21, 1828.

69. Wright, *op. cit.*, 67-68. But he points out, 52-53, that five or six years later, when Finney's respectability was more securely established, the same group joined in asking him to return to Auburn, which he did.

70. *The Independent*, October 6, 1864; *Weld-Grimké Letters*, I, 33n.

71. Finney Papers, N. S. S. Beman to Finney, September 23, 1826.

72. Josephus Brockway, *A Delineation of the Characteristic Features of a Revival of Religion in Troy, in 1826 and 1827. By J. Brockway, Lay Member of the Congregational Church in Middlebury, Vt., Now a Citizen of Troy* (Troy, 1827), 23-25.

73. *Ibid.*, 38.

74. *A Brief Account of the Origin and Progress of the Divisions in the First Presbyterian Church in the City of Troy . . . By a Number of the Late Church and Congregation* (Troy, 1827). There is no name on this pamphlet, but Wright, *op. cit.*, 70-71, ascribes it to Brockway, and a comparison of the style and content with Brockway's signed attack on the Beman-Finney revival, cited in n. 72, *supra*, makes this appear a reasonable guess. The charge that it

was a falsehood is in the Finney Papers, J. P. Cushman to Finney, December 21, 1827.

75. Quoted in Wright, *op. cit.*, 69-71. It will be noted that this is another version of the same scene whose description so enthralled an audience at Andover (*supra*, n. 29). Actually, the difference is one of degree. As Wright decorously puts it, the two versions illustrate "the extent to which the personal sentiments and sympathies of the reporter affect his account of a discourse."

76. *A Delineation* . . . , 40.

77. *A Brief Account* . . . , 21-24.

78. Finney, *Memoirs*, 202-03.

79. Beecher, *op. cit.*, II, 89-97. Italics are in the original. The Unitarian comment on the revivals is in the *Christian Examiner*, IV (1827), 242-65.

80. *Letters of the Rev. Dr. Beecher and Rev. Mr. Nettleton on the 'New Measures' in Conducting Revivals of Religion*, etc. (New York, 1828), 2-20. A long extract is in Wright, *op. cit.*, 76-79, and in Bennet Tyler's *Memoir* of Nettleton, as well as in other places.

81. A copy of this letter, dated February 15, 1827, is in the Finney Papers.

82. Beecher, *op. cit.*, II, 99.

83. Finney, *Sermons on Important Subjects*, 181-95, especially 187. The sermon was published separately in 1827. See Wright, *op. cit.*, 81n.

84. *Letters of Beecher and Nettleton*, 25-41, 42-44, 80-101.

85. Charles C. Cole, Jr., "The New Lebanon Convention," *New York History*, XXXI (1950), 389. I have pulled together the account of the conference — and there is general agreement as to the facts — from this article, covering 385-97 in the journal cited; Wright, *op. cit.*, 85-94; Finney, *Memoirs*, 211-23; and Beecher, *op. cit.*, II, 100-02.

86. Finney insisted until his dying day that the charges were entirely groundless and that the whole affair was a tempest in a teapot. A letter from him in "Foreign Correspondence," *The Independent*, April 17, 1851, reiterates his constant question: "Where . . . have I . . . led the churches astray, or unsettled pastors?"

87. Finney's account of his Boston campaign of 1831, including a delicious scene in which Beecher contradicted, or at least erroneously restated, one of Finney's arguments right in the middle of a sermon, is in Finney, *Memoirs*, 312-18.

88. Beecher, *op. cit.*, II, 102-08; Finney, *Memoirs*, 222-25; Wright, *op. cit.*, 94-95. Finney says he was "not a party" to the Philadelphia agreement, but Wright unearthed the document and found his signature on it. Finney's friends replied to the continued attack with the publication, in 1828, of *A Narrative of the Revival . . . in the County of Oneida*, emphasizing the Oneida Presbytery's full confidence in Finney's "piety and judgment." This is related in Fletcher, *op. cit.*, I, 15.

89. Finney, of course, claimed that he thrashed out his theology independently. Beecher, on the other hand, tries to leave the impression that Finney was harness-broken by reading Edwards and some of the New Haven school. (I am speaking, here, of Finney's early revival doctrines, not his later perfectionism.) A judicious evaluation is to be found in Parts I and II of Cheesebro, *op. cit.*

90. Finney Papers, Joab Seely to Finney, March 18, 1826; Silas Churchill to Finney, April 6, 1827; J. Grier to Finney, March 31 and December 29, 1828.

91. Finney Papers, Julia Peabody to Finney, June 30, 1827.

92. Finney, *Memoirs*, 234-35.

93. *Weld-Grimké Letters*, I, 11, 23.

94. Finney Papers, Zephaniah Platt to Finney, December 20, 1827.

95. Finney Papers, D. Dodge to Finney, December 18, 1827.

96. Finney Papers, Zephaniah Platt to Finney, March 10, 1828. Phelps's letter is quoted in Fletcher, *op. cit.*, I, 25-26.

97. The exact chronology of this period is quite confused by Finney and Wright. I have not thought it material to straighten it out by close examination of other sources. Sometime between the end of 1829 and the autumn of 1830, Finney put in a long period in New York. What is not clear from these two works is the date of the ending of the Philadelphia stint and the Reading and Lancaster interludes.

98. Wright, *op. cit.*, 99; Finney, *Memoirs*, 293.

99. Finney, *Memoirs*, 302-19.

100. Finney Papers, G. W. Gale to Finney, July 28, 1827.

101. Finney Papers, Daniel Nash to Finney, October 27, 1828; *Weld-Grimké Letters*, I, 15, 40.

102. Fletcher, *op. cit.*, I, 29-30.

103. *Ibid.*, 31. A sketch of Hastings, an upstate New Yorker, is in Fowler, *op. cit.*, 696-705.

104. Fletcher, *op. cit.*, I, 31.

CHAPTER V *And a Great Number Believed*

Title is from The Acts 11:21.

1. Dwight L. Dumond and Gilbert H. Barnes, eds., *Letters of Theodore Weld, Angelina Grimké and Sarah Grimké*, 2 vols. (New York, 1934), I, 14-17.

2. *New York Evangelist*, April 21, 1832, reviewing a reissue of Edwards's *Narrative of the Surprising Work of God*.

3. Peter G. Mode, *Source Book and Bibliographical Guide for American Church History* (Menasha, Wisc., 1921), 424-26.

4. See, for example, a thoroughly typical number, April 23, 1831.

5. *Ibid.*

6. *Ibid.*, September 17, 1831, "Revivals."

7. *Ibid.*, April 14, 1832, "Revival Intelligence."

8. *Ibid.*, May 26, 1832, "Revival Intelligence."

9. *Ibid.*, June 23, 1832, "Revival Department," and August 18, 1832, "Correspondence of the *Evangelist*." Italics mine.

10. Calvin Colton, *History and Character of American Revivals of Religion* (London, 1832), 30-31. A brief biographical sketch of Colton is in Charles C. Cole, Jr., *The Social Ideas of the Northern Evangelists, 1826-1860* (New York, 1954), 71n.

11. *New York Evangelist*, April 30, 1831, "Revival Measures."

12. *Ibid.*, October 8, 1831, "The Necessity of Revivals."

13. Jonathan Edwards, *Edwards on Revivals* (New York, 1832), 189-95.

14. Lyman Beecher, *Autobiography, Correspondence . . . of Lyman Beecher, D.D.*, 2 vols. (New York, 1864), II, 239-77, for the story of the Lane offer. The quotation about Unitarians' clapping their hands for joy is on page 232, the prayer of acceptance on 271 and the fear of "Catholics and infidels" on 224. The New Haven controversy is discussed intermittently, 156-238. For the details of the fight and Beecher's part in it, see Sidney Mead, *Nathaniel William Taylor, 1786-1858, A Connecticut Liberal* (Chicago, 1942).

15. George Frederick Wright, *Charles Grandison Finney* (New York, 1891), 106-08, 123-37. The story of how Oberlin profited by the troubles at Lane is told in numerous places. Beecher, *op. cit.*, II, 320-32, gives his version. Benjamin P. Thomas has a good discussion in *Theodore Weld, Crusader for Freedom* (New Brunswick, N. J. 1950). The most thorough coverage and the best starting point are

in Robert S. Fletcher, *A History of Oberlin College from Its Founding to the Civil War*, 2 vols. (Oberlin, Ohio, 1943). Finney's own story of his New York City "career" is in his *Memoirs of Rev. Charles G. Finney Written by Himself* (New York, 1876), 320-36. Gilbert H. Barnes in *The Anti-Slavery Impulse 1830-44* (New York, 1933), correctly emphasizes the connection between revivalism, the "Lane rebellion," and antislavery in the West. It must be remembered, however, that his book is making a case against the alleged predominance of New England and William Lloyd Garrison in the abolition movement, and he tends to bear down a little hard on his thesis sometimes.

16. Finney, *Memoirs*, 334-37.

17. We really need a study of American revivalists in England. Dow, Nettleton, Finney, Moody and many of their lesser collaborators spent time there. There was a strong English evangelical movement, with its own popular apostles. The influence, if any, upon each other, of the American and English developments in popular religion demands investigation as part of the whole story of trade in ideas between the United States and Great Britain — a story too often neglected.

18. Cole, *op. cit.*, 43-44. Barnes himself wrote an autobiographical work, *Life at Three-Score* (Philadelphia, 1858). The handiest summation of his views is in his *The Theory and Desirableness of Revivals* (London, 1842).

19. Whitney R. Cross, *The Burnt-Over District: The Social and Intellectual History of Enthusiastic Religion in Western New York 1825-50* (Ithaca, N. Y., 1950), 188-89; Frank G. Beardsley, *A History of American Revivals* (New York, 1904), 161-62; William F. P. Noble, *God's Doings in Our Vineyard* (Philadelphia, 1882), 401-06. There are sporadic accounts of Burchard-led revivals in the *New York Evangelist;* for example, the numbers of January 3, 1835, February 14, 1835 (in which his "great plainness and boldness" of speech is referred to), January 7, 1837, and March 25, 1837 (at which time he was in New York City). His work in Rochester is described in H. Pomeroy Brewster, "The Magic of a Voice," *Rochester Historical Society Publication Fund Series*, IV (Rochester, 1925), 273-90, although the article is mostly about Finney. See Burchard's own *Sermons, Addresses and Exhortations* (Burlington, Vt., 1836).

20. See William Baker, *The Life and Labors of the Rev. Daniel*

Baker, D.D. (Philadelphia, 1858). See also Noble, *op. cit.*, 364-89, and Beardsley, *op. cit.*, 160.

21. Cole, *op. cit.*, 76n. See David O. Mears, *Life of Edward Norris Kirk* (Boston, 1877).

22. Knapp himself wrote his own history, the *Autobiography of Elder Jacob Knapp* (New York, 1868). Sketches are also in Beardsley, *op. cit.*, 164-74; Noble, *op. cit.*, 390-401; and Cole, *op. cit.*, 33-36.

23. Swan, too, has his memoir, *The Evangelist, or, Life and Labors of Rev. Jabez Swan* (Waterford, Conn., 1873). Brief portraits are in Beardsley, *op. cit.*, 175-76, and Noble, *op. cit.*, 505-14.

24. Cole, *op. cit.*, 85-87; John N. Maffitt, *Tears of Contrition, or, Sketches of the Life of John Newland Maffitt* (New London, Conn., 1821); Moses Elsemore, *An Impartial Account of the Life of the Rev. John N. Maffitt* (New York, 1848).

25. Caughey wrote many works. His *Glimpses of Life in Soul-Saving* (New York, 1868) contains autobiographical material. For Inskip, there is a short notice in Noble, *op. cit.*, 490-94; a biography, *"I Am, O Lord, Wholly and Forever Thine"; The Life of Rev. John S. Inskip* (Boston, 1885) by William McDonald; and Inskip's own *Memorial of Rev. John S. Inskip* (Philadelphia, 1884).

26. Material on these people is fragmentary and must be hunted through such revival histories as those of Headley, Beardsley, Noble, Thompson, Conant *et al.* There are some biographies (all worshipful) and a few autobiographies. For Emerson Andrews, there is his own *Living Life, or Autobiography* (Boston, 1872) in addition to volumes of sermons and songs; for Absalom B. Earle, his *Work of An Evangelist. Review of Fifty Years* (Boston, 1881) and *Bringing in Sheaves* (Boston, 1869); for Maggie Van Cott, John O. Foster's *Life and Labors of Mrs. Maggie Newton Van Cott* (Cincinnati, 1872) and the lady's recollections, *The Harvest and the Reaper; Reminiscences of Revival Work* (New York, 1883); for Orson Parker, his own *The Fire and the Hammer* (Boston, 1877). Examples of the references to the work of these people which fill the periodicals are to be found in the *Independent*, December 2, 1852, May 22, 1856, and March 28, 1867, all under the heading "Revival Record." These references are to Parker. Mention is made of Edward P. Hammond in the same paper on November 30, 1865, "Religious Intelligence." (Hammond also has an official biography by Phineas C. Headley, *The Reaper and the Harvest*, published in New York in 1884.) Absalom B. Earle

appears in the *New York Evangelist*, under "Revival Record," on January 31, 1867. These are but a few among numerous citations. One could trace an itinerary for these men by such references, if it were a profitable enterprise, which it assuredly is not.

27. For example, the *New York Observer*, July 10, 1847; the *Independent*, April 3, 1851, "Revivals," and October 4, 1866, "Revival Record."

28. Beecher tells of his aid in founding the *Spirit of the Pilgrims* in *op. cit.*, II, 122-32. As for the general change that came over revivalism, William W. Sweet entitled a short book on the subject *American Revivalism: Its Origin, Growth and Decline* (New York, 1944) and placed the end of the "decline" in 1844. He is entirely correct in this appraisal within his own definition, since the revivals after 1844 he regards as the fruits of "professionalism." I believe, however, that the "professional" phase is itself worth further study, since it, too, had cycles of growth and stagnation, attempted to solve problems and developed leaders and techniques.

29. *New York Evangelist*, June 6, July 11, 1835.

30. *Ibid.*, March 4, 11, 1837, and July 8, 1837, quoting the *Cleveland Herald*.

31. *New York Observer*, January 20, November 2, 1844, July 5, 1845, November 4, 1848.

32. The *Independent*, February 27, October 9, 16, 1851.

33. *Ibid.*, February 8, 1855. There were peaks and valleys in the number of revivals — 1842-1843 and 1857-1858, for example, were "good" years. It might be possible to correlate these peaks and valleys with political or economic excitement and activity, but it would be a laborious work, and the prospects of reaching definite conclusions would be slim.

34. *New York Evangelist*, June 18, 1831.

35. [Orville Dewey], *Letters of an English Traveller to His Friend in England on the 'Revivals of Religion' in America* (Boston, 1828), 67.

36. *Ibid.*, 120-24.

37. Edward D. Griffin, *A Letter to a Friend on the Connexion Between the New Doctrines and the New Measures* (Albany, N. Y., 1833), 6. See also his *Letter to the Rev. Ansel D. Eddy of Canandaigua, New York, on the Narrative of the Late Revivals of Religion in the Presbytery of Geneva* (Williamstown, Mass., 1832).

38. Reported in the *New York Evangelist*, June 9, 1832.

39. *New York Observer,* March 13, 1843, "The Revival in Philadelphia."

40. Lyman H. Atwater, "The Revivals of the Century," *Presbyterian Quarterly and Princeton Review,* N.S. V (1876), 690-719.

41. *Revivals of Religion Considered as a Means of Grace; A Series of Plain Letters to Candidus, From His Friend Honestus* (Ithaca, N.Y., 1827), 13, 18.

42. Dewey, *op. cit.,* 18-19, 28.

43. *Christian Examiner,* VI (March-July, 1829), 101-30.

44. Edwards A. Park, *Memoir of Nathaniel Emmons* (Boston, 1861), 172-75. See also Heman Humphrey, *Revival Sketches and Manual* (New York, 1859), 265-66.

45. Bennet Tyler, *Memoir of the Life and Character of Rev. Asahel Nettleton, D.D.* (Hartford, 1844), 196.

46. Quoted in *New York Evangelist,* January 10, 1835.

47. Quoted in *Boston Register and Christian Observer,* July 28, 1838.

48. *New York Observer,* March 5, 1842.

49. See the discussion of Bushnell in Cole, *op. cit.,* 45-54.

50. Henry S. Commager, *Theodore Parker* (Boston, 1936), 271. These sermons were reprinted in a volume under Parker's name, *The Revival of Religion Which We Need* (Boston, 1858). There is antirevival literature in abundance for this period, both in periodicals and in pamphlet form. A sampling of the antirevival library would include, in addition to the works already cited, Menzies Rayner, *A Dissertation upon Extraordinary Awakenings* (Hudson, N. Y., 1816); "Candour" [pseud.], *Theological Pretenders, or, An Analysis of the Character and Conduct of the Rev. John N. Maffitt* (New York, 1830); "Cranmer" [pseud.], *A Few Remarks on 'Revivals' Addressed to Those Who Think* (Canandaigua, N. Y., 1830); Russell Streeter, *Mirror of Calvinist Fanaticism, or, Jedediah Burchard and Co.* (Woodstock, Vt., 1835); Sylvester Eaton, *Burchardism vs. Christianity* (Poughkeepsie, N. Y., 1837); S. B. Brittain, *Lying Wonders of Elder Jacob Knapp Exposed* (n.p., 1845); and William R. Weeks, *The Pilgrim's Progress in the Nineteenth Century* (New York, 1848). Several more are listed in Mode, *op. cit.,* 395.

51. Benjamin B. Smith, *Thoughts on Revivals* (Middlebury, Vt., 1828), 13-15.

52. *New York Evangelist,* April 7, 1832, "Revival Intelligence"; *Spirit of the Pilgrims* [Boston], quoted in *ibid.,* September 24, 1831.

53. Edward A. Lawrence, *The Life of Rev. Joel Hawes, D.D.* (Hartford, 1871), 114; Joel Hawes, *Historical Sketches of the First Church in Hartford* (Hartford, 1836), 26.

54. *New York Evangelist*, October 8, 1831, "The Necessity of Revivals."

55. *Methodist Quarterly Review*, XVII (1845), reviewing Robert Baird's *Religion in America, or An Account of the Origin . . . and Present Condition of the Evangelical Churches in the United States.* This book, published in New York in 1844, has itself considerable material on the revival system.

56. William B. Sprague, *Lectures on Revivals of Religion*, 2d ed. (New York, 1833), 213.

57. *New York Evangelist*, August 13, 1831, "Professors Department."

58. The *Independent*, April 17, 1851, "Revival Reminiscences." This was written by J. P. Thompson, one of the original editors of the paper.

59. *New York Evangelist*, April 14, 1832, quoting the *Christian Watchman*, which in turn is quoting the *Christian Spectator* of New Haven. The clipping appears in the *Evangelist's* "Revival Department." Italics mine.

60. *Christian Palladium*, March 10, 1837, "Revivals in New England."

61. Jonathan Edwards, *Treatise on Religious Affections* (New York, 1850), 109-11.

62. *New York Evangelist*, October 15, April 9, 1831. The series on "Revival Measures" began with the issue of April 14, 1832, and ran intermittently through the balance of that year.

63. *Ibid.*, August 18, 1832, "Revival Department."

64. Charles G. Finney, *Lectures on Revivals of Religion* (New York, 1868), 12-13.

65. The *Independent*, January 12, 1854, "How to Have a Revival."

66. William W. Sweet, *Religion on the American Frontier*, Vol. IV, *The Methodists* (Chicago, 1946), 303-04.

67. Knapp, *op. cit.*, 251-71. A good essay on popular culture in America could be developed out of a study of the rise of this familiar preaching style from, say, 1820 to 1860.

68. Finney's boast about introducing plain dress for clergymen and laymen's prayers is in *Lectures on Revivals*, 238-48. As for the revival hymns, here is still another fertile field for some student.

Undoubtedly, a close study of them would tell much about popular attitudes and psychology among the faithful. Leading revivalists liked to sponsor their own collections. Asahel Nettleton compiled — or at least gave his name to — *Village Hymns for Social Worship* (New York, 1828). There were also other collections which appeared from time to time. Examples are *Revival Melodies, or Songs of Zion* (Boston, 1842); Joseph Banvard, *Revival Gems* (Boston, 1858); J. Q. A. Fleharty, *The Revivalist; A Collection of Popular Hymns* (Galesburg, Ill., 1859); Edward N. Kirk, *Songs for Social and Public Worship* (Boston, 1864), *Revival and Camp-meeting Minstrel* (Philadelphia, 1867); Emerson Andrews, *Revival Songs* (Boston, 1870); and Absalom B. Earle, *Revival Hymns* (Boston, 1874).

69. The *Independent*, May 22, 1856.

70. William W. Sweet, *The Story of Religion in America*, 2d rev. ed. (New York, 1950), 310-11. The story of this much-heralded "awakening" of 1857-1858 can be gleaned from several primary sources. The preachers were vocal and happy over it, and a typical sampling of their views is in *The New York Pulpit in the Revival of 1858* (New York, 1858). Then there is a trio of books composed mostly of clippings from the press, namely, Pharcellus Church, *Pentecost; or, the Work of God in Philadelphia, A.D. 1858* (Philadelphia, 1859); William C. Conant, *Narratives of Remarkable Conversions and Revival Incidents* (New York, 1858); and S. I. Prime, *Power of Prayer Illustrated in Wonderful Displays of Divine Grace, at the Fulton Street and Other Meetings in New York and Elsewhere in 1857-58* (New York, 1858). There is also a doctoral dissertation, "The Great Awakening of 1857 and 1858," done by Carl L. Spicer at Ohio State University in 1935.

Of course, many revivalists hastened to become involved in this awakening, along with settled ministers. A few books even credit the affair to the work of Jeremiah C. Lanphier, a lay missionary of the Dutch Reformed Church in the city of New York. However, the failure of any one dominating clerical figure — or even two or three — to emerge from the entire year or so of the revival makes it clear that it was primarily a response of the laymen's organizations created by *earlier* revivals to the hard times after the panic of 1857. By that time, holding prayer meetings just came naturally.

71. Sweet, *Story of Religion in America*, 243-57.

72. *New York Evangelist*, October 8, 1831, "Revival Department."

73. Wright, *op. cit.*, 138. See also Cole, *op. cit.*, 78. The dependence of reform agencies on business prosperity is amply illustrated in individual studies of such agencies. Dwight Dumond and Gilbert Barnes, indeed, correctly refer in a footnote in their edition of the Weld-Grimké letters to "the collapse of the benevolent system" after 1837. See Vol. I, 12n.

74. *New York Evangelist*, March 4, 1837, "Communications."

75. The *Independent*, August 26, 1875, "Charles G. Finney."

76. *New York Observer*, October 5, 1844, "Two Great Revivals."

77. It is worth noting that Gilbert Barnes quite properly terminates his study of the antislavery impulse in 1844, after which it turned into a political crusade.

78. Cole, *op. cit.*, 77, 92.

79. This charge — that revival converts backslid in droves — was consistently made by opponents. It is difficult to document. An attempt was made in the *American Journal of Sociology* in that journal's early years. See Samuel W. Dike, "A Study of New England Revivals," XV (1909-10), 361-78.

80. Many of these movements are sympathetically and clearly discussed in Alice Felt Tyler's *Freedom's Ferment* (Minneapolis, 1944).

81. *New York Evangelist*, October 8, 1831, "Revival Department." For the changes in the masthead, see the numbers of April 23, 1831, January 3, 1835, and January 2, 1837. On this entire question of revivalism and reform, a new book appeared just as this chapter was being written, Timothy L. Smith, *Revivalism and Social Reform in Mid-Nineteenth Century America* (New York, 1957). Smith tries to prove that revivalism actually laid the groundwork for the "social gospel" movement of the latter part of the nineteenth century. He cites the numerous benevolent societies which sprang directly from revived churches as evidence. I think he overlooks a significant difference in approach. The benevolent associations of revivalism were aimed entirely at the conversion of individuals, after which it was expected that social improvement would be automatic. If they worked among the lowly and the fallen, it was only because they had to go where the raw materials of conversion were abundant. The proponents of the later social gospel, however, often were interested in an actual application of the ethics of Christianity to the world of private competition — in using what they considered Christian principles to build a new code of social responsibility. A more

sagacious view than Smith's, it seems to me, is contained in Clifford S. Griffin, "Religious Benevolence as Social Control, 1815-1860," *Mississippi Valley Historical Review*, XLIV (1957-58), 423-44.

82. Joshua Leavitt Papers, Library of Congress, Moses Smith to Roger Leavitt, December 14, 1836.

83. See Ralph H. Gabriel, "Evangelical Religion and Popular Romanticism in Early Nineteenth Century America," *Church History*, XIX (1950), 34-47, and also his discussion of "Christianity and the Democratic Faith," on pages 26-39 of his *The Course of American Democratic Thought*, 2d ed. (New York, 1950). See also Cole, *op. cit., passim.*

84. See Tyler, *Freedom's Ferment*, 316-27, and John A. Krout, *The Origins of Prohibition* (New York, 1924), on the temperance crusade. On the other movements see, among other things, Cross, *op. cit.*

85. Sweet, *Story of Religion in America*, 253.

86. Andrew L. Drummond, *The Story of American Protestantism* (Boston, 1951), 115-16.

87. Colton, *op. cit.*, 116-17.

88. For a most random sampling, see the *Methodist Magazine*, X (1827), 274; *New York Evangelist*, April 11, 1835, "Revivals," and October 3, 1835, "Revival Record."

89. Beecher, *op. cit.*, II, 447.

90. The *Independent*, April 9, 1863, "Our Western Correspondence."

91. Sweet, *Story of Religion in America*, 259-63.

92. Charles Lyell, *Journal of a Second Visit to the United States*, 2 vols. (New York, 1849), I, 139.

93. Finney, *Memoirs*, 230.

94. See Tyler, *Freedom's Ferment*, on nativism. The anti-Catholic note is struck frequently in the *New York Evangelist*. See, for example, "Rising Army of the Beast," June 18, 1831; a notice of the anti-Catholic paper the *Protestant*, September 10, 1831; and a clipping from *Zion's Herald*, March 21, 1835. The *New York Observer*, knowingly or otherwise, reprinted part of Poe's *The Pit and the Pendulum*, without identification, under the heading "Horrors of the Inquisition," April 8, 1843.

95. Cole, *op. cit.*, covers this matter well, 132-91.

96. See Tyler, *op. cit.;* Arthur Bestor, *Backwoods Utopias* (Phila-

delphia, 1950); and an earlier work, Charles Nordhoff, *The Commu-nistic Societies of the United States* (New York, 1875), for examples of a large literature on this subject.

97. The *Independent*, March 9, 1954, "Revivals and Reform."

98. Colton, *op. cit.*, 61-62.

99. *Ibid.*

100. *Christian Register*, April 25, 1835, "Orthodoxy Versus Revivals." Italics mine.

101. The *Independent*, January 23, 1851, "Western Correspondence."

CHAPTER VI *Troubled on Every Side*

Title is from II Corinthians 4:8.

1. Arthur M. Schlesinger, "A Critical Period in American Religion, 1875-1900," *Proceedings of the Massachusetts Historical Society*, LXIV (1930-32), 531. My summary of the crisis in religious life in the period from 1865 to 1890 is, of necessity, based heavily on secondary sources. The above-cited article (which runs from page 523 to 547 in the *Proceedings*) is very useful, comprehensive and not yet outdated. It was expanded, apparently, into the tenth chapter of the same author's *The Rise of the City* (New York, 1933), which is Volume X in the *History of American Life* series edited by Schlesinger and Dixon Ryan Fox. Three special studies have been extensively drawn upon — Aaron I. Abell, *The Urban Impact on American Protestantism, 1865-1900* (Cambridge, 1943); Charles H. Hopkins, *The Rise of the Social Gospel in American Protestantism, 1865-1915* (New Haven, 1940); and Henry F. May, *Protestant Churches and Industrial America* (New York, 1949). Other indebtedness is acknowledged in the notes which follow.

2. Merle Curti, *The Growth of American Thought* (New York, 1943), 548-54.

3. May, *op. cit.*, 47; Ralph H. Gabriel, *The Course of American Democratic Thought*, 2d ed. (New York, 1956), 171-72. An old, but standard, work on the subject of God and the findings of the laboratory is Andrew D. White, *A History of the Warfare of Science with Theology in Christendom*, 2 vols. (New York, 1896), and a modern one is Richard Hofstadter, *Social Darwinism in American Thought* (New York, 1944).

4. Schlesinger, "Critical Period in American Religion," 525-27; Curti, *op. cit.*, 540-43.

5. William W. Sweet, *The Story of Religion in America*, 2d rev. ed. (New York, 1950), 393. For other information on heresy hunts, see Schlesinger, "Critical Period in American Religion," 528-29.

6. John Rusk, *The Authentic Life of T. De Witt Talmage, The Greatly Beloved Divine* (Chicago, 1902), 296.

7. Theodore L. Cuyler, *Recollections of a Long Life* (New York, 1902), 78-79.

8. Schlesinger, "Critical Period in American Religion," 531-32.

9. Cuyler, *op. cit.*, 293-95.

10. *The Nation* is the source of the comment about a successful church being a flourishing corporation. It is quoted in Rollin W. Quimby, "Dwight L. Moody: An Examination of the Historical Conditions and Rhetorical Factors Which Contributed to His Effectiveness as a Speaker." Ph.D. dissertation, University of Michigan, 1951 (Ann Arbor: University Microfilms Publication #2637), 71.

11. Schlesinger, *Rise of the City*, 65-73.

12. *Ibid.*, 345.

13. Moody Letter Files, Moody Bible Institute, Chicago. D. W. Whittle to D. L. Moody, February 8, 1879.

14. Concerning anti-Catholic agitation and organizations, see Schlesinger, "Critical Period in American Religion," 544-46, and also Ray A. Billington, *The Protestant Crusade* (New York, 1938).

15. Paxton Hibben, *Henry Ward Beecher, An American Portrait* (New York, 1927), 332-33, 340-41.

16. Sweet, *Story of Religion in America*, 343.

17. A. V. G. Allen, *Phillips Brooks*, 2 vols. (New York, 1900), I, 380.

18. Abell, *op. cit.*, 137-65; Schlesinger, "Critical Period in American Religion," 538-40.

19. The *Independent*, February 16, 1854, "Modern Revivals." Signed "C.L.B.," the article is probably the work of Charles Loring Brace, a pioneer in religious social work.

20. Lyman Abbott, *Reminiscences* (Boston, 1915), 363-64.

21. Abell, *op. cit.*, 8-9, 118-36. See also Charles Hopkins, *A History of the Y.M.C.A. in the United States* (New York, 1951), and Herbert Wisbey, *Soldiers Without Swords, A History of the Salvation Army in the United States* (New York, 1955).

22. Hopkins, *Rise of the Social Gospel*, 7, 326. Hopkins's entire book documents the movement. See also May, *op. cit.*, especially 163-265, for a more discriminating analysis of the strength and

weakness of the "gospel." A less critical view is in Gabriel, *op. cit.*, 256-80. Abell, *op. cit.*, devotes pages 57-117 to these men and movements. His cautious conclusions are on pages 246-55.

23. Schlesinger, *Rise of the City*, 60-71.

24. Edgar Lee Masters, "The Mourner's Bench," in G. D. Sanders and J. H. Nelson, eds., *Chief Modern Poets of England and America*, 3d ed. (New York, 1946), 461.

25. See Hibben, *op. cit.*, *passim*. Henry Ward's emotional bent was sometimes a trial to him, and in fact the most spectacular episode of his career was a trial in which he was accused of seducing the wife of a parishioner and fellow editor of the *Independent*, Theodore Tilton. For a lively and impious view of these inconclusive proceedings, see Robert Shaplen, *Free Love and Heavenly Sinners* (New York, 1954).

26. Hibben, *op. cit.*, 282.

27. *Ibid.*, 130.

28. *Ibid.*, 166, 340.

29. Abbott, *op. cit.*, 161-62.

30. The *Independent*, January 9, 1873, "Our Pastoral Sketches." Italics mine.

31. *New York Evangelist*, July 11, 1835; *New York Observer*, April 8, 1843, "Parents and Children"; The *Independent*, February 26, 1852, "Sixpence a Week," copied from the *Gospel Messenger* (a missionary journal).

32. See Frank L. Mott, *A History of American Magazines*, Vol. III, 1865-85 (Cambridge, 1938), 63-89, for documentation and elaboration.

33. Rusk, *op. cit.*, 301, 372, 387, 410-11.

34. See, for example, the *Southern Christian Advocate*, a journal of the Methodist Episcopal Church South, published at Macon, Georgia, for January 26, July 20, August 10 and September 7, 1866. This is merely a sampling, which could be duplicated for any year through 1876.

35. See Hunter D. Farish, *The Circuit Rider Dismounts* (Richmond, 1938), for the complete story. On revivals in Confederate fighting forces, the book is William W. Bennett, *A Narrative of the Great Revival Which Prevailed in the Southern Armies During the Late Civil War*, etc. (Philadelphia, 1877).

36. See Henry Steele Commager, *The American Mind* (New York, 1950), 169. There is a good account of a small-town Southern

revival as late as the first decade of the twentieth century in Katherine Lumpkin, *The Making of a Southerner* (New York, 1947), 161-69.

37. Merely as an example, see the *Independent*, February 20, 1873, "Religious Intelligence."

38. *Ibid.*, March 6, 1873, "Revivals."

CHAPTER VII   *Words Easy to Be Understood*

Title is from I Corinthians 14:9.

1. Robert Boyd, *The Lives and Labors of Moody and Sankey, Giving Their Wonderful Career of Christian Conquest . . . Down to the Summer of 1876; Being a Concise Narrative of the Early Lives, Later Experiences and Grand Achievements of the Most Successful Evangelists of Modern Times* (Toronto, 1876), 359.

2. The Moody bibliography is enormous, and, happily, an effort to describe all of it through 1948 has been made in Wilbur M. Smith, *An Annotated Bibliography of Dwight L. Moody* (Chicago, 1948). Dr. Smith, of the Moody Bible Institute, reveres Moody and is himself a "fundamentalist," so that his annotations are not always perceptive or valuable, but he has collected widely. There is a most intelligent essay on books about Moody in the appendix to Paul Moody's *My Father: An Intimate Portrait of Dwight Moody* (Boston, 1938). Paul Moody correctly describes the "standard" biography to be that by his brother, William R. Moody. One version was hastily done in 1900, just after Moody's death; the revised edition, *D. L. Moody* (New York, 1930), is much more solid from a scholarly viewpoint, but uncritical and rarely cognizant of the background of the evangelist's life. Of the earlier biographies, there are two vintage periods — 1875-1877, the years of the great campaigns, and 1900-1901, the year succeeding his death. Among these, Paul Moody recommends Charles Goss, *Echoes from Pulpit and Platform* (Hartford, 1900), but I prefer William H. Daniels's *D. L. Moody and His Work* (Hartford, 1876), which has otherwise hard-to-find material on the early Chicago days, although it unfortunately ends on the eve of the greatest campaigns in the United States.

Two biographies of Moody by "rationalists" — one a religious man at bottom, the other a skeptic — are noteworthy. In 1894, Henry L. Drummond wrote an affectionate study entitled *Dwight L. Moody: Impressions and Facts*, published in New York in 1927. In

1927, Gamaliel Bradford published *D. L. Moody. A Worker in Souls*, an interesting work in which Bradford wrestled painfully, as any thoughtful critic must, with the contradictions between Moody's rudimentary theology and his genuine power. The latest full-length biography is now twenty-two years old. It is Richard E. Day, *Bush Aglow. The Life Story of Dwight L. Moody, Commoner of Northfield* (Philadelphia, 1936). This book has an advantage in that the author, then a Baptist minister in San Francisco, was able to consult the Washburne Papers, a large group of family letters held by an associate of Moody in Northfield. Unfortunately, this work is not only uncritical, but "inspirational," and written in what is without a doubt the most painful style of brummagem piety and mock archness ever committed to paper.

Moody is now sufficiently well embedded in history to be the subject of Ph.D. dissertations. There was one done at the University of Wisconsin in 1942, by B. F. Huber, entitled "D. L. Moody, Salesman of Salvation." Rollin W. Quimby wrote another at the University of Michigan in 1951, called "Dwight L. Moody: An Examination of the Historical Conditions and Rhetorical Factors Which Contributed to His Effectiveness as a Speaker." Richard Curtis submitted a doctoral dissertation at Purdue University on "The Pulpit Speaking of Dwight L. Moody," dated 1954. The Huber work is available on an interlibrary-loan basis, and the other two are on microfilm. I have only looked hastily at Huber's dissertation, but I read the other two carefully. They are limited in scope and standard-seminar in style. I have not seen an earlier dissertation on Moody done by Vernon F. Schwalm at the University of Chicago in 1915. As for other unpublished sources on Moody's life, there is a manuscript work, "Moody of Northfield," by Elmer W. Powell, a Philadelphia minister who has made a lifelong study of Moody and collected a great deal of Moodyana for the library of the Crozier Theological Seminary at Chester, Pennsylvania. Mrs. Emma Moody Fitt Powell, Moody's granddaughter, who resides in Northfield, also has some personal papers. I have not seen them or the Powell work.

Short sketches of Moody appear in many places, among them, Lyman Abbott, *Silhouettes of My Contemporaries* (New York, 1922). The periodical literature on the man is vast. Scarcely a number of *Moody Monthly*, the official publication of the Bible Institute, is without some sketch or reminiscence or tribute, often reprinted from earlier numbers. Smith has uncovered what seems to be the bulk of the magazine material available, although I am not sure how well he examined journals noted for "unbelief." I acknowledge my own indebtedness to these fugitive materials as I go along, and also to the hasty and sometimes shoddy biographies of the vintage years. There are, however, two good pieces of work among the biographies written just after Moody died and among the magazine pieces on him. Arthur P. Fitt's *The Shorter Life of D. L. Moody* (Chicago, 1900) is a good introduction to the subject. Fitt was Moody's son-in-law, and the Moody Bible Institute Colportage Association (now the Moody Press) printed the paper-covered book, which it still sells. Although reverential, Fitt's book is concise, anecdotal and knowing. An even shorter evocation of the spirit of Moody is the article by R. L. Duffus, "The Hound of Heaven," which appeared in the *American Mercury* for April, 1925. It is sharp and yet not cheap, and is cited with approval by Paul Moody.

I give this much space to the basic Moody bibliography because the man is a fascinating challenge, impossible to believe in wholly, and yet equally impossible to dislike. Even at this distance he commands a certain respect and affection, and we need to understand him if we really are to know the American mind of his generation. Someone must do the needed book, setting him against his times, which were also the times of Barnum and Rockefeller, Bryan and Ingersoll, Populism and urbanism, Darwin and Carrie Nation. The task awaits.

3. *Great Pulpit Masters*, Vol. I, *Dwight L. Moody* (New York, 1949), 75-76. Also contained in D. L. Moody, *Glad Tidings* (New York, 1876), 69.

4. Fitt, *op. cit.*, 11.

5. *Ibid.*, 17, 79. Fitt attributes the statement about cities to the year 1875.

6. J. Wilbur Chapman, *Dwight L. Moody* (New York, 1900), 54-55. Other recollections of the Moody boyhood are in Fitt, *op. cit.*, 1-18; Daniels, *op. cit.*, 4-19; and W. R. Moody, *op. cit.*, 3-27.

7. W. R. Moody, *op. cit.*, 28-31; Fitt, *op. cit.*, 17-19.

8. W. R. Moody, *op. cit.*, 33; Fitt, *op. cit.*, 19-20; Daniels, *op. cit.*, 20-21. The remark is given in a slightly different version in each case.

9. W. R. Moody, *op. cit.*, 33-35.

10. One should read William James's brilliant discussion of the effects of conversion on cheerful and gloomy temperaments in his *Varieties of Religious Experience* for more light on this.

11. Fitt, *op. cit.*, 21.
12. Chapman, *op. cit.*, 87.
13. Drummond, *op. cit.*, 56; Fitt, *op. cit.*, 23.
14. Chapman, *op. cit.*, 109.
15. W. R. Moody, *op. cit.*, 37-39, 42-43, 67; Fitt, *op. cit.*, 24-25.
16. Daniels, *op. cit.*, 31-32; Fitt, *op. cit.*, 25; W. R. Moody, *op. cit.*, 46-50.
17. Daniels, *op. cit.*, 34.
18. Bradford, *op. cit.*, 55-56.
19. Quoted in E. J. Goodspeed, *A Full History of the Wonderful Career of Moody and Sankey in Great Britain and America* (New York, 1876), 525-26.
20. This man is referred to as a "Mr. Carter" by Fitt, *op. cit.*, 27, and "Mr. Trudeau" by Daniels, *op. cit.*, 39.
21. This account of the North Market school is synthesized from several places. I have relied most heavily on Daniels, *op. cit.*, 34-75, which is quite thorough. I have also used W. R. Moody, *op. cit.*, 48-75, especially rich in reminiscences by other Chicagoans. Fitt, *op. cit.*, 27-32, is a useful condensed version. A description of Moody holding a Sunday-school picnic is in J. M. Hitchcock, "Reminiscences of D. L. Moody," *The Institute Tie*, N.S. V (1904-05), 77-78. This magazine is the forerunner of *Moody Monthly*, the Moody Bible Institute magazine which is a mine of Moodyana, under any of its various names since 1900. Chapman, *op. cit.*, 96, has enrollment figures for the school.
22. Chapman, *op. cit.*, 109.
23. Quimby, *op. cit.*, 109.
24. W. R. Moody, *op. cit.*, 75.
25. Daniels, *op. cit.*, 83-90.
26. W. R. Moody, *op. cit.*, 65-67.
27. "Dwight L. Moody as Many Men Saw Him," *Association Men*, XL (1915), 233-46. (This magazine was the official publication of the Y.)
28. Daniels, *op. cit.*, 199. Fitt, *op. cit.*, 67, says that this was after his return from a trip to England in 1867.
29. W. B. Jacobs, "D. L. Moody as a Sunday School Worker," *The Christian Workers' Magazine*, N.S. XIV (1913-14), 25-27. This is *Moody Monthly*'s ancestor under still another name.
30. Fitt, *op. cit.*, 71.
31. Daniels, *op. cit.*, 94-95. The Christian Commission, which was

basically religious in purpose, should not be confused with the Sanitary Commission, another volunteer organization designed especially to supplement the army's overwhelmed medical facilities, even though their work occasionally overlapped slightly.

32. According to W. R. Moody, *op. cit.*, 84-91, he was at the front after the battles of Shiloh, Stone River and Chattanooga, and in Richmond just after its capture. A picture of the work of the Christian Commission is given in M. H. Cannon, "The United States Christian Commission," *Mississippi Valley Historical Review*, XXXVIII (1951-52), 61-80.

33. Chapman, *op. cit.*, 181-82.

34. Daniels, *op. cit.*, 103-20; Fitt, *op. cit.*, 37-39; W. R. Moody, *op. cit.*, 98-100. Moody's technical title was "Deacon." When he went off on his evangelistic campaigns, the church was turned over to a succession of other pastors. It was burned out in the Chicago fire of 1871, and a new building raised on Chicago Avenue, which is still standing and in use.

35. Chapman, *op. cit.*, 102.

36. Daniels, *op. cit.*, 121-27.

37. This point — that Moody knew nothing but the Bible — can perhaps be a little overdone. Paul Moody, for example, in his recollections (114-15), says that his father owned a great many books and must have read some of them, since they contained marks "which could have been no other than his." On the other hand, none of this reading seemed to emerge in sermons, letters or conversation. On Moody's early Bible study see Daniels, *op. cit.*, 174-93.

38. See Fitt, *op. cit.*, 43; Bradford, *op. cit.*, 52. Bradford tries to make Moody's discovery of his preaching ability a sudden and dramatic thing, but it was not. See also Daniels, *op. cit.*, 161-69.

39. Goodspeed, *op. cit.*, 525-27. Moody used this phrase in 1876, speaking for the first time in the Chicago Avenue church, which was built during his English campaign of 1873-1875.

40. See the dissertations of Curtis, 15-54, and of Quimby, 140-84, for attempts to trace Moody's development as a speaker.

41. Daniels, *op. cit.*, 163-73.

42. Frank S. Mead, *Handbook of Denominations in the United States*, rev. ed. (New York, 1956), 50-52.

43. W. S. Manners, "D. L. Moody and His Early Contemporaries," *Moody Monthly*, XXXIV (1934), 257. Quimby, *op. cit.*, 157-59, discusses Moody's contacts with the Brethren in England.

44. J. V. Farwell, "Two Unpublished Letters of Mr. Moody," *The Institute Tie*, N.S. VI (1905-06), 181-83.

45. W. R. Moody, *op. cit.*, 108-09; Fitt, *op. cit.*, 54-55. The whole English trip is covered in the W. R. Moody book, 101-11.

46. W. R. Moody, *op. cit.*, 117-20.

47. All of this is told in various places. The prime source is Sankey's own *My Life and Story of the Gospel Hymns* (Philadelphia, 1907).

48. Several versions of this story are given, with minor variations. For lack of a better, I chose Chapman, *op. cit.*, 122-27.

49. Goodspeed, *op. cit.*, 525-27.

50. Frank G. Beardsley, *A History of American Revivals* (New York, 1904), 273-75; Daniels, *op. cit.*, 223-24.

51. Fitt, *op. cit.*, 67-70.

52. All the hasty biographies put out in 1875, on the return of Moody and Sankey to America, gave extensive space to English press reports of the great work in Great Britain. Smith's bibliography, which is broken down by date of publication, lists five full-length works for 1875, two for 1876 and one for 1877. (Smith, *op. cit.*, 1-8.) I have used, for the most part, the works by Boyd and Goodspeed already cited from among this crop.

53. It is impossible to check these figures, which vary considerably. I used an itinerary and attendance figures in Boyd, *op. cit.*, 48-207.

54. For the row over the appearance at Eton, see a report in the *Independent*, July 1, 1875.

55. Boyd, *op. cit.*, 46-47.

56. Quoted in the *Independent*, August 12, 1875, "Pebbles."

57. Boyd, *op. cit.*, 62-63; W. R. Moody, *op. cit.*, 214-15. See the *Independent*, March 25, 1875, "Religious Intelligence."

58. F. Engels, "On Historical Materialism," quoted in *Karl Marx, Selected Works*, 2 vols., ed. V. Adoratsky (New York, n.d.), II, 410-11.

59. Boyd, *op. cit.*, 205-06; W. R. Moody, *op. cit.*, 213.

60. Boyd, *op. cit.*, 214-15; W. R. Moody, *op. cit*, 200-04; Fitt, *op. cit.*, 77-78.

61. *New York Herald*, October 4, 6, 1875.

62. *Ibid.*, October 25, 1875.

63. *Ibid.*, October 24, 1875; the *Independent*, November 11, 1875, "Mr. Moody as a Preacher."

64. The *Independent*, November 11, 1875, "A Sermon by Mr.

Moody" and "Religious Intelligence," and November 25, 1875, "The Close of the Brooklyn Meetings."

65. W. R. Moody, *op. cit.*, 255-61; Boyd, *op. cit.*, 329; Goodspeed, *op. cit.*, 288-90.

66. W. R. Moody, *op cit.*, 262-63.

67 *Ibid.*, 264-71.

68. Goodspeed, *op. cit.*, 529-31.

69. W. R. Moody, *op. cit.*, 287-98; Phillips Brooks's appearance in Moody's place is referred to in A. V. G. Allen, *Phillips Brooks*, 2 vols. (New York, 1900), II, 148-50. The satires on the Boston campaign were gathered into a volume, under the pseudonym of I. A. M. Cumming, entitled *Tabernacle Sketches* (Boston, 1877). Although somewhat unfair, they are funny, and make a nice contrast to most of the reverent writing in which the story of revivalism is generally couched.

70. Smith, *op. cit.*, has an itinerary, xxii-xxiii.

71. *New York Herald*, October 8, 1875, "Moody and Sankey."

72. See Goodspeed or Boyd, *passim*, for details of how the meetings were organized. The inquiry room was so characteristic of Moody that when little Paul Moody was first shown the chapel at King's College, Cambridge, he innocently asked where the " 'quiry room" was. Paul Moody, *op. cit.*, 6.

73. Chapman, *op. cit.*, 162-63; W. R. Moody, *op. cit.*, 259.

74. Chapman, *op. cit.*, 162-63.

75. A detailed account of one such conference on tactics is in the *Independent*, April 6, 1876, "The Revival Convention." See also a "forum" synthesized from a number of accounts of such meetings in *Great Pulpit Masters*, I, 254-56. Or see Moody's own *Glad Tidings*, 461-70, or his *To All People* (Boston, 1877), 168-90, for three of these talks.

76. Quoted in Boyd, *op. cit.*, 249.

77. Moody Letter Files, Moody Bible Institute, Chicago, Moody to A. F. Gaylord, March 17, 1897. See also W. R. Moody, *op. cit.*, 419-20, and *To All People*, 181.

78. *Great Pulpit Masters*, I, 189-90, 256.

79. Chapman, *op. cit.*, 367; *To All People*, 173.

80. D. L. Moody, *Great Joy* (Chicago, 1877), 496.

81. Boyd, *op. cit.*, 98-99; W. R. Moody, *op. cit.*, 161-459, *passim*.

82. Fitt, *op. cit.*, 80.

83. W. R. Moody, *op. cit.*, 533.

84. *Great Pulpit Masters*, I, 225; *Great Joy*, 339; *Glad Tidings*, 408.
85. Quoted in Goodspeed, *op. cit.*, 274.
86. *Glad Tidings*, 83; *Great Pulpit Masters*, I, 114; W. R. Moody, *op. cit.*, 362-63.
87. Goodspeed, *op. cit.*, 565.
88. For Brooks's appearance on Moody's platform, see *supra*, n. 69. For the incidents with other collaborators, see Abbott, *op. cit.*, 206-10; Paul Moody, *op. cit.*, 183-85; and Quimby, *op. cit.*, 135.
89. See, for example, the *Presbyterian Herald and Presbyter*, November 12, 1925, a photostatic copy of which is in the files of the Moody Bible Institute. It contains an article, "Did Dwight L. Moody Favor Modernism?" The argument in this case was touched off by an article in the *Literary Digest* of the preceding September 12, in which Moody was supposed to have told Reuben A. Torrey, after the latter had had an argument with George Adam Smith, that Smith showed "more of the spirit of Christ." Torrey denied the story. Paul Moody discusses the question prudently and sympathetically, *op. cit.*, 184-99. He says, for example, that when he brought "non-Christian" friends home from Yale on vacations, Moody never embarrassed them with attempts to evangelize. Moody — Paul Moody, that is — also once publicly opined that his father would have had little sympathy with bigots of the nineteen-twenties. He promptly got his knuckles rapped by the Moody Bible Institute. See "Dr. Torrey Defends the Dead," "Mr. Paul D. Moody's Gross Calumny of His Honored Father" and "Echoes of Dr. Torrey's Defense of D. L. Moody," *Moody Monthly*, XXIV (1923-24), 49-52, 173-74 and 235-36. William, too, had his troubles with the Bible Institute. He suggested, in the 1930 edition of his biography, that the elder Moody was not entirely satisfied with what he had wrought there (373), and Dr. Smith scolds him for this, *op. cit.*, 20. See also some interesting comments on this matter in the *Christian Century* for July 12 and August 2, 1923.
90. *Great Pulpit Masters*, I, 37.
91. *Great Joy*, 100, 108. One of the problems in a discussion of Moody's technique is that there are no completely faithful reproductions of what he said. He did not write out sermons beforehand. He was, in fact, nervous about being quoted verbatim because of his lack of formal education (Paul Moody, *op. cit.*, 111). Quimby, who studied texts carefully for his dissertation, commends *Glad Tidings*, *Great Joy* and *To All People* as the best available, since they con-

tain newspaper reports, presumably stenographic, of the speeches in the New York, Chicago and Boston campaigns of 1876 and 1877, whereas other collections of Moody talks were edited. However, Curtis, in *his* thesis on Moody in the pulpit — a most exhaustive and exhausting rhetorical analysis — has an appendix in which he compares a handful of newspaper accounts of the first Philadelphia meeting, and the variations are wide indeed. Moody, a fast talker, was the despair of stenographers. Probably the three volumes commended by Quimby, which I have used most frequently, are the closest we can come to the sound of Moody. The Moody Bible Institute has a phonograph record of Moody, but he is only reading the Beatitudes from the Sermon on the Mount, and the quality of the recording is very poor. Sankey sings on the other side of the same record.

92. Quoted in Drummond, *op. cit.*, 69. Also in *Glad Tidings,* 77.

93. *Great Joy,* 329-30.

94. *Glad Tidings,* 221.

95. I have used the version in *Great Pulpit Masters,* I, 178-79. A variant version is in *Glad Tidings,* 205-06.

96. *Great Pulpit Masters,* I, 230.

97. Goodspeed, *op. cit.*, 515-16.

98. *Great Pulpit Masters,* I, 106, 108.

99. *Ibid.*, 215-18.

100. *Ibid.*, 78-79.

101. Space forbids documentation here, but the curious reader is referred, for only a few examples out of hundreds, to the following two Methodist papers: the *Southern Christian Advocate,* "Speak Gently to Each Other," December 7, 1865, "Calling the Ferryman," September 7, 1866, "A Touching Story," September 25, 1868, and "The Land Beyond the Mountains," November 20, 1868; the *Western Christian Advocate,* "Saved," January 24, 1866, "The Double Grave," May 16, 1866, and "The Dying Seaman," August 4, 1869. *Et cetera ad nauseam.* There is actually room for an interesting study of popular sentimentality in the press in the latter half of the nineteenth century. It is a facet of the mentality of the Gilded Age which has been touched on only lightly and with laughter, but it might prove revealing to explore it further.

102. See any edition of *Gospel Hymns* or *Sacred Songs and Solos,* published under Sankey's name, or Sankey's own *My Life and Story of the Gospel Hymns.*

103. For examples of Moody's control of his audiences, see Abbott,

op. cit., 194; W. R. Moody, *op. cit.*, 159, 224. The latter work contains a British journal's terse report: "Mr. Moody suffered no fools, and every symptom of the hysteria which often breaks out in such movements was promptly suppressed." See also *Great Pulpit Masters*, I, 48, and Goodspeed, *op. cit.*, 541. The Ellen Glasgow story is related in her autobiography, *The Woman Within* (New York, 1954), 34-35.

CHAPTER VIII　*Yea, What Indignation . . . Yea, What Zeal*

Title is from II Corinthians 8:11.

1. A typescript of this address is in the files of the Moody Bible Institute in Chicago.

2. This is also in a letter in the Moody Bible Institute files, quoted in William G. McLoughlin, Jr., *Billy Sunday Was His Real Name* (Chicago, 1955), 43. Of this book, I have more to say later. See n. 13, *infra*.

3. E. J. Goodspeed, *A Full History of the Wonderful Career of Moody and Sankey in Great Britain and America* (New York, 1876), 254; J. Wilbur Chapman, *Dwight L. Moody* (New York, 1900), 286.

4. *Great Pulpit Masters*, Vol. I, *Dwight L. Moody* (New York, 1949), 117, 247.

5. *Ibid.*, 225; William R. Moody, *D. L. Moody* (New York, 1930), 170-71.

6. D. L. Moody, *To All People* (Boston, 1877), 489-92.

7. Paul Moody, *My Father: An Intimate Portrait of Dwight Moody* (Boston, 1938), 164-65; *Great Pulpit Masters*, I, 49, 133, 198-99, 225.

8. See W. R. Moody, *op. cit.*, 274, 303-14, 373-80. Wilbur M. Smith, *An Annotated Bibliography of Dwight L. Moody* (Chicago, 1948), has a bibliography and other material on the Northfield schools and conferences, 64-72. Figures on the graduates of the Moody Bible Institute in its first ten years, and what became of them, are available in Margaret B. Robinson, *A Reporter at Moody's* (Chicago, 1900), 97-98.

9. Robert M. Lovett, "Moody and Sankey," *New Republic*, December 14, 1927. There is an interesting picture of the later Moody in George H. Doran, *Chronicles of Barrabas 1884-1934* (New York, 1935). Doran, later of the well-known publishing house of Double-

day, Doran, worked for Fleming H. Revell, publisher of religious books and brother-in-law to Moody, in Toronto as a young man. His chapter "The Evangelists," 359-72, is a colorful package of material on revivalism.

10. The Moody Bible Institute has a file of such letters, mostly relating to the institute alone, but touching on many matters. Random examples of Moody as a businessman in religious work are letters to T. M. Harvey, November 20 and December 14, 1889, to John Dwight, October 15, 1891, and to A. F. Gaylord, September 27, [1894?], May 26, 1897, and September 16, 1897. The nostalgic yearning for Sunday-school work is recorded in W. B. Jacobs, "D. L. Moody as a Sunday-School Worker," *The Christian Workers' Magazine*, N.S. XIV (1913), 25-27. This magazine is an earlier version of the present *Moody Monthly*.

11. Rollin W. Quimby, "Western Campaigns of Dwight L. Moody," *Western Speech*, XVIII (1954), 83-90; W. R. Moody, *op. cit.*, 339; Charles Stelzle, "The Evangelist in Present-Day America," *Current History*, November, 1931, 224-28. Quimby says that Moody could have drawn crowds in 1880 as large as those of the preceding decade if he had tried, but offers no proof. Whether Moody simply was not spending enough time on organization or had run into an ebb of religious interest, the fact remains that his crowd-catching appeal was slipping. William W. Sweet, in *The Story of Religion in America*, 2d rev. ed. (New York, 1950), 346, says that Moody's work "continued seemingly undiminished throughout the eighties and nineties," but his adverb reflects a certain doubt. Both Quimby and Sweet may be thinking of the fact that Moody staged very successful meetings in Chicago during the World's Fair of 1893-1894. See H. B. Hartzler, *Moody in Chicago; or, The World's Fair Gospel Campaign* (New York, 1894). It seems fairly clear, however, that the phenomenal interest of 1876-1877 was never quite revived.

12. Sweet, *op. cit.*, 352-53, discusses this problem and some of its consequences.

13. This point is ably made by McLoughlin in his book on Billy Sunday, but particularly in his seventh and eighth chapters, 223-97. McLoughlin made a very close study of revivalism since the Civil War for a doctoral dissertation done at Harvard in 1953. I have not been able to consult this work, since he will not permit its circulation on interlibrary loan. However, his work on Sunday, an outgrowth of the dissertation, is first-rate, and I have not hesitated to run up a

large indebtedness to it, which I am pleased to acknowledge here and
in the footnotes to follow.

14. *Western Christian Advocate*, January 27, 1869, "Treatment of
Visiting Preachers."

15. *Southern Christian Advocate*, July 11, 1876, "Machine Revivals."

16. W. H. Marsh, "Strictures on Revivals of Religion," *Bibliotheca
Sacra*, XXXIV (1877), 334-54.

17. *New York Herald*, October 6, 1875, "Moody and Sankey." For
a Universalist statement, see "Revivals and the Unchurched," *Universalist Quarterly*, XXXIII (1876). See also William B. Clarke,
"Shall the Church Rely on Revivalism or on Christian Nurture?"
The New Englander, XXXVIII (1879), 800-06. Clarke admits that revivals have their place, but "the grandest work for God," he says,
"is to seek to build up character in those who are already converted,
and in those who are to be converted. Shall He not have polished
stones in His temple?"

18. George P. Fisher, "Recent Evangelistic Movements," *ibid.*, 34-
47. But even Fisher warns that revivals may be attended with transience, vulgarization and ignorance.

19. S. L. Blake, "Extempore Preaching," *Congregational Quarterly*,
XII (1870), 378-91; W. W. Patton, "Revivals of Religion: How to
Make Them Productive of Permanent Good," *The New Englander*,
XXXIII (1874), 38-50.

20. *Western Christian Advocate*, January 17, 1868, "Foolish Objections to Revivals"; *Southern Christian Advocate*, July 17, August
28, 1868, "Revivals." Other defenses, among many, are A. H. Quint,
"Are Revivals of Religion Natural?" *Congregational Quarterly*, XI
[N.S. I] (1869), 34-41, and J. E. Twitchell, "Revivals: How Discerned and Promoted," *ibid.*, XIII [N.S. III] (1871), 551-61. For a
standard sermon in defense of the revival, see T. De Witt Talmage's
"The Broken Net," in Edward Davies, *The Boy Preacher; or, The
Life and Labors of Rev. Thomas Harrison* (Reading, Mass., 1881),
207-24.

21. McLoughlin, *op. cit.*, 189-94, documents this problem with
numerous figures and quotations.

22. Ford C. Ottman, *J. Wilbur Chapman, A Biography* (New
York, 1920), is the standard work. The introduction to the book
states that what "Boswell did for Johnson . . . Ford C. Ottman has
done for J. Wilbur Chapman." Further comment seems superfluous!

For a sample of Chapman in action, see Arcturus Z. Conrad, ed., *Boston's Awakening; A Complete Account of the Great Boston Revival Under the Leadership of J. Wilbur Chapman and Charles M. Alexander, January 26 to February 16, 1909* (Boston, 1909), 51-67.

23. The nearest thing to an official biography is Robert Harkness, *Reuben Archer Torrey, The Man, His Message* (Chicago, 1929). I am also in debt to a biographical sketch prepared by Mr. Bernard R. DeRemer, of the Moody Bible Institute. There are a few kind words about Torrey in Doran, *op. cit.*, 363-64.

24. See the works mentioned in Chapter V, n. 26. Also, D. W. Whittle, *Memoir of Philip P. Bliss* (New York, 1878), and Phineas C. Headley, *George F. Pentecost; Life, Labor and Bible Studies* (Boston, 1880). For random notes on traveling evangelists in the seventies, see the files of the *Independent* or almost any denominational paper.

25. William Baxter, *The Life of Knowles Shaw, the Singing Evangelist* (Cincinnati, 1879), 76, 152.

26. Material on Williams is hard to come by. He has a few published volumes of sermons — for example, *If Any Man Will and Other Sermons by Evangelist Milan B. Williams* (Chicago, 1899) and *Consecration* (Chicago, 1900). I have chosen these two or three random phrases from McLoughlin, *op. cit.*, 172-73. The note on his style in dress is from Doran, *op. cit.*, 363.

27. There is no lack of matter on Smith. I have used *Gipsy Smith, His Life and Work by Himself* (New York, 1906) and Edward Bayliss, *The Gipsy Smith Missions in America* (Boston, 1907). There are other versions and editions of the autobiography and some volumes of sermons available.

28. There is a good deal of print devoted to Jones. There is an autobiographical sketch in *Sam Jones' Own Book: A Series of Sermons* (Cincinnati, 1886); there are *Sam Jones' Late Sermons . . . Together with a Biography* (Chicago, 1898) and a work by his wife, Laura M. Jones, *The Life and Sayings of Sam P. Jones* (Atlanta, 1907). The most recent work appears to be Walt Holcomb, *Sam Jones; Commemorating the Centennial Year of the Birth of Sam Jones* (Nashville, 1947). There is an article by George R. Stuart, "Sam P. Jones, the Preacher," *Methodist Quarterly Review*, LXIX (1920), 419-37. Then there are commemorative volumes of particular campaigns, such as *Tabernacle Sermons of Rev. Sam P. Jones Delivered in St. Joseph, Missouri, September 27 to October 11, 1885*

(St. Joseph, Mo., 1885) and *Sam Jones at Jackson, Mississippi* (Raymond, Miss., 1888). Lastly, there are many collections of sermons. The Library of Congress card catalogue lists fourteen such volumes. Two typical ones are *Sermons and Sayings* (Nashville, 1885) and *Good News* (New York, 1886).

29. *Sam Jones' Own Book*, 62-63.
30. *Ibid.*, 110, 147.
31. *Ibid.*, 212-13.
32. Jones, *Sermons and Sayings*, 285. For other examples, see the collections of nuggets printed at the end of each sermon in the book.
33. Charles C. Sellers, *Lorenzo Dow, Bearer of the Word* (New York, 1928), 137-38.
34. *Sam Jones' Own Book*, 36; *Sermons and Sayings*, 249-50n.
35. This is on an undated sheet of the *Record of Christian Work Advertiser*, clipped to a letter dated October 26, 1898, in the file of Moody letters in the Moody Bible Institute.
36. Stelzle, *loc. cit.*, 225. I have made no effort in this chapter, or indeed this book, at encyclopedic thoroughness. Hence I do not mention here such men as L. W. Munhall, Charles Yatman, Amzi C. Dixon, Joseph Weber and a number of other people generally indistinguishable from each other. Nor am I concerned with men like Baxter McLendon who began evangelistic work at the turn of the century but had their greatest vogue after 1920.
37. Writings on Alexander are not plentiful. I have used Philip I. Roberts, *'Charlie' Alexander: A Study in Personality* (New York, 1920), mostly pages 26-46. The quotation from Torrey is on 23, and Alexander's philosophy of church music is on 48. The exhortation to "every silk hat and busted shoe" is in Ottman, *op. cit.*, in a section on Alexander, 127-35. John K. Maclean has a book, *Chapman and Alexander* (New York, 1915), which has some information. Alexander himself, in *Soul Winning Around the World* (Philadelphia, 1907), tells something of his own story. The books on Torrey and Chapman already listed show Alexander in action, as does A. Z. Conrad's compilation of reports on Chapman's Boston campaign of 1909. Three volumes by George T. B. Davis, which I did not consult, may also prove useful: *The Personal Side of Mr. Alexander* (New York, 1905), *Torrey and Alexander: Story of a World-Wide Revival* (New York, 1905) and *Twice Around the World with Alexander, Prince of Gospel Singers* (New York, 1907).
38. Frank G. Beardsley, *A History of American Revivals* (New

York, 1904), 290-95. For a sample of the Mills organization at work, see Harvey Blodgett, *Times of Refreshing* (St. Paul, Minn., 1893), an account of a Mills campaign in the Twin Cities, particularly 13-19. Two other "memorial volumes" are Joseph D. Lowden, *The Story of the Revival* (Elizabeth, N. J., 1892), and Henry Stauffer, *The Great Awakening in Columbus, Ohio* (Columbus, Ohio, 1896). McLoughlin, *op. cit.*, 40-41, has other details of the District Combination Plan.

39. McLoughlin, *op. cit.*, 9; Ottman, *op. cit.*, 120-24. Chapman's book is *Present Day Evangelism* (New York, 1903), chock-full of practical advice on everything from how to prepare a good evangelistic sermon to the weekly cost of a tent service — $119.

40. Ottman, *op. cit.*, 127-35; Conrad, *op. cit.*, particularly 16-23 for details of the organization of the Boston campaign.

41. The *Independent*, February 10, 1876, "Revival Inquirers."

42. Davies, *op. cit.*, 151. There is a protest against making standing or sitting or hand raising the means, rather than the sign, of regeneration in Lyman H. Atwater, "The Revivals of the Century," *Presbyterian Quarterly and Princeton Review*, N.S. V (1876), 690-719. See particularly 718-19, in which Atwater warns against this practice as a "coarse heresy."

43. Frederic R. Davenport, *Primitive Traits in Religious Revivals* (New York, 1902), 208-09. Bayliss, *op. cit.*, 46-60.

44. Beardsley, *op. cit.*, 290-93; Chapman, *Present Day Evangelism*, 126-27.

45. A. P. Fitt, *The Shorter Life of D. L. Moody* (Chicago, 1900), 84.

46. Bayliss, *op. cit.*, 124; Paul Moody, *op. cit.*, 195-96.

47. Jones, *Sermons and Sayings*, 23, 32, 49, 78, 85, 107, 133, 150, 186, 195, 196, 197, 200, 216, 231; Bayliss, *op. cit.*, 46-60, 110-11.

48. In the material on Sunday which follows I have drawn on a varied bibliography. McLoughlin's book appeared while this one was in the writing. It is so thorough, and its conclusions are so much in harmony with my own, that I have not felt it necessary to duplicate McLoughlin's research, and have drawn on him copiously, but not exclusively. There is a long bibliographical essay in *Billy Sunday Was His Real Name*, 311-16. Of the books mentioned in the note on secondary sources, I have used Theodore T. Frankenberg's *The Spectacular Career of Rev. Billy Sunday, Famous Baseball Evangelist* (Columbus, Ohio, 1913) and William T. Ellis, *'Billy' Sunday, The*

Man and His Message (Philadelphia, 1914), both of which are fairly adulatory. I did not use another "authorized" biography, Elijah P. Brown's *The Real Billy Sunday* (New York, 1914), since Frankenberg and Ellis are sufficiently full of paeans, and for the same reason I omitted Melton Wright, *Giant for God* (Boyce, Va., 1951), and Sunday's brief autobiography in the *Ladies Home Journal*, September, 1932-April, 1933. I did read the only critical study sustained for the length of a book, Frederick W. Betts's *Billy Sunday: The Man and Method* (Boston, 1916). Homer A. Rodeheaver's *Twenty Years With Billy Sunday* (Winona Lake, Ind., 1936) has a few veins of information on Sunday's ways and works provided by his musical director. As for Sunday's own writings, McLoughlin has a careful evaluation of their reliability and availability on pages 313-14.

The periodical literature on Sunday is enormous during the years from 1912 to 1920. I have only sampled it — most of it being ephemeral and uncritical. The individual articles which I have used are acknowledged in the footnotes which follow. Of course, after 1914, Sunday got full newspaper coverage wherever he campaigned, and a thorough investigation of him would be incomplete without exhaustive study of his "press." Again, I have relied largely on McLoughlin, but I did read, as a check, the complete reports in the *New York Herald* of Billy's climactic, summarizing campaign in New York, the Mount Everest of revivalism, April-June, 1917. I also used a file on Sunday's campaign in Detroit in the autumn of 1916 in the Burton Historical Collection of the Detroit Public Library.

49. McLoughlin, *op. cit.*, 1-5; Frankenberg, *op. cit.*, 27-59; Adrian C. Anson, *A Ball Player's Career, Being the Personal Experiences and Reminiscences of Adrian C. Anson, Late Manager and Captain of the Chicago Base Ball Club* (Chicago, 1900), 127, 133-34.

50. Ellis, *op. cit.*, 40-41; McLoughlin, *op. cit.*, 6-7.

51. Frankenberg, *op. cit.*, 81-85; McLoughlin, *op. cit.*, 8-10; Ellis, *op. cit.*, 45-55. The last-cited work is an excerpt (or excerpts) from a sermon in which Sunday discusses his Y. experiences in his own words.

52. See Frankenberg, *op. cit.*, 123-59; McLoughlin, *op. cit.*, 9-20, 45-47; Ellis, *op. cit.*, 327-28.

53. Billy as an acrobat is described in Lindsay Denison, "The Rev. Billy Sunday and His War on the Devil," *American Magazine*, LXIV (May-October, 1907), 451-68. Also see McLoughlin, *op. cit.*, 154-63,

and Ellis, *op. cit.*, 138-45. Betts, *op. cit.*, 17, refers to him as "dramatic action personified," and his washing his face out of a Thermos bottle is recorded in the *New York Herald*, May 30, 1917.

54. Denison, *loc. cit.*; Irvin S. Cobb, "Sunday as Cobb Saw Him," *Literary Digest*, June 16, 1917, 1870-74; Ellis, *op. cit.*, 69-79; Frankenberg, *op. cit.*, 226. McLoughlin thoroughly covers Sunday's preaching technique, with abundant examples, *op. cit.*, 163-88. The Sunday version of the miracle of Joshua and the sun is in McLoughlin, xix-xx. A cartoon of Sunday as "Elisha" saying, "BEAT IT," is in Ellis, *op. cit.*, between 140 and 141. Sunday's prayers, from which the quotations are taken, are made the subject of McLoughlin's examination, *op. cit.*, 176-78, and of Ellis, *op. cit.*, 271-77. A long list of "Sunday-isms" is in Frankenberg, *op. cit.*, 220-28.

55. Ellis, *op. cit.*, 102, 117-19. The entire "booze sermon," perhaps Sunday's most famous, is given on pages 86-120. The blasts at cigarette smoking and dancing are also in Ellis, 223 and 228. The complaints over "pie-counter" politicians and European "dumping" of criminals in America are to be found in McLoughlin, *op. cit.*, 175 and 147. The last four quotations are from Ellis, *op. cit.*, 201, 215, 348 and 365.

56. McLoughlin, *op. cit.*, 67-80, scrutinizes the organization of Sunday's campaigns. So does Ellis, *op. cit.*, 61-66, but much less adequately. A sense of the enormous machinery involved can be gained by actually seeing some of the original letters and memoranda. The Burton Collection's file of miscellaneous material on the Detroit campaign has, in addition to newspaper clippings, an envelope for the free-will offering, a printed form for reporting prayer meetings and a form letter to "workers" with an elaborate letterhead.

57. Such a prayer-meeting report card is in the Burton Collection file referred to in the note immediately preceding. As for Sunday's accommodations, in Detroit the party stayed at the home of Sebastian S. Kresge, the chain-store magnate, and a special car was placed at the revivalist's disposal by Henry M. Leland, president of the Cadillac Motor Company.

58. McLoughlin, *op. cit.*, 90-97, 214; Ellis, *op. cit.*, 299-302.

59. McLoughlin, *op. cit.*, 74-75, 80-89. Betts, *op. cit.*, 15, has a good picture of Rody at work in Syracuse, with a Syracuse University pennant dangling from his trombone. Joseph Collins, "Revivals Past and Present," *Harper's Magazine*, November, 1917, 856-65, has a word snapshot of Rodeheaver booming, "What hymn would *you*

like?" to an audience. Rodeheaver's own *Twenty Years With Billy Sunday* gives much of Rody's view of the nature of his work. His material on music in the tabernacle, pages 72-87, is interesting, and his comments on publicity, finances, organizational work and the delegation system are revealing.

60. Ellis, *op. cit.*, 158-66. McLoughlin, *op. cit.*, xxiv-xxvi, 97-103. The special waist-high well below the speaker's platform, where Sunday shook the hands of the trail hitters, is described on page 62, *ibid.*

61. The pamphlet is reproduced in Ellis, *op. cit.*, between pages 310 and 311. The quotation about "God's plan of salvation" is in *ibid.*, 153.

62. McLoughlin, *op. cit.*, 102.

63. The best description of Sunday's money-raising techniques and his personal income is in McLoughlin, *op. cit.*, 105-16. No one else touches on the subject of revivalism's rewards in so informed a way.

64. *New York Herald*, April 1, 9, 1917. All quotations on the New York City campaign are from this paper. Minor discrepancies in the reports of the same meetings in other New York journals did not seem serious enough to justify tracing the story through more than one daily. Page references are unnecessary, as the "Sunday story" of the day was always prominently displayed.

65. *Ibid.*, April 10, 1917.

66. *Ibid.*, April 11, 1917.

67. *Ibid.*, April 14, 16, 1917.

68. *Ibid.*, April 19, 21, 26, 1917.

69. *Ibid.*, April 28, May 4, 1917.

70. *Ibid.*, May 10, 11, 1917.

71. *Ibid.*, May 19, 20, 21, 1917.

72. *Ibid.*, May 31, June 4, 6, 1917.

73. *Ibid.*, June 12, 13, 15, 18, 1917.

74. To give only one example, the Library of Congress has a pamphlet by "Uncle Hiram," *A Money-Mad Mountebank. Billy Sunday, How He Slams Satan, Slings Slang, and Soaks Sinful Suckers* (Washington, 1914). Beginning with a denunciation of revivalism's "graft, greed and imposition," it continues in the same vein to the bitter end.

75. McLoughlin discusses the class background and impermanence of the Sunday trail hitters, *op. cit.*, 196-216, quite exhaustively. The warning against Catholic attendance at Sunday's New York meetings

appeared in the periodical *Catholic Mind*, and is quoted in the *New York Herald*, April 14, 1917, in the day's account of Sunday's doings. In Boston, Baltimore, Detroit and Syracuse, over one thousand Catholics signed decision cards, and in New York, 3690. The *Pilot*, a Catholic publication, carried an analysis of the card signers from its church in Boston, reprinted in McLoughlin, 215.

76. Betts, *op. cit.*, 41-42, tells of his frustration in following up seventeen card signers in Syracuse who gave their religious preference as Universalist.

77. McLoughlin, *op. cit.*, 52-59, illustrates the mechanics of forcing a "unanimous" invitation to Sunday on a reluctant community. Betts, *op. cit.*, 30, tells of how the bitterness engendered between critics and supporters of Sunday nearly broke up Syracuse's Evangelical Association. The Gladden story is dealt with in Frankenberg, *op. cit.*, 159-74. It should be noted that Gladden was not opposed to revivals on principle. He contributed a friendly introduction to the "memorial" volume on B. Fay Mills's meetings in Columbus. See Stauffer, *op. cit.*, 5-6.

78. John M. Mecklin, *My Quest for Freedom* (New York, 1945), 179-84.

79. "Billy Sunday Assailed by Leaders of Three Denominations," *Current Opinion*, May, 1917, 341-42.

80. *New York Herald*, May 7, 1917.

81. McLoughlin handles these charges in *op. cit.*, 234-54. Attacks on Sunday as a bulwark of privilege are of many kinds. John Reed dissected him in "Back of Billy Sunday," in the *Metropolitan Magazine* for May, 1915, an article which I have not read. A criticism of revivalism from a curious source is in Elbert Hubbard's publication, the *Fra*, VIII (1911-12), 1-5, in which Hubbard points out that when a church is dull, a revivalist can be hired, as he puts it, just like a strikebreaker.

Such attacks were begotten by the plain-spoken praise of Sunday as a "sobering" influence on the "working class." Examples of top-drawer approval are the following: Lewis E. Theiss, "Industry versus Alcohol," in the *Outlook*, August 8, 1914, the source of the statement about the C[ambria] works' reaping a quarter of a million in added efficiency after the revival. Part of this article is quoted in Ellis, *op. cit.*, 82-83. Another article in the *Outlook*, by the Reverend Joseph H. Odell, alludes again to the "higher and steadier" output in the steel mills as a result of Sunday's work. This testimonial is summarized in "Billy Sunday in the Big Cities," *Literary Digest*, April 25, 1914, 990, and an excerpt is given in Ellis, *op. cit.*, 172-73. Lastly, but by no means completing the record, is W. C. Poole, " 'Billy' Sunday and Business Men," *Methodist Review*, XCVIII (1916), 598-602, from which came the statement about the excellency of Philadelphia as a place for investment, thanks to Sunday. (The italics here are mine.) The newspaper reports of any campaign contain ample evidence that the business community found Sunday an asset.

82. George Creel, "Salvation Circus, An Estimate of Billy Sunday," *Harper's Weekly*, June 19, 1915, 580-82.

83. "Making Religion Yellow," *Nation*, June 11, 1908, 527.

84. Clipping from a scrapbook of the Reverend Levi W. Staples, lent to the author by his grandson, Hugh B. Staples. By its place in the scrapbook, the clipping, from some local paper, dates from 1914 or 1915. Lyman Abbott's judgment is in his *Reminiscences* (Boston, 1915), 465-66. Clerical praise of Sunday is abundant in the works of Frankenberg and Ellis.

85. Denison, *loc. cit.*

EPILOGUE   *All Things New*

Title is from Revelation 21:5.

Index